LOS ANGELES

AND

NEARBY ATTRACTIONS

FODOR'S TRAVEL GUIDES

are compiled, researched, and edited by an international team of travel writers, field correspondents, and editors. The series, which now almost covers the globe, was founded by Eugene Fodor in 1936.

OFFICES

New York & London

Fodor's Los Angeles:

Editor: Langdon Faust
Area Editor: Jane E. Lansky
Editorial Contributors: Chris Barnett, Mary Jane Horton, David Reed, Diana Rico, Norman Sklarewitz, Helena Zukowski
Research: William Patrick Brown, Gerry Cohen, Joseph Di Mattia, Heidi Gordon, Jennie Moffitt, Lisa Petty, Ralph Rugoff, Melisa Sanders, Holly Thomas
Illustrations: Ted Burwell
Maps and Plans: Burmar, Pictograph

SPECIAL SALES

Fodor's Travel Guides are available at special quantity discounts for bulk purchases (50 copies or more) for sales promotions or premiums. Special travel guides or excerpts from existing guides can also be created to fit specific needs. For more information write Special Marketing, Fodor's Travel Guides, 2 Park Avenue, New York, N.Y. 10016.

FODOR'S®

LOS ANGELES

AND

NEARBY ATTRACTIONS

1986

FODOR'S TRAVEL GUIDES
New York & London

ISBN 0-679-01253-2 (Traveltex edition)
ISBN 0-340-38415-8 (Hodder & Stoughton edition)

The following Fodor's Guides are current; most are also available in a British edition published by Hodder & Stoughton.

Country and Area Guides

Australia, New Zealand & The South Pacific
Austria
Bahamas
Belgium & Luxembourg
Bermuda
Brazil
Canada
Canada's Maritime Provinces
Caribbean
Central America
Eastern Europe
Egypt
Europe
France
Germany
Great Britain
Greece
Holland
India, Nepal & Sri Lanka
Ireland
Israel
Italy
Japan
Jordan & The Holy Land
Kenya
Korea
Mexico
North Africa
People's Republic of China
Portugal
Scandanavia
Scotland
South America
Southeast Asia
Soviet Union
Spain
Switzerland
Turkey
Yugoslavia

City Guides

Amsterdam
Beijing, Guangzhou, Shanghai
Boston
Chicago
Dallas–Fort Worth
Greater Miami & The Gold Coast
Hong Kong
Houston
Lisbon
London
Los Angeles
Madrid
Mexico City & Acapulco
Munich
New Orleans
New York City
Paris
Philadelphia
Rome
San Diego
San Francisco
Stockholm, Copenhagen, Oslo, Helsinki & Reykjavik
Sydney
Tokyo
Toronto
Vienna
Washington, D.C.

U.S.A. Guides

Alaska
Arizona
California
Cape Cod
Colorado
Far West
Florida
Hawaii
New England
New Mexico
Pacific North Coast
South
Texas
U.S.A.

Budget Travel

American Cities (30)
Britain
Canada
Caribbean
Europe
France
Germany
Hawaii
Italy
Japan
London
Mexico
Spain

Fun Guides

Acapulco
Bahamas
London
Montreal
Puerto Rico
San Francisco
St. Martin/Sint Maarten
Waikiki

MANUFACTURED IN THE UNITED STATES OF AMERICA
10 9 8 7 6 5 4 3 2 1

CONTENTS

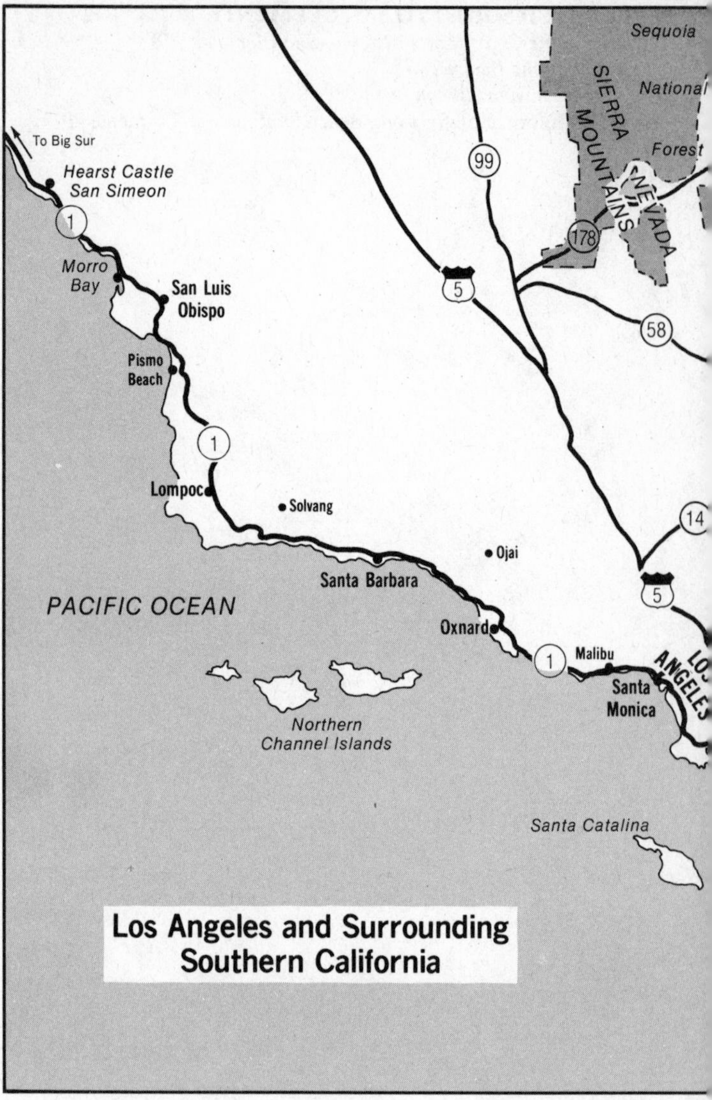
Sequoia
National
Forest
SIERRA
MOUNTAINS
NEVADA
To Big Sur
Hearst Castle
San Simeon
1
99
178
Morro
Bay
San Luis
Obispo
5
58
Pismo
Beach
1
Lompoc
Solvang
14
Ojai
Santa Barbara
5
PACIFIC OCEAN
Oxnard
1
Malibu
Santa
Monica
Northern
Channel Islands
Santa Catalina
Los Angeles and Surrounding
Southern California

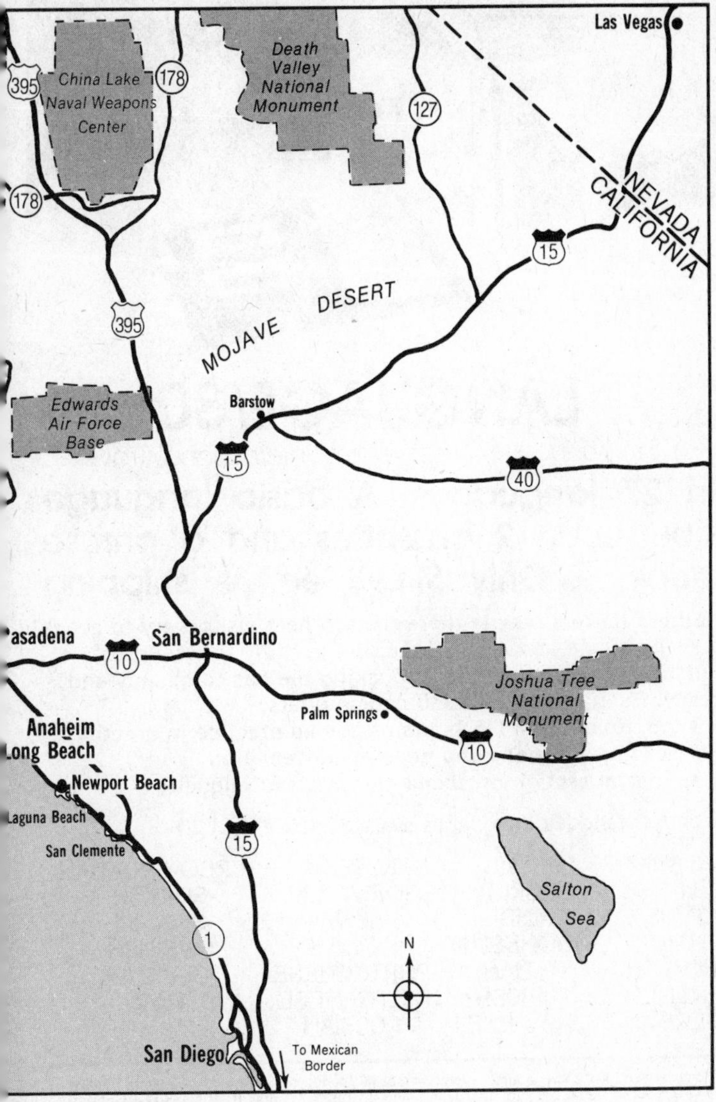

Las Vegas
Death Valley National Monument
China Lake Naval Weapons Center
395
178
127
NEVADA
CALIFORNIA
15
MOJAVE DESERT
Edwards Air Force Base
Barstow
40
Pasadena
San Bernardino
10
Joshua Tree National Monument
Palm Springs
Anaheim
Long Beach
Newport Beach
Laguna Beach
San Clemente
Salton Sea
1
N
San Diego
To Mexican Border

FOREWORD

Los Angeles has long been dubbed the "Entertainment Capital of the World." More than twelve million people spend some time in the "Big Orange" and in the surrounding Southland every year.

Fodor's Los Angeles is designed to explain just what this stimulating city is all about. It is written to help you decide what to do and where to go once you're there. The book is intended to be your tool for making some order from the chaos of possibilities. We have therefore concentrated on presenting the broadest *range* of choices offered by the city and within that range to offer *selections* that will be safe, reliable, and of value to you. We think that our descriptions will provide you with enough information on which to make intelligent choices based on your own tastes and pocketbook.

All selections and comments in *Fodor's Los Angeles* are based on the editors' and contributors' personal experience. We believe that our first responsibility is to inform and protect you, the reader. Changes are bound to affect any travel guide, however. Many changes can occur in Los Angeles while we are on press and during the succeeding twelve months or so when this edition is on sale. We welcome letters from readers on these changes or from those whose opinions differ from ours. We will revise our entries for next year's edition when the facts warrant it.

Send your letters to the editors at **Fodor's Travel Guides, 2 Park Avenue, New York, NY 10016.** Continental or British Commonwealth readers may prefer to write to **Fodor's Travel Guides, 9–10 Market Place, London W1N 7AG, England.**

Finally, a word about the "nearby attractions": Los Angeles is the major port of entry for Southern California. This book would have to be published in several volumes if we tried to cover it all. Instead, we have selected only a few of the most popular or rewarding side trips a visitor might want to add to an itinerary after arriving in the city.

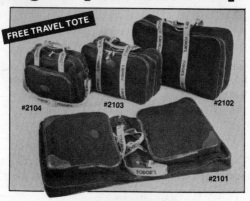

FACTS AT YOUR FINGERTIPS

FACTS AT YOUR FINGERTIPS

FACTS AND FIGURES. The third largest state in size, California's population is almost 26 million. It hosts millions of visitors yearly, and tourism has replaced agriculture as the state's number one industry.

California stretches almost 1,000 miles from the Oregon border in the north to the Mexican border in the south. It is an exciting blend of Spanish–Mexican, European, Asian, and Yankee spirits.

Los Angeles and environs are certainly an integral part of our largest western state. It's home to the aerospace industry, the glamour industries of film and television and a focal point for our nation's fashion and music. It is in fact the center for industry and agriculture in the west and boasts the largest and busiest harbor on the West Coast.

The boundaries of Los Angeles encompass more than 464 square miles and combine urban, desert, mountain, and coastal landscapes. This area is large enough to hold the cities of St. Louis, Cleveland, Milwaukee, Boston, Pittsburgh, and San Francisco, as well as the borough of Manhattan in New York City. More than 6,500 miles of roads and freeways make the Big Orange the most modern city in the United States for land transportation.

The population of Los Angeles proper is nearly three million; approximately thirteen million inhabitants live in the four-county metropolitan area.

PLANNING YOUR TRIP. If you don't want to bother making your own reservations a travel agent won't cost a cent, except for specific charges like telegrams. He gets his fee from the hotel or carrier he books for you. A travel agent can also be of help for those who prefer to take their vacations on a "package tour"—thus keeping their own planning to a minimum. If you prefer the convenience of standardized accommodations, remember that the various hotel and motel chains publish free directories of their members. Such directories will enable you to plan and reserve everything ahead of time.

If you don't belong to an auto club, now is the time to join one. It can be very helpful about routings and providing emergency service on the road. If you plan to route yourself, make certain the map you get is dated for the current year. (Highways and thruways are appearing and being extended at an astonishingly rapid rate.) Some of the major oil companies will send maps and mark preferred routes on them if you tell them what you have in mind. Try: *Exxon Touring Service,* Exxon Corporation, 1251 Avenue of the Americas, New York, NY 10020; *Texaco Travel Service,* P.O. Box 1459, Houston, TX 77001; or *Mobil Oil Corp. Touring Service,* P.O. Box 25, Versailles, KY 40383. In addition, most areas have their own maps that pinpoint attractions, list historical sites, parks, and so on. City chambers of commerce are also good sources of information. Specific addresses are given under *Tourist Information.*

VISITOR INFORMATION. In 1979 the *California Office of Tourism* (1121 L Street, Suite 103, Sacramento, CA 95814, tel. 916–322–1396) was established. Visitor information is available through that office and at the many convention and visitors' bureaus or chambers of commerce throughout the state. See individual sections for listings.

TIPS FOR BRITISH VISITORS. Passports. You will need a valid passport and a U.S. visa (which can only be put in a passport of the ten-year kind). You can obtain the visa either through your travel agent or directly from the *United States Embassy,* Visa and Immigration Department, 5 Upper Grosvenor St., London W1 (tel. 01–499 7010/3443).

No vaccinations are required for entry.

Customs. If you are twenty-one or over, you can take into the U.S. 200 cigarettes, 50 cigars, or 2 kilos of tobacco; 1 U.S. quart of alcohol; duty-free gifts to a value of $100. Don't take in meat or meat products, seeds, plants, fruits, and so on. And avoid narcotics like the plague.

Insurance. We recommend that you insure yourself to cover health and motoring mishaps with *Europ Assistance,* 252 High St., Croydon CRO 1NF (tel. 01–680 1234). Their excellent service is all the more valuable when you consider the possible costs of health care in the U.S.

Tour Operators. The price battle that has raged over transatlantic fares has meant that most tour operators now offer excellent budget packages to the U.S. Among those you might consider as you plan your trip are:

Thomas Cook Ltd., P.O. Box 36, Thorpe Wood, Peterborough, PE 3 6SB.
Cosmos, Cosmos House, 1 Bromley Common, Bromley, Kent BR2 9LX.
Holiday America, 21 Dering St., London W1R ONE.
Kuoni Travel Ltd., Kuoni House, Dorking, Surrey RH5 4AZ.
Jetsave, Sussex House, London Rd., East Grinstead RH19 1LD.
Page and Moy, 136–140 London Rd., Leicester LE2 1EN.
Speedbird, 152 King St., London W6 OQU.

Air Fares. We suggest that you explore the current scene for budget flight possibilities, including People Express and Virgin Atlantic Airways. Some of these fares can be extremely difficult to come by, so be sure to book well in advance. Also check on APEX and other money-saving fares, as, quite frankly, only business travelers who don't have to watch the price of their tickets fly full price these days. They usually find themselves sitting right beside an APEX passenger!

WHEN TO GO. With the Humboldt Current (cold) swirling toward the north of this region and the Japanese Current (warm) nudging northern coastal strips, with America's highest, coolest mountains and its deepest, sun-sizzled valleys, the humidity and temperature readings in this region are as varied as the patterns on your grandmother's favorite patchwork quilt. Here and there sea breezes cause a temperature variance of as much as 5 to 15 degrees within the limits of a single city.

Nonetheless, Los Angeles normally has a pleasant and mild year-round climate. In the summer the city's renowned smog will cause a problem for some who have respiratory ailments.

Average summer temperature is 79.5 degrees Fahrenheit; the winter average is 69.3 degrees Fahrenheit.

The rainy season usually runs from November through March. In January there usually occur the heaviest downpours, even though thunderstorms are infrequent. Summers are practically rainless. The coast may be overcast in late spring.

In fall, winter, and early spring occasional descending Santa Ana foehn winds rage from the northeast, picking up a considerable amount of dust. These winds reach speeds of 35 to 50 mph and cause a heat cover to envelope the city and surrounding areas. The most discomfort occurs in the valley regions.

CLIMATE. Seasons in Los Angeles and the Southland are not as defined as in most other temperate areas of the world. November through March brings rain, so count on needing an umbrella during a winter trip. But in June, July, August, and September there is virtually no rain at all. Smog is common during the summer months of July, August, and September.

The Pacific Ocean is the primary moderating influence; however, coastal mountains along the north and east sides of the Los Angeles coastal basin act as a buffer against extreme summer heat and winter cold occurring in desert and plateau regions. Between mild sea breezes and either hot (the Santa Ana wind) or cold winds from the interior, a variety of weather conditions results. An unusual aspect of Los Angeles' climate is the pronounced difference in temperature, humidity, cloudiness, fog, rain, and sunshine over short distances.

	Average High Daily Temp.
January	65° F
February	67°
March	68°
April	69°
May	72°
June	75°
July	82°
August	84°
September	83°

	Average High Daily Temp.
October	78°
November	73°
December	69°

WHAT WILL IT COST? This is obviously a crucial question and one of the most difficult to answer. The American Automobile Association estimates that expenses for two adults and two children driving across the country should average around $72 per day for meals, $63 for lodging, and about $8.00 for each 100 miles for gasoline (at 20 miles to the gallon). Though our own figures are slightly higher, we hope you can do it for less, and have included a number of concrete and practical suggestions for cutting costs wherever you can. A couple can travel comfortably in California for about $125 a day (not counting gasoline or other transportation costs); see below.

In some areas you can cut expenses by traveling off season, when hotel rates are usually lower. The budget-minded traveler can also find bargain accommodations at tourist homes or family-style YMCAs and YWCAs. Both California state and national parks offer limited lodgings; book early. Colleges offer dormitory accommodations to tourists during the summer vacations at single-room rates of $2.00–$10.00 per night, with meals from $0.60–$3.50. A directory of some 200 such opportunities all over the U.S. is *Mort's Guide to Low-Cost Vacations and Lodgings on College Campuses, USA-Canada* from Mort Barrish Assoc., Inc., Research Park, State Rd., Princeton, NJ 08540.

Another way to cut down on the cost of your trip is to look for out-of-the-way resorts. Travelers are frequently rewarded by discovering very attractive areas that haven't as yet begun to draw quantities of people.

If you are budgeting your trip (who isn't), don't forget to set aside a realistic amount for the possible rental of sports equipment (perhaps including a boat or canoe), entrance fees to amusement and historical sites, and so on. There are no tolls on the highways, but allow for modest bridge tolls, extra film for cameras, and souvenirs.

Typical Expenses for Two People

Room at moderate hotel or motel	$50.00
Breakfast at hotel or motel, including tip	12.00
Lunch at inexpensive restaurant, including tip	9.00
Dinner at moderate restaurant, including tip	30.00
Sightseeing bus tour	17.00
Evening drink	4.00
Admission to museum or historic site	5.00
	$127.00

After lodging your next biggest expense will be food, and here you can make very substantial economies if you are willing to get along with only one meal a day (or less) in a restaurant. Plan to eat simply and to picnic. It will save you time and money, and it will help you enjoy your trip more. That beautiful scenery does not have to whiz by at 55 miles per hour. There are picnic and rest areas, often well-equipped and in scenic spots, even on highways and thruways, and so finding a pleasant place to stop is usually not difficult. Before you leave home, put together a picnic kit.

HINTS TO THE MOTORIST. Probably the first precaution you will take is to have your car thoroughly checked by your regular dealer or service station to make sure that everything is in good shape. Second, you may find it wise to join an auto club that can provide you with trip-planning information, insurance coverage, and emergency and repair service along the way. Third, if you must have your car serviced, look for a repair shop displaying the *National Institute for Automotive Service Excellence* seal. *NIASE* tests and certifies the competence of auto mechanics in about 10,000 repair shops nationwide.

Driving in California is probably more unpredictable and challenging than in any other part of the nation. With an auto registration of some nine million, the Golden State easily outranks its two closest contenders, New York and Texas, each of which issues five and one-half million license plates. If you enter a California freeway, be sure you have a full gas tank.

California speed limits comply with federal law—55 mph. Tops for cars hauling trailers is 50, but lower limits sometimes are posted. General speed limit for school zones and residential and business districts is 25, again, except when posted. And there are special speed zones ranging from 25 to 55, depending on what the sign says at the entrance to such zones. Watch the signs: There is no state requirement for posting warning signs on radar, mechanical, or electrical speed-checking devices.

DESERT DRIVING

If you are driving to the southeast from Los Angeles into southern California, you will encounter some stretches of desert driving. Service industries across the desert have grown in number during the past decade to the point that the hazards of desert driving have been minimized. A principal point to check before crossing the hot desert should be your tires. Put them at normal driving pressure or slightly below. Heat builds pressure. If your car seems to be bouncing too readily, stop to let your tires cool. If you have a good radiator, don't bother about extra water—except for Death Valley—but keep an eye on the water gauge. Be alert for sudden sandstorms and rainstorms. If you have a car radio, keep it tuned to local stations for information about unusual weather conditions.

MOUNTAIN DRIVING

Unless you venture onto exotic mountain roads, you should have little trouble with mountain driving. Today's mountain roads are engineered for the ordinary driver. They are normally wide, well graded, and safe. Be especially wary of exceeding the speed limit posted for curves. Keep to the right. If your normal driving is at low altitudes, have a garage mechanic check your carburetor. It may need adjusting for mountain driving. If your car stalls and your temperature gauge is high, a vapor lock may be the problem. Bathe the fuel pump with a damp cloth for a few minutes.

If you get stuck on any kind of road, pull off the highway onto the shoulder, raise the hood, attach something white (a handkerchief, a scarf, or a piece of tissue) to the door handle on the driver's side, and sit inside and wait. This is especially effective on limited-access highways, usually patroled vigilantly by state highway patrol officers. A special warning to women stalled at night: Remain inside the car with doors locked, and make sure the Good Samaritan is indeed a Good Samaritan. It's easier to find telephones along the major highways these days since their locations are more frequently marked than they used to be.

HOTELS AND MOTELS. In Los Angeles or any resort area in southern California, try to reserve *well* in advance. Include a deposit for all places except motels (and for motels if they request one). Many chain or associated motels and hotels will make advance reservations for you at affiliated hostelries of your choosing along your route.

Hotel and motel chains. In addition to the hundreds of excellent independent motels and hotels throughout the state, there are also many that belong to national or regional chains. To many travelers a major advantage of the chains is the ease of making reservations en route or at one fell swoop in advance. If you are a guest at a member hotel or motel one night, the management will be delighted to secure a sure booking at one of its affiliated hotels at no cost to you. Chains also usually have toll-free WATS (800) lines to assist you in making reservations on your own. This, of course, saves you time, money, and worry. For directory information on (800) lines, dial (800) 555–1212 to see if there is an (800) number for the hotel you want to reach.

Nationwide motel prices for two people now average $60.00 a night; hotel prices start at $70.00, with the average around $75.00. This explains the recent rapid spread of a number of budget motel chains whose rates average $40.00 for a single and $50.00 for a double, an obvious advantage.

The main national motel chains are Holiday Inn, Howard Johnson's, Quality Inns, Ramada Inns, Sheraton Motor Inns, and TraveLodge. Other popular family-type motel chains include Best Western, Friendship Inn Hotels, Rodeway Inns, Vagabond Motor Hotels, and Motel 6.

Hotels and motels in all the Fodor's guidebooks to the U.S.A. are divided into categories and arranged by price: *Super Deluxe, Deluxe, Expensive, Moderate, Inexpensive.* Our ratings are flexible and subject to change. In every case, however, the dollar ranges for each category are clearly stated before each listing of establishments. We should also point out that many fine hotels and motels had to be omitted for lack of space.

Senior citizens may in some cases receive special discounts on lodgings. The Days Inn chain offers various discounts to anyone 55 or older. Holiday Inns give a 10 percent discount year round to members of the NRTA (write to National Retired Teachers Association, Membership Division, 215 Long Beach Blvd., Long Beach, CA 90801; 213–432–5781) and the AARP (write to American Association of Retired Persons, Membership Division, 215 Long Beach Blvd., Long Beach, CA 90801). Howard Johnson's Motor Lodges give 10 percent off to NRTA and AARP members (call 800–654–2000); and the ITT Sheraton chain gives 25 percent off (call 800–325–3535) to members of the AARP, the NRTA, the National Association of Retired Persons, The Catholic Golden Age of United Societies of U.S.A., and the Old Age Security Pensioners of Canada.

Los Angeles' **Bed-and-Breakfast Inns** offer a rather new approach toward visitor accommodations but are not as popular as they are two hours north of the city in Santa Barbara, as well as in other northern spots between Los Angeles and San Francisco, where the custom has really caught on.

The bed-and-breakfast establishments in and around Los Angeles County are priced conservatively, most in the moderate range. All offer highly personalized service to their guests. They're small and reservations are always required.

Ambience in these hideaways includes Victorian and Art Deco, highlighted daily by fresh southern Californian flowers and fluffy towels. Breakfast, usually special, may consist of tasty croissants or San Francisco sourdough toast, fresh fruits and juices, and wonderful coffee and teas.

Reservation services for these charming hostelries throughout California are handled by the following agencies: *American Historic Homes Bed and Breakfast,* P.O. Box 388, San Juan Capistrano, CA 92693 (714) 496–7050; *Bed and Breakfast–California Sunshine,* 22704 Ventura Blvd., Suite 1984, Woodland Hills, CA 91364 (818) 992–1984 or (213) 274–4494; *Bed and Breakfast International,* 151 Ardmore Rd., Kensington, CA 94707 (415) 525–4569 or 525–8836; *Bed and Breakfast of Los Angeles,* 32074 Waterside Lane, Westlake Village, CA 91361 (818) 889–8870 or 889–7325; *Bed and Breakfast of Southern California,* P.O. Box 218, Fullerton, CA 92632 (714) 738–8361; *California Bed and Breakfast,* P.O. Box 1581, Sacramento, CA 95818 (no phone); *California Houseguests International, Inc.,* P.O. Box 190, Tarzana, CA 91356 (818) 344–7878; *Carolyn's Bed and Breakfast Homes,* P.O. Box 84776, San Diego, CA 92138 (619) 435–5009; *Eye Openers Bed and Breakfast Reservations,* P.O. Box 694, Altadena, CA 91001 (818) 797–2055; *Napa Valley Tourist Bureau,* P.O. Box 3240, Yountville, CA 94599 (707) 944–1557; *PT International,* 1318 S.W. Troy St., Portland, OR 97219 (800) 547–1463; Also, *Bed and Breakfast Exchange* (P.O. Box 88, St. Helena, CA 94574 707–963–7756) acts as a matchmaking service, putting prospective guests with accommodations that will meet their needs.

Styles and standards vary widely, of course; generally private baths are not common, and rates are often moderate. In many small towns such guest houses are excellent examples of the best a region has to offer. Each one is different so that its advantage is precisely the opposite of that "no surprise" uniformity that motel chains pride themselves on. In popular tourist areas, state or local tourist information offices or chambers of commerce usually have lists of homes that provide spare rooms for paying guests, and such a listing usually means that the places included have been inspected and meet some standard of cleanliness and comfort and reasonable pricing. A nationwide *Guide to Guest Houses and Tourist Homes USA* is available from Tourist House Associates of America, Inc., P.O. Box 355-A, Greentown, PA 18426.

Youth Hostels. Hostels are a budget-minded alternative to hotel and motel accommodations. One must be a member of the American Youth Hostel/International Youth Hostel Federation to use its facilities at a discounted rate, but nonmembers may also stay at hostels for a slightly increased rate. There are two main hostels in the Los Angeles area, and they are open to all ages.

The *American Youth Hostel* is located in Harbor City, south of Los Angeles and close to such South Bay cities as Palos Verdes and Redondo Beach. Although sleeping bags are recommended, sheets and blankets are available to rent. There's a communal kitchen for cooking your own meals. The hostel sleeps seventy, and you may stay three days as a nonmember, five as a member.

The *Hollywood YMCA Hotel and Youth Hostel* is close to the core of the city, although the area is not safe during the evening hours. Hostelers are taken on a first-come, first-served basis. Rates are $17 for singles; $26.30 for doubles. Bring your own sleeping bag.

Both hostels offer simple accommodations. Dormitories are segregated by sex. In season it is wise to reserve space ahead; write or phone the hostel. Check with the Los Angeles Visitors Bureau (213–239–0200) or check a library for a copy of the *Official American Youth Hostels Handbook* by Michael Frome. It lists 240 or more U.S. hostels and includes maps. As an alternative (and you need not be a member), write to American Youth Hostel Association, Inc., 1332 L Street, N.W., 8th Floor, Washington, DC. 20005. If you join the association, a copy of the hostel guide and handbook will be sent to you.

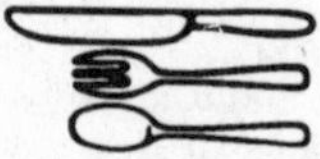

DINING OUT. The best advice for evening meals is to make reservations in advance whenever possible anywhere in the Southland but certainly in Los Angeles and in some of the resort areas, including Palm Springs.

Some restaurants, particularly in the evening, are fussy about customers' dress. For women, pants and pants suits are now almost universally acceptable. For men, tie and jacket remains the standard. Shorts are almost always frowned on for both men and women. Standards of dress are becoming more relaxed, and so a neatly dressed customer will usually experience no problem. If in doubt about accepted dress at a particular establishment, call ahead.

If you're traveling with children, you may want to find out if a restaurant has a children's menu and commensurate prices. (Many do.)

When figuring the tip on your check, base it on the total charges for the meal, not on the grand total if that total includes a state sales tax. Don't tip on tax.

RESTAURANT CATEGORIES

Restaurants located in Los Angeles proper are categorized in this volume by type of cuisine: French, Chinese, and so on, with restaurants of a general nature listed as Continental-International. Restaurants in less populous areas are divided into price categories as follows: *deluxe, expensive, moderate,* and *inexpensive.* As a general rule, expect restaurants in metropolitan areas to be higher in price than nonmetropolitan areas, although many restaurants that feature foreign cuisine are often surprisingly inexpensive. We should also point out that limitations of space make it impossible to include every establishment. We have therefore included those that we consider the best within each type of cuisine and price range.

Although the names of the various restaurant categories are standard throughout this series, the prices listed under each category may vary from area to area. In every case, however, the dollar ranges for each category are clearly stated before each listing of establishments.

TIPPING. Tipping is a personal expression of your appreciation of someone who has taken pleasure and pride in giving you attentive, efficient, and personal service. Because standards of personal service are highly uneven, you should, when you get genuinely good service, feel secure in rewarding it, and when you feel that the service you got was slovenly, indifferent, or surly, don't hesitate to show your reaction by withholding or reducing your usual tip. Remember that in many places the help are paid very little and depend on tips for the better part of their income. This practice is supposed to give them incentive to serve you well. These days the going rate on *restaurant* service is 15 percent on the amount *before* taxes. Tipping at counters is not universal, but many people leave 25¢ on anything up to $1.00 and 10% on anything over that. For *bellhops,* 50¢ per bag is usual. However, if you load him down with all manner of bags, hatboxes, cameras, coats, and so on, you might consider giving an extra quarter or two. For one-night stays in most *hotels* and *motels* you leave nothing. If you stay longer, at the end of your stay leave the maid $2.00–$3.00 per day or $5.00 per person per week for multiple occupancy. If you are staying at an *American Plan* hostelry (meals included) $1.50 per day per person for the waiter or waitress is considered sufficient and is left at the end of your stay. However, if you have been surrounded by an army of servants (one bringing relishes, another rolls, etc.), add a few extra dollars and give the lump sum to the captain or maître d'hotel when you leave, asking him to allocate it.

For the many other services you may receive in a big hotel or resort, figure roughly as follows: doorman, 50¢ for taxi handling, $1.00 for help with baggage; bellhop, 50¢ per bag, more if you load him down with extras; parking attendant, $1.00; bartender, 15 percent; room service, 10–15 percent of that bill; laundry or valet service, 15 percent; pool attendant, $1.00 per day; snackbar waiter at pool, beach, or golf club, 50¢ per person for food and 15 percent of the beverage check; locker attendant, 50¢ per person per day, or $2.50 per week; golf caddies, $1.00–$5.00 per bag, or 15 percent of the greens fee for an 18-hole course, or $3.00 on a free course; barbers, $1.00; shoeshiners, 50–75¢; hairdressers, $3.00; manicurists, $1.50.

Transportation: Give 25¢ for any taxi fare under $1.00 and 15 percent for any above; however, drivers in Los Angeles *expect* 20 percent, limousine service, 20 percent, car rental agencies, nothing. Bus porters are tipped 50¢ per bag, drivers nothing. On charters and package tours, conductors and drivers usually get $25–$30 per day from the group as a whole, but be sure to ask whether this tip has already been figured into the package cost. On short, local sightseeing runs, the driver-guide may get $1.00 per person, more if you think he has been especially helpful or personable. Airport bus drivers get nothing; redcaps in resort areas, 50¢ per suitcase; elsewhere, 40¢. Tipping at curbside check-in is unofficial, but same as above. On the plane, no tipping.

Railroads suggest that you leave 10–15 percent per meal for dining-car waiters; the steward who seats you is not tipped. Sleeping-car porters get about $1.50 per person per night. The 40–50¢ that you pay a railway station baggage porter is not a tip but the set fee that he must hand in at the end of the day along with the ticket stubs he has used. Therefore his tip is anything you give him above that, 50–75¢ per bag depending on how heavy your luggage is.

SENIOR CITIZEN AND STUDENT DISCOUNTS. Some attractions throughout the Southland offer considerable discounts to senior citizens and students. Some may require special city-issued senior-citizen identification, but in most cases showing a driver's license, passport, or some other proof of age will suffice—"senior" generally being defined as sixty-five or over for men and sixty-two or over for women. Museums, first-run and neighborhood movie theaters, and even some stores often post special senior-citizen rates. Those places offering student discounts are generally somewhat more stringent in their proof requirements—a high school or a college ID, international student traveler card, or evidence of age may be requested. Unfortunately, there is no uniformity on these matters.

DRINKING LAWS. In California the minimum age for the consumption of alcohol is twenty-one. In Los Angeles alcoholic beverages—by the bottle or by the drink—can be purchased from 6:00 A.M. to 2:00 A.M. daily. Package sales are made in liquor stores, some groceries, and drugstores. Most restaurants, bars, nightclubs, and pubs are licensed to serve a full line of beverages, whereas some have permits to serve beer and wine only. The legal age for the purchase of alcoholic beverages is also twenty-one; proof of age is required. One quart of alcohol can be imported or transported from another state or country.

BUSINESS HOURS, HOLIDAYS, AND LOCAL TIME. Los Angeles and the areas up and down the coast, like the rest of the United States, are on Standard Time from the last Sunday in October until the last Sunday in April. In April the clock is advanced one hour for Daylight Savings Time and in October is turned back an hour. The entire state lies within the Pacific Time Zone, which is three hours earlier in the day than the Eastern Time Zone, eight hours earlier than Greenwich Mean Time, and eighteen hours earlier on the clock and calendar than Sydney when Sydney is on Daylight Savings Time.

Business hours for banks are pretty much the same as those in the rest of the country, by and large 9:00 A.M. to 3:00 P.M., with some opening earlier or staying open later. Shops open at 9:00 A.M. and department stores at 10:00 or 10:30 A.M. Offices operate from 8:30 A.M. to 4:30 P.M. or from 9:00 A.M. to 5:00 P.M..

Most businesses, banks, and many restaurants close for the following holidays (the dates are for 1985): New Year's Day, January 1; Washington's Birthday (observance), February 18; Easter Sunday, April 7; Memorial Day (observance), May 27; Independence Day, July 4; Labor Day, September 2; Thanksgiving Day, November 28; and Christmas Day, December 25.

In addition, banks and some businesses may be closed on Lincoln's Birthday, February 12; Good Friday (from noon), April 5; Columbus Day (observance), October 14; Election Day (partially), November 5; and Veterans Day, November 11.

SPORTS. Southern California offers a wide variety of spectator sports throughout the year. January brings the most famous parade, the Tournament of Roses on New Year's Day. The Rose Bowl football game is held that afternoon. Although reserved seats can be bought, many people camp out on the sidewalk, using stoves, sleeping bags, chairs, and so on, a day in advance to secure ideal viewing sites. Other exciting January events include the Chinese New Year Parade, the Mounted Police Rodeo of Stars in Palm Springs, and the 90-hole Bob Hope Desert Classic in Palm Springs.

February is the month of the Pilot Pen Classic premier tennis tournament in Palm Springs, and in March the Long Beach Grand Prix features Indianapolis race cars passing through the city in a 161-mile competition.

The Dodgers and Angels open the **baseball** season in March.

Basketball, the season begins in the fall; the Lakers are at The Forum and the Clippers at the Sports Arena.

Del Mar Turf Club begins its **racing** season in July; it runs through September.

September ushers in the famous Los Angeles **County Fair** in Pomona as well as the Concours d'Elegance, the **antique car parade** in Santa Barbara.

The holiday season begins with the Los Angeles Times' NASCAR 500 at the Ontario Motor Speedway in November.

All along the coast there are **sportfishing** landings and public fishing piers. Marina del Rey has dock fishing as well as charter-boat fishing (13759 Fiji Way; 822–3625). The Malibu pier has both dock and boat fishing (23000 Pacific Coast Hwy.; 456–8030). The Redondo Beach Pier in the South Bay offers local offshore fishing (end of Harbor Dr. and Portofino Way; 372–3566). Hermosa Beach Pier has a municipal pier (end of Pier Ave., Hermosa Beach; 372–2124).

Horseback riding is popular at guest ranches in Santa Barbara and Palm Springs. Griffith Park in Los Angeles has 43 miles of horse trails. Commercial stables on the outskirts of the park, including Bar "S" Stables, Livingston Stables, Studio Stables and Sunset Ranch, offer horses for rent.

Offered up and down the coast, participant sports include swimming, surfing, sailing, skin diving, and fishing. Southern California's climate facilitates a year-round sports season. Besides the ocean, Southern California has lakes such as Big Bear, June Lake, and Lake Arrowhead for freshwater fishing, swimming, and boating. Hiking is also popular in these areas.

Golf is another popular Southern California sport. The small, well-known resort of Palm Springs alone has at least thirty-seven golf courses. See individual sections on practical information for details about each area.

Bicycling. For free maps or information regarding bike routes in the state, write to: Bicycle Facility Unit, Division of Highways, P.O. Box 1499, Sacramento, CA 95807; or call (916) 322–4314. For a copy of the 100-page guide of the Pacific Coast Bicentennial Bike Route, send $1.00, plus 6¢ tax (total $1.06) to: Caltrans, 6002 Folsom Blvd., Sacramento, CA 95817.

Los Angeles' Wheelman's Association has information on numerous bike trails; (213) 533–1707. A free bike-trail map is available to visitors at bike shops, City Hall, and the Convention and Visitors Bureau counter in the airport terminal. Rentals at bicycle shops around town and at many independent rental locations, especially along the coast, are abundant.

WINTER SPORTS. Despite the mild climate there are more than twenty established **ski** areas in southern California, half within a two-hour drive of Los Angeles. Depending on the weather, the season runs from November through March. North of Los Angeles, try the slopes of June Lake at June Mountain, Lake Isabella at Shirley Meadows, Mammoth Lakes at Mammouth Mountains, or at Sequoia National Forest at Montegicto–Sequoia, or Wolverton Ski Bowl east of Los Angeles. There is also skiing at Big Bear Lake at Crystal Ridge, Goldmine, or Snow Summit, at Running Springs at Ski Green Valley, or Snow Valley, or at Wrightwood at Holiday Hill, Mountain High, or Ski Sunrise.

Ice skating is a popular sport, especially in Los Angeles proper. Of course, skating takes place in indoor rinks where participants, dressed in summer attire, sometimes embellish their skating outfits with woolen scarfs and mittens to suggest a winter environment.

ROUGHING IT. More and improved camping facilities are springing up each year in California in national parks, national forests, state parks, private camping areas, and trailer parks, which by now have become national institutions.

A current *California State Park Camping Guide* is available for $2.00 at most State Park units or from the Department of Parks and Recreation, P.O. Box 2390, Sacramento, CA 95811, (916) 445–6477. This comprehensive brochure pinpoints all sites throughout the state and includes specific details concerning whether the campsites are developed, primitive, or contain trailer hookups. Sites especially set aside for hikers and bicyclists are noted. Parks able to accommodate group camping and those that have boat landings are designated.

For information on camping in the national park system in California, the Department of Interior offers a free booklet, available from the U.S. National Park Service, 22900 Ventura Blvd., Suite 140, Woodland Hills, CA 91364; (818) 888–3770.

Reservations are recommended for the state parks, especially in summer. There is a reservation charge plus campsite fees. Call Ticketron, (213) 216–6666 for information, but reservations must be made in person at a Ticketron outlet.

To camp in a national park or forest, there is a small fee; people are usually taken on a first-come, first-served basis. Yosemite is an exception, and in summer the valley campgrounds are on a reservation basis. Reservations are taken at the Western Regional Office, National Park Service, 450 Golden Gate Ave., San Francisco, CA 94102, (415) 556–4196, or through Ticketron, P.O. Box 26430, San Francisco, CA 94126.

For information on national forest camping write: U.S. Forest Service, 630 Sansome St., San Francisco, CA 94111, (415) 556–0122. Other useful addresses are the National Campers and Hikers Assoc., 7172 Transit Rd., Buffalo, NY 14221; and Kampgrounds of America, Inc., P.O. Box 30558, Billings, MT 59114—a very helpful commercial camping organization. Adventure Guides, Inc., 36 East 57th St., New York, NY 10022, publishes a book, *Adventure Travel (Source Book for North America),* which gives details on guided wilderness trips, backpacking, canoeing, rock climbing, covered-wagon treks, scuba diving, and more. The AAA publishes a *California-Nevada Camping Guide,* available to all members; it is revised annually.

RECREATIONAL VEHICLE PARKS. Culver City: *Rolling Homes, Inc.,* 3730 Robertson Blvd.; 673–6868. **Desert Hot Springs:** The *Golden Lantern Trailer Lodge,* Dillon Rd., has therapeutic pools. **North Hollywood:** *Valley Trailer Park,* 8250 Lankershim, takes adults only; no pets. **Oxnard:** *Wagon Wheel Trailer Lodge,* 2851 Wagon Wheel Rd. **Santa Monica:** *Beck's Deluxe Trailer Park,* 2818 Colorado Ave., adults only. **Anaheim:** *Vacationland Ltd.;* 1343 S. West Street, across from Disneyland. **Santa Barbara:** *Rancho Santa Barbara,* 333 Old Mill Rd., adults only; no pets.

FARM VACATIONS, GUEST RANCHES, HEALTH SPAS, AND RESORTS. Farm vacations continue to gain adherents, especially among families with children. Some accommodations are deluxe, some extremely simple. Here and there a farm has a swimming pool, whereas others have facilities for trailers and camping. For a directory of farms that take vacationers (including dates, accommodations, rates, etc.), write to Adventure Guides, Inc., 36 East 57th St., New York, NY 10022, for their 240-page book *Farm, Ranch, and Country Vacations.*

Circle Bar B Guest Ranch, situated in the midst of the Santa Ynez Mountains, offers an unusual combination of country living and city amenities. During the day swim, fish, horseback ride, or cook outdoors, and in the evening enjoy live theater or a private cabin with the luxuries of home. For information, write 1800 Refugio Rd., Goleta, CA 93117 (805) 968–1113.

A different approach is taken at *San Ysidro Rancho,* just outside Santa Barbara, where luxury is the key to ranching. Heated swimming pools and a French-Continental restaurant decorate the area around the stables. Celebrities often seek out the Rancho because of the beauty and solitude to be found at San Ysidro. Write 900 San Ysidro Lane, Montecito, CA 93108 (805) 969–5046.

At *Zaca Lake Resort* in the Los Padres National Forest near Santa Barbara the ranching way of life mixes with what you'd normally find in a resort area. Boating and horseback riding are the main activities at Zaca Lake, the site of many of the more memorable Western films made in America. Write P.O. Box 187, Los Olivios, CA 93441 (805) 688–4891.

Spas have been popular for several centuries in Europe, and in California they are now the rage. More and more clients of both sexes, who seek relief from high-stress jobs, are vacationing at luxury spas. Some spas are directed toward pampering their clientele, whereas others are more spartan and offer highly disciplined schedules, enabling their clientele to get back into shape or to keep the ones they have.

As an example of the former, try the *Golden Door,* a superdeluxe establishment in Escondido, California. Write to The Golden Door, P.O. Box 1567, Escondido, CA 92025 (619) 744–5777. Opened in 1958, the nation's smallest, most exclusive, and most expensive fitness center sits serenely in the Escondido Valley. Impressive Japanese architecture and gardens and an air of tranquility have drawn patrons from all over the world.

A more moderate establishment is the *Oaks* at Ojai. Low-cal meals, personalized weight control, and medical supervision constitute the name of the game. About an hour away from Santa Barbara in a picturesque setting, this elegant hotel, built in 1920, was recently reconstructed. Write 122 East Ojai Ave., Ojai, CA 93023 (805) 646–5573.

The *Bermuda Inn* is a no-frills fat farm located on the edge of the Mojave Desert, a little more than an hour's drive from Los Angeles. Weekly and daily rates include low-cal meals, exercise classes, the use of a gym, a jogging track, and a pool, as well as medical supervision. Write Joan Applegate, 43019 Sierra Highway, Lancaster, CA 93534 (805) 942–1493.

HUNTING. For current information on fees, which animals you may hunt, and seasons, write to the Department of Fish and Game, 1416 9th St., Sacramento, CA 95814, or phone (916) 445–7613. Some of the state's wildlife is protected. Deer and black bear hunting licenses are required. Pheasant, dove, and grouse shoots are often in private shooting reserves. No firearms are allowed in either the national or state parks. Big-game hunting is usually confined to national forests or public lands.

FISHING. Fishing is an all-season sport and business in the Golden State. Commercial fishermen netted over $230 million in 1980. For the sportsfisherfolk, the state's lakes and rivers abound with a great variety of freshwater fish. Several varieties of trout, salmon, bass, and catfish are especially plentiful. Saltwater catches include salmon, yellowtail, rockfish, and bass. For information, write to the Department of Fish and Game in Sacramento, listed under *Hunting.*

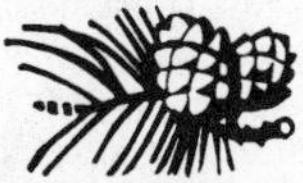

STATE PARKS. Reservations for state parks may be made through the central reservation system. For forms write the Department of Parks and Recreation, P.O. Box 2390, Sacramento, CA 95811. Reservations must be made two weeks in advance of the dates requested.

Reservations may also be made by applying in person to a local Ticketron outlet. In Los Angeles the phone is (213) 216–6666.

California's state park system involves more than 200 units spread over 850,000 acres of mountains and valleys, lakes and plateaus, rivers and deserts, forests and beaches. It also embraces many famous landmarks of the state's heritage.

Two kinds of **campgrounds** exist in the parks. Developed sites include hot showers, laundries, stoves, tables, piped drinking water, and flush toilets. The maximum stay is fifteen days; less in smaller camping areas and during peak summer months. Dogs on leashes are permitted during daylight hours only. At night your dog must stay inside your tent or in an enclosed vehicle.

About half the state's parks are in Southern California. They are strung along the Pacific Coast as beach parks. These beach parks form a chain from San Simeon Beach down to San Diego's Silver Strand and Imperial Beach next to Mexico.

The park closest to Los Angeles proper is the *Will Rogers State Historic Park,* 14253 Sunset Blvd. in Pacific Palisades. This park enshrines the beloved cowboy philospher's ranch home and mementos. "Never met a man I didn't like," said Will. Folks seem to share that feeling, for more than 225,000 visitors come callin' at his house yearly. Free polo games; more details on the park are in the *Practical Information* section.

Information on all state parks is available from the Department of Parks and Recreation, P.O. Box 2390, Sacramento, CA 95811 (916) 445–6477.

NATIONAL PARKS AND MONUMENTS. California numbers among its blessings five national parks and eight national monuments. The precise number located in Southern California depends on whose north–south demarcation is considered. (Many writers, historians, and politicians use the east–west Tehachapi Range, northeast of Santa Barbara, as the dividing line. Others claim the ten counties whose northern boundaries are parallel and slightly to the north of the 36-degree latitude. And there are those who include the four counties bordering the southern ten. *The California Information Almanac,* a state textbook, excludes Santa Barbara and San Luis Obispo counties and a portion of Kern County. It includes Inyo and part of Mono County. This interpretation extends the panhandle of southern California on the east all the way north to the same latitude as San Francisco.)

Sequoia and *Kings Canyon National parks* are considered in Southern California when one of the more generous measures mentioned above is applied. Sequoia has a visitors' center that will provide sightseeing advice. Helpful data and photographs are displayed. Campfire gatherings take place at night. Housekeeping cabins (European plan) are available at Camp Kaweah, where there also exist a coffee shop, a grocery store, a gift shop, and a gas station, all open all year. Giant Forest Lodge (American and European plan) is open from about May 24 to October 25. At Kings Canyon, the lodge, cabins, and housekeeping cabins follow the same schedule and have similar facilities. For additional information write Sequoia Kings Canyon National Parks, Three Rivers, California 93271.

Death Valley National Monument, awesome and historic, is up in the Southern California panhandle that pokes northward to the east of Los Angeles. It's weird, spooky, and memorable, covering almost two million acres. Death Valley is actually a lively place; it has many facilities ranging from rough to resort. The Mesquite Spring Campground has sixty campsites (thirty-day limit), water, and sanitary facilities. Texas Spring Campground, with eighty-five campsites, provides a trailer-parking area, water, fireplaces, and sanitary facilities. The Visitors' Center is open year round.

Joshua Tree National Monument, a 557,992-acre sprawl, preserves the unique yucca species, named by pioneering Mormons to whom its arms seemed raised in supplication in the manner of Joshua in the Bible. The Visitors' Center is at Twenty-nine Palms, and there are eight campgrounds on the valley floor. Fill your car's tank before entering.

The Channel Islands of Anacapa, Santa Barbara, Santa Cruz, Santa Rose, and San Miguel now form California's newest national park, the *Channel Islands National Park,* consisting of approximately 18,000 acres. At park headquarters in the Ventura Harbor there is a small visitors' center. All-day boat trips are scheduled from the Central Harbor aboard Island Packer Cruises (P.O. Box 993, Ventura, CA 93301, tel. 805–642–1393).

Cabrillo National Monument is without doubt within the boundaries of Southern California. It's a memorial, in the form of the Old Point Loma Lighthouse, to Juan Rodriguez Cabrillo, the Portuguese mariner who, in the service of Spain, discovered what is now San Diego Bay. The ocean view is top mast, and whale watching is another exciting pleasure from mid-December through mid-February. Pack a picnic; it'll never taste better.

For information on weather, road conditions, and campground information concerning any national park, call Parkcast, the National Park Service's recorded message at (817) 710–9488.

THEME PARKS. Within a sixty-mile radius of Los Angeles, you will find more theme or amusement parks than in any other area of the United States. Included are *Disneyland, Knott's Berry Farm, Movieland Wax Museum, Lion Country Safari,* and the *Kingdom of Dancing Stallions,* all in Orange County. (For more information on the aforementioned, see the "Anaheim/ Orange County" chapter.) Closer to the city proper, one can visit *Six Flags Magic Mountain, Marineland,* and *Universal Studios.* (See "Children's Activities" section under *Practical Information* for Los Angeles.) For a more extensive list of other such attractions, see "Sightseeing Checklist."

HINTS TO HANDICAPPED TRAVELERS. In July 1978 California's new laws concerning special privileges for handicapped people became effective. Handicapped people are now issued license plates allowing special parking privileges. The law also applies to vehicles carrying blind passengers and to people with serious heart problems. Handicapped people are now permitted to park in special blue-marked parking spaces, to park for unlimited periods in limited-time spaces, and to park free in metered spaces.

To find out what historic sites can accommodate wheelchair travelers in Los Angeles, write to the Junior League of Los Angeles, 3rd & Fairfax Sts., Los Angeles, CA 90036 for a free copy of *Round the Town with Ease.* Be sure to include a self-addressed, stamped envelope.

For general travel tips for the handicapped, write to the Consumer Information Center, Pueblo, CO 81109. Hints include requesting specially equipped hotel and motel accommodations and making reservations. Allow plenty of time if meeting bus, train, or plane schedules. Be sure the wheelchair is clearly identified if it is carried with other luggage. Check out restroom facilities, and if driving, allow frequent, refreshing breaks. Travel lightly and informally.

Additional information can be obtained by writing to the Society for the Advancement of Travel for the Handicapped, 26 Court St., Brooklyn, NY 11242. This organization has presented awards to both Ramada and Holiday Inns for their programs for handicapped guests.

Access to the National Parks, a handbook for the physically disabled, describes facilities and services at all U.S. national parks and costs $3.50. *Access Travel,* a brochure, provides information on 220 worldwide airport facilities. These publications are available from U.S. Government Printing Office, Washington DC 20402. A booklet especially for people with lung problems is available for $1.25 from George Washington University, Rehabilitation Research and Training Center, Ross Hall, Suite 714, 2300 Eye St., N.W., Washington, DC 20037.

For a free copy of Amtrak's *Access Amtrak,* a guide to their services for elderly and handicapped travelers, write to Amtrak, National Railroad Passenger Corporation, 400 North Capitol St., N.W., Washington, DC 20001. Handicapped travelers and senior citizens are entitled to 25% off regular coach fare, when the one-way coach fare is at least $40.00. A special fare is also available for handicapped children aged 2 to under 12 years. The fare is a special savings —37.5% of the applicable one-way regular adult coach fare.

The following hotels and motels will make special efforts to comply with the needs of handicapped guests. Phone or write in advance for reservations and mention any special needs or requests.

Downtown: *Alexandria Hotel,* 501 South Spring St.; The *Biltmore Hotel,* 515 South Olive St.; *Best Western Kent Inn Motel, Downtown,* 920 South Figueroa St.; *Dunes Motel,* 5625 W. Sunset Blvd.; *Holiday Inn Golden State,* 1640 Marengo Dr. at Mission Rd.; *Hyatt Regency Los Angeles,* 711 South Hope St.; *Los Angeles Hilton,* 930 Wilshire Blvd.; *Mayflower Hotel,* 535 South Grand Ave.; *Milner Hotel,* 813 South Flower St.; *Mitchell Hotel,* 1072 West 6th St.; The *New Otani Hotel and Garden,* 120 South Los Angeles St.; *Olympian Hotel,* 1901 West Olympic Blvd.; *Sheraton Grande Hotel,* 333 South Figueroa St.; *University Hilton,* 3540 South Figueroa; The *Westin Bonaventure, Los Angeles,* Fifth and Figueroa Sts.

At the airport: *Airport Century Inn,* 5547 West Century Blvd., P.O. Box 92080; *Holiday Inn–LAX,* 9901 S. La Cienega Blvd.; *Hyatt Hotel–LAX,* 6225 West Century Blvd.; *Manchester House Hotel,* 901 West Manchester; *Skyways Airport Hotel,* 9250 Airport Blvd.; *Pacifica Hotel,* 6161 Centinela Ave., P.O. Box 3200; *TraveLodge International Hotel,* 9750 Airport Blvd.; *Vista Motel,* 4900 Sepulveda Blvd.

Marina Del Rey: *Marina City Club Hotel,* 4333 Admiralty Way; *Marina International Hotel,* 4200 Admiralty Way; *Marina del Rey Hotel,* 13534 Bali Way; *Marina del Rey Marriott,* 13480 Maxella Ave.

Santa Monica–Malibu: *Hotel Carmel,* 201 Broadway, Santa Monica; *The Huntley Hotel,* 1111 2nd St., Santa Monica; *Inn at Santa Monica,* 530 Pico Blvd., Santa Monica; *Miramar-Sheraton Hotel,* 101 Wilshire Blvd., Santa Monica; *Palm Motel,* 2020–14th St., Santa Monica; *SeaShore Motel,* 2637 Main Street.

Hollywood: *Franklin Motel,* 1824 N. Beachwood Dr.; *Holiday Inn–Hollywood,* 1755 N. Highland Ave.; *Cine Lodge/Howards Weekly Apartments,* 1738 North Whitley; *Ramada Inn–Hollywood,* 1160 North Vermont Ave.

Mid-Wilshire, Los Angeles: *The Ambassador,* 3400 Wilshire Blvd.; *Executive Motor Inn–Mariposa,* 457 South Mariposa Ave.; The *Hotel Chancellor,* 3191 West 7th St.; *Hyatt Wilshire Hotel,* 3515 Wilshire Blvd.; *Wilshire Dunes Motor Hotel,* 4300 Wilshire Blvd.; *Wilshire–Orange Hotel,* 6060 West 8th St.

Beverly Hills/West Los Angeles: *Bel Air Sands Hotel,* 11461 Sunset Blvd.; *Beverly Wilshire Hotel,* 9500 Wilshire Blvd.; *Century Plaza,* 2025 Avenue of the Stars; *Holiday Inn Westwood Plaza Hotel,* 10740 Wilshire Blvd.; *Los Angeles*

West TraveLodge, 10740 Santa Monica Blvd.; *L'Ermitage Hotel,* 9291 Burton Way; *Ramada Inn–Beverly Hills,* 1150 South Beverly Drive; *Westwood Marquis Hotel,* 930 Highland Ave.

POSTAGE. At press time, rates for international mail from the United States are as follows: *Surface* letters to Canada and Mexico are at the U.S. domestic rate: 22¢ for 1 ounce or under, 39¢ for 2 ounces or under, but these rates actually involve airmail carriage to those countries. Surface letters to other foreign destinations are 44¢ each half ounce up to 2 ounces. *Airmail* letters to foreign destinations other than Canada, Mexico, and some Caribbean and South American countries are 44¢ for ½ ounce, 88¢ for 1 ounce. Postcards to domestic destinations, Canada, and Mexico are 14¢; 33¢ to any foreign destination. Standard international *aerogram letters,* good for any foreign destination, are 36¢ but, of course, nothing may be enclosed in them. Postal rates are no exception in periods of inflation; so check before you mail in case they have gone up since press time.

SECURITY. Take a good look at a map before exploring Los Angeles. This is an extremely seductive city, and it looks safer than it really is. There are some areas, in fact, that should be avoided—especially after daylight hours.

Stay away from south-central Los Angeles along the Imperial Highway and around the Sports Arena and Colliseum in Watts unless absolutely necessary. When you must be in that part of town, ride with your car doors locked, and park in secured parking lots.

Hollywood Blvd., with all its neon and bright lights, is also a haven for pickpockets and street criminals. Although a stroll along the Walk of Stars shouldn't be discouraged, take caution.

Don't leave money or valuables in your hotel room. Be sure to lock your door—even when you intend to stay in your room briefly. Use safe-deposit boxes offered by hotels for valuables; they are usually free.

Carry most of your funds in traveler's checks, and be sure to record the numbers in a separate, secure place. Watch your purse or wallet. Enjoy casual acquaintances—but at a distance. Never leave your car unlocked or valuable articles in plain sight in the car even if it is locked. Terminal counters and hotel check-in desks are also favored spots for lurking opportunists.

Since it isn't hard to have a safe vacation in Los Angeles, it would be too bad to let a little carelessness spoil it.

EMERGENCY TELEPHONE NUMBERS. In Los Angeles during emergencies, dial "0" and ask the operator to connect you immediately with the appropriate agency. The direct-dial number for the police in Los Angeles is 625–3311; for medical emergencies call 483–6721; and for fire, call 384–3131.

AN INTRODUCTION TO LOS ANGELES

by
JANE E. LASKY

Jane Lasky is a contributor to the Los Angeles Times Syndicate. She writes travel columns for both Esquire *and the inflight magazine for Republic Airlines, and contributes to such publications as* Palm Springs Life, Los Angeles Magazine, Travel Agent, Bon Appetit, *and* Emmy. *She is a resident of Los Angeles.*

On an acclaimed public television documentary called "LA, LA, Making it in LA," which chronicles struggling performers, a particularly naive yet charmingly enthusiastic actor observed: "Los Angeles is a place you dream of coming to and yet when you get here, you can still keep dreaming."

The surrounding landscape—towering skyscrapers, sun-baked deserts, rambling mountain ranges, miles of beaches, and the ubiquitous palm trees—is so unbelievably diverse that it enhances the unreal quality of the region. When you take account of the fact that this is the home of the movie and television industry, the mass producers of Technicolor dreams for the entire world, you can understand why so many visitors pinch themselves during their first encounter with Los Angeles.

This is a metropolis that possesses urban statistics that may well jolt back into consciousness the sun-and-fun-besotted mind:

The city contains more cars than Detroit.

Some 6,500 miles of road and freeways exist within city limits.

Los Angeles alone is bigger than the entire state of Rhode Island.

More than 130 legitimate theaters, 36 dance companies, 29 symphony orchestras, 35 museums, 17 opera and light opera companies, and 74 movie theaters enrich the life of Los Angeles.

Los Angeles boasts 46 colleges and 15 universities.

Every year 12.1 million people visit the city, and 75 percent of them come back for a second look.

Although these statistics may seem overwhelming, one fact may help the visitor relax and enjoy his or her visit: It's virtually impossible to do everything during one trip to Los Angeles. After all, as the city's slogan suggests, "LA's the place"—just do it at your own pace.

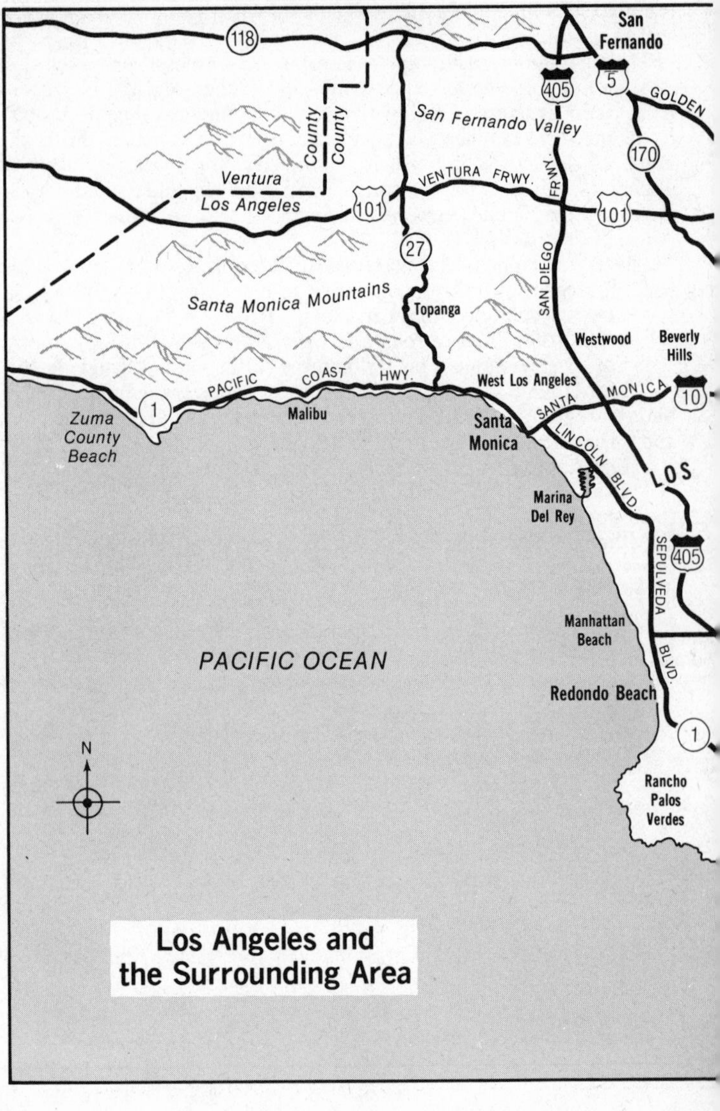

118
San Fernando
405
5
GOLDEN
Ventura County
Los Angeles County
San Fernando Valley
170
Ventura
Los Angeles
VENTURA FRWY.
101
101
27
SAN DIEGO FRWY.
Santa Monica Mountains
Topanga
Westwood
Beverly Hills
West Los Angeles
PACIFIC COAST HWY.
SANTA MONICA
10
1
Zuma County Beach
Malibu
Santa Monica
LINCOLN BLVD.
LOS
Marina Del Rey
405
SEPULVEDA BLVD.
Manhattan Beach
PACIFIC OCEAN
Redondo Beach
1
N
Rancho Palos Verdes
Los Angeles and the Surrounding Area

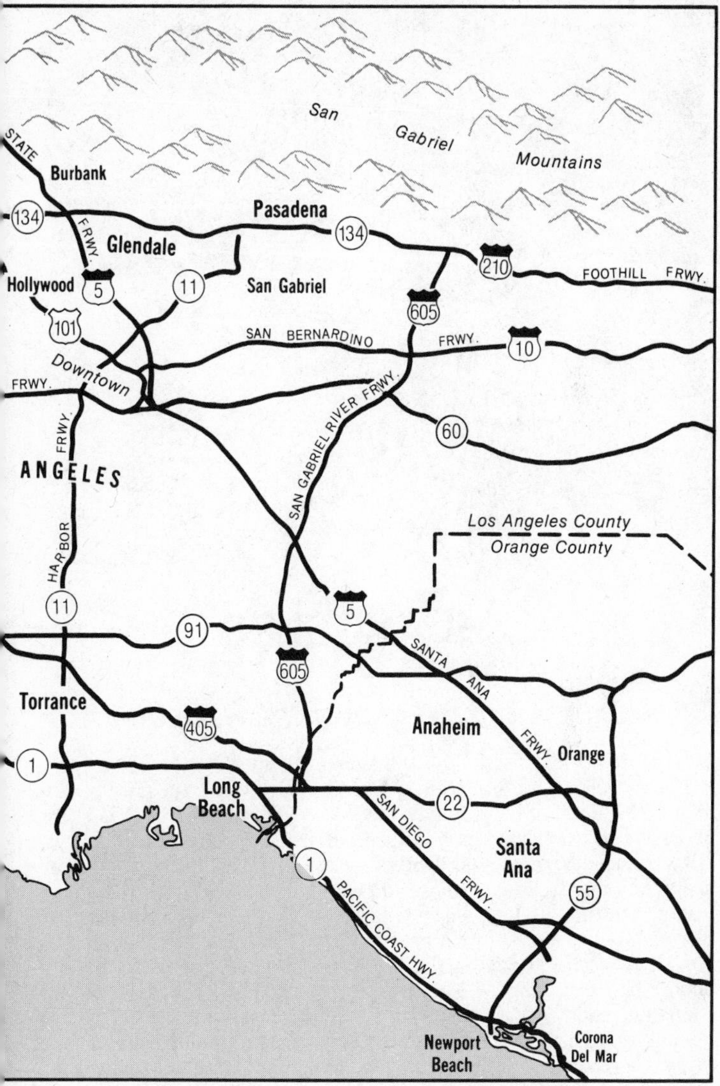
San Gabriel Mountains
STATE FRWY.
Burbank
134
Pasadena
Glendale
134
210
FOOTHILL FRWY.
Hollywood
5
11
San Gabriel
605
101
SAN BERNARDINO FRWY.
10
Downtown
FRWY.
SAN GABRIEL RIVER FRWY.
60
HARBOR FRWY.
ANGELES
Los Angeles County
Orange County
11
5
91
SANTA ANA FRWY.
605
Torrance
405
Anaheim
Orange
1
Long Beach
22
SAN DIEGO FRWY.
Santa Ana
1
55
PACIFIC COAST HWY.
Newport Beach
Corona Del Mar

LOS ANGELES

Exploring the City over the Rainbow

Los Angeles: The Big Orange, El Lay, Tinseltown, the City of Angels. Why does one place have so many different names? Perhaps because Los Angeles is not just one city; it's a collection of towns, villages, neighborhoods, and other assorted places, all connected by geography and freeways, where you can find practically anything. For instance, although Los Angeles is the entertainment capital of the world, the city also offers a growing list of cultural attractions. Los Angeles is one of the few cities in the world where people are able to choose between lying on a sunny beach or going skiing. Looking for something more stimulating than leisure-time activities? There is the possibility of visiting state-of-the-art computer technology centers and firms where aerospace research is underway that just might put a man (or a woman) on Mars in the next few years.

Maybe a fantasy diversion is what you had in mind. Here again, Los Angeles is the place for you. Less than an hour away is the world-famous Disneyland, and in the surrounding area are many other amusement parks filled with all kinds of rides and attractions. Just want to see a movie? Well, you can do that, or you can see how they're made by taking the Burbank or Universal Studios tour. Or get tickets to a prime-time television show and watch your favorite stars go through their paces.

There are the usual kinds of visitor pastimes here, too—such things to do as shopping and sightseeing. If you'd care to do a little gambling, you don't have to go all the way to Las Vegas: the race track circuit in Los Angeles is always active. At any time of the year you can find thoroughbreds racing at Santa Anita, Hollywood Park, or Del Mar. In addition, quarter horse races and trotters can be seen throughout the year at Los Alamitos Race Track.

If you'd prefer not to be a spectator, plenty of small shops offer roller skates or bicycles for rent. You can even rent a Rolls Royce if you like to travel in style.

When you get hungry, you'll have to do some choosing. There are about 16,000 restaurants in Los Angeles, *not* counting franchises and fast food parlors. They range from pure fun to extremely fine. Because of the ethnic mix in the city, one can find cuisine from all over the world in Los Angeles, as well as good old American fare.

Why does Los Angeles offer so much variety? Possibly because the city has attracted people from all over the world. Most have brought with them their dreams for a better life. Los Angeles is a city built on fantasy, hope, and wishes, a place beyond the rainbow, where even today dreams really do come true—sometimes.

The Early Days

Most people are surprised to learn how big Los Angeles is. Founded in 1769 by Spanish missionaries, the village in its early days was a sleepy little farming community that flooded every time a sizable rain came.

Although Los Angeles served briefly as the capital of California, most of the growth in the state took place in the north, especially during San Francisco's gold rush days in the mid-1800s. During those years, the fertile Los Angeles valleys provided miners up north with food, but the city, hampered by lack of water, grew only modestly.

It was another kind of "gold" that brought settlers to Los Angeles: citrus fruits. Cheap railroad fares and the promise of easy-to-grow, easy-to-sell citrus fruits attracted thousands to Southern California at the turn of the century. Black gold, in the form of rich oil deposits, was

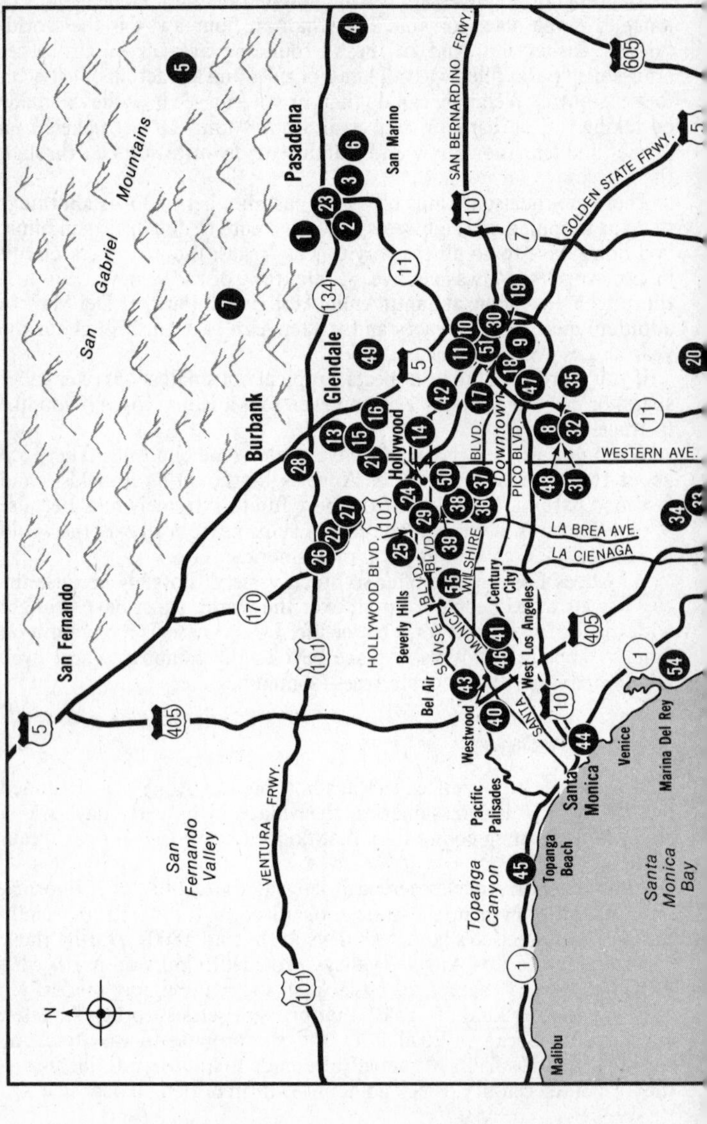
San Gabriel Mountains
San Fernando
Burbank
Glendale
Pasadena
San Marino
Hollywood
Beverly Hills
Bel Air
Westwood
Century City
West Los Angeles
Downtown
Pacific Palisades
Topanga Canyon
Topanga Beach
Santa Monica
Venice
Marina Del Rey
Malibu
San Fernando Valley
Santa Monica Bay
VENTURA FRWY.
SAN BERNARDINO FRWY.
GOLDEN STATE FRWY.
HOLLYWOOD BLVD.
SUNSET BLVD.
SANTA MONICA BLVD.
WILSHIRE BLVD.
PICO BLVD.
WESTERN AVE.
LA BREA AVE.
LA CIENAGA
N

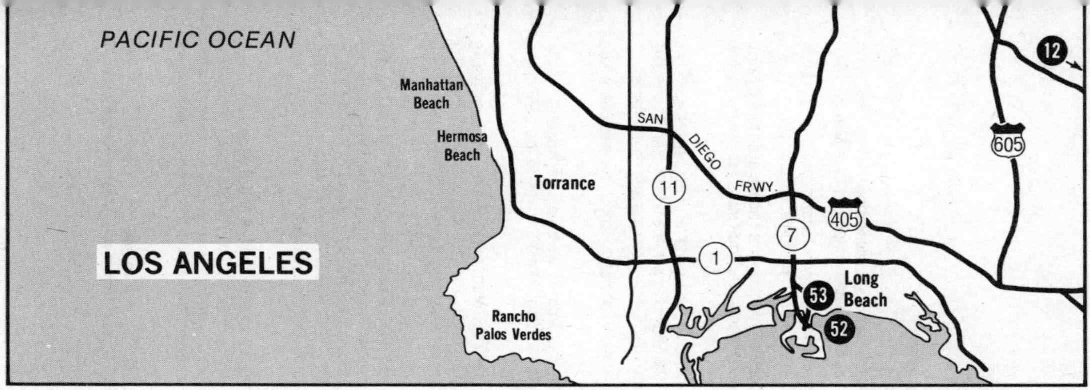

Points of Interest
(Add'l info. on following 2 pages)

1) Rose Bowl
2) Norton Simon Museum
3) Pasadena Civic Auditorium
4) Santa Anita Racetrack
5) Mt. Wilson Observatory
6) Huntington Library Gallery
7) Descanso Gardens
8) USC Campus & Medical Center
9) Littly Tokyo
10) Chinatown
11) Dodger Stadium
12) Anaheim Stadium, Disneyland, Knott's Berry Farm, Anaheim Convention Center
13) L.A. Zoo
14) Barnsdall Park
15) Griffith Park
16) Greek Theater
17) Civic Center
18) Music Center
19) City Hall
20) Watts Towers
21) Griffith Park Observatory
22) Hollywood Sign
23) Hollywood Bowl
24) Pantages Theater
25) Mann's Chinese Theatre
26) Universal Amphitheatre
27) Universal Studios
28) NBC Studios
29) Huntington Hartford Theatre
30) Union Station
31) Coliseum
32) Exposition Park
33) Hollywood Park Racetrack
34) The Forum
35) Shrine Auditorium
36) L.A. County Art Museum
37) La Brea Tar Pits
38) Farmer's Market
39) CBS TV City
40) Pacific Design Center
41) Shubert Theater
42) ABC Entertainment Center
43) UCLA
44) Santa Monica Civic Auditorium
45) J. Paul Getty Museum
46) Mormon Temple
47) Los Angeles Convention Center
48) California Museum of Science and Industry
49) Forest Lawn Memorial Park
50) Paramcunt Studios
51) Olvera St.
52) Queen Mary/Spruce Goose
53) Long Beach Convention Entertainment Center
54) L.A. Int'l Airport
55) Beverly Center

LOS ANGELES AREA

(Italic numbers refer to map and legend on previous pages)

Olvera Street. Cobblestoned, historic Olvera Street is a bustling strip of shops and open booths selling souvenirs and mementos of all kinds, many imported from Mexico. *(51)*

Little Tokyo. A short hop away from Olvera Street between 1st and 3rd Streets is Little Tokyo, with a wealth of restaurants, shops—and even a Buddhist temple. *(9)*

Chinatown. Close to Little Tokyo is Los Angeles' Chinatown, an active area along North Broadway where hundreds of tiny shops, restaurants, and food stores share only a few blocks of space. *(10)*

Downtown. Bordered by 1st Street, Olympic Blvd., Alameda, and Figuero Streets lies the city's downtown district, which includes the Music Center, the flower market, the garment district, the Bonaventure Hotel, and the ARCO Plaza (shops and restaurants).

Exposition Park. Close to the downtown area, Exposition Park is the site of the Los Angeles Museum of Natural History. *(32)*

The Boulevard. Wilshire Boulevard takes you from downtown Los Angeles to the Pacific Ocean, showing off lots of the city in between. Along the way to the beach, the sixteen-mile street passes Beverly Hills, Westwood, and Santa Monica.

Miracle Mile. The stretch of Wilshire Blvd. between Vermont Ave. and La Brea Ave. is known as the Miracle Mile. At the mile's end is Hancock Park, location of the famous La Brea Tar Pits, along with the George C. Page Museum, devoted to displays of prehistoric relics, many retrieved from the nearby tar.

Hollywood. The most well-known street in Hollywood is Hollywood Blvd., where the star plaques embedded in pavement beneath your feet make up the notable Walk of Fame, commemorating the greats of the entertainment industry. At the end of this walk is a monument to movies, Graumann's (now Mann's) Chinese Theatre. Also in Hollywood are Paramount Studios, ABC and CBS Studios, Griffith Park, the Hollywood Bowl, and the highly visible Hollywood sign.

West Hollywood/Fairfax Area. The Farmer's Market is located at 3rd Street and Fairfax Avenue: 20 acres of sights, including souvenir shops, restaurants, and fresh-produce stands. The Fairfax area is considered to be the heart of Los Angeles' Jewish community, and also has loads of open-air markets featuring fresh produce and baked goods. *(38)*

Beverly/La Cienega. At Beverly and La Cienega is a mammoth shopping mall, the Beverly Center, which houses more than 100 shops, 18 movie theaters, and seemingly endless eating establishments. *(55)*

Sunset Strip. A scenic view of a different kind can be found along Sunset Blvd.'s infamous strip, located between Crescent Heights Blvd. and Doheny Drive in Beverly Hills. Found on the Strip are some of the most creative billboards in the world, advertising current motion pictures or recently released record albums. The Strip is the location of the legendary Hollywood hotel favored by celebrities, Chateau Marmont, and also of a large number of restaurants catering to a wide range of tastes.

Beverly Hills. The glitz of the Strip ends as suddenly as it begins at Doheny Blvd. where Sunset Blvd. enters the glamorous and world-renowned city of Beverly Hills. Suddenly the sidewalk gives life to perfectly manicured lawns and the palatial homes of movie stars and entertainment-industry biggies.

Century City. Once the backlot of Twentieth Century Fox Studios, today Century City is a 180-acre tribute to modern architecture and the Los Angeles business world.

Westwood. Here nationalities of all kinds meet and mix creating an interesting street life. Westwood has much to offer, such as the University of California at Los Angeles (UCLA) and the actual village itself, with a dozen movie theaters, nearly as many book stores, and all manner of restaurants.

Bel Air. While not as well known as Beverly Hills, this area is equally spectacular in terms of real-estate. Upon driving through the white wrought-iron gates, you'll see some of the gigantic homes beyond—some of them, of course, owned by the stars who rule in Hollywood.

Santa Monica. This portion of town offers an interesting juxtaposition of the old and the new on its Main Street. You'll find some of the trendiest shops, restaurants, and bars anywhere, while nearby you will catch glimpses of the good old days. Take a walk along Santa Monica pier, which juts out into the Ocean.

Venice. There is no shortage of street life along the three-mile stretch of beach in Venice; sidewalk cafés, street vendors, roller skaters, bike riders and sidewalk entertainers. Canals in the area slightly remind the visitor of the Italian Venice.

Marina del Rey. A recently developed area, the Marina is home to thousands of boats, everything from sampans to yachts and schooners. The marina's harbor—one of the largest on the West Coast, and completely man-made—offers scenic boat tours.

Malibu. North of Santa Monica lies a city that is virtually synonymous with California: Malibu. Surfing here is a religion. On this stretch of the Pacific Coast Highway there are several restaurants where one can sit out over the water's edge and absorb some of the Mailbu state of mind.

San Fernando Valley. For years, the Valley was considered suburbia, but now it has come into its own right, boasting fine restaurants, shopping, and several major movie studios—not to mention Beautiful Downtown Burbank.

Pasadena. Several of the main streets are lined with quaint little shops and architecture reflecting the city's early days. Some of Pasadena's claims to fame are the Norton Simon Museum, the Pasadena Library, the Rose Bowl, and Pasadena Center.

San Marino. South of Pasadena lies San Marino, home of magnificent homes and one of Southern California's most remarkable landmarks, the Huntington Library, Botanical Gardens, and Art Gallery.

discovered in the area at about the same time and further increased the influx of would-be settlers.

Oddly enough, it was a development on the East Coast that eventually gave Los Angeles its most famous industry. Shortly after Thomas Edison developed valuable motion picture equipment in his New Jersey studio, it became apparent that the mild weather and the good sunlight of Southern California formed a more suitable environment for producing movies. And ever since the early 1900s, the Los Angeles area has been the center of the world's film business.

Los Angeles continued to thrive as its economy diversified and its population grew. Today it is the second largest metropolitan area in the United States. Yet, despite its growth, Los Angeles has managed to retain much of its early charm.

An Overwhelming Experience

"It's so spread out!" If you find yourself exclaiming about the vastness of the city during a visit to Los Angeles, don't be surprised. It's true. Los Angeles city proper isn't all that big (64 square miles as opposed to San Francisco's 49), but the Greater Los Angeles Basin, which encompasses the other towns as well, extends from the Pacific Ocean's shores 60 miles inland to the San Bernardino and San Jacinto mountain ranges and takes in all the territory between Santa Barbara and San Diego, a range of about 464 square miles. Now *that* is big, but not intimidating. The people and the pleasant weather combine to make Los Angeles one of the easiest places in which to live.

Los Angeles has been maligned on several counts: its size, the intricately entangled freeway system, the smog, and the shallow "sun worshipper" mentality. Some of these criticisms are based on fact: The place is large, no doubt about it. The freeways can be confusing, but, on the other hand, what better way to get around such a vast area than via huge arteries that keep the traffic flowing? A good map and paying attention to the roadsigns will enable you to find your way around. The smog, a natural by-product of the freeways and the geography of the city, which is located between an ocean and several mountain ranges, is another story. Fortunately, not every day is smoggy, and many Angelenos seem to be immune to the effects of unclean air. As for being inhabited by people who do nothing but sip drinks at their poolsides, that assessment is far from the truth. Some of the finest universities in the world are located here, as are some of the nation's best museums and art galleries. Although the film and television industries often overshadow it, Los Angeles has a bustling theater community that consists of a large number of Broadway-type theaters and a seemingly endless number of smaller showcases, which feature hopefuls who sometimes go on to stardom.

In addition to the universities, museums, art galleries, and theaters, there are innumerable bookstores that specialize in everything from fine first editions to pulp paperbacks and comic books. That should be enough nonalcoholic pleasure to keep anyone satisfied.

The Angeleno

Over the years, thanks to television and films depicting the southern California area, a stereotypical Angeleno has emerged: blond, tanned, athletic, and clad in swimwear. This image of the Southern Californian seems to persist for good reason. Just one visit to a beach area and you'll see why. Because of the magnificent weather, sun lovers in Southern California can enjoy their favorite pastime nearly every day. And they do. It's only during the few cool, cloudy days each year that the beaches aren't occupied by sun-streaked blond surfers and sunbathers.

But the stereotypical Angeleno is only one member of the Los Angeles population. If you travel inland, you'll find a wide-ranging mix of people, and most of them are from somewhere else. Surprising as that sounds, you'll rarely meet a native Southern Californian. The city is primarily made up of people from other places who've come here to find the good life.

Does it exist? Is the quality of life here better than it is elsewhere? It's a difficult question to answer, but most residents seem quite content with their lives. Feel free to take a poll of your own, however. Angelenos love to talk about their city and their lives.

Besides serving as a second home for transplanted Easterners and Midwesterners, Los Angeles is a melting pot comprising a substantial foreign-born population. The largest group is Mexican-Americans, and the city also has a number of Chinese, Japanese, Korean, Filipino, South American, English, Armenian, Israeli, and Polish residents, a rich assortment of ethnic communities scattered throughout the city.

The Original Los Angeles

Because of the city's vastness, it's difficult to get a clear idea of how to approach it. But if you think of it as a giant meal and try to take it just one course at a time, you'll find it easier than trying to cover too much territory in one day. Remember that Los Angeles is a basin more or less circular in shape. The best way to see the area, therefore, is to go in circles.

A convenient place to begin is at one of Los Angeles' oldest streets, now named Olvera Street. Although Los Angeles isn't a city suited to walking, this downtown district—encompassing Olvera Street, Chinatown, and Little Tokyo—lends itself to daytime walking tours.

Olvera Street is where the first settlers established a homestead, which still stands. Tours go through the Avila Adobe, built in 1818, the city's oldest extant home. One can see the furnishings of an early California family. Cobblestoned Olvera Street itself is now a bustling strip of shops and open booths selling souvenirs and mementos of all kinds, many imported from Mexico. Here you can get a colorful serape, a pinata, a first-rate enchilada, or tooled leather goods without crossing the border. Often there is outdoor entertainment such as folk dancers and mariachi bands performing in the plaza. It's no wonder that Olvera Street ranks as the city's number one tourist attraction.

A short walk from Olvera Street is Union Station Passenger Terminal, the city's central train station. Nearly fifty years old and covering 50 acres of ground, Union Station retains its historic charm. Still used today, it is filled with original furnishings.

Another short hop away from Olvera Street, between First and Third Streets, is Little Tokyo, which contains a wealth of Japanese restaurants, shops, and even a Buddhist temple. The Japanese Village Plaza provides a mall setting for a number of shops. Nearby is the New Otani Hotel, which contains several fine restaurants serving sushi and other traditional Japanese fare. Next to the hotel is Weller Court, a retail shopping area of department stores and boutiques. At the Japan Cultural Arts Center is the new Japan America Theater, which showcases Kabuki and koto presentations.

A new spotlight on the redeveloping downtown area is on the Museum of Contemporary Art on the edge of Little Tokyo. For the time being, MoCA is in a 1940s warehouse at Central and 1st, and appropriately titled The Temporary Contemporary until the hard opening of the museum in 1986.

Not far from Little Tokyo is Los Angeles' Chinatown—an active area on North Broadway where hundreds of tiny shops, restaurants, and food stores share only a few blocks of space. One can sample *dim sum,* tiny traditional Chinese pastries, sip some tea, and perhaps buy a silk kimono or hand-painted fan. At night Chinatown takes on another aspect when several of the city's premier punk rock clubs open their doors and the plaza fills with an assortment of colorful young people. (Most of the older citizens seem to have gone home.)

Yes, There Is a Downtown

Many people (some of them are Los Angeles residents) claim that there is no downtown Los Angeles. But there is. In the area roughly bounded by First Street on the north, Olympic Boulevard on the south, and Alameda and Figueroa on the east and west, respectively, lies the city's center.

Like many city centers, it has its share of unsavory characters. But don't let that stop you from visiting it; it has plenty of interesting sites.

At the north end of the district is one of the renowned landmarks, the Music Center. A forty million dollar monument to Los Angeles' cultural community, it consists of three theaters. At the Dorothy Chandler Pavilion, the Los Angeles Philharmonic Orchestra, the Civic Light Opera, and the Joffrey Ballet perform. The Ahmanson Theater offers entertainment in a Broadway vein. And the Mark Taper Forum is home for some of Los Angeles' experimental plays, as well as more conventional fare.

The Los Angeles Times Building, taking up an entire city block at First and Spring Streets, houses the West's largest newspaper operations. Tours are offered.

The Los Angeles Mall on North Main Street is two blocks of double-decker shopping, plus dining and convenient parking facilities. The Los Angeles Children's Museum, with its wonderful "hands-on" displays, is at the north end of the mall.

On Wall Street near Eighth is the Los Angeles Flower Market, one of the largest in the nation. Although most business is transacted in the wee hours of the morning (when there's also the most excitement), there is still plenty to see throughout the day.

Also worth a visit in the downtown area is the Pacific Stock Exchange, a miniversion of the one in New York. The visitors' gallery on the second floor overlooks the often frenetic activities.

Also downtown is the garment district on Los Angeles Street between Fourth and Tenth, where clothing of all sorts (some by major designers, others not) is sold at cut-rate prices.

The oldest library in Los Angeles, built in 1926, is downtown on Fifth Street. This central library features beautiful Spanish tiles, a second-floor rotunda, and an outstanding collection of Californiana.

There are two very good spots in the downtown area to get one's bearings. One is the observation area on the 27th floor of City Hall. The other is at the Westin Bonaventure Hotel's rooftop lounge, which revolves, displaying different vistas of the city as you relax and take in the view. Downtown Los Angeles boasts many old architectural wonders, but the shimmering cylinders of the Bonaventure are certainly one of the most dramatic constructions of recent origin.

Other sights in the downtown area include the Bradbury Building, an architectural wonder built in 1893 on S. Broadway, the Arco Plaza, which features some fine art displays, shops, restaurants, and the World Trade Center. For something with more of an ethnic flavor—almost any ethnic flavor in the world—check out the Grand Central Market,

Points of Interest

1) Chinatown
2) Union Station
3) Olvera Street
4) Los Angeles Mall
5) City Hall
6) Music Center
7) Federal Building
8) Little Tokyo
9) Grand Central Market
10) Bradbury Building
11) World Trade Center
12) Bonaventure Shopping Gallery
13) Arco Plaza Visitors Information Center
14) Central Library
15) Pershing Square
16) RTD/Greyhound Bus Terminal
17) California Mart
18) Convention Center

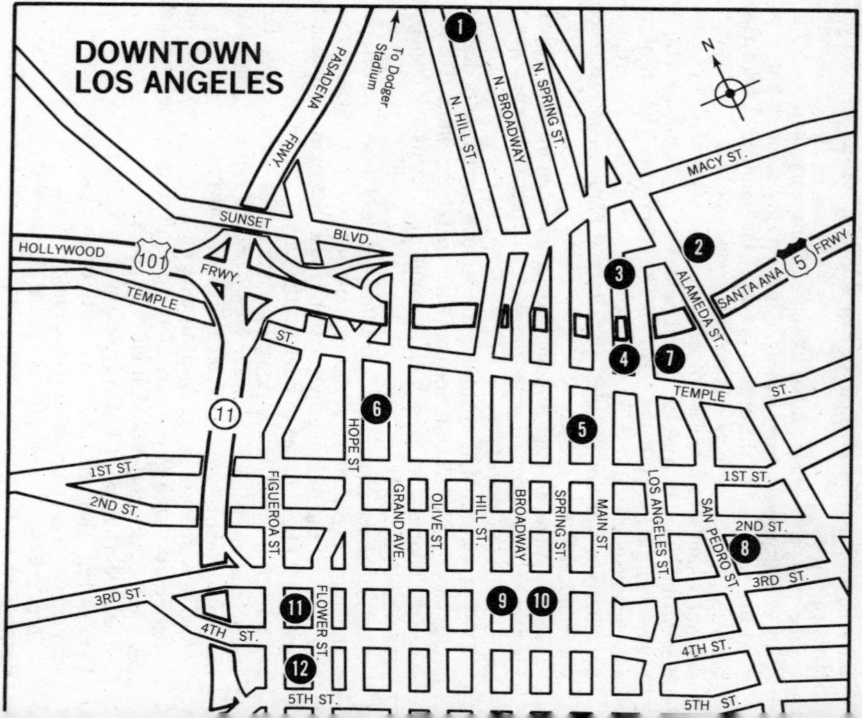

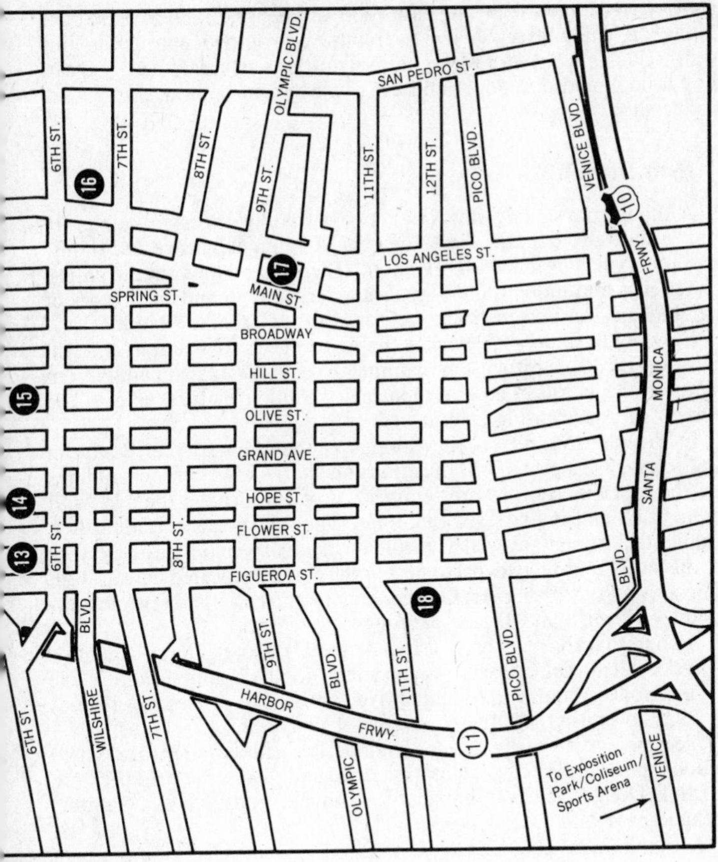
OLYMPIC BLVD.
SAN PEDRO ST.
6TH ST.
7TH ST.
8TH ST.
9TH ST.
11TH ST.
12TH ST.
PICO BLVD.
VENICE BLVD.
10
16
LOS ANGELES ST.
FRWY.
17
SPRING ST.
MAIN ST.
BROADWAY
HILL ST.
15
MONICA
OLIVE ST.
GRAND AVE.
SANTA
14
HOPE ST.
FLOWER ST.
6TH ST.
8TH ST.
13
FIGUEROA ST.
BLVD.
18
BLVD.
9TH ST.
BLVD.
11TH ST.
PICO BLVD.
HARBOR
6TH ST.
WILSHIRE
7TH ST.
FRWY.
11
OLYMPIC
To Exposition Park/Coliseum/ Sports Arena
VENICE

a vast cavern filled with shops for food and delightful oddments of all kinds, on Third Street. A less well-known downtown spot is St. Vincent's Court on Seventh Street, a lovely little courtyard where you can buy a book and a bouquet and even enjoy them both at an open-air coffee shop.

Near Downtown

Although not strictly downtown, two of the city's finest museums are only a short drive south. The California Museum of Science and Industry honors achievements in aviation, space technology, mathematics, electricity, and industrial design. Some learning, "hands-on" types of exhibits are fun and instructional for both children and adults.

Close by in Exposition Park is the Los Angeles Museum of Natural History. Its displays focus on mammal, bird, and artifact exhibits from all over the world. The development of motion pictures is also the subject of a fascinating exhibit here.

In the same vicinity is the campus of the University of Southern California, a leader in both education and sports. Many of the buildings on the spacious campus are reminiscent of Ivy League schools, with their brick and ivy-covered buildings. The school has a leading film studies department, as well as medicine, dentistry, and pharmacy. One of the few gerontology departments in the nation is located here as well. The university's Fisher Art Gallery houses sixteenth- and seventeenth-century Flemish and Dutch paintings.

Also in this area are three of Los Angeles' major stadiums. The Los Angeles Memorial Coliseum is the site of football games, motorcycle racing, rodeos, and other competitive sports. The coliseum was built in 1932 to house the Olympic events of that year.

Nearby is the Sports Arena, a modern, enclosed structure where indoor sporting events, such as basketball and tennis, are held. Farther north is Dodger Stadium, home of Los Angeles' most famous National League baseball contenders.

The Boulevard

Since the Los Angeles Basin is round in shape and not everyone wants to traverse the entire circumference of the place, there is an alternative. You can take Wilshire Boulevard from downtown Los Angeles to the Pacific Ocean. Along the way to the beach, the 16-mile street passes by Beverly Hills, Westwood, and Santa Monica before it runs to the ocean. Like New York's Fifth Avenue or Chicago's State Street, Wilshire is filled with banks, shops, department stores, and myriad stop offs. (In fact, a neat little four-hour capsule tour of Los

Angeles can be accomplished by taking Wilshire from its point of origin to the beach, continuing on the Pacific Coast Highway up to Sunset Boulevard, and then following Sunset all the way back downtown.)

The stretch of Wilshire between Vermont and La Brea referred to as the Miracle Mile—the world's only linear downtown—contained the city's first commercial establishments adapted to motorized transport in the 1920s. At the end of Miracle Mile is Hancock Park, the location of the famous La Brea Tar Pits and the George C. Page Museum, devoted to displays of prehistoric relics, many of them retrieved from the nearby tar.

Adjacent to Hancock Park is the Los Angeles County Museum of Art, a worthwhile stop. A major collection of Impressionist paintings and an excellent sculpture garden are permanently on display. In addition, major national exhibits are frequently booked. The museum consists of three buildings and the sculpture garden. The four-story Ahmanson Gallery displays collections spanning the history of art and culture. Among its offerings are works by Picasso, modern-day American painters, and early Asian artisans. The Frances and Armand Hammer Wing features contemporary art and visiting exhibitions. The Leo S. Bing Theater shows retrospectives of Hollywood classics.

Hollywood

Following Wilshire will provide you with a pleasant overview of the city; but to get to the main sights, other routes are required. In Los Angeles, the foremost sight and the "city within the city" is Hollywood. Once synonymous with glamour, Hollywood is now a shadow of its former self.

The area is roughly bounded by Vermont Avenue on the east, La Brea on the west, Melrose on the south, and Franklin on the north. The best known Hollywood street within the city, though, is Hollywood Boulevard. It still offers a wealth of sights. Beginning at the eastern edge, at Vermont and Hollywood Boulevard, the first attraction is Barnsdall Park, a former estate designed by Frank Lloyd Wright. It now houses the municipal Art Gallery and a Junior Arts Center where exhibits by local artists and festivals celebrating creativity are held. There are tours of Hollyhock House, oil heiress Aline Barnsdall's former residence, which still contains some of the original furnishings from the 1920s. Hollyhock House was recently restored.

Farther west along the boulevard is the Pantages Theater, a former movie palace that has been refurbished and now presents Broadway musicals.

Continuing west: The famous intersection of Hollywood and Vine is nearby, but visitors may notice that it is not quite what it used to be.

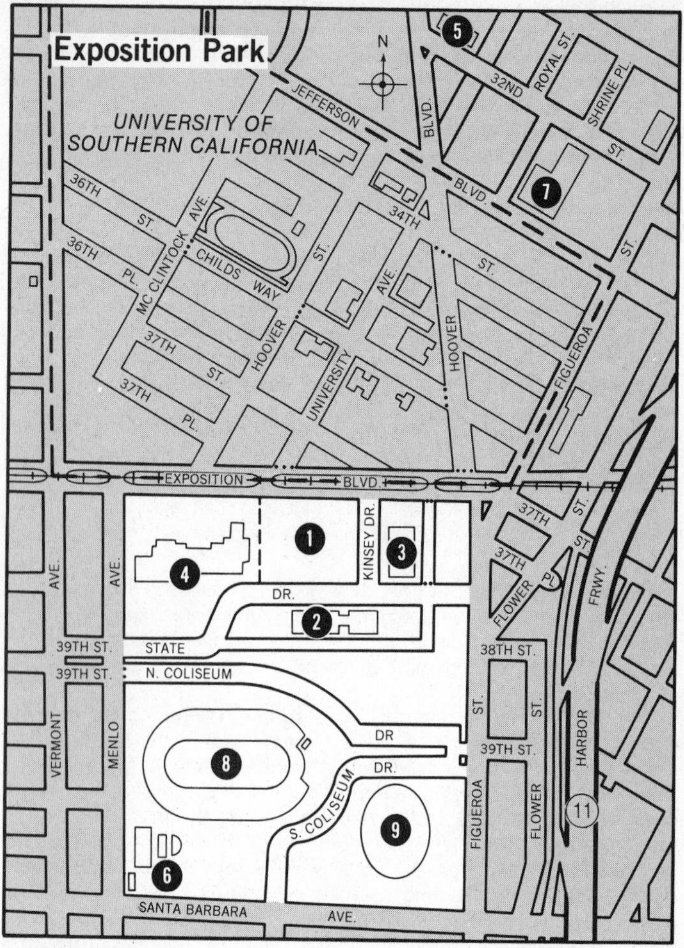

Points of Interest

1) Exposition Park Rose Garden
2) California State Museum of Science and Industry
3) The Space Museum
4) Los Angeles County Museum of Natural History
5) Hebrew Union College and Skirball Museum
6) Swimming Stadium
7) The Shrine Auditorium
8) Los Angeles Memorial Coliseum
9) Sports Arena

Nevertheless, this stretch of Hollywood Boulevard between Vine and La Brea is fun to stroll. North on Vine is an architectural wonder, the Capitol Records building, shaped like a stack of records with a needle on top. In addition, there are endless novelty and book shops, as well as lots of movie memorabilia and poster shops. The stars embedded in the pavement beneath your feet, commemorating the greats of the entertainment industry, make up Hollywood's Walk of Fame. At the end of this walk is a monument to the movies, Grauman's (now Mann's) Chinese Theater. Even the most jaded traveler can have fun trying to match foot- and handprints with those of their favorite stars. And even if you're not going in to catch a movie, take a peek at the lobby of the theater. It's a wonderful reminder of the splendor that once was Hollywood.

The equally extravagant Egyptian Theater is located across the street from the Chinese. Also nearby, just one block east, is the Hollywood Wax Museum, containing lifelike replicas of immortal stars.

Speaking of movies, where is the industry that once made Hollywood great? A fair share of it is still in Hollywood. Paramount Studios is just south of Hollywood Boulevard, at Melrose and Valentino. And in that neighborhood there are many small, independent studios, film-developing labs, and other auxiliary services—such as plant rental outlets that can create a whole jungle on a soundstage—that supply the film industry with its magic.

There are two major television studios on the edges of Hollywood: ABC is located on Prospect Street, at the eastern fringe, and CBS is on Beverly Boulevard, to the south.

Griffith Park

Just north of Hollywood Boulevard is one of the city's jewels—Griffith Park. Comparable to New York's Central Park or Chicago's Lincoln Park, this quiet haven contains a zoo, lovely scenic drives, playgrounds, an observatory, and all the other amenities traditionally associated with a major city park. It also offers some extravagant vegetation and, from its high points, vistas unmatched anywhere else in the city.

Farther west a bit, a familiar Hollywood trademark can be seen up in the hills. The world-famous Hollywood sign spells out the name of the city in 45-foot high letters that weigh a total of 480,000 pounds. Erected in 1928, the sign originally read, "Hollywoodland"—an advertisement for Hollywoodland Realty. The *land* fell off, and what was left was simply *Hollywood*—which stuck. The sign fell into further disrepair over the years but was refurbished and rededicated in 1978.

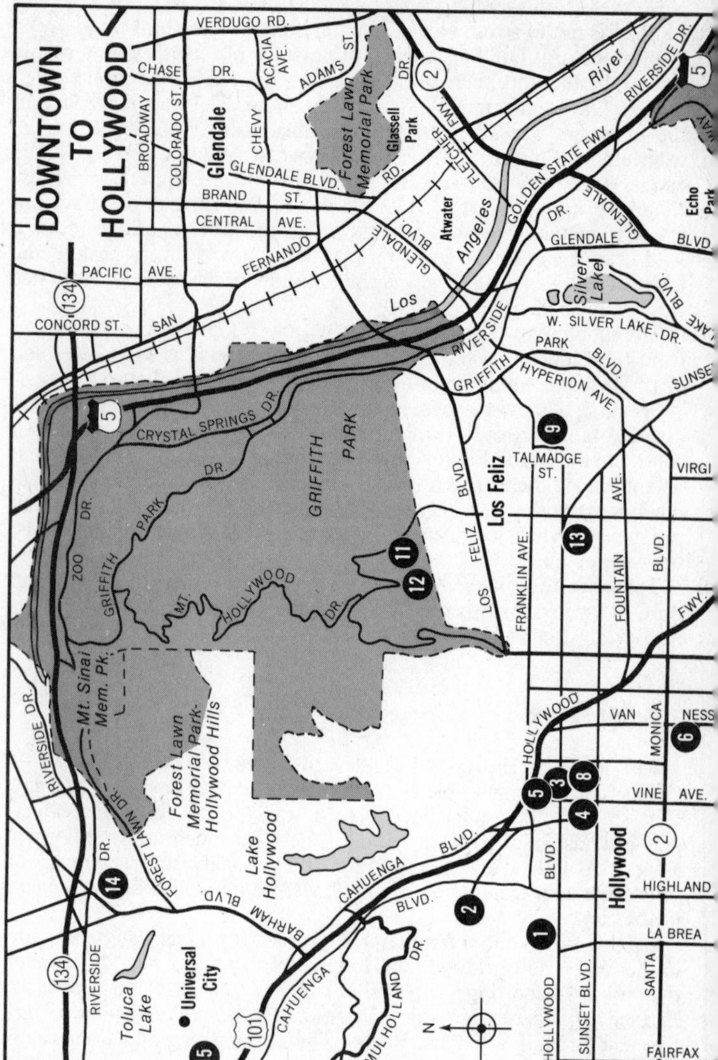
DOWNTOWN TO HOLLYWOOD
VERDUGO RD.
CHASE DR.
BROADWAY
COLORADO ST.
Glendale
ACACIA AVE.
CHEVY
ADAMS ST.
Forest Lawn Memorial Park
Glassell Park
DR.
GLENDALE BLVD.
RD.
BRAND ST.
CENTRAL AVE.
SAN FERNANDO
PACIFIC AVE.
CONCORD ST.
134
2
5
FLETCHER FWY.
Los Angeles River
RIVERSIDE DR.
GOLDEN STATE FWY.
GLENDALE BLVD.
Atwater
Echo Park
GLENDALE DR.
GLENDALE BLVD
Silver Lake
W. SILVER LAKE DR.
RIVERSIDE
GRIFFITH
PARK BLVD.
HYPERION AVE.
SUNSET
CRYSTAL SPRINGS DR.
GRIFFITH PARK DR.
GRIFFITH PARK
ZOO DR.
MT. HOLLYWOOD DR.
LOS FELIZ BLVD.
Los Feliz
TALMADGE ST.
FRANKLIN AVE.
FOUNTAIN AVE.
VIRGI
SANTA MONICA BLVD.
FWY.
HOLLYWOOD
VAN NESS
VINE AVE.
HIGHLAND
LA BREA
FAIRFAX
Hollywood
HOLLYWOOD BLVD.
SUNSET BLVD.
Mt. Sinai Mem. Pk.
Forest Lawn Memorial Park-Hollywood Hills
Lake Hollywood
CAHUENGA BLVD.
BARHAM BLVD.
FOREST LAWN DR.
RIVERSIDE DR.
RIVERSIDE
Toluca Lake
Universal City
CAHUENGA
101
MULHOLLAND DR.
N
1
2
3
4
5
6
8
9
11
12
13
14
15

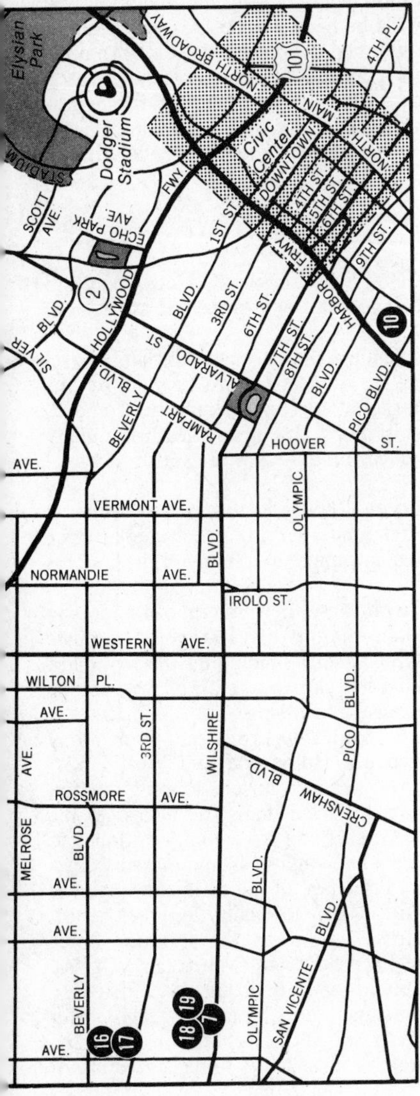

Points of Interest

1) Mann's Chinese Theatre
2) Hollywood Bowl
3) Pantages Theater
4) Huntington Hartford Theatre
5) Capitol Records, Inc.
6) Hollywood Memorial Park
7) Hancock Park
8) CBS Studios
9) ABC TV
10) Los Angeles Convention and Exhibition Center
11) Greek Theatre
12) Observatory
13) Hollyhock House, Barnsdall Park
14) Burbank Studios
15) Universal Studios
16) CBS Television Studios
17) Farmer's Market
18) Los Angeles County Museum of Art
19) La Brea Tar Pits

Just to the west of the sign is another of Los Angeles' major cultural attractions: the Hollywood Bowl, a home of the Los Angeles Philharmonic Orchestra. Busiest in the summer, the bowl, a natural amphitheater set in a hillside, sponsors concerts by some of the greatest conductors and musical performers in America. Most of the performances are in the evening, under the stars, and picnicking on the grounds before a concert is one of the supreme summer pleasures in Los Angeles.

West Hollywood

In the area known as West Hollywood, between Hollywood and Beverly Hills, run Fairfax and La Cienega Boulevards, two streets that offer a number of diversions.

At Third Street and Fairfax Avenue is the Farmer's Market, a novel shopping area that once served the Depression-era farmers of Los Angeles. Today the Farmer's Market offers convenient parking and 20 acres of sights, including souvenir shops, restaurants featuring many kinds of cuisines, and fresh produce stands—as well as a small wine-tasting room.

Continuing north on Fairfax, you'll find a lot of open-air markets featuring fresh produce and baked goods. Fairfax is considered to be the heart of Los Angeles' Jewish community, and many of these stores offer kosher products.

At Beverly and La Cienega is an absolutely mammoth shopping mall, the Beverly Center, which houses more than 100 shops, 14 movie theaters, and endless eating establishments—including the landmark Hard Rock Café. The rest of La Cienega is made up of restaurants, shops, and art galleries that encourage browsing.

If you are interested in the unusual, check out the shops along Melrose Avenue, which runs between Hollywood and West Hollywood. This area has recently blossomed as a novel shopping district. It is filled with one-of-a-kind and imported items from all over the world. The merchandise includes everything from funky antiques to sophisticated clothing to new wave and high-tech home furnishings. Melrose Place, a short street that branches off the main thoroughfare near La Cienega Blvd., is known for its high-quality antiques.

Another "must see" on Melrose Avenue is the stunning "blue whale"—officially known as the Pacific Design Center, an all-glass-panel building of the brightest blue that caused quite a controversy when it was unveiled. The dust has since settled, but the design center still attracts its share of attention. Although it is full of shops specializing in interior furnishings, the proprietors sell only to registered interior designers and decorators. It's a fun place to window-shop.

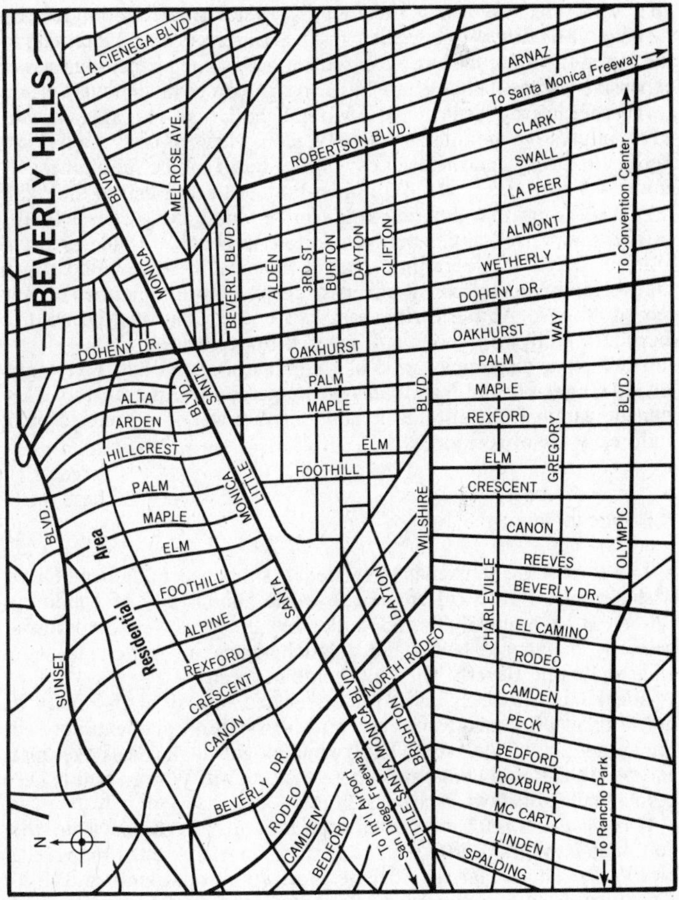
BEVERLY HILLS
LA CIENEGA BLVD
MELROSE AVE.
ROBERTSON BLVD.
ARNAZ
To Santa Monica Freeway
CLARK
SWALL
LA PEER
ALMONT
WETHERLY
DOHENY DR.
OAKHURST
WAY
PALM
MAPLE
REXFORD
ELM
CRESCENT
CANON
REEVES
BEVERLY DR.
EL CAMINO
RODEO
CAMDEN
PECK
BEDFORD
ROXBURY
MC CARTY
LINDEN
SPALDING
GREGORY
CHARLEVILLE
OLYMPIC
BLVD.
To Convention Center
To Rancho Park
SANTA MONICA BLVD.
BEVERLY BLVD.
ALDEN
3RD ST.
BURTON
DAYTON
CLIFTON
DOHENY DR.
OAKHURST
PALM
MAPLE
ELM
FOOTHILL
WILSHIRE BLVD.
ALTA
ARDEN
HILLCREST
PALM
MAPLE
ELM
FOOTHILL
ALPINE
REXFORD
CRESCENT
CANON
BEVERLY DR.
RODEO
CAMDEN
BEDFORD
LITTLE SANTA MONICA BLVD.
Residential Area
SUNSET BLVD.
DAYTON
NORTH RODEO
BRIGHTON
LITTLE SANTA MONICA
To Int'l Airport San Diego Freeway
N

A glimpse of "how the other half lives" can be seen in two nearby areas. The first, Laurel Canyon, is located at the borderline of Hollywood and West Hollywood. The street itself, also named Laurel Canyon, winds its way along the foot of several small mountains. By turning off on any of the smaller residential streets and continuing to the top of the mountain, you can see not only some prime examples of expensive California real estate but also some exceedingly lovely views.

Another nearby scenic drive is Mulholland Drive. This area is divided by impressive mountains where fabulous views of both the flat San Fernando Valley and the flat Los Angeles Basin can be simultaneously enjoyed. These views extend for miles both to the left and to the right.

A scenic view of a different kind can be found along Sunset Boulevard's infamous "strip," between Crescent Heights Boulevard and Doheny Drive. It is here that some of the most creative billboards in the world are located. Most advertise current motion pictures or new record albums. At the Strip's east end is the Chateau Marmont, a legendary Hollywood hotel still favored by celebrities.

The Strip is also the location of a number of restaurants catering to a wide range of tastes. Nightclubs are numerous in this area, too. They run the gamut from ultrafashionable, private watering holes to punk and heavy metal rock clubs.

Beverly Hills

The glitz of the Strip ends as suddenly as it begins at Doheny Drive, where Sunset Boulevard enters the world-famous city of glamorous Beverly Hills. Suddenly the sidewalk street life gives way to expansive, perfectly manicured lawns and palatial homes, all representative of what the name Beverly Hills has come to mean.

The fabulous Beverly Hills Hotel is located here, right off Sunset. Its quiet Spanish Colonial Revival architecture and soft pink exterior belie the excitement inside, where Hollywood moguls make deals over margaritas in the Polo Lounge and where such stars as Warren Beatty keep permanent bungalows as second homes.

It is on this stretch of Sunset, especially during the daytime, that you'll see hawkers peddling maps of stars' homes. Are the maps reliable? Well, that's a matter of debate. Stars do move around, and so it's difficult to keep any map up to date. But the fun of looking at some of these magnificent homes, irrespective of whether they're owned by a star at the moment, makes many people buy such maps and embark on tours.

Any map of stars' homes will almost certainly include a drive up Beverly Glen, which is not actually in Beverly Hills. The homes along

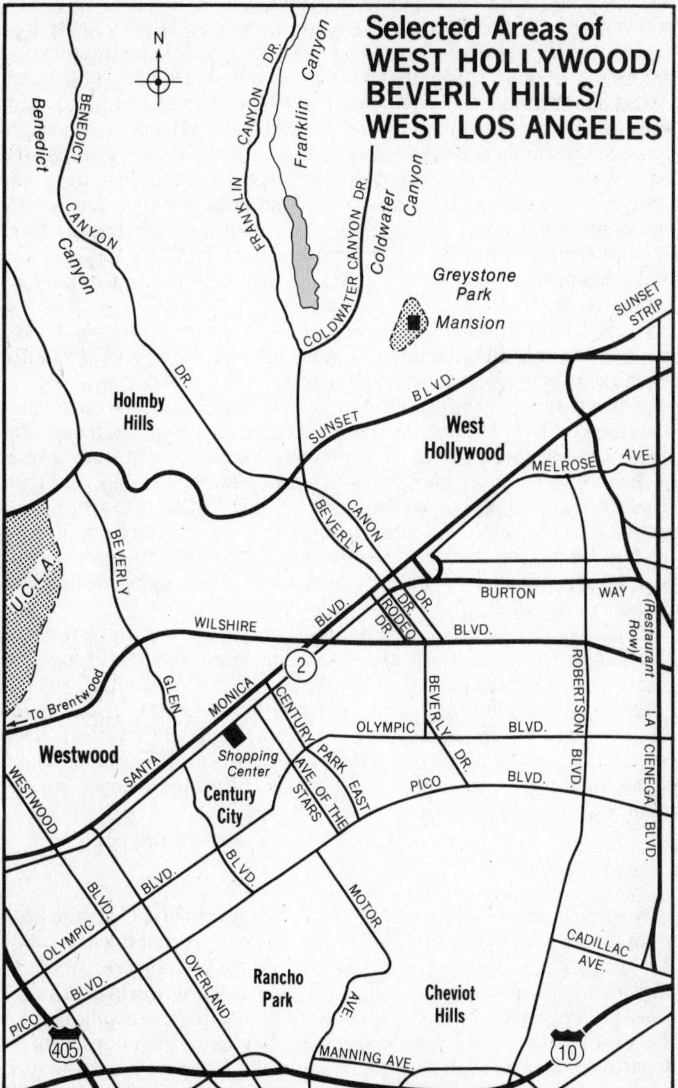
Selected Areas of
WEST HOLLYWOOD/
BEVERLY HILLS/
WEST LOS ANGELES
N
Benedict
BENEDICT
CANYON
Canyon
DR.
FRANKLIN
CANYON
DR.
Franklin
Canyon
COLDWATER CANYON DR.
Coldwater
Canyon
Greystone
Park
Mansion
SUNSET
STRIP
Holmby
Hills
SUNSET
BLVD.
West
Hollywood
MELROSE
AVE.
U.C.L.A.
BEVERLY
BEVERLY
CANON
BURTON
WAY
(Restaurant
Row)
WILSHIRE
BLVD.
RODEO
DR.
DR.
DR.
BLVD.
2
To Brentwood
GLEN
SANTA
MONICA
CENTURY
PARK
EAST
BEVERLY
DR.
ROBERTSON
BLVD.
LA
CIENEGA
BLVD.
OLYMPIC
BLVD.
Shopping
Center
Westwood
Century
City
AVE. OF THE
STARS
PICO
BLVD.
WESTWOOD
BLVD.
BLVD.
BLVD.
MOTOR
AVE.
OLYMPIC
BLVD.
OVERLAND
Rancho
Park
Cheviot
Hills
CADILLAC
AVE.
PICO
BLVD.
405
MANNING AVE.
10

this street are a lot more posh than the Laurel Canyon variety. This is where many of the people you'll see in Beverly Hills actually live.

Beverly Hills itself was incorporated as a city early in the century and has been thriving ever since. As a vibrant, exciting city within the larger city, it has retained its reputation for wealth and luxury, an assessment with which you will agree as you drive along one of its main thoroughfares, Santa Monica Boulevard. Rolls Royces, Mercedes Benzes, and Bentleys are as common as Chevrolets might be in another town. The same can be said for the shops. Within an area of only a few square blocks are some of the most exotic, not to mention high-priced, stores in southern California. Here one can find such items as $200 pairs of socks wrapped in gold leaf and stores that take customers only by appointment.

On Wilshire Boulevard in Beverly Hills are a number of fine department stores, including Neiman-Marcus, Bonwit Teller, and Saks Fifth Avenue, as well as an Abercrombie and Fitch.

A fun way to spend an afternoon is to stroll famed Rodeo (pronounced ro-DAY-o) Drive between Santa Monica Boulevard and Wilshire. Some of the names of shops may be familiar to you since several of them supply clothing for major network television shows, and their names often appear among the credits. Others such as Gucci have a worldwide reputation. Fortunately, browsing is free (and fun), no matter how expensive the store. Several nearby restaurants have outside patios where you can sit and sip a drink while watching the fashionable shoppers striding by.

Santa Monica Boulevard splits into two portions in Beverly Hills. The southern route, known as Little Santa Monica, runs through the heart of the shopping district. The other—"Big Santa Monica"—is one of the city's main thoroughfares. As you drive along, take a look at the attractive and varied landscaping at the north side of this street. Each block deploys different plants: cactus, roses, and so on. The landscaping enhances the attractive drive and provides pleasing diversion for the numerous joggers who run through the "park."

Century City

West of Beverly Hills is a new "city"—Century City. Once the back lot of the Twentieth Century Fox film studio (before that it was cowboy star Tom Mix's ranch), today Century City is a 180-acre tribute to modern architecture and the Los Angeles business world. Although most of Century City contains office buildings, there is much here for the visitor to see. The huge Century City Shopping Mall houses major department stores, such as Bullock's and the Broadway, and smaller, boutique-type shops.

The three-level ABC Entertainment Center is located near the prestigious Century Plaza Hotel, where many political functions are held. The entertainment center is a complex of shops, restaurants, and theaters. Here you can dine on anything from a hot dog to fine French or Italian cuisine. Then drop by the Shubert Theater for a Broadway play, or take in a film at one of the twin movie theaters. There is a branch of the Playboy Club located here, and ABC has a ticket booth offering tickets to shows to be taped that week.

Near Century City—just around the corner, in fact—is the lot of Twentieth Century-Fox Studios. Production is still undertaken here, and the public is not permitted inside. You might be able to get a glimpse of the sets from the studio driveway.

Just west of the Century City area is a magnificent building in a style completely different from most others in the city. The Mormon Temple, located on Santa Monica Boulevard, is situated on a hilltop where it projects over a picture-perfect lawn. At the Visitors Center you can watch a movie about the interior of the temple, but visitors are not permitted inside the building.

Westwood

Continuing west on Santa Monica Boulevard, you'll come to Westwood, an exciting area that includes the University of California at Los Angeles (UCLA). Here nationalities of all kinds meet and mix, creating an interesting street life. In fact, it is in Westwood that many people encounter what they consider to be a city—an area containing a lot of milling people, day and night.

Westwood has a lot to offer, which explains why it attracts so many people. Not only is there the fine university, which sponsors a vast number of extension courses for those who cannot attend school full time, but there is also the "village" itself, which houses a dozen movie theaters, nearly as many book stores, and restaurants of all sorts. This is also one of the few places in Los Angeles where you can enjoy New York City-type sidewalk entertainment: Strolling minstrels, mimes, and magicians perform for the crowds and can be enjoyed at all hours.

The UCLA campus is located just north of the village. It is an enormous parklike area that's fun to explore. The Dickson Art Center, for example, has an outdoor sculpture garden where visitors can admire some fine works of modern art. The Student Union is open to all, and so if you're a Bruin buff, you can pick up souvenirs of all kinds. Free maps are available at the entranceways to the campus.

North of Westwood, just off Sunset Boulevard, is the legendary neighborhood of Bel Air. Although not as well known as Beverly Hills, it is equally spectacular in terms of real estate. Just take a drive through

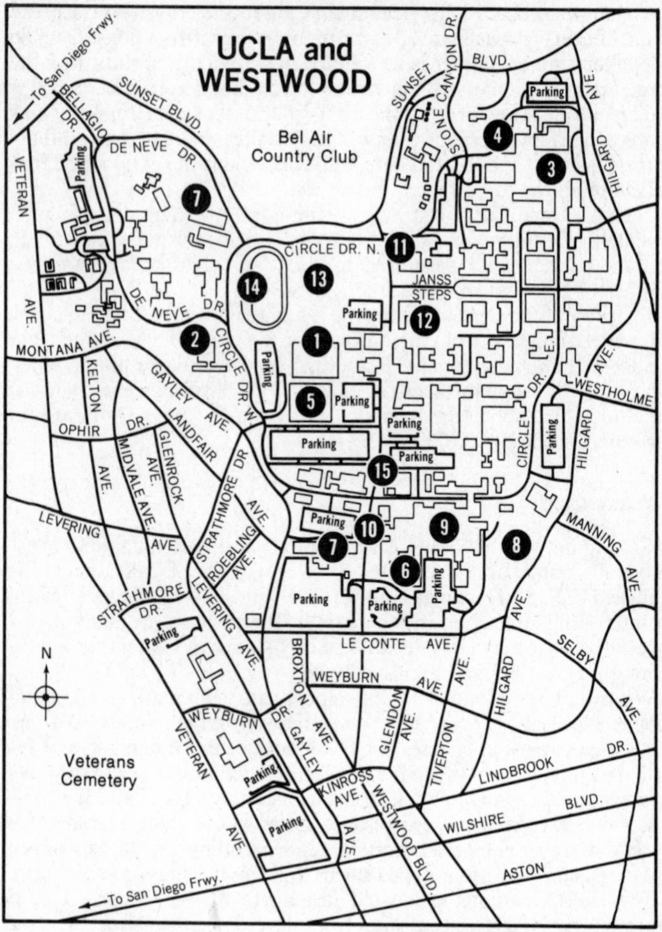

Points of Interest

1) Pauley Pavilion
2) Dykstra Hall
3) Franklin Murphy Sculpture Garden
4) Dickson Art Center
5) Spaulding Field
6) Stein Eye Institute
7) Tennis
8) Botanical Gardens
9) Center for Health Sciences
10) Westwood Plaza
11) Women's Gym
12) Men's Gym
13) Athletic Field
14) Drake Track Stadium
15) Central Tickets Office

the white wrought-iron gates marking the entrance, and you'll see why. Some of these palatial estates are, of course, owned by stars, but again, it's difficult to tell which ones. Unfortunately, many of the houses are screened from public view by lush vegetation and clever landscaping.

Santa Monica

West of Westwood is Santa Monica, a pleasant town bordered on its west side by Palisades Park. This two-mile stretch of green offers magnificent views of the ocean and the beaches below. Picnicking here is a wonderful way to spend an afternoon.

Although the city of Santa Monica is known for its clear air and proximity to the ocean, it has an abundance of shopping opportunities. Santa Monica Place is an enclosed mall containing hundreds of shops, and the downtown city itself was converted to a pedestrian mall, with plenty of room to stroll.

Santa Monica offers an interesting juxtaposition of the old and the new. On its Main Street you'll find some of the trendiest shops, restaurants, and bars. Nearby you can get a glimpse of the good old days by taking a walk along the Santa Monica Pier, which juts out into the ocean. Here, where the Redford–Newman film, *The Sting,* was filmed, are arcades, bumper cars, and merry-go-rounds, all the kinds of amusements not usually found in cities any more. Fishing from the end of the pier is permitted, and anglers can be found there day and night.

Venice

South of Santa Monica is an area that has achieved a distinctive reputation. Venice, California, has frequently been the subject of discussion for several reasons. At one time, Venice was a typical ocean beach community, then it was developed by Abbot Kinney, a well-to-do man with a dream. Kinney decided to build in Southern California another Venice modeled on the city in Italy. At the turn of the century, he did just that, replicating even the canals.

The area prospered in the early days when the amusement parks, gondola rides, and seaside hotels drew large numbers of tourists. Then the place lost its importance as newer attractions were developed in other places and oil interests caused a major shift in the city's economic base. Eventually Venice fell into disrepair. Attracted by the low rents, a large number of senior citizens and artists moved there and enjoyed the peaceful little community until the Los Angeles real-estate boom eventually attracted developers to Venice again. The construction of several high-rise condominiums displaced long-time Venice residents, and the citizens protested vehemently that a way of life was being destroyed.

Although development has not stopped, Venice has managed to retain its great charm and color. There is no shortage of street life along the three-mile stretch of beach in Venice; here one can find sidewalk cafés and street vendors, as well as roller skaters and bicycle riders acting out fast-paced performances. Although rents have gone up, artists still favor the pleasant climate of Venice, and art galleries abound. It's fun to walk here; roller skates and bicycles can be rented. Weekends are the busiest but also the most lively times.

Marina Del Rey

In contrast to Venice, Marina Del Rey is not a beach community; it's a boat community. A recently developed area, the marina is home to endless numbers of boats, including everything from sampans to yachts and schooners. During the Christmas holidays there is a nighttime parade featuring many of the marina's boats emblazoned with lights and other holiday decorations.

The marina's harbor—one of the largest on the West Coast and completely man-made—offers tours, or you can rent any one of a variety of boats and tour independently. There are some lovely restaurants offering seaside dining, but since the windowside tables fill up fast, reservations, when accepted, are advised.

Marina Del Rey's Undersea Gardens on the waterfront offers an unusual view from more than one fathom below the sea, where fish and divers put on a show in a natural environment.

South Bay and Beyond

At this point, it is necessary to leave the circle that encompasses the Los Angeles Basin for a tour of the magnificent south coastline. Traveling south from Marina Del Rey, you should arrive at the South Bay in about twenty minutes. This area is known primarily for offering, on a smaller scale, all the kinds of beach activities that are so popular in Los Angeles. The South Bay area consists of three small cities: Redondo Beach, Hermosa Beach, and Manhattan Beach. Each one contains a series of small shops and restaurants and a stretch of beach offering great opportunities for light surfing, swimming, and sunbathing.

Since the South Bay is close to the Los Angeles International Airport, a number of aviation and aerospace firms are based here. Some, such as TRW, permit tours.

An old and famous jazz club, the Lighthouse, is located in Hermosa Beach, and in Redondo Beach there is the King Harbor marina complex, with restaurants, a jazz club, and a lot of boats.

A bit farther south of the South Bay is an area that even some residents of Los Angeles aren't familiar with. The Palos Verdes Peninsula, comprised of five cities, is considered to be something of a bedroom community for the Los Angeles area. But it is more than that, and one trip along Palos Verdes Drive will tell you why. It contains some of the area's most beautiful scenery. Here visitors will see unparalleled seacoast vistas highlighted by rocky cliffs, a most unusual glass and redwood building named the Wayfarer's Chapel (designed by Frank Lloyd Wright), and nearly inaccessible beaches.

Besides its natural beauty, Palos Verdes is also known for its amusement park, Marineland. There are dozens of rides and entertaining displays here. Visitors can even go snorkeling if they wish by renting the appropriate gear and then plunging in.

Farther south is Los Angeles Harbor, where both the Port of Los Angeles and the Port of Long Beach are located. In Los Angeles Port is a shopping center done in a rustic seaside motif. Nearby is the *Queen Mary* ocean liner providing tours as well as hotel rooms for those who would like to stop and investigate the area further. Alongside is the world's largest airplane, Howard Hughes' *Spruce Goose,* also a touring facility.

Only twenty-one miles from Los Angeles Harbor is the jewellike Santa Catalina Island. This lovely little place can be reached by sea or by air. Although automobiles are not allowed on the island, tours of all kinds are available. They afford a wide variety of scenery, including oceanfront as well as mountainous terrain and even a charming seaside city, Avalon. Two things not to be missed here are the grounds of the Wrigley Estate, once owned by the chewing gum king, and the Avalon Ballroom, a relic from the island's glamourous past. Diving buffs rave about the clear water off Catalina and the many coves where they can practice their favorite sport without interruption. The nighttime harbor tours are spectacular. (Santa Catalina is covered in the chapter *Long Beach South to San Clemente.*)

Malibu

North of Santa Monica, our coastal starting point, lies a city that is virtually synonymous with California: Malibu. The subject of movie and television cameras, Malibu is less a city than a state of mind. As they drive up the coast, visitors are often perplexed when they realize that much of Malibu is invisible. And indeed it is.

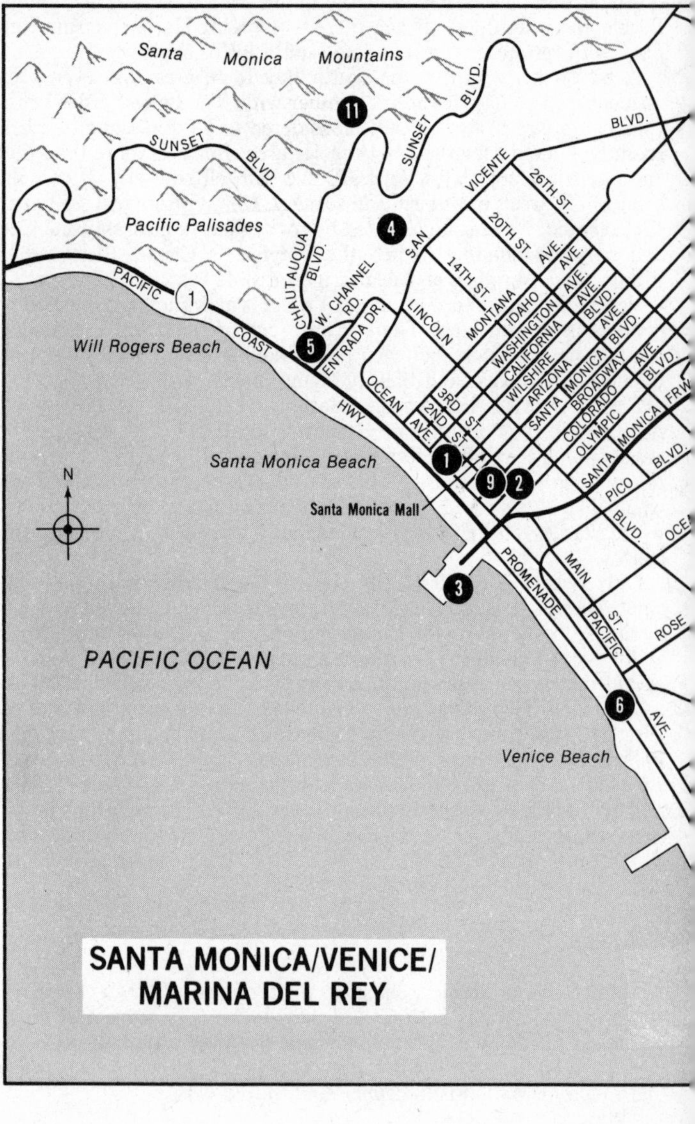

SANTA MONICA/VENICE/
MARINA DEL REY

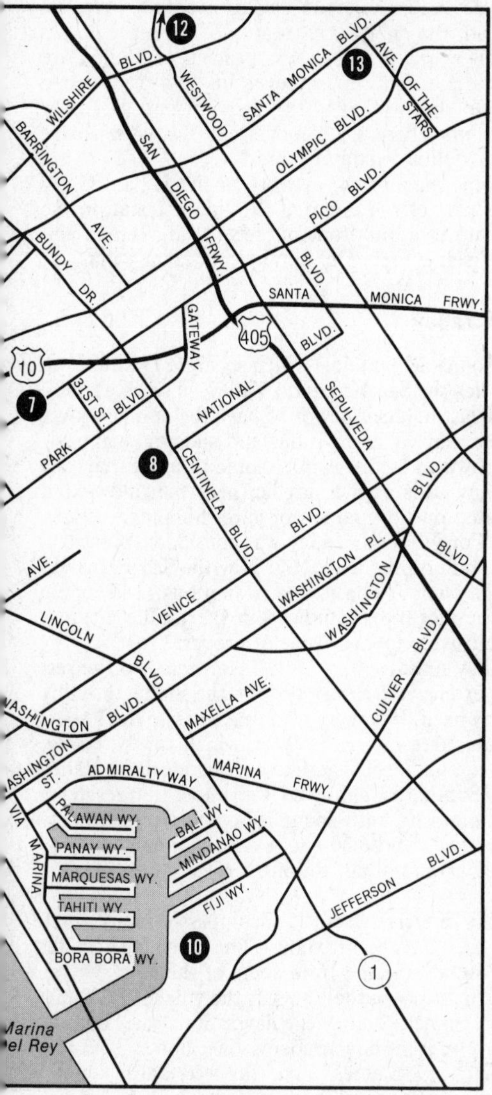

Points of Interest

1) Palisades Park
2) Santa Monica Place
3) Santa Monica Pier
4) Santa Monica Canyon
5) Castle Rock
6) Ocean Front Walk
7) Santa Monica College
8) Santa Monica Airport
9) Mayfair Music Hall
10) Fisherman's Village and Undersea Gardens
11) Will Rogers State Park
12) U.C.L.A.
13) Century City

Malibu Colony, a residential area noted for its extraordinary wealth, isn't visible from the road. But the natural beauty of the place makes a drive up the coast well worth the time. The beaches of Malibu are spectacular. Surfing here is a daily ritual—even on cold days, when surfers wear wetsuits. On this stretch of the Pacific Coast Highway there are several restaurants where one can overlook the water's edge and absorb some of the Malibu "state of mind."

You can also view some magnificent artwork at the J. Paul Getty Museum in Malibu. As part of the estate of the "richest man in the world," this museum features a multitude of pieces from Roman and Greek antiquity and is itself a replica of an ancient Italian villa.

The San Fernando Valley

Just over the Santa Monica Mountains, which separate Malibu from the Los Angeles Basin, lies the San Fernando Valley, once an agricultural center. Only in the last half century or so have the orange groves and family farms yielded way to subdivisions and shopping centers.

The Valley, as it's known to locals, is now home to more than one million people. For many, this area is idyllic; neat bungalow- and ranch-style homes situated on tidy parcels of yard. Shopping centers are never too far away. For years the Valley was considered suburbia, a bedroom community and nothing more. But now the San Fernando Valley is coming into its own: It boasts fine restaurants, a shopping center, and even several major movie studios—in short, all the things that used to belong exclusively to Los Angeles proper.

As remote as the Valley may seem, it is well connected to the rest of Los Angeles via the extensive freeway system, the lifeline used by residents to get to the city itself. If you are planning a trip to the Valley, try to avoid the rush-hour freeway traffic jams, which can be brutal. The Ventura, Hollywood, and San Diego freeways connect the Valley to various other parts of Southern California. Remember that residents travel to the city in the morning until about 10 A.M. and return home between the hours of 3:30 P.M. and 6:30 P.M. Although a resident may not mind spending an hour and a half driving a twenty-mile stretch, you may.

The Valley sounds like one entity, but it encompasses many small communities that are related only by proximity. The following account contains a sampling of sights selected from some of them.

At the far northwestern corner of the Valley is the village of Calabasas. This little town has retained some of the flavor of its early days as a stagecoach stop. Many present-day residents own horses (the real estate ads read "Minirancho, 1½ acres"), and the feed store is one of the town's most active spots. The rural, homey atmosphere of Calabasas blooms every autumn during the annual Pumpkin Festival, which brings out the locals in celebration of the city's rural roots.

Continuing eastward, you will come to the city of Encino, where Indian tribes settled more than 200 years ago. These settlers left behind the adobe buildings where they lived and raised livestock. The buildings at Los Encinos State Historic Park on Moorpark Boulevard are open for touring.

Continuing our circular tour to the area north of Encino will lead to the Saugus–Newhall area where a number of sites of interest are found. Perhaps the best known is Magic Mountain, an amusement park. Here you can wander through 200 acres of entertainment, including live stage shows featuring name performers, super roller coasters, water slides, and a host of other attractions. There are plenty of places where you can stop off for a bite to eat or to pick up a souvenir.

In nearby Newhall is the William S. Hart Park, where the silent-screen cowboy once lived. There are numerous items of interest focusing on the star's film career, and there are displays associated with the early days of the American West.

In Valencia, to the south, is a noted school, the California Institute of Arts, established by Buena Vista (a Disney company) as a place devoted to the study of the arts. It contains an art gallery and represents a striking example of contemporary architecture.

Returning to the San Fernando Valley: The next area of interest is Studio City, which is indeed the home of a major studio. CBS has deployed a major portion of its operations here, and both television movies and television shows are filmed on the premises.

Universal City, the home of Universal Studios, as well as of numerous record companies and businesses related to films, has one prominent landmark that serves as a guide for visitors. "The Black Box," as the tower is known to locals, is actually the studios' executive office building. But because it towers above the landscape, it looks like a futuristic monolith.

The Universal Studios Tour offers an all-inclusive introduction to the way in which motion pictures are made. Included are demonstrations covering makeup, stunts, special effects, trained animals, and other treats. The tour, conducted by a guide, is kept up to date. It gives glimpses into the making of current motion pictures and television programs. Stars often participate in the tour, and audience participation is encouraged. Camera-rental facilities are available, and a number of gift shops, snack bars, and several restaurants are located on the tour grounds.

Just a mile or so east of Universal City is Burbank, a city made famous because of the many references made to it by comedians. Beautiful downtown Burbank is the home of a number of record studios and film companies, including Disney, Warner Brothers, and Columbia, as well as the NBC Television Studios on Olive Avenue. NBC offers tours and tickets for those who would like to attend a taping of a television show.

Next door to Burbank is Glendale, the location of the world-famous Forest Lawn Cemetery, where reproductions of entire churches from all around the world decorate the magnificent grounds. Although Forest Lawn is a cemetery, it's also a tourist attraction because of its many copies of art treasures. Don't hesitate to stop here.

Griffith Park's Travel Town, containing outdoor displays of classics in transportation, and the Los Angeles Zoo, with its "cast of thousands," are located in Glendale. Like the famous San Diego Zoo, the one in Los Angeles keeps animals in environments as similar to their natural ones as possible. The zoo boasts a large number of endangered species among its extraordinary collection. Another special feature is the baby animal nursery, where visitors can see tiny animals being cared for.

San Gabriel Valley

Although it seems like one continuous stretch, the San Fernando Valley gives way to the San Gabriel Valley in the Pasadena area. The San Gabriel Valley has a number of museums, magnificent gardens, and stately homes reflecting the gracious life-style of an earlier era.

Pasadena is perhaps most famous because it is the site of the annual Tournament of Roses Parade and football game. The Rose Bowl, where the tournament is held, is actually part of the larger Brookside Park, where picnicking, hiking, and golfing facilities are available.

The city of Pasadena represents an interesting blend of yesterday and today. Several of the main streets are lined with quaint little shops whose architecture reflects the city's early days. The library is a monument to buildings of another era. Several blocks away from the downtown district is the Pasadena Center, a contemporary cluster of buildings housing shops and conference areas.

Another expression of Pasadena's claims to fame is the Norton Simon Museum, 411 W. Colorado Blvd., with its wide-ranging collection of fine art. There is something here from almost every culture in the world, and most centuries are well represented, too. Besides the art collection, there is the building itself, a modern-day architectural statement that evokes a feeling of timelessness.

In the neighboring city of La Canada are the lovely Descanso Gardens, where camellias bloom spectacularly during the spring months. Besides the veritable cornucopia of camellia bushes, there is a rose garden, endless bulb flowers, and a small Japanese tea house, dispensing souvenirs and, of course, tea.

South of Pasadena is the city of San Marino, the site of magnificent homes and one of Southern California's most remarkable landmarks, the Huntington Library, Botanical Gardens, and Art Gallery. Once a tycoon's estate, the Huntington grounds are now devoted to some of the finest plant collections in the world, including a Shakespeare garden, one of the most complete cactus gardens to be found anywhere, and an herb garden. The Art Gallery is home to Gainsborough's *Blue Boy* and other well-known pieces. In addition, the library contains a Gutenberg Bible and first editions of works by Shakespeare, Ben Franklin, and others.

Another remarkable garden lies just to the east of the Huntington in the city of Arcadia: the Los Angeles State and County Arboretum containing more than 100 acres of plants, flowers, and trees. A number of films and television shows have been shot at the arboretum's gardens.

Nearby is the Santa Anita Race Track, where a string of snowcapped mountains provides the backdrop for some of the area's finest thoroughbred racing. The clubhouse is of Spanish architecture and tiling. Those who arrive early in the day can take a tram ride through the stable area conducted by a guide who provides a running commentary on the horses and the people "backstage" at the track.

Above the San Gabriel Valley, in the San Gabriel Mountains, is Mt. Wilson Observatory. The site of the 100-ton Hooker telescope provides outstanding views of the surrounding area, and displays set forth an explanation of the science of astronomy.

To the east of the San Gabriel Valley is the Pomona area, where the annual Los Angeles County Fair is held. Once a prime winemaking region, the Pomona area is now known because of the fair and the fine Arabian horses housed at the Kellogg Ranch. Nearby, on Foothill Boulevard, is Rancho Santa Ana Botanic Gardens displaying exclusively California vegetation, with nature trails.

The Mountain Resorts

Continuing east, you will come to the San Bernardino Mountains. At their peak is one of Southern California's prime recreation areas: the resorts of Lake Arrowhead and Big Bear Lake, which provide year-round opportunities for boating, swimming, and water- and snow-skiing in an atmosphere of fresh, pine scented air reminiscent of an alpine resort. All kinds of cabins, motels, and condominiums can be rented through realtors in the area. Almost any kind of sporting goods can be rented in the area. Lake Arrowhead, the more urbanized of the two, has a lakeside shopping mall. Although the winding mountain roads are not for everyone, don't miss Rim of the World Drive. The stretch of road at the edge of the mountain offers some of the finest vistas available anywhere.

The Desert Resorts

Just below the mountains of Lake Arrowhead–Big Bear lies one of California's most publicized attractions, Palm Springs, where swimming pools nearly outnumber the residents, and golf courses abound. Graceful, tree lined Palm Canyon Drive offers sophisticated shopping opportunities and some very fine restaurants as well as nightlife. (See the chapter on Palm Springs in this book.)

Actually, Palm Springs is the best known of the string of cities, including Rancho Mirage, Cathedral City, La Quinta, and Palm Desert, in this desert oasis. At the end of the string is Indio, where an annual Date Festival, featuring camel races and date flavored milkshakes, is held every winter.

While in Palm Springs, don't miss the aerial tram that takes a handful of people on a long climb to the top of Mt. San Jacinto. In the wintertime snow is usually very much in evidence, even though the temperature at the tram's origin might have been 80 degrees.

In the Palm Springs area there are exhibits of interest to those who would like to learn more about the desert. At the Desert Museum elaborate dioramas show desert life; the museum also houses fine collections of art and Indian artifacts.

At the Living Desert Reserve in Palm Desert are all kinds of desert vegetation, along with explanations of how many of the plants are used today and how many were used in the past.

Heading back toward Los Angeles from the desert communities, you will approach two state parks worthy of a visit. Anza Borrego Desert State Park is an enormous desert preserve encompassing more than 600 miles of roads, plenty of camping and hiking trails, and historic spots, including old stagecoach stations. At the nearby Joshua Tree National Monument, picnicking, camping, hiking, and rock climbing are permitted, but the main attraction is provided by thousands of majestic Joshua trees. Although these high-desert plants appear to the casual observer to resemble cactus, they are members of the lily family. Joshua Tree encompasses more than 800 square miles of varied terrain and includes wildlife preserves and self-guided nature trails.

Back to the Beginning

If you continue west on Interstate 10 when you leave the desert areas, you will end up right back at our starting point, downtown Los Angeles. The circle is complete, although by now it is more of an irregularly shaped ellipsis. But at least, our overview should have given you a general feel for the area that should help you in deciding which areas you'll be going back to visit.

PRACTICAL INFORMATION FOR LOS ANGELES

HOW TO GET THERE. There are, of course, four common ways to get around in the United States: plane, train, bus, and car. Usually, if you plan to travel long distance, it is cheaper to go by plane than by rail. But for distances under 300 miles, the train is cheaper and may be faster too because the station is sometimes in the middle of town and you won't have to take a long ride to and from the airport. Another benefit of rail travel is seeing the scenery, which can't be observed when flying.

For short trips between cities, buses offer the same sightseeing advantage as trains but are usually cheaper and may provide more frequent service.

By bus. *Continental Trailways* (213–742–1200) and *Greyhound* (213–620–1200) bus routes provide a vast array of scheduled trips, allowing travelers from all U.S. areas to come close to their vacation destinations and often to reach them directly. Focal points to consider are the same as those for trains. Currently both offer unlimited train passes at $189—7 days; $249—15 days; $349—30 days. Children under 12 pay half-price and under 5, they travel free. The great distance involved in traveling around southern California may make these passes advantageous.

Contact your travel agent or a nearby Greyhound or Trailways office for information about special tours to and in the area you would like to visit. Also, ask your travel agent about special tours to the area you plan to see. Keep in mind that you will be alloted only a certain amount of time in any one place, and the allocation of time depends on your tour itinerary.

By air. In the Los Angeles area, two major airports bring in visitors: Los Angeles International Airport (LAX) is the larger; Burbank operates a smaller domestic terminal in the San Fernando Valley. Among major airlines serving either or both of these airports are *American, Capitol Air, Delta, Eastern, Republic, TWA, United,* and *Western.* Some of the international carriers serving LAX are *Air Canada, Air France, AeroMexico, Air New Zealand, UTA, British Airways, Continental, China Airlines, Qantas, Mexicana, World Airlines,* and *Pan American.*

Also serving the Los Angeles area are regional airlines, which offer many scheduled flights from the cities mentioned above as well as from other metropolitan areas. Regional airlines include *Air Cal, PSA (Pacific Southwest Airlines),* and *Western.*

Discounts are usually available to members of the family who are traveling together. Thirty-day excursion fares and special low fares for senior citizens as well as for members of the armed forces are also offered by many airlines that may also offer stand-by reduced rate fares. All special fares are subject to restrictions requiring the traveler to make the trip when the airlines are least busy, usually midweek. Savings can range from 15 to 50 percent over regular coach fares, but since discounts change frequently, it is best to consult your travel agent for the most recent exact rates.

To accommodate those travelers who require transportation to and from LAX, try the *Flyaway Service.* This ground transportation line has two locations: in West Los Angeles, at 1401 S. Sepulveda Blvd., and in San Fernando Valley, at 7610 Woodley Ave. Both locations offer nonstop service to the airport at a nominal fee.The *Super Shuttle* (9625 Bellanca Ave., L.A.; 213–777–8000) is another economical method of traveling to and from the airport. Cost is $15 for the first person and $5 for each additional passenger. Plan at least two hours for the trip to the airport. Upon arrival, after picking up baggage, use the terminal's courtesy phone to request shuttle service for outbound trips from the airport. The vehicle will arrive within 10 minutes.

By train. Amtrak's *Coast Starlight* is a superliner train that offers service to Seattle–Portland and Oakland–San Francisco and south to Los Angeles. A special bedroom is available for handicapped passengers traveling with a companion. Superliner sleepers offer an economy bedroom for two, family bedroom accommodations for two adults and two children, and deluxe bedrooms with sofa and reclining swivel chair. Connecting with the *Coast Starlight* in Martinez, Amtrak's *San Joaquin* train travels through the Central Valley, the gateway to three national parks: Yosemite, Kings Canyon, and Sequoia.

For more information, see your local travel agent or call Amtrak, at 800/ USA–RAIL, for details on discounts and excursion fares; Family-A-Fare and discounts for the handicapped and senior citizens are also available. Ask for the "Rail America" West tour book that lists different plans that enable travelers to save money.

Also available on the *Coast Starlight* are one- and two-day tours to Yosemite National Park and a two-day train tour to Hearst Castle. Daily service is available to Stockton, Merced (Yosemite), Fresno, Bakersfield, and San Joaquin Valley points.

Los Angeles' Amtrak Union Station, one of the last grand railroad stations to be built in this country, is located at 800 N. Alameda St.

TELEPHONES. The area code for Los Angeles proper is 213. Part of the area has been split off and given the 818 area code. The communities to go into 818 of interest to visitors are the San Fernando Valley, Glendale, Pasadena, and Burbank. You do not need to dial the area code if it is the same as the one from which you are calling. Information (known as directory assistance) is 411 locally. When trying to find a number, be aware of which section of the city you are seeking—Los Angeles has many different sections with so many different telephone books and different telephone companies (two: Pacific Telephone and General Telephone). When direct-dialing a long-distance number from anywhere in Los Angeles, you must dial the number "1" (one) *before* you dial the area code and the number itself. An operator will assist you on person-to-person, credit-card, and collect calls if you dial "0" first. Pay telephones still start at 10 cents.

HOTELS AND MOTELS. Los Angeles offers almost any kind of accommodation, from a simple motel room, which permits you to park right in front of your room, to a posh hotel such as the Beverly Hills, where an attendant will park your car and whisk you off to a spacious room or to your own bungalow.

Because Los Angeles is so spread out—the city is actually a series of suburbs connected by freeways—it is possible to obtain clean, decent accommodations at low priced motels that place you only a little distance from the mainstream of the city.

The best known Los Angeles hotels—the Century Plaza, the Beverly Wilshire, the Beverly Hills, and the Westin Bonaventure among them—are sleek, fashionable establishments in the hub of the city; they are high-priced luxury hotels providing many restaurants and conveniences.

European-style hotels are also prospering here; they provide personalized attention, rooms that are often minisuites, and a concierge to perform services. These hotels are usually small and gracious and often present you with baskets of fruit, bottles of wine, and/or place fine chocolates on your pillow at night. L'Ermitage Hotel is high on the list, in both price and amenities; it offers elegant suites, original artwork, and a gourmet dining room for guests only. The Westwood Marquis and Le Bel Age offer similarly intimate accommodations.

It is best to plan ahead and reserve a room; hotels usually offer special prices for weekend visits or may offer tickets to amusement parks or plays. A travel agent or the Sunday Travel Section of *The Los Angeles Times, The Los Angeles Herald Examiner,* or *The Los Angeles Daily News* can aid you in your efforts.

Most hotels take all major credit cards but check in advance to be sure.

Hotels are listed in categories, determined first by location: Downtown, Mid-Wilshire, Hollywood, Beverly Hills, West Los Angeles, Santa Monica, Marina Del Rey–Venice, South Beach Cities, San Fernando Valley, and San Gabriel Valley. They are further divided, under location, into categories determined (roughly) by the price of a room for two people, on the European plan (i.e., no meals). These price categories are: *Deluxe,* $110 and up; *Expensive,* $70 to $110; *Moderate,* $35 to $70; and *Inexpensive,* under $35.

DOWNTOWN

Deluxe

The Biltmore Hotel. 515 S. Olive St.; 624–1011; (800) 421–0156 nationwide; (800) 252–0175 in California. This Los Angeles historical landmark near beautiful Pershing Square has recently undergone renovation and restoration to the tune of $35 million. The lobby ceiling was hand painted by Italian artist Giovanni Smeraldi, and imported Italian marble and plum-colored velvet grace the hotel's Grand Avenue Bar, a local meeting spot. Since the Biltmore first opened in 1923, this impressive property has hosted such dignitaries as Mary Pickford, J. Paul Getty, Eleanor Roosevelt, Princess Margaret, and several of our nation's presidents. Award-winning European architecture. Bernard's is a critically acclaimed suburb Continental restaurant. Private, swank health club in a Roman-bath motif. Modern updated guest rooms. Banquet and meeting rooms serve up to 1,200; special club floor boasts library, wide-screen-TV theater, and pocket-billiards room. 1,022 rooms. No CB.

Hyatt Regency, Los Angeles. 711 S. Hope St.; 683–1234; (800) 228–9000. One of the largest downtown hotels, it prides itself on atmosphere and service. Each room has a wall of windows that takes advantage of the city view. Atop this 25-story building is Angel's Flight, a revolving restaurant and lounge. Glass-enclosed skylight. The hotel is part of downtown's Broadway Plaza, comprising 35 fine shops and restaurants, including Hugo's V, offering gourmet fare. There also is the Los Angeles Racquet Club, providing fine tennis and health club facilities at an extra cost. Parking is $12.50 per day. 500 rooms.

Los Angeles Hilton Hotel. 930 Wilshire Blvd; 629–4321. On Los Angeles' most accessible street, this hotel offers a restaurant, a lounge, a 24-hr. coffee shop, a pool, and large banquet and meeting rooms. Parking is expensive. 1,200 rooms.

Sheraton Grande Hotel. 333 South Figueroa St.; 617–1133; (800) 325–3535. New 14-story, 550-room mirrored hotel near Dodger Stadium, Chinatown, Music Center, in the Bunker Hill District downtown. Three restaurants; outdoor pool; 23 meeting rooms; four movie theaters. Limo service available. Privileges at Los Angeles Racquet Club.

Westin Bonaventure Hotel. Fifth and Figueroa; 624–1000; (800) 228–3000. John Portman's striking masterpiece, this 35-story, circular towered, mirrored glass high rise is in the heart of downtown. This superstructure includes outside elevators, five acres of ponds and waterfalls in the lobby, several restaurants, including Beaudry's Gourmet, and the Bona Vista revolving lounge at the top. Grand ballroom seats 3,000; just one of the features of this complete convention hotel. Pool; five-level shopping gallery inside. Popular Sunday brunch in atrium lobby. Parking is expensive. 1,474 rooms.

Expensive

Best Western Inn Towne. 925 S. Figueroa St.; 628–2222; (800) 528–1234 in California. A three-story hotel 1½ blocks from the convention center and right down the street from the famous 24-hour Pantry Restaurant. Room service; pool; facilities for the handicapped. Parking is free. 170 rooms.

Holiday Inn Convention Center. 1020 S. Figueroa; 748–1291; (800) 238–8000. Various athletic teams visiting the city stay at this newly renovated hotel, next door to the convention center. It offers the lovely Courtyard Restaurant, a pool, a laundry room, and complimentary garage parking. Amtrak offers a weekend package at this Holiday Inn. 193 rooms.

The New Otani Hotel and Garden. 120 S. Los Angeles St.; 629–1200; in California (800) 252–0197; nationally (800) 451–8795. A fusion of international design and human-scale concepts, this ultramodern hotel surrounds a beautiful Japanese garden with running stream and waterfalls. Visitors at the hotel especially like the fine restaurants: A Thousand Cranes, offering classic Japanese cuisine; Commodore Perry's, boasting steak and lobster; and the Genji Bar, with notable jazz entertainers. Each room has a refrigerator, an alarm clock, a phone in the bathroom, and concrete walls for great noise control. Large conference center inside. 446 rooms.

University Hilton, Los Angeles. 3540 S. Figueroa St.; 748–4141. If you're doing business at USC, the coliseum, or the sports arena, you will find that this is the best hotel in the area. All rooms have a view of the pool area, the lush garden, or the nearby USC campus. Coffee shop; Trojan Horse Restaurant; lounge. Courtesy shuttle service to both LAX and the Amtrak station. The hotel is well equipped to handle banquet meetings and conventions. Parking at $2 per day. 241 rooms.

Moderate

Alexandria Hotel. 501 S. Spring st.; 626–7484; (800) 421–8815. This turn-of-the-century charmer strives for Old World elegance. Pleasurable Victorian accommodations; nightclub; fine restaurant. This landmark hotel is in the heart of the financial district close to the convention center and City Hall. Room service; facilities for the handicapped. 500 rooms.

Best Western Kent Motel. 920 S. Figueroa; 626–8701; (800) 528–1234. Two blocks from the convention center and near the famous Pantry Restaurant. Inside: an Italian restaurant and cocktail lounge. Pool. Parking is free.

Executive Motor Inn–Mariposa AAA. 457 S. Mariposa; 380–6910. This Spanish-style hotel is relatively new. Pool; sauna. Offers refrigerators. AAA-member discount. Spanish, Chinese staff.

Figueroa Hotel. 939 S. Figueroa; 627–8971; (800) 421–9092; in California (800) 331–5151. This charming 55-year-old Spanish-style hotel is across the street from the historic Variety Arts Theatre. There's a 24-hr. coffee shop in the building and a pool with a Jacuzzi. On the Gray Line Sightseeing tour route. Parking is free. Airport service every hour. 280 rooms.

Holiday Inn, L.A. Downtown. 750 Garland Ave.; 628–5242; (800) 465–4329. Restaurant; cocktail lounge; pool. Pets allowed. Plenty of free parking. Holiday Inn's usual professional staff. 201 rooms.

Holiday Lodge Motel. 1631 W. 3rd; 483–4920. One of the only downtown hotels with an outdoor garden complete with trees. Tourists will find the atmosphere friendly. Coffee shop; pool. Free parking. 60 rooms.

Los Angeles Plaza Hotel. 1640 Marengo Dr.; 223–3841; (800) HOLIDAY. About as close as one can get to Dodger Stadium and, of course, Chinatown. Restaurant and lounge; laundry service; babysitting service. Parking is free.

Vagabond Motor Hotel. 1904 W. Olympic; 380–9393; (800) 854–2700 nationwide; (800) 522–1555 in California. Near the convention center. This hotel is also convenient to several area restaurants. Rooms were recently renovated. On the Gray Line route. Free parking. 54 rooms.

Inexpensive

City Center Motel. 1135 W. 7th Street; 628–7141 (hotel gives permission to call collect for reservations). Near the downtown Hilton, this small hotel allows small pets. Pool; laundry rooms. Quiet rooms. Parking on premises. 42 rooms. No CB.

Friendship Inn–Motor Deville. 1123 W. 7th; 624–8474. Well located downtown, near the Hilton, this reasonably priced hotel boasts a coffee shop and a pool and is on the Gray Line tour. Parking is free. 63 rooms.

Los Angeles Huntington Hotel. 752 S. Main St.; 627–3186. One block from main Greyhound depot, this hotel is inexpensively priced. Not many services but very clean. Vending machines off main lobby for 24-hr. quick-food service. No parking. 200 rooms. MC, V.

Milner Hotel. 813 S. Flower at 8th; 627–6981. Across the street from the Broadway Plaza, three blocks from the central library, and four blocks from the convention center. A very clean building recently renovated. Coffee shop; hotel restaurant; popular bar decorated in old-Hollywood theme: Scarlett O'Hara adorns the wall. 175 rooms. MC, V.

Oasis Motel. 2200 W. Olympic; 385–4191. Near Little Korea, this hotel is a favorite with Korean tourists. Sports enthusiasts find the Oasis convenient to the sports arena. Pool. Free parking. 70 rooms.

Orchid Hotel. 819 S. Flower St.; 624–5855. One of the smaller downtown hotels, very reasonably priced. No frills but clean; Laundromat on the premises. No parking at the hotel but plenty of public lots close by.

Royal Host Olympic Motel. 901 W. Olympic; 626–6255. Clean, friendly atmosphere. Convenient to convention center. 52 rooms.

Stillwell Hotel. 838 S. Grand; 627–1151. One of Los Angeles' oldest hotels, the Stillwell has kept its charm throughout the years. On-premises Indian restaurant. No parking at the hotel but plenty nearby. 250 rooms. AE.

MID-WILSHIRE

Expensive

The Ambassador. 3400 Wilshire Blvd.; 387–7011; (800) 421–0182, nationwide; (800) 252–0385 in California. Aptly called the city within a city, this hotel is situated on 160 acres and is surely one of the most exquisite in Los Angeles. The "city within"—built in 1921—includes a health club, three restaurants, a putting green, a jogging track, a travel agency, a post office, 17 shops . . . the list goes on. The hotel is well equipped to handle conventions and banquets in a number of meeting rooms. (Check regarding group rates.) On occasion the Ambassador is used as a set for filming a number of television shows and feature films. Parking charge. 500 rooms.

Hyatt Wilshire. 3515 Wilshire; 381–7411 (800) 228–9000. One of the larger hotels on Wilshire Blvd., this 12-story building has a newly renovated interior. The lobby is enhanced by a grand piano played by a concert pianist. The Hyatt's corporate clients often utilize the property's large banquet and meeting rooms (up to 400 people). Extras include the Hyatt Regency Club, a full security floor, a lounge, a disco, room service, and same-day laundry service. Parking charge. Sunday champagne brunch. 397 rooms.

Sheraton Towne House. 2961 Wilshire; 382–7171; (800) 325–3535. Howard Hughes slept (and lived) here. One of Sheraton's finest establishments, this hotel was built in the 1920s. It prides itself on its country-estate setting, with marble fireplaces and cedar-lined closets. Tennis; swimming in an Olympic-size pool. Coffee shop; Garden Room for fine dining. Right across the street from Bullocks Wilshire, a fine example of the city's best Art Deco architecture. Parking charge. 300 rooms.

Moderate

Best Western Executive Motor Inn–Mid-Wilshire. 603 S. New Hampshire; 385–4444; (800) 528–1234. A block from the Wilshire financial district. Pool; sauna; Jacuzzi; laundry. Parking is free. 90 rooms.

Cloud Motel. 3400 W. 3rd Street; 385–0061. This hotel is centrally located between downtown Los Angeles and Hollywood. Business types especially find the hotel convenient, for it is near the Wilshire commercial district but not on the busy boulevard. Rooms done in a modern decor. Coffee shop; pool. Free parking. 130 rooms.

Royal Viking Motel. 2025 W. 3rd Street; 483–8691. Near St. Vincent's Hospital, the Royal Viking is quite small in terms of number of rooms but big in terms of friendliness. Large security parking lot for guests at no extra charge. American-Chinese restaurant. On the Gray Line tour. Car rentals; laundry service; pool. Large suites available to accommodate up to 6 guests. 38 rooms.

Wilshire-Dunes Motor Hotel. 4300 Wilshire; 938–3616. A bit west of the financial district, this hotel offers a coffee shop and a pool. Parking is free. 60 rooms.

HOLLYWOOD

Deluxe

Château Marmont Hotel. 8221 Sunset Blvd.; 656–1010. Despite is location on the Sunset Strip among giant billboards and a lot of glitz, this castle of Old World charm and French Normandy design is offered to its guests as a secluded hideaway convenient to all Hollywood's hot spots. A haunt for many show-business personalities and discriminating world travelers since it opened in 1927. All kinds of accommodations are available, including fully equipped cottages, bungalows, and a penthouse. Garden; pool; patios. 62 rooms. No CB.

Le Bel Age Hotel. 1020 N. San Vicente Blvd., West Hollywood; 854–1111. Wonderful location. All-suite, European-style hotel with distinctive restaurant featuring fine Russian meals with French flair. Many extravagant touches, like 3 telephones with 5 lines in each suite, courtesy limousine service, original art, private terraces with city views.

Le Dufy Hotel. 1000 Westmont Dr., West Hollywood; 657–7400. New 121-suite luxury property, with a rooftop heated pool, whirlpool, spa, sauna, and sundeck. Great for business travelers. Near Restaurant Row.

Le Mondrian Hotel. 8440 Sunset Blvd., West Hollywood; 650–8999. Not only does this new all-suite business hotel have fine art works on the inside, but the entire structure is a monument to the Dutch artist after whom the hotel is named. The exterior of this 12-story hotel is actually a giant of a surrealistic mural. Private, chauffeured limo at each guest's disposal. Nouvelle cuisine at Cafe Piet. Convenient to major recording, motion picture and television studios. 188 suites.

Sunset Marquis Hotel. 1200 Alta Loma Rd.; 657–1333; (800) 692–2140 (U.S.); (800) 858–9758 (Calif.) This three-story property near La Cienega and Sunset offers nightly entertainment. Jacuzzi, complimentary breakfast, garden area with lovely landscaping. Parking is free. 115 rooms.

Expensive

Hollywood Roosevelt. 7000 Hollywood Blvd.; 469–3802. Currently closed for renovation until spring, 1985, this hotel was once considered to be the state-of-the-art in Hollywood glamour and luxury. Alas, the Roosevelt, over the years, fell into disrepair. But, in true Hollywood fashion, this site of the first Academy Awards makes its comeback this year (1985), thoroughly restored right down to the ornate lobby and elegant courtyard. Olympic-size pool and Tropicana Bar in the courtyard. Across from the famous Chinese Theater and its illustrious footprints. Airport bus service; car rentals on premises; group rates. Free parking. 380 rooms plus 90 poolside lanais.

Hyatt on Sunset. 8401 W. Sunset Blvd.; 656–4101; (800) 228–9000. In the heart of the Sunset Strip, this Hyatt is a favorite of music-business executives and rock stars. Penthouse suites and some rooms with private patios. Rooftop pool. Daisy's Restaurant features everything from hamburgers to steak and lobster; cocktail lounge. Garage; parking lot.

Moderate

Beverly Sunset Hotel. 8775 SUnset Blvd.; 652—0030; (800) 421–3323. You'll find people in the music business frequenting this high-service hotel offering the beautiful Café Chez Pierre overlooking Sunset Blvd. Recently renovated. Pool. Free parking. 60 rooms.

Dunes Motel. 5625 Sunset Blvd.; 467–5171. Across the street from two television stations, so you'll find studio people around and about this hotel. American Restaurant and cocktail lounge. Parking is free. 56 rooms.

Farmer's Daughter Motel (Best Western). 115 S. Fairfax; 937–3930. Across the street from the fabulous Farmers Market shopping and CBS Television City, the hotel is especially proud of its good service. Steak house; pool. Free parking. Cantor's 24-hr. New York–style deli is down the street.

Franklin Motel. 1824 N. Beachwood Dr.; 464–1824. This fairly new hotel has a AAA rating and is immaculate. Close to Bronson Canyon and Griffith Park. Weekly rates available for rooms with kitchenettes. 24 rooms.

Hallmark House Motor Hotel. 7023 Sunset Blvd.; 464–8344. Near the wax museum, this hotel offers free security parking, which is not easy to find elsewhere in Hollywood. Pool. Small pets allowed. 24-hr. coffee shop nearby. 72 rooms.

Hollywood Highland Motel. 2051 N. Highland Ave.; 851–3000. Here's something unusual—a free Continental Chinese breakfast is offered at this hotel, just steps from the Hollywood Bowl. Pool; laundry rooms. Free parking. 53 rooms.

Hollywood Holiday Inn. 1755 N. Highland Ave.; 462–7181; (800) 238–8000. You can't miss this one. It's one of the tallest buildings in the heart of Hollywood. 23 stories, topped by Windows, a revolving restaurant-lounge. Features include a safekeeping box in each room. The location is minutes from the Hollywood Bowl an Universal Studios and only fifty paces from Hollywood's Walk of Fame. Gray Line stop. Free parking. 468 rooms.

Sunset–La Brea TraveLodge. 7051 Sunset Blvd.; 462–0905 in California; otherwise, (800) 255–3050. Just around the corner from the Chinese Theatre, this hotel offers friendly service. The rooms have recently been refurbished. Facilities for the handicapped; babysitting service; Laundromat across the street. Free parking. 43 rooms.

Sunset Plaza Hotel. 8400 Sunset Blvd.; 654–0750; (800) 252–0645; (800) 421–3652. Situated on the Sunset Strip, this hotel is a favorite with show-business people. Rooms are modern, in the mode of the Los Angeles open-air style. Parking is free. AE, MC, V.

Vermont Sunset TraveLodge. 1401 Vermont Ave.; 665–5735; (800) 255–3050. This hotel is in East Hollywood, right next to Children's Hospital and near Griffith Park. Pool; direct-dial phones. Near several restaurants. Free parking. 71 rooms.

Inexpensive

Bevonshire Lodge Motel. 7575 Beverly Blvd., near Fairfax, West Los Angeles–Hollywood; 936–6154. Close to CBS and the Farmers Market, this 25-room family-style motel has a pool and free parking. On Gray Line route.

Hollywood Downtowner Motor Hotel. 5601 Hollywood Blvd.; 464–7191. In the heart of Hollywood. You'll find this hotel one of the most reasonably priced in the area. Pool; babysitting service.

Hollywood La Brea Motel. 7110 Hollywood Blvd.; 876–8000. Near all Hollywood Blvd. attractions. Pool. Free parking. 30 rooms.

Hollywood Premier Hotel. 5333 Hollywood Blvd.; 466–1691. Near Western Ave., this hotel is just down the street from Griffith Park's loveliest spot, Ferndell, a perfect place to have a picnic or just relax. The hotel offers room service from their coffee shop. Pool. Free parking.

Howard's Weekly Apartments. 1738 N. Whitley; 466–6943. A popular hotel with oriental visitors. You'll find it quite reasonable. Charges are by the week exclusively, but there is a three-day, three-night miniweek special. The apartments are one block off Hollywood Blvd. Laundry room. Reservations are a must. 138 units. MC, V.

Saharan Motor Hotel. 7212 Sunset Blvd.; 874–6700. Near La Brea Ave., this hotel has a babysitting service and facilities for the handicapped and allows small pets. Pool. Plenty of free parking. 63 rooms.

BEVERLY HILLS

Deluxe

Bel Air Hotel. 701 Stone Canyon Rd.; 472–1211. Charming, secluded hotel, lovely gardens, trees, flowers, and a creek complete with swans. This celebrity mecca contains a dining room with Old World atmosphere, a cocktail lounge, and entertainment. Fine service. Distinctively furnished rooms and suites. Heated pool.

Beverly Comstock. 10300 Wilshire Blvd.; 275–5575. Small, well-appointed 50-room hotel. All suites.

Beverly Hills Hotel. 9641 Sunset Blvd.; 276–2251. Beautiful grounds with tropical plants on 12 acres. A California landmark. Lovely rooms; quiet location. Movie stars often occupy the bungalows. Breakfast and lunch are served on the Loggia and adjoining outdoor patio. Lunch and dinner served in the Lanai Restaurant overlooking the pool. The famous Polo Lounge is here. Tennis courts; poolside service. Heated pool. Screening room; country-club feeling. Parking at various prices.

The Beverly Hilton. 9876 Wilshire Blvd., at Santa Monica; 274–7777. Large hotel complex, 600 well-decorated rooms, broad selection of restaurants and shops. Trader Vic's and L'Escoffier are two of the city's renowned restaurants. Theater-ticket desk; limousine service; pool. Free coffee in lobby for hotel guests. Underground parking at $6 a day.

Beverly Wilshire Hotel. 9500 Wilshire Blvd.; 275–4282. European in atmosphere and decor with personal service and extras to match. The garden swimming pool is lovely. Sauna bath. Great restaurants, including El Padrino, Hernando's Hideaway, and La Bella Fontana. Limousine service to airport. Multilingual staff.

Century Plaza Hotel. 2025 Ave. of the Stars, Century City; 277–2000; (800) 228–3000; from Alaska and Hawaii, (800) 228–3000. One of the area's largest hotels offers fine style and amenities. Handsomely designed by Minoru Yamasaki. Each room has a refrigerator, a lanai, and a view. The hotel has several restaurants, including Yamato and the Vineyard. Dancing and entertainment. Pool. In the heart of Century City. No pets.

L'Ermitage Hotel. 9291 Burton Way; 278–3344. (800) 282–4818 in California; otherwise, (800) 421–4306. This hotel of Old World charm offers all the modern conveniences to ensure the highest standards in accommodations and services. Opened in 1976, it has won the Mobil Five-Star Award and the AAA Five-Diamond Award, the only West Coast hotel to garner both. Near Beverly Hills, elegant shopping, and Twentieth Century-Fox, this gem offers 117 suites with parquet entries, sunken living rooms with fireplaces, wet bars, and private balconies. Café Russe, a fine dining place, is reserved exclusively for hotel patrons and their guests. The café offers French cuisine amid a collection of 19th- and 20th-century oils by European masters. 24-hr. in-suite service, complimentary Continental breakfast. Chauffeured limousine within Beverly Hills. Rooftop garden available for dining. Pool; whirlpool; spa; private solariums.

Overnight shoeshine; basket filled with fresh fruit, newspapers, mineral water. Parking underneath building for guests only.

Le Parc Hotel. 733 North West Knoll, West Hollywood (between Beverly Hills and Hollywood); 855–8888; (800) 421–4666, nationwide; (800) 252–2152 in California. This intimate European-style hotel is housed in a modern low-rise building in a lovely residential area. Received a presidential citation in recognition of superior design from the Society of American Registered Architects. Each of the 154 suites includes a living room with a fireplace, a kitchenette, a stocked cocktail cabinet, and a private balcony. Near Farmers Market, the Los Angeles County Art Museum, and CBS Television City. Guests will especially enjoy their own private eaterie, Café le Parc, which is reserved exclusively for them. In-suite service from 7:00 A.M. to 10:30 P.M.; complimentary Continental breakfast. Colorful rooftop garden; lighted tennis; heated pool; whirlpool spa; sauna; exercise room. Complimentary covered security parking and chauffeured limo to Hollywood and Beverly Hills from 9:00 A.M. to 9:00 P.M. Special "Le Weekend" consists of accommodations for two nights, a champagne brunch, a basket of fruit, and cocktails to welcome guests to the hotel.

Expensive

Beverly Pavillon Hotel. 9360 Wilshire Blvd.; 273–1400; (800) 421–0545. (800) 441–5050 (Calif.). In the heart of Beverly Hills, this property is popular with commercial clients. Pool; restaurant; laundry. Valet parking $6. 109 rooms.

Beverly Rodeo. 360 N. Rodeo Dr.; 273–0300. With modern elegance throughout its 100 units, this small Beverly Hills hotel features Café Rodeo, an outdoor eaterie popular with the locals. Newly renovated, the hotel contains a sun deck, a free garage, and an intimate bar and lounge. Convenient to fashionable shopping. 100 rooms.

Ramada Beverly Hills. 1150 S. Beverly Dr.; 553–6561; (800) 228–2828. A large high-rise property in the heart of Beverly Hills. Affordable rates. Room service; meeting rooms; cocktail lounge. Close to Rodeo Drive, Century City, and Twentieth Century-Fox. Parking adjacent at no extra charge. Haunt of movie stars and musicians. 260 rooms.

Moderate

Beverly House Hotel. 140 S. Lasky Dr.; 271–2145. Small and friendly establishment near Century City. Laundry. Parking is free. 50 rooms.

Beverly Terrace Motor Hotel. 469 N. Doheny; 274–8141. Pentagon-shaped hotel with a roof terrace. Close to Melrose antique stores. The hotel attracts an international clientele. Scully's Restaurant. Pool. Good security. Parking is free.

WEST LOS ANGELES (INCLUDING WESTWOOD AND BRENTWOOD)

Deluxe

Westwood Marquis. 930 Hilgard Ave.; 208–8765; (800) 352–7454 in California; otherwise, (800) 346–0410. Corporate and entertainment personalities like this elegant property. Breakfast and lunch are served on the Garden Terrace. The Dynasty Room features Continental cuisine. European teas are served in the afternoon in the Westwood Lounge. Pool; sauna; phones in bathrooms; laundry. Banquet and meeting rooms. Near UCLA campus. Parking $6 per day. 225 suites (no two are alike).

Expensive

Century Wilshire. 10776 Wilshire, West Los Angeles; 474–4506. A European-style hotel offering mostly suites, many with kitchenettes. Near UCLA and Westwood. The clientele is mostly European. Pool; laundry; room service but no restaurants. Parking is free.

Holiday Inn–Brentwood Bel Air. 170 N. Church La.; 476–6411. Near UCLA and the I-405, this 17-story, round establishment is popular with corporate and college clients. Van shuttle to UCLA. Outdoor kennels for animals. Parking is free.

Holiday Inn of Westwood. 10740 Wilshire Blvd.; 475–8711. Near UCLA. Pool; laundry; restaurant. Free parking.

The New Bel Air Sands Hotel. 11461 Sunset Blvd.; 476–6571; (800) 421–6649 nationwide; (800) 352–6680 in California. Recently renovated. Here you'll find "a bit of the Bahamas in Bel Air." Putting green; tennis courts; cocktail lounge with live entertainment; pool. DC, MC, V.

Moderate

Best Western Royal Palace Hotel. 2528 S. Sepulveda Blvd.; 477–9066; (800) 528–1234. Pool and sauna are both available in this small, 32-room hotel right off I-405. All suites. Parking is free and so is morning coffee.

St. Regis Motor Hotel. 11955 Wilshire Blvd.; 477–6021. Near UCLA and Westwood Village. Many restaurants close by. Cocktail lounge and El Capote Restaurant inside. Pool. Parking free to guests. 50 rooms.

Stardust Motor Hotel. 3202 Wilshire Blvd.; 828–4584. Near UCLA and Westwood Village, this hotel offers a pool and ample parking for patrons and their guests. Multilingual staff. 33 rooms.

SANTA MONICA

Deluxe

Miramar Sheraton. 101 Wilshire Blvd.; 394–3731. This hotel is "where Wilshire meets the sea," close to all area beaches and across the street from Pacific Palisades Park. Landscaping incorporates the area's second-largest rubber tree. Group rates available. Two restaurants and a lounge. 276 rooms.

Expensive

Holiday Inn. 120 Colorado Ave.; 451–0676. Close to many restaurants, major shopping centers, the beach, and the Santa Monica Pier, this hotel offers a heated pool, laundry facilities, meeting and banquet rooms, and room service. Free guest parking. 128 rooms.

Huntley House. 111 2nd St.; 451–5971. One block from miles and miles of magnificent white-sand beaches, this 17-story hotel is on a quiet street overlooking the ocean. Dining is always a pleasure; home-cooked meals for breakfast and lunch are served in the patio restaurant. The area is hopping with restaurants (one on the roof), nightclubs, and 350 shops and boutiques. Also available are facilities for swimming, jogging, biking, tennis, and boating. Room service; laundry facilities; banquet and meeting rooms. Free guest parking. 210 rooms.

Pacific Shore. 1819 Ocean Ave., 451–8711; (800) 241–3848 nationwide; (800) 532–3733 in California. Formerly the Royal Inn of Santa Monica, this modern building is one-half block from the beach in the heart of Santa Monica. Attractive rooms. Heated pool; sauna; therapy pool; Jacuzzi; laundry facilities; same-day valet service; Ajax Rent a Car; gift shop; lounge bar. Surrounding the hotel is a variety of restaurants. Parking is available in a patrolled lot at no fee to guests. 172 rooms.

Moderate

Breakers Motel. 1501 Ocean Ave.; 451–4811. This two-story building is only a minute from the beach and is known for its well-maintained rooms. Heated pool; color TV. Free parking. 34 rooms.

Stardust Motor Hotel. 3202 Wilshire Blvd.; 828–4584. Friendly hotel service at motel rates. Multilingual staff. A distance from the beach in the heart of the Santa Monica shopping area. Amenities include color TV, room service, and laundry facilities. Free parking. 33 rooms.

Inexpensive

Carmel Hotel. 201 Broadway; 451–2469. Built in the 1920s, this charming hotel offers fun and excitement for the entire family. Very close to the beaches, shopping, and theaters. Color TV. Restaurants specializing in seafood are nearby. Free parking. 110 rooms. No CB.

AIRPORT

Expensive

Airport Park Hotel. 600 Ave. of Champions; 673–5151. "Lets be friends" is the motto of this hotel, on the grounds of the Hollywood Park racetrack, next door to the Forum, and close to major freeways. There is live entertainment in the Picadilly Circus Lounge; the Thoroughbred coffee shop offers superb eating for the casual diner; pool; 24-hour shuttle to LAX. 350 rooms.

Amfac Hotel Los Angeles. 8601 Lincoln Blvd.; 670–8111; (800) 227–4700 nationwide; (800) 622–0838 in California. This hotel is in a quiet residential area perfect for jogging, tennis, and golf. Full services are provided; excellent dining in the Bistro Restaurant. Airport transportation, shuttle service to Fisherman's Village. 754 rooms.

Holiday Inn–LAX. 9901 La Cienega Blvd.; 649–5151; (800) 238–8000. This newly decorated, international-style hotel is ideal for families as well as business types. Full group facilities. Dining room; the 2001 Lounge has live entertainment featuring acts from Las Vegas, San Francisco, and the East. Multilingual telephone operators; tour information. 403 rooms.

Howard Johnson's Airport Hotel. 5990 Green Valley Circle, Culver City; 641–7740; (800) 654–2000. Another fine Howard Johnson accommodation, 2 mi. north of LAX. Just right for the commercial traveler. Close to the Fox Hills Shopping Mall. 24-hr. restaurant; pool; laundry; banquet facilities; meeting rooms. Free airport transportation. 200 rooms.

Hyatt Hotel–LAX. 6225 W. Century Blvd.; 670–9000; (800) 228–9000. An elegant, 12-story building decorated in earth tones and brass. The hotel closest to LAX, Hollywood Park, and Marina del Rey. With business travelers in mind, it boasts large meeting rooms with ample banquet space. Bilingual staff; concierge on duty 24 hr. a day. Great location. 600 rooms.

The Los Angeles Marriott. 5855 W. Century Blvd.; 641–5700; (800) 228–9290. A truly luxurious hotel, which describes itself as being "one of the city's most active and successful." Artwork depicting significant historical events and scenes from Academy Award-winning movies is hung throughout the hotel, giving a feeling of early California. For relaxation, try the heated pool, complete with swim-up bar, or the patio featuring a prize-winning landscape of native as well as tropical plants and flowers. Three lounges for backgammon or dancing. Gourmet-trained chefs work in all three restaurants, and for business there are high-toned conference rooms featuring the Marriott Hall of Cities. Each holds up to 100 conferees and contains a sound system, a TV hookup, and projection booths with a multispeaker system. 1,020 rooms.

Pacifica Hotel. 6161 Centinela Ave.; 649–1776. Conveniently situated 3 mi. north of LAX and a few minutes from Marina del Rey, this deluxe Spanish-American-style hotel is convenient for business people. Elegant as well as casual dining. Health spa; tennis courts; saunas; therapy pool. The Celestial Lounge has lively entertainment and dancing. The California Suite, with beautiful decorations and its own indoor pool, is extra special. Package rates, special "Fly Fresh Honeymooners' Package." 375 rooms. No CB.

Ramada Inn. 6333 Bristol Pkwy., Culver City; 670–3200; (800) 228–2828 nationwide. A thoroughly modern high rise conveniently near the airport and shopping. Room service; Garden Room Lounge, pool with bar. Free airport transportation every half hour. 260 rooms.

Sheraton Plaza la Reina. 6101 W. Century Blvd.; 642–1111. A luxurious high-class, 15-story hotel befitting its name, which means "Plaza of the Queen." This Sheraton provides the perfect climate for business and leisure travelers alike. 96 meeting rooms, with in-house audio-visual equipment, can accommodate groups of up to 1,000. Three restaurants include a 24-hr. coffee shop, Landry's for steak, lobster, and sushi, and Le Gourmet for Franco-Japanese cuisine that continually garners awards. Three lounges; live entertainment; multilingual concierge; room service; currency exchange; direct international dialing from guest-room telephones. Built to conform to Los Angeles' most stringent fire code. Also, 48 of the 810 rooms were specifically designed for the handicapped. Parking at $4 per day.

Moderate

Airport Century Inn. 5547 W. Century Blvd., at Aviation; 649–4000; (800) 421–3939. A garden-atmosphere hotel designed with an emphasis on comfort.

24-hr. coffee shop; complete conference facilities; in-house banquet and party catering. Continental cuisine and libations are offered in the elgant Centurian Lounge. There are many personal touches in this warm, friendly family inn—a true value. 150 rooms.

Manchester House Motel. 901 W. Manchester; 649–0800. Small, comfortable, and hospitable, this hotel offers full limo service to and from LAX. Heated pool; car rental arrangements. Suites for large families and interconnecting rooms. 47 rooms. AE, MC, V.

Skyways Airport Hotel. 9250 Airport Blvd.; 670–2900. Within seconds of the airport, this semimodern, two-story hotel offers free limo service to and from LAX. Laundry; room service; coffee shop; color TV. Free hotel parking. 93 rooms.

Vista Motel. 4900 Sepulveda Blvd.; 390-2014. A cozy hotel that has a Spanish-style courtyard and is centrally situated for beaches and freeways and is 10 min. north of LAX. Free parking. 19 rooms. MC, V.

Inexpensive

Geneva Motel. 321 W. Manchester Blvd., Inglewood; 677–9171. Centrally situated among the airport, the Forum, and Hollywood Park. Near many restaurants. Tours and car rentals available. Color TV. Free guest parking. 30 rooms.

Sand Motel. 5330 W. Imperial Hwy.; 641–7990. Clean, small, homey accommodations; convenient to LAX and freeways. Excellent Japanese restaurant on premises. Tour bus; free airport transportation available. Free parking. 52 rooms.

Skylark Motel. 11512 Aviation Blvd.; 643–9121. Only 2 mi. from airport. Pleasant atmosphere. 24-hr. restaurant; laundry; cocktail lounge; kitchenette in every room. Free parking. 43 rooms.

MARINA DEL REY–VENICE

Deluxe

Marina City Club Resort Hotel. 4333 Admiralty Way; 822–0611; (800) 221–8843 nationwide; (800) 282–2212 in California. Just 7 min. from LAX, Marina City Club hosts discerning world travelers and top corporate executives in a lovely 30-acre property right on the water. Full recreational facilities on premises. Sports facilities include three swimming pools, six lighted tennis courts, paddle-tennis courts, racquetball courts, and full-service health spas. There are three restaurants, nightly entertainment including a disco, and dancing, and meeting and banquet facilities. 24-hr. security; free valet parking; valet cleaning; room service; pro shop; clothing boutique. Golf, sailing, boating, or fishing can be arranged by the hotel staff. 120 suites.

Marina del Rey Marriott Inn. 13480 Maxella Ave.; 822–8555; (800) 228–9292. Just a 10-min. drive from the beach and LAX, this Marriott Inn is also within walking distance of Fox Hills shopping mall, which houses a four-movie theater and a slew of shops. The pool-area surroundings are enhanced by trees and foliage, and a goldfish pond makes Sunday brunches by the water exceptionally nice. Meeting and banquet rooms; game room; restaurant; Jacuzzi. 281 rooms.

Expensive

Marina del Rey Hotel. 13534 Bali Way; 822–1010; (800) 421–8145. Completely surrounded by water, this deluxe waterfront hotel is on the marina's main channel, making cruises and charters accessible. It houses five meeting rooms and is within walking distance of shopping and Don the Beachcomber's Restaurant. Full catering. Beautiful gazebo area for parties.

Marina International Hotel and Villas. 4200 Admiralty Way; 822–1010; (800) 421–8145. Directly across from an inland beach, this hotel is unique for its village style of luxury decor featuring such rooms as "The King Tut Hut" and "Old Hollywood." Very private accommodations. Boat charters available for as many as 90 people. Dining in the elgant Crystal Fountain for Continental cuisine. Jacuzzi. 110 rooms, 25 villas.

Moderate

Marina-Pacifica Hotel and Apartments. 1697 Pacific Ave., Venice; 399–7770; (800) 421–8151. Quaint European intimacy is the only way to describe Los Angeles' only contemporary beachfront hotel. On Venice Beach, it features rooms with fireplaces and kitchens and an indoor-outdoor café. For the active traveler, there are ocean swimming, roller-skating along the strand, racquetball, and tennis. Central. 92 rooms; one-bedroom apartments available.

SOUTH BAY BEACH CITIES

Deluxe

Barnabey's Hotel and Restaurant. 3501 Sepulveda Blvd., at Rosecrans, Manhattan Beach; 545–8466. Modeled after a 19th-century English inn, with four-poster beds, lace curtains, and antique decorations. Enclosed greenhouse pool. Rosie's Bar resembels a cozy pub, with live entertainment. Barnabey's Restaurant features Continental cuisine and curtained private booths. Afternoon tea. Adjacent health club, $2 per day use. Weekend packages. 128 rooms.

Expensive

Portofino Inn. 260 Portofino Way, Redondo Beach; 379–8481. A complete resort in the middle of the harbor, this inn is on a human-made finger of land near King Harbor. Attractive rooms, most with kitchenettes. Heated pool; room service; restaurants; laundry facilities; meeting rooms. Bike rentals and tennis nearby. 136 rooms.

Moderate

Hacienda Hotel. 525 N. Sepulveda Blvd., El Segundo; 615–0015; (800) 421–5900 nationwide; (800) 262–1314 in California. Uniquely designed, the Hacienda provides tour advice, free transportation to two shopping malls in the area, 24-hr. limousine service, Jacuzzi, two pools, 24-hr. room service, and complete meeting and banquet facilities with the finest audio equipment available for any business assembly. 660 rooms.

Hi-View Motel. 100 S. Sepulveda Blvd., Manhattan Beach; 374–4608. Quaint and simple, with kitchenettes available in several rooms; only 1 mi. from the beach. Small pets allowed. 22 rooms.

Quality Inn. 4111 Pacific Coast Hwy., Hawthorne, Torrance; 378–8511; (800) 228–5151. In a lovely residential area with commercial services just 2 mi. from the Pacific. Facilities at the inn include an outdoor pool with an attractive sundeck. Kitchenettes in most rooms; courtesy car to airports; valet and babysitting services; coffee shop; cocktail lounge with live entertainment. 120 rooms.

Sea Sprite Ocean Front Apartment-Motel. 1016 Strand, Hermosa Beach; 376–6933. This charming motel was built in the 1900s and is one of the only buildings on the beach. Heated swimming pool; laundry facilities; playground. Kitchenettes available. Near restaurants and free parking. Known to be a well-managed, clean family resort. 55 rooms.

Inexpensive

Malahini Motel. 14329 E. Whittier Blvd., Whittier; 698–6731. This modern building offers laundry facilities, a heated pool, and color TV. Convenient to many ethnic restaurants, including Chinese, Mexican, and Italian. Not far from a major shopping center; easy freeway access. 31 rooms. AE, MC, V.

SAN FERNANDO VALLEY

(818 Area Code)

Expensive

Beverly Garland's Howard Johnson Resort Lodge. 4222 Vineland Ave., North Hollywood; 980–8000. Popular with business and entertainment folk, this seven-story property suggests a country-club atmosphere, with private balcony patios and sliding view windows. The lodge is on the historic El Camino Real; all rooms have AM-FM radio and color TV. Swimming and wading pool; cocktail lounge. Parking is free. 258 rooms.

Burbank Airport Hilton. 2500 Hollywood Way, Burbank; 843–6000. Directly across the street from the Hollywood-Burbank Airport. Close to major TV and movie studios. Pool; saunas; whirlpool spa; video-game room; gift shop; babysitting service; meeting facilities. Free parking. 280 rooms.

Carriage Inn. 5525 Sepulveda Blvd., Van Nuys; 787–2300. Modern motor hotel with attractive rooms. TV; free breakfast coffee and newspaper; coffee shop; bar; dining room; heated pool.

Sheraton Universal. 333 Universal Terrace Pkwy., Universal City; 980–1212. A large, 23-story hotel. You're likely to see the stars here. Two restaurants; rooftop pool; sauna; whirlpool spa; exercise room. On the grounds of Universal City, where you'll see the newly renovated Universal Amphitheatre and tour the world's largest movie studio. Overlooks Hollywood. 500 rooms.

Sportsman Lodge Hotel. 12825 Ventura Blvd., Studio City; 769–4700. An English country-style establishment with a resort atmosphere. Beautiful gardens with waterfalls and an unusual mountain pool stocked with live trout. Guest rooms are quite large, and the pool is Olympic size. Restaurant with American and Continental cuisine and coffee shop providing room service. Studio suites with private patios are available. 196 rooms.

The Valley Hilton. 15433 Ventura Blvd.; 981–5400. One great feature of the hotel is location: It's situated at the intersection of the 405 (San Diego) and 101 (Ventura) freeways. Like all Hiltons, this hotel stands behind its excellent service and comfort. Aside from being a great location for tourists, this hotel is also well equipped for conventioneers. Its banquet and meeting rooms accommodate up to 500 people. 210 rooms in all, including plush executive suites.

Moderate

Burbank TraveLodge, L.A. 1112 N. Hollywood Way, Burbank; 845–2408; (800) 255–3050. Near the NBC, Universal, and Warner Bros. studios, this small hotel dishes up a warm, friendly atmosphere. Courtesy services include coffee in each room and a bus to the Hollywood-Burbank airport. 28 rooms.

Holiday Inn–Burbank. 150 E. Angeleno St., Burbank; 841–4770; (800) 465–4329. This Holiday Inn is very large and is near all major Burbank studios. It features full service, including a restaurant and lounge with fireplace. This hotel, according to the management, has the most sophisticated fire-control system available. 45 banquet and meeting facilities, the largest accommodating up to 300. The five-story converted parking structure is free. 375 rooms.

Holiday Inn of Van Nuys. 8244 Orion Ave., Van Nuys; 989–5010; (800) 238–8000. Next to the Busch Brewery (tours conducted); this hotel is off the Roscoe exit of I-405, near Magic Mountain and Universal. Cable television with current movies; Pipers Restaurant; lovely outdoor pool. Parking is free. 126 rooms.

Mission Hills Inn (Best Western). 10621 Sepulveda Blvd., Mission Hills; 891–1771. At the northern end of the San Fernando Valley; get a true taste of the California lifestyle at this hotel, with its 120 spacious rooms surrounding a large pool with flower gardens and palm trees. Just 10 min. from Magic Mountain and blocks from the San Fernando Mission. Restaurant; cocktail lounge; room service. Parking is free. 120 rooms.

Safari Inn. 1911 W. Olive, Burbank; 845–8586. Used frequently for location filming, this hotel offers high-standard services. There is a fine French restaurant, Leserene, on the premises, along with a pool and a Jacuzzi. Suites available with bars. 110 rooms.

St. George Motor Inn. 19454 Ventura Blvd., Tarzana; 345–6911. This English Tudor–style hotel is near the southwest end of the San Fernando Valley close to the Warner Studios ranch. Services available include TV, a heated pool, a Jacuzzi, suites with kitchenettes at reasonable rates, and parking for both cars and RVs. Near such restaurants as Victoria Station, Charlie Brown's, and several fast-food outlets. 57 rooms. AE, MC, V.

TraveLodge Sepulveda. 8525 Sepulveda Blvd., Sepulveda; 894–5721. You'll find this fine hotel just down the street from Western Bagel (open 24 hr. and offering the best bagels in town). Very clean; swimming pool and restaurant on property. Laundromat nearby. Parking is free.

SAN GABRIEL VALLEY

Expensive

Holiday Inn–Pasadena. 303 E. Cordova St., Pasadena; (818)449–4000; (800) 465–4329. Situated next to the Ice Capades Ice Rink and convenient to the Rose Bowl and Super Bowl. (To obtain a room during those times, please make reservations well in advance of your arrival.) Tennis courts; swimming pool; popular champagne brunch available every Sun.

Huntington-Sheraton Hotel. 1401 South Oak Knoll, Pasadena; (818)792–0266. A picturesque old resort hotel on 23 landscaped acres in a beautiful, quiet neighborhood near the Huntington Library, this establishment is more than 70 years old and is one of Pasadena's most spectacular buildings. Recreational facilities include a putting green, tennis courts, and an Olympic-size pool. In addition to the main building, the hotel offers poolside cottages comprising one to seven bedrooms. Daily to monthly rates available. First-class restaurant, lounge. 525 rooms.

Pasadena Hilton. 150 S. Los Robles Ave., Pasadena; (818)577–1000. This Hilton prides itself on "rich fabrics, fine woods, lush plants, and a distinct European ambience." Enter the lobby, where you'll find Fanny's piano bar, and ride the elevator to Skylights, a gourmet penthouse restaurant, with its panoramic views of the city and the mountains. Close to the Rose Bowl and Pasadena's historic civic center. Convention facilities. 264 rooms.

Moderate

El Dorado Motor Inn. 140 N. Azusa Ave., West Covina; (818) 331–6371. Just off I-10. An inexpensive motor inn, with many of the luxuries of a hotel, set in a garden atmosphere. Newly refurbished interior with a Spanish-style decor. Therapy pool; swimming pool; wading pool; restaurants; banquet and meeting rooms; daily valet service. Cocktail lounge. Free parking for guests. 85 units.

Holiday Inn Montebello. 7709 E. Telegraph Rd., Montebello; 724–1400; (800) 465–4329. Conveniently situated near the Santa Ana Freeway and next to the City of Commerce, this hotel caters to the businessperson as well as the tourist. Restaurant, pool, cocktail lounge. Parking is free. 148 rooms.

Rodeway Inn and Valley Racquet Club. 840 S. Indian Hill Blvd., Claremont (in Los Angeles County); (714) 621–4831. Off San Bernardino Fwy. Reservations necessary during the L.A. County Fair and the Ontario Races. Sauna; swimming pool; Jacuzzi. AE, MC, V.

YOUTH HOSTELS

For those on tight budgets, Los Angeles youth hostels offer clean accommodations, a communal atmosphere, and reasonable rates. Youth hostels are available to American Youth Hostels/International Youth Hostel Federation members at discounted rates and to nonmembers at less than $10 per night. (American Youth Hostel Association, 1332 L St., N.W., 8th floor, Washington, D.C. 20005).

A false impression about youth hostels is that they are offered only to students. On the contrary, hostels welcome people of all ages who have an adventuresome spirit—students and nonstudents alike. The only requirement for registration may be willingness to perform a simple chore or a task.

The two main hostels in Los Angeles are located near popular places of interest. Both are accessible to public transportation lines.

L.A. International Youth Hostel. 1502 Palos Verdes Drive North, Harbor City, CA 90710; (213) 831–8109. Located in a hilly area that was once a reservation for the Suangna tribe, the hostel overlooks the Long Beach Harbor area. Once serving as a naval barracks, the structure was renovated four years ago to accommodate hostelers. It is minutes away from Redondo, Hermosa, and Palos Verdes beaches and Port O'Call Village. The #232 bus takes you from LA International Airport to the hostel.

It's recommended that visitors bring sleeping bags, but bed sheets and blankets are available for a rental charge of $1 per night. The hostel has separate men's and women's dormitories, with toilet and shower facilities. The communal building consists of a fully equipped kitchen where hostelers can save money by cooking meals, a dining area, a reading room, a lounge area, a television room, and a large patio area—the only place smoking is allowed.

Dutch, French, German, and Spanish are spoken by staff members who are great conversationalists eager to give information on Los Angeles or hostel services. It is best to make reservations if you plan to stay during the summer or if you will be traveling with a large group. The hostel sleeps 62 and has a tendency to reach maximum occupancy during July and August. Check-in time is between 4:00 and 11:00 P.M., and check-out time is between 7:30 and 9:30 A.M. Nonmembers are allowed to stay up to three days and members up to five, but arrangements can be made ahead of time for a longer visit. Rates are $8.25 for nonmembers and $6.25 for members.

Most of hostel visitors are in the 18–30 age range, usually cross-state or cross-country travelers. A sign in the hostel reads "The basic premise of hosteling is to leave a place better than one found it." In this regard, simple chores such as wiping a table or sweeping a floor are expected to be performed by hostelers. No maid service is offered and so hostelers are continually encouraged to pick up after themselves.

The hostel is between Western Avenue and Gaffey Street near Pacific Coast Highway and is two miles from the Harbor (#11) Freeway. It is a 25-minute walk from bus #232's stop.

The Hollywood YMCA Hotel and Youth Hostel. 1553 N. Hudson Ave., Hollywood; (213) 467–4161. Unwinding in the saunas, floating in the pool, or, if you feel up to it, exercising with weights in the gymnasium is one way to end a day of sightseeing in Hollywood. All this, along with aerobic classes and other programs, are available to guests of both the hotel and the youth hostel. In a strategic location for those touring via public transportation, the Hollywood YMCA is accessible to several bus lines going to Disneyland, Universal Studios, or the beaches and is less than a mile from the Hollywood Greyhound Bus Terminal.

The hotel consists of single and double rooms available for both men and women. The decor is modest but clean. Guests share the bathroom and shower facilities located in the hallway. Check-out time is 11:00 A.M., and it is best to make reservations between mid-May and late August. Rooms are not offered on a weekly basis.

The youth hostel provides separate sleeping quarters for men and women. Blankets are available, but it is best to bring your own sleeping bag. Check-in time is 7:45 P.M. and all are required to check out by 8:00 A.M. because the rooms used as sleeping quarters are also used for YMCA activities during the day and evening. Hostelers are taken on a first-come-first-served basis and allowed to stay up to seven days. Longer visits can usually be worked out. Showering facilities are in the men's and women's locker rooms. Women must shower before 11:00 P.M. or after 7:00 A.M. Belongings can be stored in closets available to hostelers.

There are no kitchen facilities, but the YMCA has a patio restaurant on the premises. It serves Middle Eastern dishes, Turkish coffee, pastries, healthful drinks, and sandwiches. Umbrella-covered tables and plants make up the Garden Café's decor. The restaurant is open from 7:30 A.M. to 8:30 P.M.

Vending machines, a TV set, and computer games are in the patio areas—the only place smoking is permitted. The hostel lounge contains a piano, chess and backgammon games, tables, and large sofas and is reserved exclusively for hostelers who want to meet and enjoy one another's company. Hotel and hostel guests are encouraged to use all the facilities, including the gym and spa areas, and to participate in YMCA services and programs, such as exercise classes, weight control programs, and psychological counseling provided at no additional charge. Tourist information is available at the front desk or from the hostel attendant.

Hotel rates are $17 per night for a single room and $26.30 for a double. Visa, Mastercard accepted. Hostel rates are $6 per night for Youth Hostel members and $8 for nonmembers. Proper I.D. is required and used as collateral when checking out equipment.

The neighborhood of the Hollywood YMCA is not safe during the evenings. Hotel and hostel guests, especially women, are asked to be extremely cautious when walking in the area and not to walk unaccompanied.

HEALTH SPAS. Southern California is probably *the* fitness capital of the country, boasting more health and reducing spas per potbelly and double chin than any other state in the nation. There's a spa tailored to fit every bulging waistline and budget and to cater to almost all needs. If your shape could use some remodeling—and your body a little rejuvenation—a visit to one of the area's top spas could be just what you need.

From The Ashram, with its spartan regimen of hard exercise and good, natural eating, to La Costa, with its luxurious amenities, to an inexpensive hotel in the beautiful countryside offering outdoor activities and hiking, the choices are endless.

A month is optimum for a stay at the serious health resort; but since this time span is unrealistic for most people, weekly programs are designed to provide the most benefit within that length of time. Many spas also offer daily rates for quick pick-me-ups. Even though the selection is large, these spas—especially the more popular ones—fill up quickly, so book as far in advance as possible. And check prices: They change frequently.

Prices can be steep—up to $2,675 at The Golden Door—but health spas offer invaluable benefits. Clients invigorate their systems, release the tensions of the everyday world, and get their bodies in shape. Here is a sampling of spas within a day's drive (many much closer) from Los Angeles. Go out and get healthy!

La Costa Hotel and Spa. *Super Deluxe.* Rancho La Costa, Carlsbad, CA 92008; (619) 438–9111. At this world-famous, posh health resort do as much or as little as you like. Rates vary, from $130 to $750 a day. The high end is for a five-bedroom home and so price per person depends on occupant number. Weekly rate is $2,000 per person, single occupancy and $1,500 per person, double occupancy. Guests hobnob with stars such as Ava Gardner and Ali McGraw. The usual amenities, such as exercise classes, massage, sauna, and swimming, are available. There is an impressive sports complex offering tennis courts and golf.

Night life at La Costa is more active than at most spas. Guests dine among strolling violinists and dance or converse to music. Movies are available both in the theater or in the rooms. Located 40 minutes from San Diego, a few minutes from the Pacific Ocean, and not far from Mexico.

The complete spa program for men and women offers not only a medical evaluation and a special diet, but also skin analysis and review, herbal wraps, yoga, the daily use of sauna, whirlpool, solarium, and gym facilities. The food gets rave reviews; executive chef Willy Hauser creates such lunches as broiled sherried grapefruit, cucumbers vinaigrette, braised chicken chasseur, fresh carrots with fine herbs, and peach parfait—all totalling only 284 calories.

The Golden Door. *Super Deluxe.* 3085 Reynard Way, San Diego, CA 92103; (619) 295–3144. The "creme de la creme" of health spas, this one is the model for many other such establishments around the world. Founded by its present owner, Deborah Szekely, in 1959 and in its present home since 1975, The Golden Door is a posher version of Rancho La Puerta, also founded by Szekely and her husband.

Beautiful people such as actress Christina Ferrare (who has been visiting the spa for nearly a decade), her friend Joanna Carson, and designer Bill Blass frequent The Golden Door. Small classes allow for a great deal of supervised exercise and health programs centered on the individual. The hefty price tag of $2,675 per week is thought to be well worth it by guests. The Golden Door is predominantly for women, although there are special men's weeks nine times a year and couples' weeks about seven times a year.

A typical day at The Golden Door can include any number of activities and treatments: body contouring, water exercises, back-strengthening exercises, yoga, steam, meditation, and herbal wraps. The atmosphere here—although relaxing—is one of serious work and serious pampering.

The physical environment also adds to the relaxed atmosphere: The spa complex includes one of the largest Japanese-style buildings outside Japan. It was constructed in the spirit of a classic honjin inn that has served the nobility in Japan since feudal times. The graceful, low buildings have exotic roof lines and tiles that reflect the blue of the sky. The gem-studded golden door is reached by a 141-foot wooden footbridge. The grounds, with citrus trees and thickets of evergreen, encompass 157 acres, with 1,000 feet of outdoor walkways and three courtyards. The entrance gates are surrounded by camellias, fuschias, and spring flowers. A teahouse and Koi pond on the grounds complete the picture.

Another inviting aspect of The Golden Door is its cuisine. Large selections of natural foods are prepared gourmet style. Much of the menu—fresh vegetables, fruits, and herbs, is grown in The Golden Door's gardens. The diet is low calorie, low sodium, and low cholesterol.

The Ashram. *Deluxe.* P.O. Box 8009, Calabasas, CA 91302; (818) 888–0232. *Deluxe* in the context of The Ashram does not denote the meaning that we usually attach to that word, even at $1,300 a week. Guests do not go to The Ashram to be pampered; they go there to work *hard.* Ashram directors Anne-Marie Bennstrom and Catharina Hedberg know how to get the body in shape, and they do not fool around.

Everyone entering The Ashram is put through a cardiovascular stress test (included in the fee) to determine how far he or she can exert himself/herself. Then a specialized program is prescribed. The diet consists of raw foods and various kinds of therapeutic fasting. All the attire that a guest will need, except for personal items and sneakers, is provided. The Ashram encourages guests to bring books and hobby items, but the real emphasis here is spiritual renewal—best attained by taking yourself away from the world for a couple of days.

"During your short stay with us," says a letter from the directors, "we would like you to receive the optimum program conducive to your physical, mental, and spiritual well-being. To insure this please plan to retreat from the world for this one time in your life, and let your business associates, family, and friends know ahead of time. Even a phone call has proven a disruptive influence in our daily routine at The Ashram."

A typical day at the Ashram begins with morning meditation at 6:30, breakfast at 7:30, followed by a 2–2¼ mile walk. At 11:00 A.M. there is a weight class; at 12:00 P.M. water exercise; at 1:00 P.M., lunch; at 4:00 P.M., jogging, and at 5:30 P.M., walking. In the evening, at 7:00, is yoga, and finally, at 8:00, dinner. The evening program, from 9:00–10:00, consists of movies, discussions, tips on home follow-up.

Monaco Villa Reducing Resort. *Expensive.* 371 Camino Monte Vista, Palm Springs. (619) 327–1261. Features a variety of low calories, fitness and exercise programs as well as hot therapy and massages. Cost: $95 per person, per day. Seven units.

The Oaks at Ojai. *Expensive.* 122 East Ojai Ave., Ojai, CA 93023; (805) 646–5573. This spa is run by another physical fitness "celebrity," Sheila Cluff.

A noted expert in the field of physical fitness, Cluff's philosophy about exercise and fitness is employed in this spa and at the Palms.

A two-hour drive from Los Angeles, the Oaks' rates range from $79 per person per day to $110 per person per day. The prices are flexible, and there is a two-day minimum. The usual extras—massage, facials, makeup, hair salon, and so on—are available at extra cost; the fitness program combines a diet of low-calorie gourmet food and a choice of twelve fitness classes per day. Meals are planned so that its easy to set your sights on the suggested 750 calories a day. Some of the more determined guests take in only 500 and some don't diet at all. Meals are in three courses. Tennis and golf are available nearby.

The Palms at Palm Springs. *Expensive.* 572 No. Indian Ave., Palm Springs, CA 92262; (619) 325–1111. Also run by Sheila Cluff, this spa is similar to the Oaks. The rates are slightly higher: from $84 a day for an adjoining double to $155 a day for a single cottage. Special deals are often offered. The location is a big plus for the Palms: All the shopping, sports, and sightseeing activities in Palm Springs are easily accessible. The Palms offers twelve fitness programs each day together with personalized attention and healthy food.

Rancho La Puerta. *Expensive.* P.O. Box 69, Tecate, Baja, CA 92080, (619) 478–5341. One of the oldest spas, established by spa pioneers Deborah and Edmond Szekely in 1940. Rancho La Puerta is a more humble version of The Golden Door. A European philosopher and chemist, Edmond Szekely was one of the first to show an interest in preventive medicine.

Today Deborah Szekely is one of the most respected experts in her field—health spas. She personally directs Rancho La Puerta and The Golden Door. Also known for her work with the President's Council on Physical Fitness, Szekely has earned many nationwide honors.

Rates for the one-week program range from $779 per person in a double-occupancy cabana to $1,194.85 each for a double- or triple-occupancy villa. This spa offers a complete exercise program from sunup until sundown, along with a low-cholesterol, low-sodium, low-calorie, and high-energy diet that contains minimal artificial chemicals and preservatives. After-hours activities include a camera clinic, Indian pot painting, and pottery; seminar topics include transactional analysis, behavior modification, assertiveness training, and more.

Zane Haven. *Expensive.* P.O. Box 2031, Palm Springs, CA 92263; (619) 323–7486. $550 double occupancy (subject to change) for five days and four nights. Program based on weight training and fitness; a selection of weight-training regimens, as well as aerobic exercises and stretching, is offered in a fully equipped gym. Nutritional counseling is also available. Each session is limited to only eight people.

Swimming pool, sunbathing facilities, and a sauna. Zane Haven is a 15-minute walk from downtown Palm Springs. It is a place that will enable you to combine a vacation with an introduction to weight training and healthful living.

The Grove. *Moderate.* 32281 Riverside Drive, Lake Elsinore, CA 92330; (714) 674–1501. Daily rates range from $49 to $99; special weekly rates are available. Located 75 miles south from Los Angeles, it is a modern spa dedicated to helping guests take off weight and condition their bodies. Low-calorie meals, behavior modification, and exercise help attain these goals. Indoor and outdoor pools, a sauna, a whirlpool, and tennis available nearby.

Meadowlark Health and Growth Center. *Moderate.* Meadowlark Center for Holistic Health, 26126 Fairview Ave., Hemet, CA 92343; (714) 927–1343. Since 1959 Meadowlark has been reestablishing a balance in their clients' lives through diet, nutrition, and exercise. The program costs from $395 to $475 a week, per person, not including such extras as nutritional counseling. This facility focuses on holistic health under the guidance of Evarts Loomis, M.D., F.A.C.S., a health practitioner in the field. Activities include walking, swimming, lectures on body awareness, yoga, and discussions on journal keeping. Guided fasting is featured. Outdoor activities also include jogging and bicycling. Located on a 20-acre estate at the foot of the San Jacinto Mountains.

Alive Polarity Murrieta Hot Springs. *Inexpensive* 28779 Via Las Flores, Murrieta, CA 92362; (714) 677–7451. Murrieta Hot Springs, in the European health spa tradition, offers mud baths in mineral waters, healthy vegetarian cuisine, and beautiful surroundings. The 46-acre facility, near Lake Elsinore, has two mineral pools and an Olympic-size swimming pool; various special programs—Feel Alive, Self-Growth, Fit 'n' Trim, among others—add to the attractiveness of this place. Prices vary depending on the program.

A typical rate is $32.35 per night, double occupancy. Available at extra cost although sometimes part of a special package, are massage, facial, tennis, gravity balancing, and medical services.

Glen Ivy Hot Springs. *Inexpensive.* 25000 Glen Ivy Road, Corona, CA 91719; (714) 737–4723. At the base of the Santa Ana Mountains and the Temescal Valley, Glen Ivy Hot Springs is a good place for a day visit. The Luiseno Indians nicknamed this area temescal (meaning sweathouse) after the mud saunas they built around the hot springs. Established in 1890, the spa has changed with the times. Reproductions of old pictures trace the history of the spa. The same mineral springs are still flowing, and the mud is thought to be good for skin and circulation. Be careful though; bring some old clothes because the mud can stain. Extras include massage, eucalyptus blanket-wrap treatments, private mineral baths, and chiropractic treatment by appointment. The daily rate is $9.75 on weekends for everyone; during the week, $8.50 for adults and $7.50 for seniors and children 12 and under. (Prices subject to change so check first.)

Jacumba Hotel Hot Springs Resort. *Inexpensive.* P.O. Box 466, Jacumba, CA 92034; (619) 766–4333. This reasonably priced resort is located between Tijuana and Mexicali. Weekly rate, double occupancy, is $203.04; daily and monthly rates are also available. Jacumba is a quiet village in a high desert oasis 70 miles east of San Diego. Visitors bathe in mineral waters, swim, and explore such attractions as an old stagecoach trail, a mine, and tunnels. The hotel features two hot springs mineral pools and two outdoor pools. Good desert hiking.

Wheeler Hot Springs. *Inexpensive.* 16825 Maricopa Hwy. (just north of Ojai); (805) 646–8131. Both hot and cold mineral baths are offered here, in redwood tubs. There is a staff of masseurs and a century-old restaurant serving organically prepared food. Private tubs are $7.50 per half hour and massage is $20 for a half hour.

GUEST RANCHES. Travelers looking for a more unusual vacation might be interested in checking the guest ranches that are located in the area surrounding Los Angeles. Although the accommodations vary widely, most offer a glimpse of California country living, complete with horses, unspoiled acreage, and fresh air. Those listed here are not more than three hours away from Los Angeles, and in all cases the drive itself is memorable. A word of caution: Plan a guest ranch vacation in advance; many of these facilities are booked months ahead of time.

The Alisal. *Expensive.* P.O. Box 26, Solvang, CA 93463; 805/688–6411. Although sometimes called an upscale dude ranch, this retreat is not gussied up by slick buildings and gourmet fare. The food, served restaurant-style, is typically Western and extremely plentiful. Accommodations are simple, mini ranch houses, each with fireplaces and none equipped with television or telephones. The 10,000-acre Alisal, actually a working cattle ranch of 2000 head, borders Ronald Reagan's 688 acres. Seven tennis courts, swimming pool, hot tub, 18-hole golf course, croquet, volleyball, archery. Children's program. Rates: $176 double occupancy for single with twins, $204 double for two-room studio suites.

San Ysidro Ranch. *Expensive.* 900 San Ysidro Lane, Montecito, CA 93108; (805) 969–5046. Just outside Santa Barbara, it offers a taste of the luxurious side of ranch living. Peace, quiet, and privacy are in abundance here, along with three tennis courts, a heated swimming pool, stables, and a French-Continental restaurant. Celebrities often seek out San Ysidro Ranch because of the solitude it offers. In fact, John and Jacqueline Kennedy honeymooned here. Rates range from $99–$349, double occupancy.

Apple Valley Inn. *Moderate.* P.O. Box 5, Apple Valley, CA 92307; (619) 247–7271. Near Victorville in the scenic Apple Valley, it offers a taste of Western-style ranch life with none of the inconveniences. Visitors here can browse through the Roy Rogers and Dale Evans memorabilia on display or take part in activities that range from horseback riding and hayrides to swimming and boating, tennis and volleyball. Campfire cookouts and stagecoach rides through the desert trails round out the experience. Rates are $47–$58, double occupancy.

Cholame Creek Ranch. *Moderate.* P.O. Box 8-R, Cholame, CA 93431; (805) 463–2320. A 5,000-acre homestead about a three-hours' drive north from Los Angeles, it gives guests a choice of lodging in either a ranch house or a cowboy-style bunkhouse. Horseback riding is a featured activity here, with summers being devoted exclusively to teaching children (ages 8–16) all about equitation. All ages are welcome the rest of the year. Among the activities are all kinds of ranch "chores," including branding, as well as camping, cookouts, and the chance to pick up bits of history from nearby Indian sites. Rates are $40 to $60 daily, American Plan.

Circle Bar B Guest Ranch. *Moderate.* 1800 Refugio Rd., Goleta, CA 93117; (805) 968–1113. Situated in the midst of the magnificent Santa Ynez Mountains, one of Southern California's most lovely natural settings, the Circle B offers an unusual pairing of both country living and city amenities. By day, visitors can enjoy swimming, outdoor cooking, mountain hikes, and horseback riding (at an extra charge). Evening offerings include live theater presentations in the barn-style theater. Dinner, a show, overnight accommodations, and breakfast are $117 for two.

Zaca Lake Resort. *Moderate.* P.O. Box 187, Los Olivos, CA 93441; (805) 688–4891. In the Los Padres National Forest near Santa Barbara, it is not strictly a guest ranch, but a blending of resort and ranch, where movie crews used to come to film Westerns in a California environment. Zaca Lake Lodge, built in the 1920s, sits on the very edge of the natural lake, with the guest cabins a short walk away. Boating and horseback riding are the two main activities, or you can just stroll through the pine forests where squirrels and deer play. Privacy is assured; there are no phones in the cabins. Cabins are $69; day use is $3.00 ($1.50 for children 12 or younger).

HOW TO GET AROUND. The Los Angeles Basin takes up 464 square miles, and so, needless to say, there's a lot of ground to cover. Whether you are walking, busing, or driving, it is a good idea to become familiar with a map of the city before venturing out on your own. Take notes on how to get to and from each destination so that you will avoid getting lost, and always travel with telephone numbers of the hotel concierge or friends so that they can talk you back to your original destination should you lose your way.

By bus. You may have heard that a tourist in Los Angeles is helpless without a car. Well, **the Southern California Rapid Transit District** (otherwise known as RTD) believes differently. Local buses cost 85 cents and 10 cents for each transfer, so it's certainly a bargain considering the distances that can be covered for that price.

RTD also has bus service to *Los Angeles International Airport.* All airport-bound bus lines run to and from a point located just outside LAX at 98th Street and Vicksburg, where a line 608 Minibus picks up passengers and takes them to their terminals within the airport complex. Line 608 operates in and out of LAX from 5:00 A.M. to 1:00 A.M. the following day. Buses make trips approximately every fifteen minutes throughout the day and about every twenty minutes in the late evening. As a passenger traveling on the regular bus lines to the airport, you should ask the operator for a free transfer to line 608. For more information, call RTD at (213) 626–4455, or, for timetables, write RTD, Los Angeles, California 90001.

Hop on the #602 minibus for 25 cents and tour the downtown area of the city. Each ethnic section such as Chinatown, Olvera Street, and Little Tokyo, is covered. You will also see City Hall, the Music Center for the Performing

Arts, Arco Plaza, and the California Mart, where you can do some shopping at bargain prices. From this point, board RTD Line #83 and head westbound, stopping off along the way at any one of Los Angeles' major attractions. To find out more about the self-guided tours, phone RTD at (213) 626–4455, or visit any of the ten RTD Customer Service Centers: Arco Plaza, 505 S. Flower Street, Los Angeles; RTD/Greyhound Station, 208 E. 6th Street, Los Angeles; RTD Headquarters, 425 S. Main Street, Los Angeles; RTD El Monte Station, 3501 N. Santa Anita Ave., El Monte; Hollywood, 6249 Hollywood Blvd., Hollywood; S. Central L.A., 5425 Van Ness Ave., Los Angeles; in Van Nuys at 14435 Sherman Way; South Bay, 1811 Hawthorne Blvd., Redondo Beach; in the Wilshire area at 5738 Wilshire Blvd.; and in Long Beach at 18 Long Beach Blvd., Long Beach.

By car. While visiting Los Angeles it really is helpful to have a car at your disposal if possible. Many car rental agencies operate around town, especially on Century Blvd., the street opposite Los Angeles International Airport. Car rental rates charged by a given company are the same regardless of the location from which you rent; so pick up your car at the most convenient spot. It would also be best to arrange for car rentals before visiting Los Angeles to ensure that you will be able to rent the car of your choice.

Once you've secured a car, the next step is to learn to drive in Los Angeles, really an experience in itself. Maps outlining the freeway system are essential; the Southern California Automobile Club has put together "Triptiks" to Los Angeles, guides that will take you to your destination. AAA provides special area maps that give useful details about all kinds of recreational activities. Also available are county maps, city maps, and special guide publications that blend accurate map coverage with information on campgrounds, golf courses, parks, boat-launching sites, coastal surfing areas, and other points of interest.

The next step in learning to drive in Los Angeles is to understand the city's extensive *freeway system.* Los Angeles is served by more than thirty freeways; eight radiate from the downtown freeway loop and, with the exception of the Golden State Freeway, are named for their major destinations. By traveling the freeways, you will also familiarize yourself with the metropolitan Los Angeles area.

The #405, or San Diego, Freeway runs north to south, stretching from the San Fernando Valley south down to San Diego. This is an excellent freeway to use as an approach to Los Angeles from LAX, for it runs parallel to the coastline from Santa Monica on south.

The #10, or Santa Monica Freeway, runs east/west and loops off the San Diego Freeway (#405) beginning in Santa Monica and then continues east toward San Bernardino, where it is then called the San Bernardino Freeway. This freeway is particularly effective when your destination is somewhere between Santa Monica and the downtown area.

Beginning in the northwest area of Los Angeles (San Fernando Valley) and diagonally dividing the city is the #5, or Golden State, Freeway. You can travel on this freeway as far north as San Fernando Valley; however, the name of the

Freeway changes at the intersection of the #10 Freeway, for you will be heading south at this point. The new name, the Santa Ana Freeway, reflects the fact that your direction at that point has changed.

Also traveling north to south is the Harbor Freeway, or #11. It stems from the #11 Pasadena and finishes at Los Angeles Harbor.

Other freeways traveling into the Pasadena/Glendale area are the Glendale Freeway, which runs north to south, and the #210, or Foothill Freeway, which intersects with the #2 and runs east to west. Stretching from Ventura County on east is the Ventura Freeway, or the #134 East/West. You can use this freeway to travel to the San Fernando Valley or north/east to Pasadena.

The #101, or Hollywood, Freeway runs north to south in Hollywood and then shifts direction and heads east to west out toward Pasadena, merging with the #134 Freeway. This freeway can take you to the San Fernando Valley as well as connect you to the necessary freeways to take you west to the beach.

At the beach, Route 1, also called the Pacific Coast Highway (PCH), runs right along the coastline and is one of the world's most beautiful drives. Many freeways will lead you to this highway.

There is a method to this madness on the freeway system. AAA has many maps to assist visitors driving to Los Angeles, an exceptionally good one being *The Guide to Los Angeles Freeway System.* Now you're ready to drive in Los Angeles. Gather up your maps and start driving.

By limousine and cab. Los Angeles is an unusual city; although the four-county metropolitan area is home to thirteen million people and about eleven million visitors come here year after year, the cab system is not like that of any other major American city. You will probably not be able to hail a cab on the street, unless by chance you happen to be in Hollywood or on a major boulevard.

To call a cab, you must phone one of the many taxi companies that operate in Los Angeles. A few of the more reputable companies are: *Independent Cab Co.* at (213) 385–5397 or 385–TAXI. *United Independent Taxi* at (213) 653–5050. United Independent accepts MC and V.

For total luxury and a real taste of the Los Angeles way of life, try a limousine. It's the most relaxing way to view a city of this caliber. Limousines come equipped with everything from a full bar and telephone to a hot tub and a double bed—depending on your needs.

Most travel agencies will be able to suggest a reputable limo service suited to your requirements. Contrary to popular knowledge, a limo service is not all that much more expensive than other forms of transportation. Consider hiring a limo if you have a group of eight or fewer that want to travel together. (The fare can be split, making it extremely reasonable.) After all, since you're here on vacation, you might as well let someone else do the driving if you possibly can.

A few limo services are: *Dav-El Livery* at (213) 550–0070; *Le Monde Limousine* (213) 271–9270, (818) 990–8440, (800) 874–5432; and *Beverly Jade Limousine Service* (213) 829–1009.

TOURIST INFORMATION. *The Greater Los Angeles Visitors and Convention Bureau* has multilingual aides to assist you in making your sightseeing plans. The Bureau operates in three convenient locations.

The Downtown Visitors Information Center, (213) 239–0200), located in the Atlantic Richfield Plaza at 6th and Flower Streets, B Level, L.A. 90071, is open Monday through Friday, 8 A.M. to 5 P.M. In addition to walk-in service, this center will also mail the bureau's vacation-planning material to soon-to-be visitors to the city.

The Hollywood Visitors Information Center, (213) 239–0290, is open Monday through Thursday, 9:00 A.M. to 4:00 P.M. and Friday from 9:00 A.M. to 6:00 P.M. in the Pacific Federal Bank Building at 6801 Hollywood Boulevard, on the corner of Hollywood and Highland.

All three locations offer free information on attractions, public transportation, hotel and motel accommodations, restaurants, and Los Angeles nightlife. In addition, bimonthly special calendars, climate information, and information on self-guided tours of Los Angeles and Southern California are available to aid the uncertain traveller.

There is a *Visitors Information Center* at the airport, located in the Tom Bradley Terminal (both departure and arrival areas) 205 Worldway, LAX (213) 215–0606. Open 8 A.M. to 9 P.M. seven days.

Beyond the Greater Los Angeles Visitors and Convention Bureau, each community in this sprawling metropolis maintains either a specialized tourism bureau or a chamber of commerce. Here is a sampling; for those areas not listed, consult directory assistance.

Beverly Hills Visitors and Convention Bureau, Chamber of Commerce, 239 South Beverly Dr., Beverly Hills 90212; (213) 271–8174; open 9:00 A.M. to 5:00 P.M., Monday through Friday.

Santa Monica Visitor Information Center, 1430 Ocean Ave. in Palisades Park; (213) 393–7593. Open 10:00 A.M. to 4:00 P.M., seven days a week.

Pasadena Convention and Visitors Bureau, 300 East Green St., south of the Pasadena Mall; (818) 795–9311. Open 9:00 A.M. to 5:00 P.M., Monday through Friday.

Because Los Angeles covers such a large area, telephone assistance can save the visitor considerable time and energy. For beach and surfing conditions, call (213) 451–8761; for road conditions, call (213) 626–7231; for the weather, call (213) 554–1212;

California magazine and *Los Angeles* magazine are published monthly and incorporate extensive listings of restaurants, shopping, museums, children's activities, theater events, and films, as well as happenings in the world of art, dance, and music. All reflect the true pulse of the city.

This sprawling city also offers three daily newspapers, *The Los Angeles Times, The Daily News,* and *The Los Angeles Herald Examiner.* They keep up with city goings-on from day to day. The *Times'* Calendar Section gives information on films, theater events, and so on, and that information is also provided in the

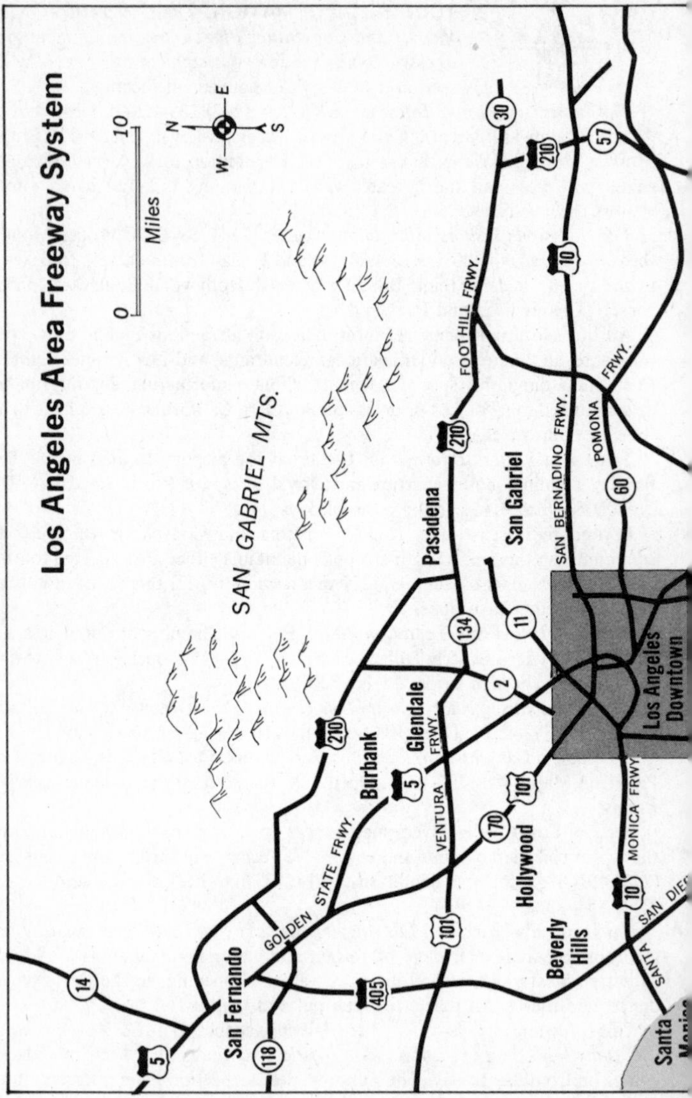
Los Angeles Area Freeway System
0
10
Miles
N
E
S
W
SAN GABRIEL MTS.
San Fernando
Burbank
Glendale
Pasadena
San Gabriel
Hollywood
Beverly Hills
Santa Monica
Los Angeles Downtown
GOLDEN STATE FRWY.
VENTURA FRWY.
GLENDALE FRWY.
FOOTHILL FRWY.
SAN BERNADINO FRWY.
POMONA FRWY.
SANTA MONICA FRWY
SAN DIEGO
5
14
118
405
101
170
210
2
134
11
30
57
10
60

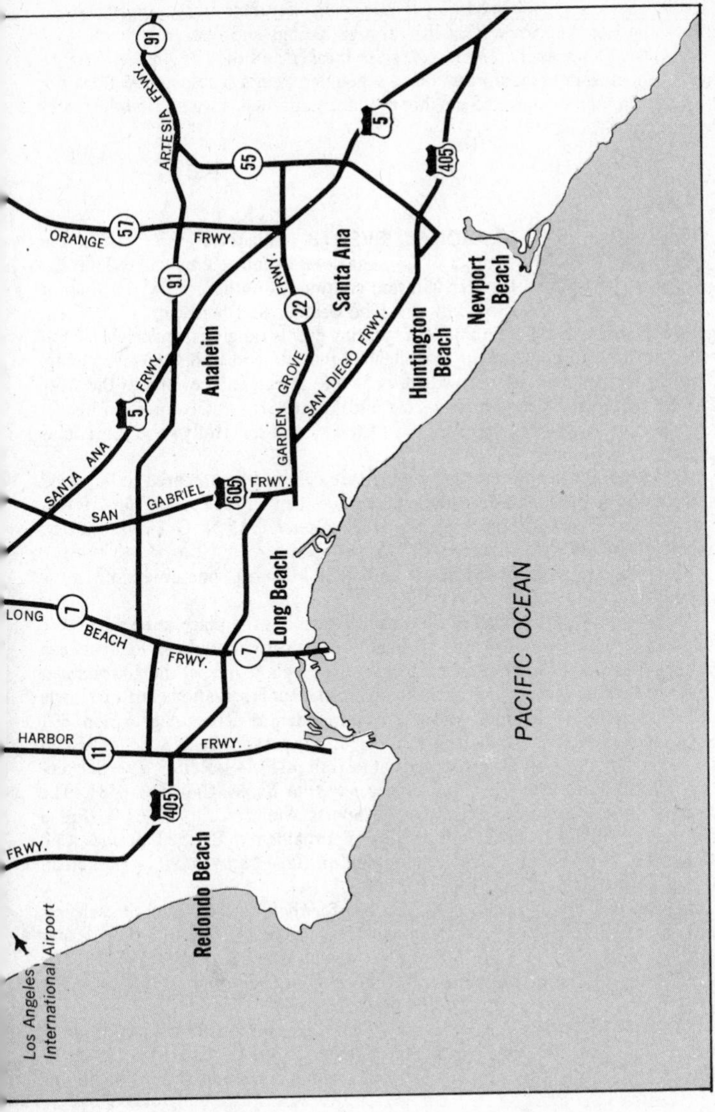
ARTESIA FRWY.
91
55
5
405
ORANGE
57
FRWY.
Santa Ana
FRWY.
22
GARDEN GROVE
SAN DIEGO FRWY.
Newport Beach
Huntington Beach
Anaheim
SANTA ANA
5
FRWY.
SAN GABRIEL
605
FRWY.
Long Beach
LONG
7
BEACH
FRWY.
7
HARBOR
11
FRWY.
405
FRWY.
Redondo Beach
Los Angeles International Airport
PACIFIC OCEAN

Herald's Style Section. On Sunday these papers offer their most complete coverage of the Los Angeles way of life through listings and feature articles.

Two free newspapers, *The Los Angeles Weekly* and the *Los Angeles Reader,* are excellent sources of information on scheduled events. These publications can be found in many stores and neighborhood restaurants as well as in bookstores and movie theaters.

SEASONAL EVENTS. Whatever the season, the weather in Los Angeles is usually summerlike. Thus the traveler will find continuous outdoor as well as indoor special events. The weather and landscape of Los Angeles contribute to a great number of sporting events ranging from celebrity golf tournaments and horse racing to volleyball tournaments and stock-car racing. And the city's streets lure crowds of people to attend such events as the Rose Parade in January, Chinese New Year and Mardi Gras at Olvera St. in February, the Los Angeles Street Scene in October, and the Hollywood Christmas Parade in November.

As a general rule, outdoor happenings are free, but be prepared to buy food and souvenirs. Indoor events usually take place at either the *Los Angeles Convention Center* (Pico and Figueroa), the *Music Center* (135 N. Grand), or at the *Sports Arena* (3939 S. Figueroa).

The phone numbers listed below are in the 213 area code unless otherwise indicated.

January. On the first day of the year, Pasadena is the place to be. Get there before sunrise, or rough it and spend the night on Colorado Blvd. (between Orange Grove and Sierra Madre) to be assured a good view of the *Tournament of Roses Parade.* Grandstand seats are available, but reservations must be made at least a month in advance. Write the Tournament of Roses Association, 391 S. Orange Grove Blvd., Pasadena, CA 91105. The parade begins at 8:40 A.M. and is followed by the Rose Bowl football game. Call (818) 449–ROSE. The Convention Center hosts the *Greater Los Angeles Auto Show.* Call 748–8531. The *Beverly Hills Dog Show* is held at the Sports Arena. Call 748–6131. For a leisurely stroll, there's the L.A. Open Golf Tournament in Pacific Palisades. Call 482–1311. At the end of the month, the *Harlem Globetrotters* do their basketball tricks at various locations. Call (818) 906–1234.

February. Crowds gather in Chinatown for the *Chinese New Year* celebration, a colorful display of costumes and great fireworks. Call 617–0396. Later in the month is the *Mexican Mardi Gras* down Olvera St. Call 625–5045. The Convention Center hosts two events: the *Southern California Boat Show* (471–1151) and the *Custom Car and Hot Rod Show* (588–1934).

March. The world's largest *Camellia Show* takes place at Descanso Gardens, where more than 100,000 camellia plants are in full bloom. Call (818) 790–5571. *Filmex* in Century City presents film buffs with a marathon of films, including premier releases as well as some classics. Call 856–7707. March 19 marks the traditional day for the *return of the swallows* to San Juan Capistrano Mission.

April. A parade of colorfully decorated animals takes place for the *Blessing of the Animals* at Olvera St. Call 625–5045. On Easter Sunday the traditional *sunrise service* is held at the Hollywood Bowl. Hollywood Park *thoroughbred racing* begins its run in Inglewood through mid-July. Call 419–1500. Orchids, cacti, and other exotics are on display to commemorate the *L.A. Zoo Plant and Garden Day.* Call 666–4650. Artists and musicians gather for a weekend at Beverly Hills Park on Santa Monica Blvd. for an *Affaire in the Gardens.* Art work on sale, live music, and a lot of food. Call 550–4864. Near the end of the month, see the *Ice Capades* skate for ten days at the Forum. Call 469–2767.

May. The *Los Angeles Civic Light Opera* begins its stay at the Music Center (through September). Call 972–7200. Every Saturday and Sunday of the month the *Renaissance Faire* celebrates in Agoura. (From Los Angeles, take the Ventura Freeway to the Agoura offramp). Find a costume and prepare for a day in the life of Renaissance Man. Call (818) 889–3150. On the first weekend of the month is the *Westwood Sidewalk Arts and Crafts Show.* Call 475–4574. Olvera St. presents the *Cinco de Mayo* celebration on the fourth and the fifth. Call 625–5045. Beginning on about the tenth is *Auto Expo/LA* at the Convention Center. Call 748–8531. Catch a free boat ride and tour the harbor at San Pedro during *World Trade Week.* Call 519–3508. On the third weekend of the month, artists and musicians gather at Beverly Hills Park on Santa Monica Blvd. for an *Affaire in the Gardens.* Artwork on sale, live music, and a lot of food. Call 550–4864.

June. The *Greek Theater* begins its season of outdoor concerts at Griffith Park (through September). Call 216–6666. The *Whale Festival* is at Cabrillo Beach. Call 548–7562. The *Playboy Jazz Festival* takes place at the Hollywood Bowl. Call 972–7200. The *Beverly Hills Dog Show* returns to the sports arena for a spring show.

July. *Ringling Bros./Barnum and Bailey Circus* occupies the Forum in Inglewood from mid-July through mid-August. Call 673–1300. *Symphonies Under the Stars* concerts begin at the Hollywood Bowl and are highlighted by a Fourth of July celebration by the Los Angeles Philharmonic. Another way to spend American Independence Day is to lounge in the sun at Venice Beach. When the sun goes down, you can see spectacular *fireworks* over the Pacific Ocean. For biking fans, the *Coca Cola Super Bowl of Motorcross* comes to Anaheim Stadium. Call (714) 553–3333. Another beach event is the *Malibu Festival of Arts and Crafts* during the last weekend of the month. Call 456–9025.

August. The *San Fernando Valley Fair* at Devonshire Downs takes place early in the month. It features rides, games, crafts, animals, and a lot of food. Call (818) 368–6202. Surfers from all over gather at such beaches as Hermosa, Manhattan, Redondo, and Torrance for the *International Surf Festival.* Call 545–4502. In Santa Monica, take in the *Sports and Art Festival* during the last two weeks of the month. Call 393–9975.

September. Los Angeles celebrates *its birthday* on the sixth by holding festivities at Olvera St. Call 625–5045. The *Los Angeles County Fair* in Pomona has everything from livestock judging and pie tastings to carnival rides and game booths. Call (714) 623–3111. Recently, the downtown *L.A. Street Scene* has become a tradition in the streets adjacent to City Hall. Artisans and cultural groups from the city gather to present their exhibits and goods. Musicians play, people dance in the streets, exotic foods are served, all enhancing your enjoyment. Call 626–0485. More than 100 *gymnasts* perform in outdoor competition on the beach just south of the Santa Monica pier. Call 458–8311. Another *Affaire in the Garden* takes place in Beverly Hills Park (see listing under April). The horses are running for the *Oak Tree Thoroughbred Horse Races* at Hollywood Park in Inglewood from late September through October. Call 677–7151.

October. At the beginning of the month is the *Budweiser Grand Prix* at the Riverside International Raceway (714–653–1161) and the *Westwood Arts and Crafts Show* (475–4574). The *Los Angeles Chamber Orchestra* begins its series of performances in Pasadena (818–796–2200) and the *Glendale Symphony* and the *Los Angeles Philharmonic* begin their six-month schedules at the Music Center. Call 972–7211. If you would rather ski but can't find any snow, at least have a look at the latest equipment and clothes for the slopes at the *Ski Show* at the Convention Center. Call 748–8531. During the last weekend of the month, witches and goblins gather at Hancock Park for the *Festival of Masks* Parade and the Masquerade Ball. Call 934–8527.

November. The Dorothy Chandler Pavilion at the Music Center features the *New York City Opera.* Call 972–7211. For philatelists, the *Stamp Expo Pacific* is at the Convention Center in the middle of the month. Call 748–8531. The holiday festivities begin the Sunday after Thanksgiving down Hollywood Blvd. See your favorite stars and celebrities join Santa Claus at the *Hollywood Christmas Parade,* a motor arcade of vintage vehicles. Call 469–2337. Also at this time, the zany *Doo-Dah Parade* wends its way through the streets of Pasadena. Call (818) 796–2591.

December. The closing of the year marks a month of parades. *Christmas parades* are in abundance during the first half of the month in Los Angeles, Covina, El Monte, San Pedro, Glendora, Pacoima, and El Segundo. Call the Chamber of Commerce of each city to find out when and where. There's the *City of the Christmas Story* in Santa Monica along Palisades Seaside Park, where lighted Nativity scenes are set up to be viewed by motorists. Call 393–9825. A beautiful show of lights reflecting on the water takes place at the *Christmas Lighted Boat Parades* in San Pedro (832–7272) and Marina del Rey (821–0555). At Olvera St. on each evening from the sixteenth through the twenty-fourth at 7:00 P.M. is *Las Posadas.* This nightly event begins with a children's choir singing carols, followed by a candlelight procession through the decorated street, which depicts the journey of Joseph and Mary. Each evening is climaxed by children breaking a piñata full of goodies. Call 625–5045. The day after Christmas *thoroughbred horse racing* begins at Santa Anita in Arcadia. It continues through mid-April. Call (818) 574–7223.

FREE EVENTS. In Los Angeles every day is a free event in terms of nature; The sun, sand, and ocean alone can fill a vacation. But there are plenty of other free activities, events, and cultural attractions to keep busy even those with limited budgets. (All telephone numbers listed below are in the 213 area code.)

Free concerts take place at the *Triforium* (at the Los Angeles Mall, corner of Temple and Main Sts.). This building was originally designed to symbolize the city of Los Angeles; here, right near City Hall, free noontime concerts are offered every day. Many feature recorded music from a tape library, but at least once a week there is live entertainment.

Even though winter in Los Angeles is not at all harsh, the outdoor concert scene thrives a bit more during the summer months. Outdoor *Concerts on the Green* in Barnsdall Park, 4800 Hollywood Blvd., are held on Sunday afternoons in the summer at 4:00 P.M. Classical concerts are sponsored by the Cultural Affairs Department of Los Angeles, and there are also free performances—drama, dance, comedy—at the Gallery Theater in the same park.

On Sunday evenings during July and August, *Stough Park* in Burbank is the site of free evening concerts at 7:30. The big band sound and smaller musical groups are the bill. *Concerts in the Sky,* on the pool deck of the Bonaventure Hotel, 404 S. Figeroa St., take place Monday, Wednesday, and Friday at noon throughout the summer. Several artists are featured. (To find out who is appearing, call 972–7211.)

Another summer concert series, the *Watts Towers Jazz Concerts,* is offered on Sunday afternoons at 1765 East 107th St. The towers of Simon Rodia provide a splendid backdrop for some of the best sounds in jazz. Because the schedule is a bit uneven, call 569–8181 for more information. The Los Angeles State Historical Park at the Plaza in *El Pueblo de Los Angeles* has Mexican music and celebrations on Thursday evenings during the summer. The festivals, which serve to encourage the audience to sing and dance, take place at 6:30 and 8:30.

In Santa Monica at Lincoln Park on 7th St. and Wilshire Blvd., afternoon concerts are held one Sunday a month. The *Outdoor Summer Band Schedule* features many different kinds of music from marches to jazz. (Call 458–8323 for further information.) Summer musical entertainment can also be heard on some Sunday afternoons at the *William Grant Still Community Arts Center* at 2520 West View St., Los Angeles. Jazz, big band, and other kinds of music are sponsored by this community center. (For details call 734–1164.)

Finally, a fall musical series takes place at the *John Anson Ford County Cultural Arts Theater* at 2580 Cahuenga Blvd., East, in North Hollywood. This multifaceted presentation offers dance, jazz, and many other kinds of music. It is sponsored by the Los Angeles Board of Supervisors, the Performing Arts Commission, and the Department of Parks and Recreation. For more information call 461–7140.

Free festivals, including musical events, abound in Los Angeles throughout the year (see *Seasonal Events*). Some, such as the Pasadena *Tournament of Roses Parade* on the first of the year, are real "California events," and others, such as the Chinese New Year in February, are special events in many cities. March marks the *Return of the Swallows* to San Juan Capistrano; and also in March is *National Mime Week;* although it is celebrated in various areas of the city, the closing celebration occurs in Venice (call (714) 494–3100 for details). *Cinco de Mayo* is an especially Californian, or southwestern, celebration. This day of Mexican Independence is celebrated throughout the city; one of the largest gatherings takes place at the El Pueblo de Los Angeles State Historical Park.

Another Los Angeles celebration devoted to one of its special ethnic groups is *Nisei Week* in August. This Japanese festival in Little Tokyo at First and San Pedro Sts. offers tea ceremonies, dances, martial arts demonstrations, and other examples of Japanese cultural traditions.

Another southern California festival takes place at the San Gabriel Mission in September. At the *Community Fiesta* such traditional rites as blessing the animals are performed. For more information call (818) 282–5191. One of the most exciting celebrations in the city is the *Los Angeles Street Scene,* which takes place in October on all the downtown streets around City Hall. Eleven stages are set up, and the entertainment is nonstop. For information call 626–0485. *Christmas parades* in cities and in harbors fill the month of December. There are boat parades in Los Angeles Harbor, Marina del Rey, Newport Harbor, and Dana Point.

In addition to festivals and musical entertainment, Los Angeles offers a variety of visual art. Throughout the year communities open their streets to displays of local artists. *The Los Angeles Times, The Los Angeles Daily News,* and *The Herald Examiner,* as well as local papers such as *The LA Reader* and *The LA Weekly,* have information on these shows as well as other free events that might be available when you are in town. Art in progress is one of the attractions at the *Santa Monica Fine Art Festival* in August at Palisades Park. The *Santa Monica Art Show* in October takes place in the open-air Santa Monica Mall. There are street entertainers as well.

At Century City in April the *Spring Festival* hosts an exhibition of art for four days. And one of the well-attended showings is the *Westwood Sidewalk Art and Craft Show* in May. Strolling musicians will serenade you as you look at the art displayed throughout the streets of Westwood Village.

As you might expect of the capital of the movie business, Los Angeles offers free movie showings. Here is a list of the places where you can see *free films: The Natural History Museum,* check *The Los Angeles Times* or call 746–0410; *the Beverly Hills Library* shows screen classics; *the UCLA Meinitz Auditorium* often shows offbeat films, 825–2345; *the Hearst Theater* in the Museum of Science and Industry offers old movies, 744–7400; *the Norris Theater* at USC shows classics on Saturdays and Sundays, 743–2311; and *the Santa Monica Community College District* at 1900 Pico Blvd. offers "Sunday Afternoon at the Movies" at which classic movies are shown on Sundays at 2:00 P.M.

There is more. Live theater freebies can also be had. The *Free Public Theater Festival* from mid-July to the end of August is the largest free theater offering. Productions take place at the Gallery Theater in Barnsdall Park as well as at smaller parks in communities around town. Call 665–5148.

Works in progress and free performances can sometimes be seen at the *Los Angeles Theatre Center,* 296 N. Western Ave. Call 464–5603.

In addition to scheduled free events, many things in Los Angeles can be experienced. The *Walk of Fame* on Hollywood Blvd. from Vine to Orange is one of the most popular attractions. Over a thousand stars, each with a plaque of his or her own, are represented on this walk. In the same vein, a visit to the famous *Mann's Chinese Theater* at 6925 Hollywood Blvd. will enable you to view famous hand and foot imprints. Elizabeth Taylor, Shirley Temple, and Clark Gable are only a few of the stars whose imprints are immortalized.

For present-day stargazing, charity sports activities are a good choice. An *Arthritis Run-a-Thon* is held in Griffith Park each December. The *Beverly Hills–Perrier 10K* is also held in December. It pits local celebrities against each other in various unique events. The *All Star Celebrity Softball League* begins practice in April at Rancho Park at Motor Ave. and Pico Blvd. Stars playing raquetball can be caught at the *Motion Picture/Television Industry Raquetball Classic* in October. The Greater Los Angeles Visitors and Convention Bureau can provide additional information on these events.

And for those who are not satisfied with watching celebrities but want to see the "business" firsthand, there are opportunities to attend the taping of *television shows.* Most networks prefer to process ticket requests sent through the mail. Write to CBS at 7800 Beverly Blvd., LA 90036, and to NBC at 3000 W. Alameda, Burbank 91523. ABC makes things easier by providing ticket booths at ABC TV Center, 4151 Prospect Dr., ABC Vine Street Theater, 1313 N. Vine, ABC Entertainment Center, Plaza Level, 2040 Ave. of the Stars and Glendale Galleria in Glendale. You can call 557–7777 to see what is available.

TOURS. By bus, car, or boat there is a lot to see in and around Los Angeles. All forms of transportation provide a good overview of this vast city and its surrounding environment. Motor travel provides an excellent way to discover what the Big Orange is all about.

By bus. The largest of the sightseeing companies in the Southland is *Gray Line Tours Co.* of Los Angeles. Offices, branches, and travel desks are operated in hotels throughout Southern California.

For a large enough group, Gray Line will tackle any special tour anywhere the group wants to go. All Gray Line Tours make pickups at major hotels in Hollywood and Beverly Hills and then join other sightseers for a mass departure from Gray Line, 1207 W. 3rd St. in Los Angeles (downtown).

Among Gray Line tours are *Pasadena and Huntington Library, Hollywood, Beverly Hills Movie Star Homes, Farmers Market, Twentieth Century-Fox Universal Studio Tour,* including studios and sites of interest in Hollywood and Beverly Hills.

Listed under "Sightseeing Tours" in the yellow pages are a number of small companies offering individualized tours, multilingual guides, and personal chauffeurs who will drive your car or theirs. Some recommendations: *Starline Sight-*

seeing Tours, 6845 Hollywood Blvd., Hollywood 90028; (213) 463–3131, goes to movie stars' homes in Beverly Hills as well as to Universal Studios.

L.A. Today Tours focuses on seven areas of Greater Los Angeles, each of which includes scenic beauty, art, shopping, and historical development: the downtown area, Wilshire West, Hollywood, Pasadena and East, the Valley, South to Long Beach, and West to the Pacific Ocean. For reservations, phone or write Elinor Oswald, LA Today, 14964 Camarosa Dr., Pacific Palisades, CA 90272; 454–5730.

Butterfly Express (8530 Wilshire Blvd.; 553–9141) offers luxury tours by limousine contrasting the historical and cultural parts of Los Angeles with the contemporary. Along with the general tour, there are special excursions focusing specifically on architecture and Hollywood. Also, tours can be custom designed to particular interests.

By boat. Sightseeing boat trips leave from the piers and docks at Malibu, Pierpoint Landing at the Port of Long Beach, from the foot of Magnolia Ave. in the city of Long Beach itself, and from Fisherman's Wharf in Redondo Beach.

Catalina Terminals, Inc. (P.O. Box 1948, San Pedro CA 90733; 213–514–3838) has tours via ship from San Pedro to Santa Catalina Island. The tour offers a glass bottomed boat, inland motor trips, a seal colony, and scenic drives.

Long Beach/Catalina Cruises (same address as Catalina Terminals, Inc., above) offer one of three modern boats to Catalina Island. There are also harbor tours at Long Beach, including a close-up water view of the *Queen Mary* and Howard Hughes's *Spruce Goose.* For information call *Starline,* 6843 Hollywood Blvd., Hollywood CA 90028, at (213) 463–3131. *Long Beach Harbor Helicopters* (same address as Catalina Terminals, Inc., above) tour the area after lift-off from San Pedro's Ports o'Call Village.

SPECIAL-INTEREST TOURS AND SIGHTSEEING

As a major American city with all the corresponding attributes, Los Angeles offers quite a diversified array of attractions to the visitor no matter what his or her tastes. From the many cultural activities here to the host of major universities and the galaxy of famous people in their architecturally amazing homes, the Big Orange is a city that has something for everyone. Below is a sampling of unique, special-interest tours in and around Los Angeles. (For Long Beach, see the chapter *Long Beach South to San Clemente* at the end of the book.)

Public tours of the *Music Center* downtown at 135 N. Grand are sponsored by The Music Center Operating Company and conducted by the Symphonians, a dedicated group of volunteers who offer this service to visitors at no charge. During the week, the tour will take you inside all three theaters (the Mark Taper, the Dorothy Chandler Pavilion, and the Ahmanson), where history and architecture, as well as the artwork decorating the hall and the wall of these beautiful buildings, will be discussed. On Saturdays, the tour is centered on the Dorothy Chandler Pavilion. From May through October, tours can enjoyed Monday, Tuesday, Thursday, and Friday at 10:00 A.M., 10:30 A.M., 11:30 A.M., 12 noon, 1:00 P.M. and 1:30 P.M. On Saturdays throughout the year tours are given every half hour beginning at 10:00 A.M. and ending at 12:30 P.M. Tour availability changes daily. For information call 972–7483.

A tour of the *California Institute of Technology* (Cal-Tech) at 1201 E. California St. in Pasadena provides a general walking tour of the grounds. The first stop along the walk is the Campus Building, where student life is discussed. As the tour progresses through the grounds, tour guides will point out interesting sites and the history of the school. Also mentioned on the tour is an overview of the vast research conducted on this lovely campus. One especially interesting stop at Cal-Tech is the Seismological Building, where semiprecious stones and minerals found not only in California but all over the world are displayed. Tour hours are Monday, Thursday, and Friday at 3:00 P.M. and Tuesday and Wednesday at 11:00 A.M. The duration of the tour is one hour. For more information, call (818) 356–6328.

Located in the heart of downtown Los Angeles on one hundred fifty acres of rolling green hills is the *University of Southern California* (USC). Here specially trained tour guides give walking tours of the campus, which is known for its exceptional athletic department. A few points of interest on the tour are the Tommy Trojan Statue, notorious for its appearance at football games as the USC symbol; the Annenberg School of Communications; and renowned Heritage Hall, a building dedicated to athletes.

Another portion of the tour takes the visitor through the school's multimillion dollar performing arts center, which was dedicated by George Lucas and Steven Spielberg. The equipment in these buildings is comparable to that found on professional soundstages. The Mudd Hall of Philosophy may look familiar to you; it has been used quite often in a number of films. Tours, which are free, last approximately forty-five minutes; they are held on the hour Monday through Friday from 10:00 A.M. to 2:00 P.M. Call 743–2983 and prearrange your tour. Parking instructions will be given on the phone.

At the *University of California, Los Angeles* (UCLA), in Westwood at 405 Hilgard Ave., many different kinds of general public tours are offered. A Day at UCLA is one; ten tours featuring the serene Japanese Gardens, as well as the beautiful Botanical Gardens, are conducted every Friday. For art enthusiasts, the Frederick Wight Art Gallery is open for viewing.

Materials for a self-guided tour are available in the UCLA tour office located on campus. This kind of do-it-yourself tour enables the visitor to choose what to see on campus. A self-guided tour of the Japanese Gardens is also available, but a reservation is necessary. These special tours can be prearranged on Tuesdays between 10:00 A.M. and 1:00 P.M. or Wednesdays between 12 noon and 3:00 P.M. For a group of ten or more, tours are conducted on Friday between 10:00 A.M. and 3:00 P.M.

Minilecture discovery tours at UCLA are conducted on Thursdays. On this walk, one department is visited each week. The Green Thumb Tours in the spring and fall focus on the beautiful landscape and foliage.

Other points of interest during a general UCLA tour are the Ackerman Student Union, the Student Store, the Bookstore, and the campus's eighteen libraries. Visitor information: 825–4338; tour reservations: 206–8147.

On the *Stars' Homes Tours* you can peek at the celebrities' hideaways in a few hours. Plan this self-guided tour through charming Beverly Hills and Bel Air residential areas by consulting maps that can be purchased from street vendors and from Hollywood specialty shops. A sneak preview: Judy Garland once lived at 1231 Stone Canyon Rd. in Bel Air; Rudolph Valentino lived at *Falcon's Lair,* 1436 Bella Dr. in Beverly Hills; Charlie Chaplin lived at Breakaway House at 1085 Summit Dr. in Beverly Hills; Douglas Fairbanks and Mary Pickford lived at Pickfair, 1143 Summit Dr. in Beverly Hills; and Lionel Barrymore lived at 802 North Rexford Dr. in Beverly Hills.

Inside Hollywood Tours brings visitors face to face with stars of the silver screen. Designed for groups (minimum size: twenty), these tours can be arranged through American Express Tours or Trade Wind Tours. On one of these tours, participants take a walking tour of NBC and then dine in the studio commissary. Then they view an NBC television taping and are given personalized gifts or door prizes.

Inside Hollywood Tours' "Spotlight on Beverly Hills" is operated weekdays only. Visitors see selected homes of the stars and spend some time at the Academy of Motion Picture Arts and Sciences.

For further information on Inside Hollywood Tours write P.O. Box 283, Tarzana, California 91356, or call (818) 344–0663.

Hollywood Fantasy Tours runs a two-hour excursion covering dozens of Hollywood highlights. Included are Charlie Chaplin's old studio and Rudolf Valentino's grave. The open-air double-decker buses leave every hour starting at 8:30 A.M. from 1721 North Highland Ave., Hollywood 90028. Phone 469–8184.

Architecture is an intriguing aspect of Los Angeles. From older edifices to sleek, handsome, high-rise buildings to fantasy architecture, there is quite a diversity that reflects the tastes and styles of the city during different stages of growth. Many of the city's buildings, designed by such world-famous architects as Frank Lloyd Wright and Richard Neutra, are exceptional.

You may want to consider self-guided tours of some of these fascinating buildings: Frank Lloyd Wright's Hollyhock House, built from 1917 to 1920, at Barnsdall Park, 4800 Hollywood Blvd. in Hollywood; the Bradbury Building, at 304 S. Broadway, downtown, with its outstanding iron decoration; the ornate Byzantine architecture of the Cathedral of Saint Sophia at 1324 S. Normandie Ave. in Los Angeles; the Gamble House at 4 Westmoreland Pl. in Pasadena (luncheon is served; reservations necessary)—a charming example of the Greene and Greene California bungalow style; Los Angeles' first brick house, La Casa Pelanconi at 33–35 Olvera St., now a restaurant; Lovel House, 4616 Dundee Ave.; Queen Anne Cottage, 301 N. Baldwin, part of the Los Angeles State and County Arboretum; fabulous Watts Towers at 1765 E. 107 St. in Los Angeles, which was thirty-three years in the making; Casa de Adobe, 4603 N. Figueroa St. in Los Angeles, which replicates a Spanish hacienda.

Each spring, home tours of private homes designed by master builders and architects can be arranged. Check with information at the Los Angeles County Museum of Art (857–6111) to find out when this tour is scheduled.

To see the architecture as well as an overview of the artwork and the performing arts in Los Angeles, try the *Los Angeles Cultural Connection* at 2228 Benecia Ave. in Los Angeles. Group tours.

Art Tours of Los Angeles at 2864 Motor Ave. (870–2549), helps visitors experience the contemporary art explosion in the city. Tours take you to Venice and Melrose Ave., art communities and melting pots of current trends, styles, and influences. Reservations are necessary.

Los Angeles Conservancy Cultural Tours at 623-CITY offers a guided walking tour of downtown Los Angeles to view the city's historical architecture, California's Broadway Theater district, and the lavish movie palaces of the 1920s. Reservations are necessary; the fee is $5.00.

Hollywood on Location, 8644 Wilshire Blvd., Beverly Hills 90211 (213–659–9165), publishes a location list that pinpoints where and when filming of major movies and television series around Los Angeles are happening. Cost is $19 for list of locations, all necessary maps, and information brochure. Transportation is up to you. Start any time. Most shooting goes on until midnight, often until dawn. More action on weekdays than weekends.

MOVIE AND TELEVISION TOURS

Before Los Angeles became one of the nation's largest and fastest growing cities in the 1920s, it had been a kind of rural nirvana. Surrounded by bean fields and orange groves, its climate was temperate all year long; grassy plains, snow-capped mountains, ocean, and even the desert were easily accessible.

This was the Hollywood that Cecil B. De Mille, a struggling actor turned director from New York, found when, a few days before Christmas in 1913, he arrived in Hollywood. He came to film *The Squaw Man* for the Jesse Lasky Feature Play Company, a notable movie in that it was the first feature ever made. De Mille rented a barn on the corner of Selma Ave. and Vine St.

The Squaw Man changed Hollywood. It marked the beginning of a new era for Los Angeles and the fledgling moving-picture business. Within a few years, Hollywood replaced New York as the capital of the film industry and became a symbol of glamour, fame, and riches to millions. Today movie studios look nothing like De Mille's barn (which still stands at Vine near Yucca—see *Historical Sites* for further details.) They are huge, technically sophisticated production centers and account for one of Los Angeles' most important industries. A few of them, along with the newer television studios that flourish here, are open to the public.

Universal Studios. 100 Universal Pl., Universal City. Call (818) 508–9600 for information. Discover what really goes on behind the scenes in Hollywood. The five-hour Universal tour is an enlightening and amusing day at the world's largest television and movie studio. (It stretches across more than 400 acres, many of which are traversed during the course of the day by trams featuring witty running commentary provided by enthusiastic guides.)

Visitors experience the parting of the Red Sea, an avalanche, and a flood. They live through an encounter with a runaway train and an attack by the ravenous killer shark of *Jaws* fame. They endure a confrontation by aliens armed with death rays—all without ever leaving the safety of the tram.

Visitors are taken through a New England village, an aged European town, and the same New York street that Kojak and Columbo once walked. They examine giant props and see children lift up "automobiles." Also on display are a mobile forest and a Western jail. At this point in the tour, visitors relax in the snack bar and picnic area before going on to the Entertainment Center, the longest and the last stop of the day.

At the Entertainment Center visitors stroll around to enjoy various shows. In one theater animals beguile you with their tricks. In another you can pose for a photo session with the Incredible Hulk. Visit Castle Dracula and confront a variety of terrifying monsters. At the Screen Test Theater, visitors may find themselves being filmed as extras in films already released and now recut to include them.

Recent additions to the tour include access to more of the back-lot filming areas. Another attraction, which opened in the summer of 1982, is the Comedy Screen Test Theater.

Admission fees: $11.50 for adults, $8.50 for children ages three–eleven. For children under three, admission is free. Summer hours: open daily from 8:00 A.M. to 6:00 P.M. and during the other seasons, Monday through Friday, 10:00 A.M. to 3:30 P.M., Saturday and Sunday from 9:30 A.M. to 4:00 P.M.

Burbank Studios. Warner Brothers and Columbia Pictures share the lot at Burbank Studios, 4000 Warner Blvd., Burbank. A guided walking tour is available. Called the VIP tour, it is limited to groups of twelve adults. Reservations are essential; no visitors are allowed without them. (Call 818-954–1008.)

Because the tours involve a lot of walking, dress comfortably and casually. This tour is somewhat instructional, more technical, and more centered on the actual workings of filmmaking than the tour at Universal.

Visitors can also make reservations to dine in the studio commissary, the Blue Room, after the tour.

NBC Television Studios. NBC Television Studios (3000 W. Alameda Ave., Burbank, 840–4444 or 840–3572), offers a one-and-one-half hour guided tour of the largest color TV facilities in the United States. During the tour, visitors will have communication satellite and videotape processes explained to them. Studio I, where the *Tonight* show is filmed, is also part of the tour, as is the huge prop warehouse.

Tickets are available for tapings of NBC shows (see below).

Tours take place daily, 9:00 A.M. to 4:00 P.M. except in the summer when the studio opens at 8:30 A.M. Admission fees are $4.50 for adults, $3.75 for children ages five–eleven. Children under five are admitted free when accompanied by an adult. Free parking.

KCET: Los Angeles' Public Television Station. A behind-the-scenes look at television production is available to the general public at KCET, Los Angeles' public television station, located at 4401 Sunset Blvd. in Hollywood. On this tour you will walk through sound stages where special television productions (such as Steve Allen's *Meeting of the Minds* and Carl Sagan's *Cosmos*) were taped for nationwide broadcast. KCET's satellite system has an instantaneous feed throughout the world, which allows the station to pull any information occurring twenty-four hours a day. This satellite, along with the many different kinds of television cameras and equipment found on the sound stages, will be discussed in detail during the tour. Also seen on the tour is KCET's legitimate theater, which dates to the early 1920s.

Free tours are available Tuesday and Thursday at 10:00 A.M. or 11 A.M. These tours should be prearranged by contacting the volunteer department of the station at 667–9242. The tour is an hour-and-a-half in length.

Television Shows. There's no better opportunity to see a television show being produced than in Los Angeles, and TV show tickets are easily obtained throughout the Los Angeles area.

Each network maintains a ticket booth located at its respective studio, and each is open during the hours of 9:00 A.M. and 5:00 P.M. The studios suggest that those interested in seeing a particular show phone ahead to be assured of ticket availability and show times.

Phone numbers for each network are:

ABC: 557–4396
CBS: 852–2345
NBC: (818) 840–3537
KTLA (Channel 5 in Los Angeles): 460–5500
KTTV (Channel 11 in Los Angeles): 856–1425.

Most tickets can be obtained the day of the performance; however, on shows such as *Johnny Carson,* NBC will mail tickets if you live more than 150 miles outside Los Angeles and if you allow six weeks for delivery. Write to NBC Ticket Office, 3000 W. Alameda Ave., Burbank, CA 91523.

Free tickets are also available outside Mann's Chinese Theater in Hollywood, at the Universal Studios Tour, and at the Hollywood Greater Los Angeles Visitors Bureau (see *Tourist Information,* above).

Mann's Chinese Theater. A no fuss, self-made tour at Mann's Chinese Theater (at 6925 Hollywood Blvd.) is on the top of most movie buffs' sightseeing lists. Opened by Sid Grauman in 1927 for the premiere of Cecil B. De Mille's *King of Kings,* this theater was the subject of much fanfare.

Mann's Chinese is famous for its courtyard filled with the impressions of more than 150 movie stars' handprints, footprints, and signatures sealed in concrete—a tradition that began accidentally (or so the legend goes) when Norma Talmadge stepped in wet cement at the first premiere. Modern-day celluloid stars (including R2D2 and Darth Vadar of *Star Wars*) and long-ago lovelies (such as Marilyn Monroe and Judy Garland) are remembered in this historical Hollywood setting. For information, call 646–8111.

PARKS. The extensive Los Angeles park system provides a welcome oasis after the myriad concrete freeways and urban sprawl. The Los Angeles Department of Parks and Recreation provides helpful information on locating and identifying park facilities. Call 485–5555.

The vast park system offers everything from small, grassy knolls for picnicking and relaxing to huge wilderness areas offering a wide spectrum of recreation facilities, including tennis courts, golf courses, and lakes.

The Parks Department also sponsors various activities such as marathon races, interpark sports contests, poetry readings, art shows, and chess tournaments. During summer the Los Angeles Free Public Theater sponsors performances in the parks featuring Shakespeare and contemporary plays. For a schedule of events and activities, check *The Los Angeles Times* Sunday "Calendar" section, *The Herald-Examiner's* Friday "Style" section, the *Los Angeles Reader,* the *Los Angeles Weekly,* or *Los Angeles* or *California* magazines. Each has special listings on upcoming activities.

Barnsdall Park. 4800 Hollywood Blvd., Los Angeles. The Hollyhock House, the first California residence designed and built by Frank Lloyd Wright, is hidden amid the bustle of Hollywood by a hillside olive grove. There is an ample picnic area, and tours of the remarkable house are free. Also located in the park is the Junior Arts Center, a facility offering arts and crafts classes and theater arts instruction to children. The Municipal Art Gallery exhibits feature a changing lineup of local talent primarily in a contemporary vein.

El Pueblo de Los Angeles State Historical Park. 420 N. Main St. (Mailing address: 845 N. Alamita St., Los Angeles, 90012). Tours are offered at the historic buildings that make up this park, the founding site of Los Angeles in 1781. Adjacent to Olvera St., the city's oldest thoroughfare, is the park itself, also known as the Old Plaza, a cobblestone square filled with shops, restaurants, and entertainment facilities—all suggestive of the atmosphere of a real Mexican village.

Elysian Park. Entrances on Academy Rd., Stadium Wy., Scott Ave., Los Angeles. This 575-acre park is on hilly acreage overlooking downtown Los Angeles and the San Gabriel Valley. Much of the park is still wilderness, and there is a 10-acre rare-tree grove completely labeled for convenient identification. The recreation center has volleyball and basketball courts. Plentiful play areas for the children, nature trails for hiking, plus nine picnic spots round out the park's offerings. Perched on the southeast corner, high above the smog, is Dodger Stadium, home of the Los Angeles Dodgers professional baseball team.

Ernest E. Debs Park. 4235 Monterey Rd., Los Angeles. A 306-acre wooded park that includes a 1½-acre lake available for boating and fishing. The park is also designated a bird sanctuary. Picnicking is welcomed.

Exposition Park. Figueroa at Exposition Blvd., Los Angeles. This beautiful park was the site of the 1932 Olympics, and the impressive architecture still stands. Adjoining the University of Southern California, Exposition Park is the location of two major museums: the California Museum of Science and Industry and the Natural History Museum. Also included in this 114-acre park is the Los

Angeles Swimming Stadium (home of Los Angeles aquatic competitions), which is open to the public during the summer, and the Memorial Coliseum, the site of college football and soccer games. There are plenty of picnic areas on the grounds, as well as a sunken rose garden that is lovely for strolling. (See the map of Exposition Park in the *Exploring Los Angeles* section, above.)

Forest Lawn Memorial Park. 1712 S. Glendale Ave., Glendale. This 300-acre formally landscaped area features a major collection of marble statuary and art treasures, including a replica of Leonardo da Vinci's *The Last Supper* done entirely in stained glass. In the Hall of the Crucifixion–Resurrection is one of the world's largest oil paintings incorporating a religious theme, *The Crucifixion* by artist Jan Styka. The picturesque grounds are perfect for a leisurely walk. Forest Lawn was the model for the setting of Evelyn Waugh's novel *The Loved One*.

Forest Lawn Memorial Park—Hollywood Hills. 6300 Forest Lawn Dr., Hollywood. Just west of Griffith Park on the north slope of the Hollywood Hills, this 340-acre "sister" park to Forest Lawn Glendale is dedicated to the ideal of American liberty. Featured are bronze and marble statuary, including Thomas Ball's 60-ft. Washington Memorial and a replica of the Liberty Bell. There are also reproductions of Boston's Old North Church and Longfellow's Church of the Hills. A film entitled *The Many Voices of Freedom* is shown daily, and Revolutionary War documents are on permanent display.

Griffith Park. Entrances on Los Feliz Blvd. at Vermont, Western, and Riverside Dr. and off the Golden State Fwy. at the Los Feliz exit. Donated to the city in 1896 by mining tycoon Griffith J. Griffith, this is the largest city park in the United States. It contains 4,000 acres. There are seemingly endless picnic areas, as well as hiking and bridle trails. Travel Town, with its miniature railroad, is a favorite for kids. Pony riding is also available. The park is home to three major golf courses, a driving range, and tennis courts. A swimming pool and soccer fields are nearby. The world-famous Los Angeles Zoo, which includes the Children's Zoo, is on the park's north side. Here animals can be seen in environments as close to their natural habitat as possible. The Griffith Park Observatory and Planetarium is located on the park's south side, high atop the Hollywood Hills, where visitors can enjoy stargazing or view the various astrological exhibits on display. The Western Ave. entrance is the location of Fern Dell, a half mile of shaded area that includes paths winding their way amid waterfalls, pools, and thousands of ferns. A small nature museum is centered on the many species of ferns growing there. (Map overleaf.)

Hancock Park. Curson Ave. at Wilshire Blvd., Los Angeles. This attractively landscaped park is the location of the La Brea Tar Pits, the George C. Page Museum, and the Los Angeles County Museum of Art. At the bubbling asphalt of the Tar Pits, replicas of prehistoric beasts recreate fateful ventures into the tar. The George C. Page Museum houses discoveries from the pits and other sites in the park. During the summer months there are usually ongoing excavations for fossilized animals on the grounds, and visitors are welcome to watch the painstaking search. Fossilized animals aren't the only type to be found here; look for rabbits that hide among the shrubs and trees.

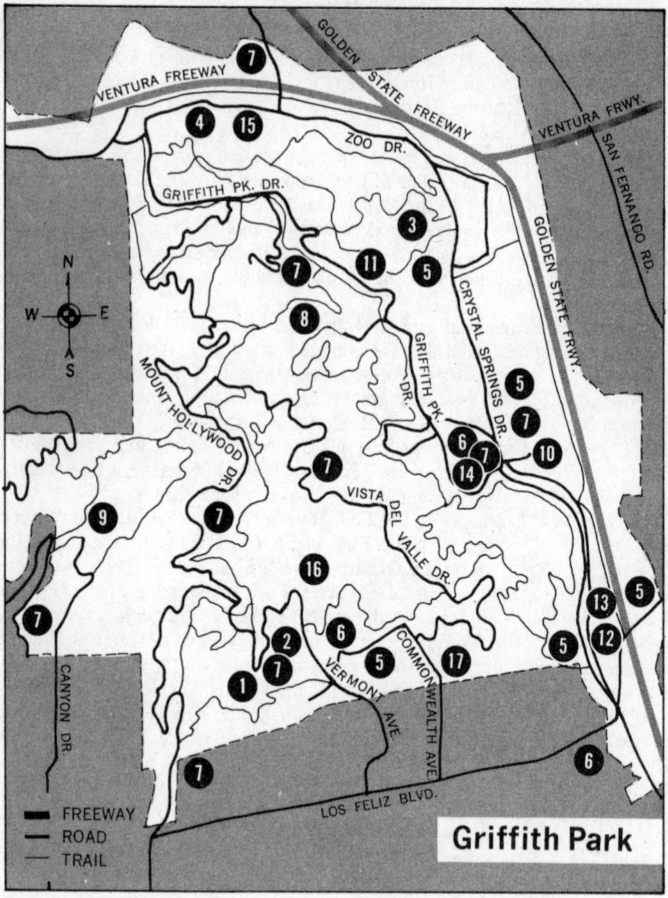

Points of Interest

1) Observatory and Planetarium
2) Greek Theater
3) Los Angeles Zoo
4) Travel Town
5) Golf Course
6) Tennis Courts
7) Picnic Grounds
8) Griffith Park camp
9) Hollywoodland Camp
10) Ranger Visitor Center
11) Driving Range
12) Stables, Pony and Stage Ride
13) Miniature Railroad
14) Merry-Go-Round
15) Los Angeles Live Steamers, Inc.
16) Bird Sanctuary
17) Park Nursery

Highland Park. 6150 Piedmont Ave., Los Angeles. Located in a suburban area also called Highland Park, this spot has plenty of picnic space amid the sycamores. It's a favorite for family get-togethers.

Hollywood Bowl. 2301 N. Highland Ave., Los Angeles. Nestled in the Hollywood Hills is a natural amphitheater, the Hollywood Bowl, famous for its outstanding cultural events ranging from free symphony concerts on Sundays to the three-day Playboy Jazz Festival. There are picnic tables in the surrounding area; baskets of sandwiches, salads, and wine can be purchased on the premises. Bring sweaters and a blanket for night performances because no matter how hot it is during the day, nights tend to get chilly. For program information call 876–0232.

John Anson Ford Theater. 2580 Cahuenga Blvd., East Los Angeles. Just a short distance from the famed Hollywood Bowl in Hollywood, near the Universal Studios lot, is this amphitheater and picnic area. The outdoor theater hosts theatrical events and concerts and is the home base for the Free Public Theater Foundation's Shakespeare productions, available in the summer months at no charge. Sometimes a deer or a raccoon will venture into the park from the nearby hillsides. As with the Hollywood Bowl, performances are outside; bring warm clothing in the evenings.

Lincoln Park. 3501 Valley Blvd., Los Angeles. Located in a predominately Mexican–American neighborhood, this park offers bilingual activities and has basketball and tennis courts. Picnicking under the trees.

Los Encinos State Historical Park. 16756 Moorpark, Encino. Located in the San Fernando Valley, this park's main attraction is the early California dwelling, complete with grounds, all of which are furnished with historically accurate furniture, household goods, and tools. Tours are available Wednesday through Sunday.

MacArthur Park. 2230 W. 6th St., Los Angeles. This lovely park, sprawling under majestic palm trees, features a large lake that is available for boating in the summer months. During the 1920s and 1930s, MacArthur Park was the hangout for the elite, a favorite spot for a leisurely stroll, boating, or an afternoon concert. Unfortunately, the park now suffers from urban blight and is frequently the gathering place for loiterers—who have been unable, however, to diminish the park's beauty. On Sunday afternoons impromptu music played by jazz musicians who gather to "jam" is still offered. The park is, of course, the inspiration for the famous song "MacArthur Park."

North Hollywood Park. 11430 Chandler Blvd., North Hollywood. Just off the Hollywood Freeway at Magnolia, this impressive park has baseball diamonds, a swimming pool, lighted tennis courts, and a beautiful Spanish-style library. In front of the library stands a bronze statue of Amelia Earhart, the famed aviatrix. There are many picnic spots under the trees and plenty of open space for volleyball nets.

Palisades Park. 851 Alma Real Dr., Pacific Palisades. Between West Los Angeles and the Pacific Ocean, just off Sunset Blvd., is this exclusive area where many stars and entertainment moguls reside. The park is lush with palms and eucalyptus trees, and there are plenty of picnic areas, and hiking trails.

Plummer Park. 1200 N. Vista, Los Angeles. This small 6-acre park in West Hollywood is especially geared to the elderly. There is a senior citizen center where organized activities take place. Most days horseshoes, shuffleboard, checkers, and croquet matches are scheduled. The park also contains tennis courts, a children's playground, and a bird sanctuary, plus the historic Plummer House that is open for tours on Sundays. Picnic tables are available.

Roxbury Park. 471 S. Roxbury Dr., Beverly Hills. This centrally located park is under the Beverly Hills Parks and Recreation's jurisdiction. It offers a softball diamond, tennis courts, and lawn bowling, as well as excellent youth programs, including monthly summer theater productions performed on a portable stage. Shaded picnic areas surround the grassy park.

Silverlake Park. 1850 W. Silverlake, Los Angeles. Adjacent to a reservoir, this park offers grassy picnic areas, volleyball and basketball courts, tennis courts, and plenty of space for soccer or jogging, favorite activities here.

Sycamore Park. 4702 N. Figueroa Ave., Los Angeles. Near Highland Park, this area offers shaded picnicking amid the towering sycamores.

REGIONAL PARKS

Banning Mansion and Park. 401 E. M St., Wilmington. An 1864 mansion built by General Phineas Banning, founder of the city of Wilmington, sits on the grounds of this landscaped park, complete with gardens. Tours on Wednesday, Saturday, Sunday, 1:00, 2:00, 3:00, and 4:00 P.M. Park and children's playground are open daily. Picnic areas are plentiful. No fee, but small donations are requested.

Brookside Park. Pasadena. At the junction of Hwys. 134 and 210, or Colorado Blvd. and Orange, lies the Arroyo Seco Glen, a valley that is the home of Brookside Park and the world-famous Rose Bowl. The park rambles along a sparkling creek and offers many hiking trails in the hillsides. Tennis, basketball, and volleyball courts are located at the park's recreation facilities.

Catalina Island. Officially Santa Catalina Island could be called a park. The Wrigley Foundation donated most of the island to the federal parks system, and it has been designated a wildlife preserve. There are plenty of outdoor activities here, including tennis courts, golf courses, riding stables, and a beautiful cactus garden, plus guided tours of the bays in glass-bottom boats and tours of the island's interior, where wildlife, some of which is endangered, and indigenous vegetation are abundant. To help preserve the natural habitat, a regional park of 41,000 acres is being developed for backpacking, hiking, camping, and general public use.

Chatsworth Park. Off Hwy. 118 in the San Fernando Valley, west on Chatsworth St., is this unusual park made up of scattered boulders and rocks. The area has served as the location of many Western movies and television shows. The children's playground includes a stockade, a log house, and a cannon, all of which have often formed the background for films.

Jesse Owens Park, 9651 S. Western Ave. This park of twenty acres features a gymnasium, a field house, an indoor swimming pool and basketball, volleyball,

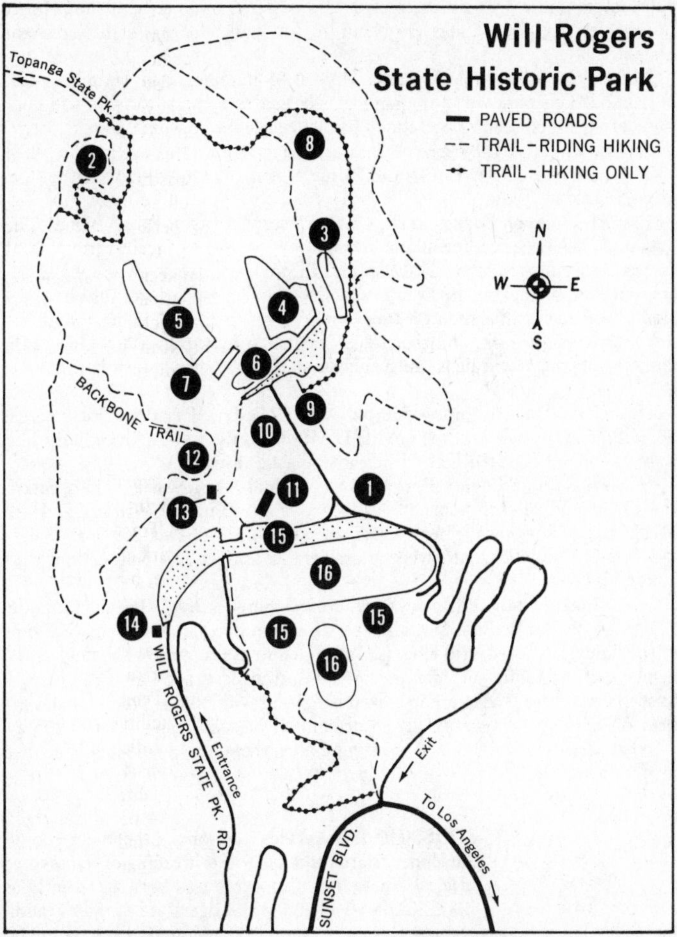

Points of Interest

1) Picnic Area
2) Inspiration Point
3) Roping Arena
4) Heart Canyon
5) Mitt Canyon
6) Riding Arena
7) Stables
8) Bone Canyon Corral
9) Nature Center
10) Lawn Area
11) Will Rogers' Home
12) Visitor Center Store
13) Tennis Courts
14) Contact Station
15) Parking
16) Polo Fields

badminton, and tennis courts, plus a senior citizen's center with shuffleboard and horseshoes. Picnic sites are plentiful. The park also has a three-par golf course.

Malibu Creek State Park. Santa Monica Mountains, about six miles north of Malibu. This park features a nature walk guided by a ranger who will point out native animals and vegetation. Birds are plentiful, which should delight those who like to identify species. Because the nature walks are leisurely paced, children and the elderly can join in. Bring a picnic lunch to enjoy at the stops along the way.

Placerita Canyon County Park. 19150 Placerita Canyon Rd., Newhall. This 350-acre park is perfect for hiking. There are eight miles of trails through both flat and hilly terrain along a stream and through oak trees. Overnight or day camping and picnicking are available. There is an equestrian area for horseback riding and a ½ mile ecology trail centered on flora and fauna. Gold was discovered in the park, and the site is designated by the so-called Oak of the Golden Dream. Naturalists are available at the park headquarters to answer questions.

Oak Grove County Park. 4550 N. Oak Grove Dr., Pasadena. Picnic areas are nestled in the oak trees next to the Devil's Gate Reservoir. An eighteen-hole frisbee course is located here; bring your plastic discs.

William S. Hart County Park. 24151 Newhall Ave., Newhall. This park is the ranch and former home of legendary silent film star William S. Hart. Western and cowboy mementos and art are on view. This 259-acre facility includes picnic tables and barbecue braziers as well as overnight camping accommodations.

Will Rogers State Historic Park. 14253 Sunset Blvd., Pacific Palisades 90272. In the Pacific Palisades, this twenty-seven-acre park was once the home of the famed humorist Will Rogers. The ranch house is open to the public, and displays of mementos and manuscripts are arranged exactly as if Rogers still lived there. There is also a horse-exercising ring with stable; polo matches are held on Sundays. There are fields for softball or soccer and a lot of grassy, wooded acreage for hiking and roaming. Sorry, there's no picnicking. (See map in this section.)

ZOOS. The **Los Angeles Zoo,** one of the major zoos in the United States, is noted for its breeding of endangered species. An Indian rhinoceros was born as recently as 1982. Koala bears and white tigers are the latest addition. This 113-acre compound holds more than 2,000 mammals, birds, amphibians, and reptiles. Animals are grouped according to the geographical areas where they are naturally found—Africa, Australia, Eurasia, North America, and South America. A children's zoo features a baby animal nursery where small, newborn mammals can be seen in incubators. At the baby animal compound, larger newborn mammals can be seen at close range. Another area popular with children is the barnyard, where they can walk among gentle animals such as lambs, goats, and chickens.

There are also a couple of new features at the zoo: A walk-through bird exhibit with more than 50 different species from all over the world; and, for a dollar, you can actually ride a camel, elephant, or Clydesdale horse.

Located in Griffith Park, at the junction of the Ventura and Golden State Fwys. Open daily, 10:00 A.M. to 6:00 P.M. (summer), and 10:00 A.M. to 5:00 P.M. (the rest of the year). No one is admitted an hour before closing. Adults $4.00; children ages 5 through 15 and senior citizens, $1.50. Children under 5, free. Baby strollers and wheelchairs can be rented. There is tram service around the perimeter of the zoo. Snack stands and two picnic areas are located on the grounds. Recorded general zoo information can be obtained by calling 666–4090; guided tours and further information are available by calling 664–1100.

Marineland. 6600 Palos Verdes Drive South, Rancho Palos Verdes; (213) 377–1571 or 541–5663. This seaside zoo and theme park offers an unusual view of aquatic animals in beautiful surroundings. Live shows star sea animals and birds such as Orky and Corky in the whale show. Other animal-actors include sea lions, macaws, and dolphins. The Marineland Animal Care Center affords the curious a view of the care of sick or wounded animals. The Baja Reef is the first man-made aquarium in which you can swim among the fish. Visitors are given a wet suit, snorkel, mask, and fins to use and swim in the tank with 2,000 fish; there are viewing ports for those who would rather just watch. Also worthwhile is the Sky Tower—an elevator ride that lifts 344 feet above the sea for a panoramic view of the coastline.

GARDENS. Although Los Angeles is known primarily for its sunny weather, movie stars, and freeways, a closer look reveals, among other things, some of the finest botanical gardens in the world. Not merely collections of cacti and palm trees, these gardens include exotic flowers, plants, and trees from all over the world. Several of the gardens have provided backdrops for many films and television shows. Others are the focal point of important botanical research.

The Huntington Library, Art Gallery, and Botanical Gardens. On Oxford Road in San Marino. The Huntington has been a landmark ever since it was founded by rail tycoon Henry E. Huntington in the early 1900s. The Huntington has established a reputation as one of the most extraordinary cultural complexes in the world, annually receiving more than half a million visitors—and for good reasons. The library contains six million items, including such treasures as a Gutenberg Bible. In the library's hallway are five tall hexagonal towers displaying important books and manuscripts. Other rooms contain books dating to the 11th century.

The art gallery, devoted to British art from the 18th and early 19th centuries, possesses the original *Blue Boy* by Gainsborough and Lawrence's *Pinkie.*

The Huntington's awesome 130-acre garden, formerly the grounds of the estate, now includes a twelve-acre Desert Garden featuring the largest group of mature cacti and other succulents in the world, as well as a Japanese Garden with traditional Japanese plants, stone ornaments, a moon bridge, a Japanese house, a walled Zen Garden, and a Bonsai Court.

Besides these gardens, there are collections of azaleas and 1,500 varieties of camellias, the world's largest public collection. The 1,000-variety rose garden displays its collection historically so that the development leading to today's roses can be observed. There are also herb, Shakespeare, and palm gardens, plus a newly completed jungle garden.

Because of the Huntington's vastness, a variety of tour options is available for visitors. They include: a 12-minute slide show introducing the Huntington; an hour-and-a-quarter guided tour of the Gardens; a 45-minute audio tape about the art gallery (which can be rented for a nominal fee); a 15-minute introductory talk about the library; and inexpensive, self-guided-tour leaflets.

In 1980 the first major facility constructed on the Huntington grounds in more than sixty years opened. The five million dollar Huntington Pavilion offers visitors unmatched views of the surrounding mountains and valleys, while housing a bookstore, displays, and information kiosks as well. Both the east and the west wings of the pavilion display paintings on public exhibition for the first time. The Ralph M. Parsons Botanical Center at the pavilion includes a botanical library, a herbarium, and a laboratory for research on plants.

Open Tuesday through Sunday, 1:00 P.M. to 4:30 P.M. Reservations are required for Sunday visits (818–449–3901). Call 792–6141 for general information and public programs.

To get there: From the west take the Ventura Fwy. (#134) and exit at the Hill St. offramp. Follow this street east to Allen, and proceed south to the Huntington. From the east take the 210 Fwy. to the Allen offramp and continue south to the Huntington.

Los Angeles State and County Arboretum. 301 N. Baldwin Ave., Arcadia. Contains 127 acres of native and exotic plants. The rotunda inside the main entrance features displays of those currently in bloom, including rare orchids and other flowers seldom seen. The Arboretum's demonstration home gardens were designed to provide homeowners with ideas for gracious outdoor-living landscaping. Other attractions at the Arboretum include the begonia house, with about 200 varieties of begonias, and the nearby tropical greenhouse, featuring orchids, bromeliads, ferns, and other exotics in a rainforest setting.

To simplify things for the visitor, many of the more than 5,000 kinds of plants on the Arboretum's grounds are arranged in geographical sections, based on the plants' place of origin. In these individual areas you can see vegetation thriving as it does in its natural habitat. Included are plant life from Australia, South Africa, North America, Asia, the Mediterranean, and South America.

The Arboretum's historical section features buildings, along with appropriate flowers and plants, from different times in California's colorful past. The result is a colorful mixture of Victorian, adobe, and railroad-depot architectures.

One of the most popular sites at the Arboretum is Lasca Lagoon, one of the few natural freshwater lakes in southern California. The lagoon may look familiar: It has been used as a jungle setting for movies and television series, including *Tarzan* and *Fantasy Island.*

Open daily from 9:00 A.M. to 4:30 P.M. Adults, $1.50; senior citizens and students with ID, 75¢; children under 5, free. Third Tuesday of each month, all admissions free. Call (213) 446–8251.

How to get there: From the east or west, take the Foothill Fwy. (#210) to Baldwin Ave. and go south to the entrance. From the south, take the San Bernardino Fwy. (# 10) to Baldwin Ave. and go north to the entrance.

Descanso Gardens. 1418 Descanso Dr., La Canada. Once part of the vast Spanish Rancho San Rafael that covered more than 30,000 acres. Descanso Gardens now encompasses 155 acres of native chaparral-covered slopes. A forest of California live oak trees furnishes a dramatic backdrop for thousands of camellias, azaleas, and a four-acre rose garden. Descanso's Tea House features pools, waterfalls, and a gift shop, as well as a relaxing spot to stop for refreshments. Flower shows, including chrysanthemum, daffodil, camellia, and bonsai competitions, are held at various times of the year. Guided tours are available; trams traverse the grounds.

Open daily from 9:00 A.M. to 4:30 P.M. Tea House open Tuesday through Sunday, 11:00 A.M. to 4:00 P.M.; closed Mondays. Adults $1.50; senior citizens and students with ID, $.75; under 5 free. Call (818) 790–5571.

How to get there: Take the Glendale Fwy. (# 2) to Verdugo Blvd., exit. At second light—Alta Canada Rd.—turn right and proceed to Descanso Gardens parking lot.

South Coast Botanic Garden. 26300 Crenshaw Blvd. on the Palos Verdes Peninsula. (213) 377–0468. A study in recycling. This eighty-seven acre garden environment has been transformed from a landfill into a place of serenity and beauty. Visitors will find guided bird walks (more than 240 different bird species have been sighted here), plant identification photos, exhibits and display materials, and small wildlife at the man-made lake. There are plenty of trails and paths, as well as a tram. Among the plants to be found at South Coast Botanical Garden are flowering trees, palms, ornamental figs, legumes, redwoods, succulents, and eucalyptus.

Open daily from 9:00 A.M. to 5:00 P.M. Closed Christmas. Adults, $1.50; senior citizens and students with ID, 75¢; children under 5, free. Tram tours, $1.50 per person. Third Tuesday of each month, all admissions free.

How to get there: From the north, take the San Diego Fwy. (#405) to the Crenshaw offramp. Continue south on Crenshaw to the gardens.

Exposition Park Rose Garden. Menlo Ave. near Exposition Blvd. A rose lover's dream come true. Here, in a seven-acre sunken garden, more than 17,000 roses are on display. During the months of April and May, the height of the flowering season, the fragrance coming from the rose garden and the array of magnificent flowers attract more than 45,000 visitors *weekly.*

Many all-American award-winning roses grow at Exposition Park; the range includes everything from miniature tea roses to six-inch diameter blooms, in every hue imaginable. A magnificent fountain and four summery gazebos provide respite from the busy city that surrounds the garden.

Open daily from 9:00 A.M. to 5:00 P.M. Call (213) 485–5529.

How to get there: Take the Harbor Fwy. (# 11) south to the Santa Barbara Ave. exit. Then follow signs to Exposition Park.

Wrigley Memorial and Botanical Garden. 1400 Avalon Canyon Rd. in Avalon on Catalina Island. A living tribute to William Wrigley Jr., the chewing-gum magnate who helped develop Santa Catalina Island. The Wrigley Memorial, with its spectacular circular staircase leading to the top of the eighty-foot observation tower, is constructed almost completely of materials obtained from the island itself. Surrounding the memorial is the garden, a thirty-seven acre showcase for Catalina's native plants. Surprisingly enough, this little island has an even better climate than the Southern California mainland, and so plants, including St. Catherine's lace and the wild tomato, that cannot survive at any of the Los Angeles gardens grow here. Cars are not permitted on Catalina Island, but a tram connects the garden with downtown Avalon island plaza. Open daily from 8:00 A.M. to 5:00 P.M. Admission is 50¢; children under 12, free.

The Virginia Robinson Gardens. In Beverly Hills, 6.2 acres of terraced gardens surrounding the former home of Virginia Robinson of the J. W. Robinson Department Store clan. A trained guide will take you on an hour tour of the gardens and the exquisite exteriors of the main house, guest house, servants' quarters, swimming pool, and tennis court. A highlight of the tour is the collection of rare and exotic palms.

Two tours daily, Tuesday through Friday at 10:00 A.M. and 1:00 P.M. Adults, $3.00; children, students, and senior citizens, $2.25. Phone (213) 466–8251. Since the garden's administration is trying to keep a low profile to avoid congestion in the cul-de-sac where this garden is situated, visitors must call for reservations and be told the address and how to get there.

Rancho Santa Ana Botanic Garden. 1500 N. College, Claremont (714) 626–3922. Now more than 50 years old, Rancho Santa Ana specializes in plants native to California. Here an extensive library, research labs, classrooms, and systematic collections contribute to research, conservation, and graduate work in botany. Although these functions are not open to the public, the grounds of the garden are. Located at the foot of the San Gabriel Mountains, with Mount Baldy looming on the horizon, the gardens are perhaps at their best between February and June, when desert plants such as manzanitas, California lilacs, tree poppies, and bush anemones burst forth in an array of colors seldom seen anywhere.

A home demonstration garden here offers homeowners suggestions on how to use California native plants in landscaping. Other attractions include a rock garden, a coniferous forest, Joshua tree woodland, and a desert and dune garden. Open daily from 8:00 A.M. to 5:00 P.M. Closed Christmas, New Year's Day, July 4th, and Thanksgiving. Admission free.

How to get there: Take the San Bernardino Fwy. (#10) east to the Indian Hill Blvd. exit. Go north on Indian Hill to Foothill. Take Foothill east to College Ave. Turn left into the grounds there.

BEACHES. More so, perhaps, than even Disneyland or Hollywood, Los Angeles beaches are memorable. Each has its own mood and flavor. Histories vary, as do sizes and locations, but all are within an hour's drive of downtown Los Angeles in normal (non-rush-hour) traffic.

Take any main east/west street (such as Wilshire, Santa Monica, or Olympic Blvds.), travel as far west as possible, and eventually you'll reach the Pacific Ocean. Pacific Coast Highway (PCH), California Route 1, follows the coast. Starting at the northern end is illustrious Malibu, the home of dozens of stars. The scenery here, including miles of rugged cliffs, is spectacular. It is a city by the ocean that offers plenty to do and see and is a welcome magnet for both residents (many of whom also have homes in the city proper) and visitors.

South along the cliffs on PCH, all the southerly beaches spread before your eyes. Santa Monica is the next stop; as beach communities go, this city has one of the strongest reputations. Scene of the famous Muscle Beach of the "beach blanket" movie genre and hangout for the perennial beach boy in a wet suit, Santa Monica seems the essence of the beach experience. This beachiness, however, takes a different turn as you leave family-oriented Santa Monica.

Although Venice Beach has recently been subject to a bad press, it boasts one of the most fascinating histories of the area. A bit similar to SoHo in New York City and other artists' habitats, Venice seems somewhat sinister but electric. During the day the boardwalk is congested with all manner of rollerskaters, hippy types, street entertainers and other folk having all kinds of fun.

South from Venice is Marina del Rey, one of the largest man-made venues of its type. Thousands of colorful boats are surrounded by residences, hotels, and restaurants. Beaches here are scarce, but the area is still fascinating to explore. Playa del Rey, farther south, is an old-fashioned beach town. Connecting Playa del Rey with El Segundo is Dockweiler State Beach, which is surrounded by a bizarre-looking steam-generating plant. Dockweiler is the unofficial home of area hang gliders.

The communities farther south—Manhattan, Redondo, and Hermosa—are old beach cities that, through the years, have added to California's reputation for surf, sand, and fun. These communities swarm with visitors all summer long. On any given evening after surfers have grounded their boards, the main strip—Manhattan Beach Blvd.—looks like a scene out of the movie *American Graffiti.* The cruising culture here is still built on fast cars, loud radios, and knowing everyone who drives by. It is an interesting place in which to watch and mingle.

MALIBU

World famous Malibu Beach stretches twenty-seven miles along the coast from Ventura County to Santa Monica. Old Beach Boy songs and Frankie Avalon movies depict Malibu as a swinging, surfing town—a teenager's paradise—but it is really much more.

The Malibu Colony is actually a community of well-to-do and well-known people. With coastal homes ranging from one million dollars to over four million

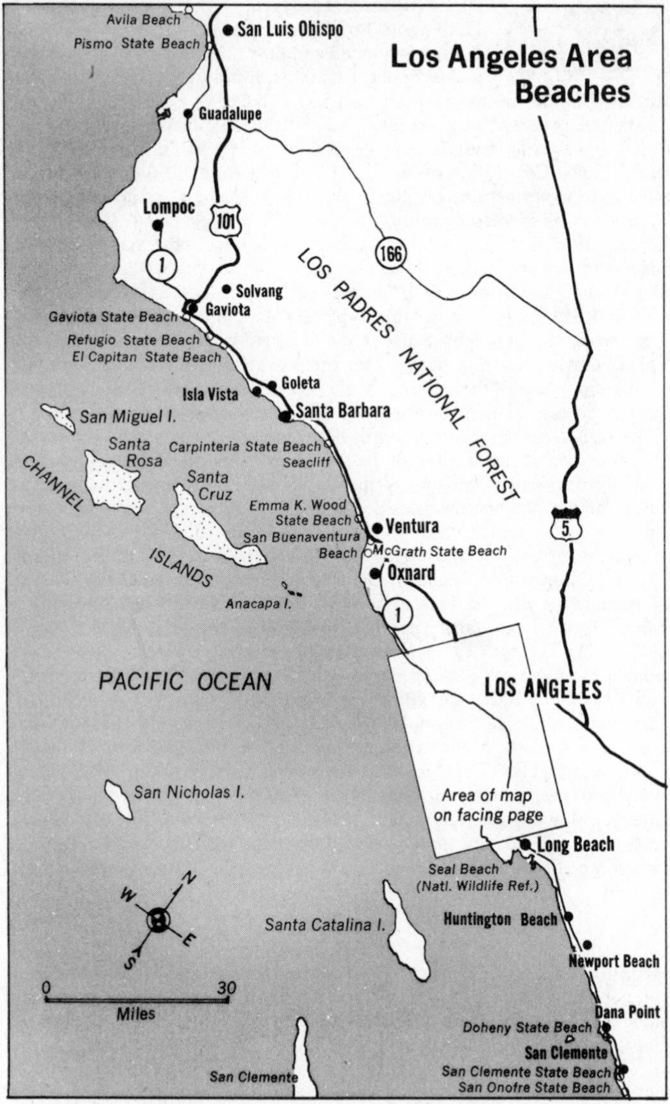
Los Angeles Area Beaches
Avila Beach
Pismo State Beach
San Luis Obispo
Guadalupe
Lompoc
101
1
166
Solvang
Gaviota
Gaviota State Beach
Refugio State Beach
El Capitan State Beach
Goleta
Isla Vista
Santa Barbara
LOS PADRES NATIONAL FOREST
San Miguel I.
Santa Rosa
Carpinteria State Beach
Seacliff
Santa Cruz
CHANNEL
ISLANDS
Emma K. Wood State Beach
San Buenaventura Beach
Ventura
McGrath State Beach
Oxnard
5
Anacapa I.
1
PACIFIC OCEAN
LOS ANGELES
San Nicholas I.
Area of map on facing page
Long Beach
Seal Beach (Natl. Wildlife Ref.)
Huntington Beach
Santa Catalina I.
Newport Beach
N
W
E
S
0
30
Miles
Dana Point
Doheny State Beach
San Clemente
San Clemente State Beach
San Onofre State Beach
San Clemente

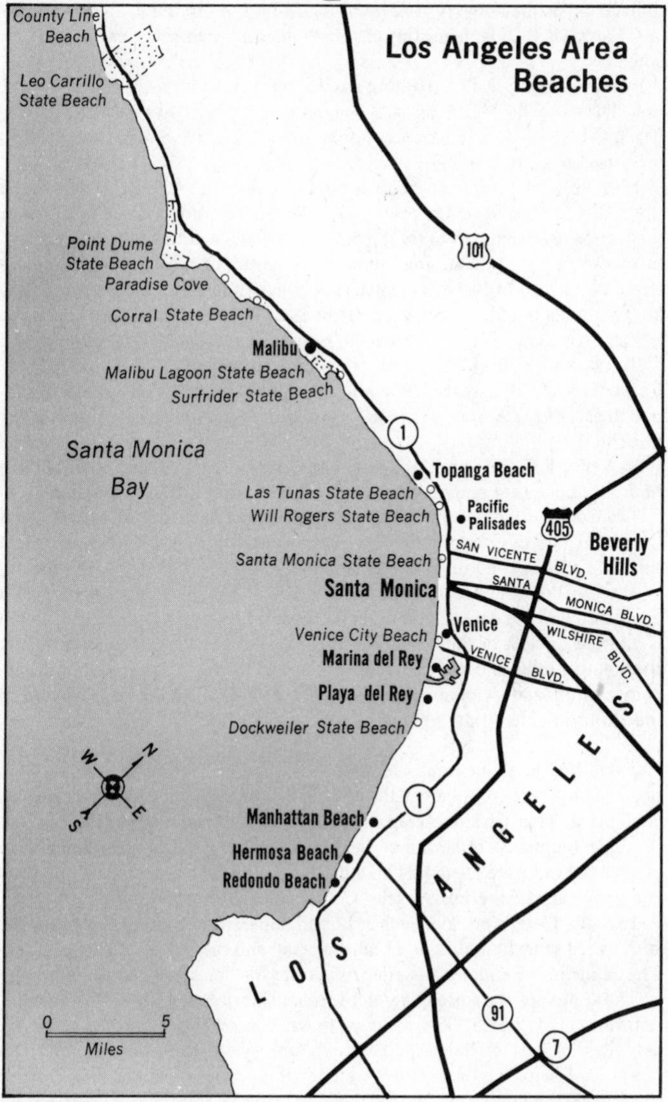
Los Angeles Area Beaches
County Line Beach
Leo Carrillo State Beach
Point Dume State Beach
Paradise Cove
Corral State Beach
Malibu
Malibu Lagoon State Beach
Surfrider State Beach
Santa Monica Bay
Topanga Beach
Las Tunas State Beach
Will Rogers State Beach
Pacific Palisades
Santa Monica State Beach
Santa Monica
Venice
Venice City Beach
Marina del Rey
Playa del Rey
Dockweiler State Beach
Manhattan Beach
Hermosa Beach
Redondo Beach
Beverly Hills
SAN VICENTE BLVD.
SANTA MONICA BLVD.
WILSHIRE BLVD.
VENICE BLVD.
LOS ANGELES
101
405
1
91
7
N
E
S
W
0
5
Miles

dollars and as the home of residents such as Barbra Streisand, Johnny Carson, and Larry (J. R.) Hagman, this city resembles a beachfront version of Hollywood.

Malibu is a physically arresting environment. It is surrounded by the stunning Santa Monica Mountains and canyons and valleys that sweep inland to the beach. Although rock slides are common here during the rainy season, residents seem to remain undaunted.

Most beaches along the Malibu coast are private. But where there are accessways, it is legal to be on the beach—despite the lack of rest room facilities and lifeguards. A better bet is to try the public beaches. (A listing follows.) Approximately six, all great for surfing, sunning, and swimming, exist along the Malibu stretch of ocean. Most have lifeguards and health facilities, concession stands, and water fountains. If you want to give surfing a try, surfboard rentals are available at *Zuma Jay,* 22775 Pacific Coast Hwy. (456–8044).

To take in a little of Malibu's local color, visit the *Malibu Pier,* 23000 Pacific Coast Hwy. Fisherman, tourists, and locals mingle here. For a meal or just a bite to eat, *Alice's Restaurant* (456–6646) at the beginning of the pier is a local favorite.

In Ventura County and heading south toward Santa Monica, the following Malibu beaches are public:

The County Line Beach (half in Malibu and half in Ventura County) is good for surfing; a rocky ocean floor, however, makes it impossible to swim or body surf. There is also no lifeguard, so confine your visit to walking and looking.

Leo Carillo State Beach, quite an active beach, is divided into three separate areas: two with no name, and one, called Secos, known for its surfing. Camping is allowed on part of the beach; and Leo Carillo has the added attraction for the younger folks of caves to explore and crawl through. Scuba diving, surfing, body surfing, and swimming are also good at Leo Carillo. Rock piles form on the shore in interesting configurations, making intimate spots perfect for a picnic.

Zuma Beach, about 5 miles long, is the largest of the Malibu beaches. Many people come here from "the Valley"; it is a good family recreational area that contains a large parking area, concession stands, rest rooms, showers, and drinking fountains. In terms of the ocean, body surfing and swimming are good—and there are lifeguards on duty during the days in season. Zuma Beach is also the site of the Los Angeles County lifeguard exhibition.

Paradise Cove, a private beach at Point Dume, costs $3 to enter. Point Dume, with its red sandstone cliffs, is a beautiful spot, and the beach is clean and sandy. The *Sandcastle Restaurant* is a local favorite for breakfast, lunch, and dinner.

The section of **Paradise Cove** on the other side of Point Dume is the county's notorious nude beach. The focus of much controversy in recent years, it is actually not very secluded, and voyeurs and photographers have been troublesome. The police department watches this area closely for illegal doings; nonetheless, many people congregate here, especially on weekends.

Corral Beach is a narrow strip of land two miles west of Pepperdine University. Parking and other facilities are scarce, but this beach is usually less crowded than most others and is a good place to retreat to from the packed beaches.

Malibu's **Surfrider Beach,** near the pier, is a world-famous beach, with some of the best surfing in Southern California. This is also the site of the International Surfing Contest at the end of September, when waves usually reach from three to five feet. (During the summer the waves are usually only one to three feet.) This beach is sometimes very crowded, but it is a good place for people watching.

Las Tunas Beach, just left of Las Tunas Canyon, is a good surf-fishing beach. Sunbathing is good, too, but be careful of the steel groins set in the water to hold the sand. The last Malibu beach, closest to Santa Monica, is **Topanga Canyon Beach.** At the foot of Topanga Canyon and near the illustrious Getty Museum, this beach is good for swimming and has some fishing areas.

Besides the beaches, Malibu contains many establishments for fine food and interesting atmosphere: The *Showboat,* 22718 W. PCH, has a counter that overlooks the ocean; the *Charthouse,* 18412 W. PCH, and *Moonshadow,* 20356 W. PCH, also have great views. A wonderful jazz club, *Pasquales* (22724 W. PCH), has gained in popularity recently.

SANTA MONICA

You'll notice the family flavor of the Santa Monica beach area, particularly on weekends. When the local masses take to the waves, there is a good chance you will find most of them here.

Temescal Canyon, below Pacific Palisades, is the entrance for the main section of **Will Rogers State Beach.** This beach, three miles long, contains volleyball courts, rest rooms, showers, and lifeguards. It is extremely clean. Pack your own volleyball and be sure to arrive early on weekends; the parking areas fill up quickly.

Castle Rock—the section of Will Rogers north of the junction of Sunset Blvd. and PCH—is small and cozy. There is very good body surfing in this area. Farther south, at Santa Monica Canyon, is where you will find many famous people whiling away the hours between jobs. Will Rogers attaches to **Santa Monica city beaches** here for miles and miles of oceanfront fun.

Presently and historically Santa Monica is a beach haven. Families seeking solace from their daily routine and pleasure seekers have come here for many years. The old pier is standing, although almost a third of it has been washed away in severe winter storms. The pier and carousel (which is open on weekends) bring the visitor back to the time when beaches were synonymous with saltwater taffy and striped bathing costumes. Although updated with the latest electronic games, this is an interesting place in which to wander and imagine what it was like when movie stars and famous people came here for vacations. The movie *The Sting* used this pier as a backdrop to convey a sense of the past; it is still a great place to watch people. Fish eateries dot the pier; *The Lobster* at the beginning of the pier is one of the most popular.

Santa Monica also has Palisades Park, on a cliff above the ocean. Joggers, skaters, and walkers can enjoy a respite from the bright sun and a picnic amid this lush greenery. Just as Santa Monica is a beach community, it is also a thriving business community. Although many stores sell surfboards and bathing suits, others sell sophisticated "worldly" items. The recent revitalization of Main Street, which starts just blocks away from the beach area, has made Santa Monica an exciting place to spend a rainy afternoon.

For those who favor active beach sports more than rambling along the shore, there is the bike path. Bike-rental outlets and roller skate rentals can be found along the boardwalk. (See Venice section for bike and skate rental stores.) The bike path that goes for miles and miles starts in Santa Monica. This path follows the ocean, detours in Marina del Rey, then goes back to the ocean, and continues along the coast all the way south to Redondo Beach.

VENICE

If Santa Monica is where to go with the family for a peaceful day of fun, Venice is where to go for excitement and the exotic. People do not go to Venice to sit on the beach; instead, they take in the throng of people and activities on the boardwalk.

Venice began as the dream of Abbot Kinney who wanted to turn it into a replica of Venice, Italy. And for a while his dream came true. (There are still some canals to attest to this.) Hollywood stars used to flock here to take advantage of the romantic gondoliers and one of the largest roller coasters ever built.

Over the years the flavor of Venice has changed. It is a West Coast version of New York's Greenwich Village, and many of the same kinds of people live here—actors, writers, poets. There is also a large contingency of punk rockers sporting pink, green, and other lively shades of hair. The weekend is the best time to visit the boardwalk, which follows miles of beach, but it can be hard to find a place for your feet among a thousand others. Every inch of boardwalk seems filled with a roller skate or a bicycle wheel, or another intrepid pedestrian. The place is abuzz with street performers—musicians and comedians—in the summer. Swami X is a popular fellow; he spends some of his time here and the rest in Washington Square Park in Greenwich Village. There are also people in booths selling clothing, jewelry, souvenirs, and art. And when you get tired from all the walking, the *Sidewalk Café,* 1401 Ocean Front Walk, right near the Venice Pavilion, is a great indoor–outdoor café in which to sit and take in all the activity. And if you feel like treating yourself to lunch, dinner, or a health shake, the *Figtree Cafe,* at 429 Ocean Front Walk, is a recent addition to the area.

If you'd like to join in the confusion, bicycle rentals are available at the *Venice Pier Bike Shop,* 21 Washington St. (823–1528), where they rent everything from five-speed two wheelers to tricycles.

For wheels that go directly on your feet, *Roller Skates of America,* 64 Windward Ave., and *Skatey's,* 22 Washington St., offer roller skates by the hour or by the day.

MARINA DEL REY

South a bit from Venice is the illustrious home of the "swinging singles," Marina del Rey. An extremely young and vibrant residential area and a visitor's delight, the marina is made up of a maze of boats, restaurants, shopping, great walking paths, and a beach. The main road through the marina—the largest man-made marina in the world—is Admiralty Way.

On one end is Via Marina, and just as the road curves is the location of the only public beach in the marina. A small crescent in the harbor area, this is a good beach for children because there are no waves. It can get very crowded on summer weekends, but the rest of the time it is fine. There is a public parking lot here, and it is a good place to start a walk around the area.

On the other end, on Fiji Way, is Fisherman's Village—a recreation of a Cape Cod-type fishing village. Interesting shops and restaurants line the street, and on the other side is the water and a good view of the thousands of boats docked in Marina del Rey.

The marina channel (near the beach—continue on Via Marina) is another great vantage point. Walk down the pier into the water, and you can see planes taking off from nearby LAX Airport every couple of minutes. To the right you can see north to Santa Monica and farther. And all around all kinds of sailboats and yachts are entering and leaving the channel. The area just north, known as the Marina Peninsula, boasts a wide beach that goes all the way to Venice. But during the summer the parking situation is impossible.

Admiralty Way is an oasis filled with many restaurants to refresh you after a busy day of walking, sightseeing, and sports activities. As a result of being filled with young professionals and many visitors from all over the world, the range of restaurants and the types of cuisine in the marina are staggering. From the exclusive, members-only (unless a guest of the hotel) Marina City Club to the new *Red Onion* for good Mexican food and dancing afterwards, this street is called Restaurant Row.

PLAYA DEL REY

Just south of Marina del Rey is Playa del Rey. At the turn of the century this was the site of one of the most popular seaside resorts in the area. It had a three-story pavilion, a restaurant, a bowling alley, a 50-room hotel, an automobile speed-racing track, and a boat-launching harbor. Holiday crowds used to rush here to ride two cable cars that offered a magnificent aerial view of the beach and mountains. This ended in 1913 when a fire destroyed everything.

Today Playa del Rey is still a popular beach community. The beach is wide and the surf is usually calm. Facilities include lifeguards, rest rooms, showers, drinking fountains, basketball courts, picnic tables, and barbeque grills. Ten yards from the beach is the lovely Del Rey Lagoon. This is a large plot of green grass surrounding a pond; and there are basketball courts and barbeque pits.

Outside Playa del Rey, going south to El Segundo, is **Dockweiler State Beach.** The landscape here is an eerie reminder of the industrial nature of Southern California: There is a steam-generating plant out in the water, a green structure with imposing smoke stacks. Perhaps not the most peaceful of beaches, with this view and the jets taking off from nearby LAX, this beach has one definite attraction: It is the unofficial site of hang gliding in southern California. It is thrilling to watch these daring men and women glide through the air on wings. Another reason to go to Dockweiler is the fact that it is the only Los Angeles beach with fire rings; if you want a primitive beach barbeque, this is the place. Firewood is sold along the beach, which has ample parking.

MANHATTAN BEACH

The South Bay communities begin here, and these beaches offer some of the cleanest sand and nicest settings in the area. Manhattan Beach is a small, young community, a health-oriented place; joggers, skaters, and runners can be seen on the street at all times.

It is said that when the Beach Boys went to the beach, this is where they came. They lived in nearby Hawthorne. The Manhattan Beach pier offers fishing; the pier pavilion, a roadhouse built in 1921, is covered with stucco and roofed with Spanish tile. Today the roadhouse is used by biology, geology, and chemistry students as an ocean-study center.

The beach is clean and has lots of room to spread out, but the only drawback is the parking—available only on the street. This beach is a hangout for teenagers in the summer. At night Manahattan Beach Blvd. becomes *the* cruising street. Just as the Beach Boys sang, the street is packed with cars of people who know each other, and the air buzzes with the sound of hundreds of radios.

There are a few establishments that have been around a long time and are almost a part of the community. Beach bars with a real local flavor include *Grunions, Brennan's* and *La Paz.* And for dining with a terrific view of the ocean there is *Orville and Wilbur.*

HERMOSA BEACH

Hermosa Beach (*hermosa* means beautiful in Spanish) is appropriately named: It stretches two miles along a lovely section of the coast. After the turn of the century this area was a summer haven for movie stars and other wealthy people. Today single-family homes and condominiums, along with some businesses and restaurants, line the Strand.

The beach itself is great for swimming and body and board surfing. Pole, bait, and tackle rentals are available at the Hermosa Beach Pier. Again, parking is only on the street.

The community of Hermosa Beach is artistically oriented. Small shops with unusual items line Pier Ave., one block east of the beach. And there are many good food establishments. *The Lighthouse,* 30 Pier Ave., offering great acts nightly, is the oldest jazz club in Southern California.

Twice a year, on Memorial Day and Labor Day weekends, local artists and artists from around the country come out en masse to the Fiesta de Las Artes—an arts and crafts festival.

REDONDO BEACH

The next stop along the beach is Redondo. Its marina is its main distinction. Although not quite as well known as Marina del Rey, *Kings Harbor* is quite similar, with boats, restaurants, and apartments overlooking the colorful port.

During the 1800s much of the shipping trade in Los Angeles was centered here, but with the opening of the harbor at San Pedro, that changed. Today Redondo's marina and beach area attracts sailing, swimming, and fishing enthusiasts from all over Southern California. Shops, restaurants, and fresh-fish stores abound on the Redondo Beach pier alongside the harbor. The *Murata Pearl Company,* 233K Fisherman's Wharf on the Redondo Pier (379–4915), is a unique jewelry store featuring pearls, rings, and pendants. Choose an oyster from the tank near the store window. Each one has a cultured pearl in it—sometimes two!

The beach itself starts at the pier and extends south about two and a half miles. Condominiums and single-family units line the Esplanade. This is where the bike path from Santa Monica ends. There are fire pits on the sand and volleyball courts at the beach.

Also near the marina is Seaside Lagoon, a warm saltwater pool dug out of the sand. Besides swimming, the lagoon area offers picnicking, a playground, and volleyball courts. Private parties can be arranged here for day or evening. There is an admission charge.

WATER SPORTS. Los Angeles has abundant and diverse water recreation, including skin diving, snorkeling, surfing, sailing, pleasure boating, swimming, and wind surfing.

There are many **swimming pools** located throughout the area. Two of the most popular are Griffith Park Pool, at the intersection of Riverside and Los Feliz; and the Magnolia Pool at Magnolia Park, just off the Hollywood Fwy. at Magnolia, in the San Fernando Valley. Both are Olympic-sized; Magnolia Park also offers a second, smaller pool. Moreover the Magnolia Pool is in the middle of a lovely tree-lined park. Another popular pool, located in Exposition Park near downtown Los Angeles, is also Olympic size; in fact it was used in the 1932 Olympics. Thispool is used for summertime recreation and for college meets.

If **paddle boating** is your idea of fun, you can do just that at MacArthur Park during the summer months. Loll about this man-made lake in the beautiful setting of palm and sycamore trees and dream to your heart's content.

The Los Angeles City Department of Parks and Recreation (485–5515) will provide information on locations, fees, and hours of these city facilities.

For the intrepid sports person, **wind surfing** is at the height of popularity in Los Angeles. Rentals and lessons are available at *Wind Surfing West,* 4047 Lincoln Blvd., Marina del Rey (821–5501).

Sailing enthusiasts can rent boats all around the Marina del Rey area. Among others: *Rent-A-Sail,* 13560 Mindanao Way (822–1868), offers 14- to 25-foot sloops, Hobie 16 catamarans, gas-powered boats, and lessons. Rent-A-Sail also has an outlet at 13757 Fiji Way in Fisherman's Village (822–2516). Here, again, they have sailboats for rent (no catamarans or lessons though) and electric power boats for public use.

For high-budget travelers, *Charter Concepts,* 13757 Fiji Way (823–2676), charters yachts, 40 to 140 feet long. Skippers are available for hire.

Fun Fleet, 13723 Fiji Way (822–1151), offers harbor cruises all year round. Boats leave every hour.

Boats offering sport fishing and sightseeing tours leave daily from the Redondo Beach Marina, 181 N. Harbor Drive (374–3481). Boat rentals are available here, but the reservation office is open Monday through Friday only, so be sure to call weekdays for a weekend boat.

FISHING is a common pier activity in Los Angeles. *Malibu Pier Sport Fishing,* 2300 Pacific Coast Highway (456–8030), offers two boats, both approximately 60 feet, for a group fishing experience. The full-day boat, leaving at 7:00 A.M. each day, features deep-sea fishing for rock cod in the winter and surface fishing during the summer. Surface fish such as halibut and bonita are regulars here, whereas warm summer waters attract bass and occasionally yellowtail and barracuda as well. Half-day boats, leaving at 8:00 A.M. and 1:00 P.M. daily, take you surface fishing all year around.

At the *Redondo Sport Fishing Company,* 233 N. Harbor Drive (372–2111), you can arrange half-day and full-day charters, excursions, and pole rentals.

A real California activity—grunion hunting—takes place on the beach from March through August. These small fish spawn on the beach at night, and finding them can be quite an experience. On the first day they are spotted each year, local tradition dictates that everyone meet them on the beach for a party. Grunions are edible, but they have a hard time swimming for miles and miles to spawn, so people interested in the environment go only to witness an interesting natural phenomenon.

See also *Water Sports,* above.

PARTICIPANT SPORTS. Los Angeles is an athlete's paradise. Year-round sunshine, geographic variety, and a near-perfect climate combine to create the sport activist's haven. From hiking (or skiing in winter) in the mountains to surfing and swimming at the beaches, outdoor enthusiasts are certain to find ample recreation here.

Because Los Angeles is such a sprawling metropolis, it is advisable to do some planning with a map before attempting your sporting adventure. For instance, if you want to drop the kids at the beach and buzz on over to the San Fernando Valley for golf, you may find yourself spending the greater part of the day just traveling between activities. There are two excellent resources that will inform you of what activities are available in the area in which you are staying or the part of town you would like to see: The City of Los Angeles Dept. of Recreation and Parks, 200 N. Main Street, 13th floor, City Hall East, Los Angeles (485–5515), and Los Angeles County Parks and Recreation Dept., 433 S. Vermont Ave., Los Angeles (738–2961). These agencies are more than happy to assist in locating recreational areas for tennis, hiking, bridle paths, golf, swimming, basketball, soccer, shuffleboard, and so on.

Because the Los Angeles area is so large, and space in our book is so limited, listed below are only some of the more popular recreation facilities.

Golf. Golf courses abound in the Los Angeles area. In urban Griffith Park alone there are three public golf courses: *Harding Golf Course,* an eighteen-hole course at the entrance of Los Feliz Ave. and Riverside Dr.; *Wilson Golf Course,* another eighteen-hole course, also to be found by entering the park at Los Feliz and Riverside Dr.; and *Roosevelt Golf Course,* a very popular nine-hole course at the Vermont entrance. The Griffith Park courses are quite hilly.

Near Beverly Hills is the *Rancho Park Golf Course,* an eighteen-hole course at 10460 W. Pico Blvd., Los Angeles. Nearer the beach is *Penmar Golf Course,* a popular flat nine-hole course at 1233 Rose Ave., Venice.

In the San Fernando Valley, in what is referred to as the Sepulveda Dam Basin, lie perhaps the longest, straightest, flattest, fairways you might ever encounter. It is advisable to keep in mind that these courses have very little shade in summer. The courses include *Woodley Golf Course,* eighteen holes—pure heaven for those who are prone to losing balls; there are no trees, brush, or water hazards on this course, which is located at 6331 Woodley Ave., Van Nuys. *Balboa Golf Course* at 16821 Burbank Blvd., Encino, offers eighteen holes. Here you will also find *Encino Golf Course,* an eighteen holer, Balboa's twin.

Other popular courses listed in "Golf Digest" include the *Riviera* at Pacific Palisades and *Brookside* in Pasadena.

Special pitch 'n' putt golf courses include *Holmby Hills,* an eighteen-hole course, at 601 Club View Dr., Los Angeles, and *Rancho Park,* a nine-hole, three-par course, at 10460 W. Pico Blvd., Los Angeles, alongside the regular course *Los Feliz Pitch N' Put* is a nine-hole course at 3207 Los Feliz Blvd.

Driving ranges are available at the Balboa, Encino, Rancho Park, and Wilson/Harding courses, above.

Contact the Los Angeles City and County Parks and Recreation Depts. for more information, fees, availability, and additional courses.

Tennis. Courts, most of which are lighted at night, are located in most parks. Try Griffith Park's ample, well-lit courts not far from the intersection of Los Feliz and Riverside Dr. These courts, except for the daytime hours between 11:00 A.M. and 3:00 P.M., are rarely unoccupied. Be prepared to pay an hourly fee anywhere, unless courts are available at your accommodations. A popular pay-by-the hour tennis club, available to the public, is the *Racquet Center* in North Hollywood, 5252 Coldwater, near Universal Studios. For reservations, call (818) 985–8686.

A few hotels offer tennis clinics, weekend classes, and make courts available to guests. The Century Plaza in Beverly Hills has eight outdoor rooftop courts featuring John Gardiner's famous clinics. The Sheraton Town House, at 2961 Wilshire Blvd., offers four indoor courts; Al Secunda, pro. The Ambassador Hotel, on the Wilshire Corridor at 3400 Wilshire, shares ten outdoor courts with a local private tennis club and offers clinics on weekends. The Los Angeles Bonaventure, downtown Los Angeles, reserves eight courts from the Los Angeles Racquet Club. The Marina City Club in Marina Del Rey has six outdoor courts for guests.

For additional club or tournament information, contact the Southern California Tennis Association, 609 N. Cahuenga Blvd.; 208–3838.

Racquetball and Handball. Rapidly becoming the most popular participant sport in the area. Courts for the sports are offered at most YMCAs for an hourly rate, and courts are also available at the *Racquet Center of Pasadena,* 920 Lohman Lane, 258–4178; and at the *Sherman Oaks Health Club,* 5300 Coldwater Canyon, in North Hollywood, (818) 985–8686. Both centers are clean, fairly new, and offer equipment and locker rental. They have small sport shops in the lobby areas. Their courts are well lighted and clean.

Jogging. Angelenos jog everywhere: on sidewalks, along busy streets, in parks, or at high school and college tracks. The best place to jog, however, is definitely at the beach. There are miles and miles of sandy strand, and the air is not congested with smog, a real problem for visitors not conditioned to it and often at unhealthy levels during the summer and early fall at points farther inland. Redondo Beach maintains an area along the beach called "the Strand," designated especially for runners. Several marathons feature this course throughout the year.

Great Shape, a health club on 11980 San Vicente in Brentwood, offers free coed hiking and jogging clinics weekly. Clinics, featuring world-class marathoners, are also available twice a week. For information, call 820–6602. Great Shape is advertised as a women's health club, but classes are for both men and women.

Besides the beach, favorite places for jogging include San Vicente Blvd. from Brentwood to Santa Monica, where runners jog along a wide, grassy meridian under the shade of coral trees. This path ends at the Palisades high above the Pacific Ocean, where there are benches and grassy lawns on which to rest. Griffith, Will Rogers, and Elysian parks are all good places to run unobstructed from most traffic. Griffith Park is very hilly and crowds of motorists arrive on weekends. Generally, you will find the least amount of traffic on the valley side. Elysian and Will Rogers have light traffic, especially on weekdays. These roadways are also hilly. The *Sepulveda Dam Recreation* area in the San Fernando Valley offers jogging near the golf courses. This area is very flat, and the smog can be troublesome. For information and updates on races, pick up a copy of *City Sports,* at any newsstand.

Bicycling and Roller Skating. Both these sports are extremely popular and often vie with each other for the right of way, especially in the famous beach walkway between Venice and Santa Monica. The area is crowded, especially on weekends when everyone tries to crowd onto the paved pathways extending along the beach from the Santa Monica pier to the Venice pier. (The bike path actually ends farther south, to Redondo Beach.) There are plenty of rental shops in Venice and right under the Santa Monica pier.

Other areas are not recommended; bicycling and roller skating in unprotected areas can be dangerous.

There are, however, many roller skating rinks in the area: *Moonlight Rollerway Skating Rinks,* 5110 San Fernando Rd., Glendale, (818) 241–3630; *Skateland* 18140 Parthenia St., Northridge, (818) 885–1491 or (818) 885–1142.

There is an excellent source book for the bicycle trouper who insists on cycling about the city: *Bicycle Touring in Los Angeles* by Weltman and Ellis; it's available in public libraries or in bookstores.

Exercising and Weightlifting. All the beautiful bodies on the beach in Los Angeles weren't born that way, they worked hard at it. If you wish to partake of some of that hard work here are a couple of places to do it: *Gold's Gym,* 364 Hampton Drive, Venice, (213) 392–3005 is world famous. The gym, open from 5 A.M. to 10 P.M. Monday through Friday, and 8:00 A.M. to 6:00 P.M. on weekends has a clientele of hard-core body builders. Nautilus machines and free weights are featured. The daily rate is $7.00, and the weekly rate is $20.00.

Exercising classes, from Jane Fonda's Workout (213–652–9464 in Beverly Hills or 818–986–1624 in Encino), to Holiday Health Spas, to YMCAs and YWCAs, are available all over the Los Angeles area. Check the local phone books for information about the gym or salon nearest you. (Remember that each area has separate phone books: North Hollywood, Glendale, Los Angeles, Beverly Hills, West Los Angeles.)

Horseback Riding. Riding is especially popular in the valleys, where most of the horse owners and stables are located. *The Los Angeles Equestrian Center* at Griffith Park (480 Riverside Dr., Burbank, 818–840–9063) has lessons for all levels as well as hourly rates to ride through 50 miles of wooded Griffith Park trails.

Azusa Canyon Stables rent horses and feature both western and English saddles; call 334-7000 for information and directions. Other stables for horse rental include *Hansen Dam Equestrian Center* in Lakeview Terrace, 896–6514; *Livingston Stables* in Burbank, 843–9890; and Sunset Hollywood Stable in Hollywood, 469–5450 (the latter offers at dusk a special "starlight" ride through Griffith Park over to Burbank on Fridays only).

Many more exciting adventures such as hang gliding (see also *Beaches,* above), soaring, glider flying, and hot-air ballooning can be found in the Riverside County and San Bernardino sections near the cities of Hemet, Perris, Antelope Valley, and Victorville, all within a day's trip from Los Angeles.

Enjoy your stay and take advantage of our year-round sunny playground. Be certain to contact the state, city, and county park systems to ensure that you enjoy the 800,000 acres of recreational facilities available for fun and adventure in and around Los Angeles. (For further details, refer to the *Parks* section of this guide.)

HIKING. Most of the large city parks such as *Griffith, Brookside, Elysian,* and *Will Rogers* have wilderness paths. Griffith and Elysian perch atop the Hollywood Hills and offer spectacular views of downtown and Hollywood to the south or the Valley and the mountains to the east. When hiking, keep in mind that these are wilderness areas and that you may be hiking in an area that does not provide drinking water. Elysian Park features a wooded botanical area with a wide variety of trees. Please check the *Parks* section for further information.

Placerita Canyon Park in Newhall is especially geared to the hiker, for it has well-marked trails of varying length for the amateur hiker as well as the more seasoned hiker. Information is available on the natural wildlife and flora, and rangers are available for any questions. This canyon park is in dry, oak tree, rocky terrain typical of the San Gabriel Mountains.

In the Angeles National Forest are several hiking trails, including Spruce Grove, Mt. Lowe, Cooper Canyon, and Altadena. These trails are in dry, mountainous regions, and drinking water is not available. For information on hiking in these areas, contact the National Forest Service Parks at (818) 790–1151.

For further information on area hiking, outings, and so on contact the Sierra Club, 2410 Beverly Blvd., 387–4287.

WINTER SPORTS. Los Angeles area mountains offer many fine skiing opportunities from December to April. There are a dozen ski areas offering more than 150 ski runs and nearly 70 lifts and tows within a two-hour drive of downtown Los Angeles. With fickle California weather, the natural snowfall may not suffice, so most resorts have on hand artificial snow machines to ensure winter skiing. The resorts that use snow-making machines are Snow Summit, Snow Forest, Goldmine, Snow Valley, Mountain High, and Holiday Hill. Big Bear's snow-making operation is one of the largest in the world.

Regular runs can be found at *Mammoth* to the north and *Mt. Waterman, Mt. Baldy,* and *Kratka Ridge* much closer to home, a scant two-hours drive into the San Bernardino Mountains. A bit farther south in the San Bernardinos are *Goldmine, Snow Summit, Snow Valley, Big Bear, Arrowhead,* and *Table Mountain.* Most offer lifts and beginner's, moderate, and advanced runs. Rates tend to be somewhat lower than most resorts around the country.

Summit Express bus service to the Big Bear area departs from several Los Angeles locations. Advance lift tickets are a must for the Big Bear area. Also available is airport-ski transportation; call Mountain Air Service, (714) 585–2511. For reservations, package deals, or information, contact Big Bear Chamber of Commerce at (714) 866–5652 or Big Bear Lake's Tourist and Visitor Bureau at (714) 866–4601.

For any information on other ski area resorts, feel free to contact any sporting goods store; they are helpful and have the latest information on skiing and road conditions. *Sport Chalet,* at 920 Foothill Dr., La Canada (near Pasadena), (213) 684–0545, is very knowledgeable.

Ice Skating. This sport is very popular in the dry basin that has never experienced an icy winter. Try *Ice Capades Chalet Ice Arena,* 6100 Laurel Canyon Blvd., North Hollywood, (818) 985–5555; *Ice Skating Center* in Pasadena (818–578–0800) and *Ice Capades Chalet Ice Arena,* 555 Deep Valley Dr., Rolling Hills Estate (818–541–6630); *Pickwick Ice Arena,* 1001 Riverside Dr., Burbank, 846–0032. Rinks have adjacent skating shops for rentals and sharpening and refreshment areas.

SPECTATOR SPORTS. Angelenos are people on the move, whether it be jogging, running, surfing, playing tennis, or on through the whole gamut of indoor and outdoor sports. But when not participating themselves, they are avid fans, and there is never a day when you can't settle down into a stadium seat and see sporting action. Take your pick.

Baseball. Get the Dodger Blue Fever at the Dodger Stadium. The season starts early in April and runs through early October. For ticket information, call 244–1400.

Golf. The Glen Campbell Los Angeles Open will be played in late February at the Riviera Golf Course in Los Angeles. It starts on Wednesday with the pro-am. The big-money tourney starts on Thursday and runs through Sunday.

Thoroughbred Racing at Santa Anita Park in Arcadia. Champion jockeys ride internationally rated thoroughbreds. The $500,000 Santa Anita Handicap is run around late April. The 320-acre park is located at the junction of 285 W. Huntington Dr. and Colorado Pl. For more information call (818) 574–7223.

Starting late April and continuing through mid-July, Hollywood Park in Inglewood near Los Angeles International Airport offers sixty-six days of racing. Races are run Wednesday through Sunday, with special promotions on Memorial Day, the Fourth of July, and closing day. Post time is 2:00 P.M. The 350-acre park includes such features as picknicking in the infield, a fully supervised children's playgroup, gift shop, and a variety of restaurants. Total seating capacity is 34,000, with parking for 31,000 cars. For ticket information, telephone 419–1500.

Harness racing is at Los Alamitos. Prearranged group tours are available.

Basketball. The Los Angeles Lakers represent the NBA at its best at the Los Angeles Forum in Inglewood. The Clippers have moved from San Diego to L.A. and will be playing at the Sports Arena, 3939 S. Figueroa; (213) 748–6131.

Boxing. At the Olympic Auditorium (213) 749–5171 in downtown Los Angeles and at the Forum (213) 673–1300.

Boat Racing. Marinas in Los Angeles host all classes of sailboat races, and, on special occasions, powerboat competition and surfing contests.

Auto Racing. Long Beach Grand Prix, April 1–3, draws more than thirty of the world's top Formula One drivers and close to two hundred thousand spectators for the three days of celebrity and pro-racing. The course snakes around twelve turns and covers 2.13 mi. through the city's streets. Prize money tops $1.5 million. Ticket information is available from Long Beach Grand Prix Association, 110 W. Ocean, Suite A, Long Beach, CA 90802.

Collegiate athletics are not only big in Los Angeles but offer visitors the opportunity to see top-flight teams in action. The Bruins teams of the **University of California at Los Angeles** (UCLA) go nonstop virtually year round.

Basketball. Intersectional as well as Pacific 10 competition played at Pauley Pavilion at the UCLA campus in Westwood.

Football. First home game in September through the November intercity clash with the University of Southern California (USC). All UCLA home games played at the Rose Bowl, Pasadena.

Baseball. Late January through mid-May; home games are played at the Jackie Robinson Stadium on campus.

Fencing. Late January through late March at the UCLA Men's Gym.

Rugby. On campus at the North Athletic Field, early January through early April.

Swimming. At the Sunset Canyon Recreation Center, early January through mid-February.

Volleyball. At Pauley Pavilion, late January through early April.

Track and Field. At Drake Stadium on campus, late February through late April. (Some meets are dual events with the women's track team.)

For UCLA ticket information and schedule details, call (213) UCLA 101.

The Trojans of the **University of Southern California** (USC) offer a full slate of collegiate athletics for visitors. Telephone: (213) 743–2620.

Basketball. Games start early in January; home games are played at the Sports Arena adjoining the USC campus and continue into early spring.

Football. The Trojans kick off their season in September and wrap up against UCLA in November.

Baseball. Begins at Dedeaux Field on campus in late January and continues on through mid-May.

Volleyball. At the campus gym starting in late January and continuing through late April.

Regatta. Starts in March with crew races for men and women at the Los Angeles harbor, Berth 192, or Bellona Creek, and continues through May.

BABYSITTING SERVICES. Don't be reluctant to bring the children to Los Angeles. Daytime activities are plentiful, and for those evenings when parents want to be out on the town, the city offers reliable babysitting sources.

Babysitters Guild, Inc., Agency. (213) 469–8246. The largest babysitting agency covering the greater Los Angeles area, including the San Fernando and San Gabriel valleys and Beverly Hills. The agency, in business for over thirty-five years, is bonded and licensed by the state. There is a minimum fee of $19.50, travel included, with a four-hour minimum. The base rate after the first four hours is $5.50 per hour.

We Sit Better. (818) 997–1421. Covers the San Fernando Valley, Bel Air, and Brentwood. Four-hour minimum, $17.50; each additional hour, $4.25. Transportation fee, $3.50. Experienced sitters aged 25 years and up.

Other options: *Community Service Agency* (Box 108, Woodland Hills, CA 91365; 818–880–4552); *Moms Care Unlimited* (13455 Ventura Blvd., Suite 233, Sherman Oaks, CA 91423; 818–783–6667).

CHILDREN'S ACTIVITIES. From the area's many amusement parks to the simple pleasures of a day swimming or playing in the sand at the beach to a trek to one of Los Angeles' excellent museums, this city will not fail to delight children. (For *Long Beach* and *Orange County* attractions, see the separate chapters at the end of the book.)

Places listed below are popular year-round attractions of special interest to children. The beauty of these southern California attractions is that they are not strictly kiddie oriented; adults will undoubtedly find as much pleasure in experiencing most of these activities as will the children.

A more comprehensive source of information on weekly children's activities is *The Los Angeles Times'* Sunday Calendar section that contains listings in the Family Activities column. This column includes announcements of special events oriented toward children, museum hours, exhibitions, and other current events that would be of interest to the entire family.

MUSEUMS

Angel's Attic. 516 Colorado Ave., Santa Monica; 394–8331. This toy museum is nonprofit, sponsored by the Angels for Autistic Children of the Brentwood Center for Educational Therapy. Forty dollhouses are in the collection, the oldest dating back to the early 1800's. Exhibits change every three months, and other items on display include miniatures, dolls, and toys. Tea is served. Open 12:30–4:30 Thursday, Friday, Saturday, and Sunday, or by appointment. $3 for adults, $2 for seniors, $1 for children.

Cabrillo Marine Museum. 3720 Stephen White Dr., San Pedro; 548–7562. A multilevel marine and nautical museum featuring aquariums with live sealife and exhibits of stuffed sharks, whales, and marine history. Children will love maneuvering nautical equipment and rummaging through old whale bones. The museum is adjacent to a grassy picnic area, playground, and the beach. Open Tuesday through Friday, noon to 5:00; weekends, 10:00 to 5:00. Closed Monday. Free, but parking costs $3.

California Museum of Science and Industry. 700 State Dr., Exposition Park, Los Angeles; 744–7400. With one section geared solely to children, this museum is also of great interest to adults. Each exhibit demonstrates a scientific or a mathematical principle, clearly labeled and explained. Children can operate the exhibits by punching buttons, twisting knobs, or pulling levers. Open daily 10:00 to 5:00. Free.

George C. Page Museum of La Brea Discoveries. 5801 Wilshire Blvd., Hancock Park, Los Angeles; 936–2230. In conjunction with the La Brea Tar Pits, the Page Museum houses over one million prehistoric fossils recovered from the Tar Pits. Excellent displays, films, and exhibits recreate the skeletons and histories of the prehistoric animals that once roamed the Los Angeles basin and have been perfectly preserved for thousands of years in natural asphalt. In the lab area, everyone is welcome to view the ongoing painstaking recovery of the fossils from the tar. During summer months an excavation on the grounds is usually in progress and can be viewed from a roped-off area. Open Tuesday through Sunday, 10:00 A.M. to 5:00 P.M. closed Monday. Adults, $1.50; 75 cents for students, children and senior citizens. Admission is free on the second Tuesday of each month.

Kidspace. 390 S. El Molino Ave., Pasadena; (818) 449–9143. A museum where kids can talk to a robot, direct a radio or television station, visit a medical clinic, or test skills in observation and changing environments. A special "Human Habitrail" challenges children by changing architectural environments and "Illusions" teases one's ability to perceive what is real and what is an illusion. School year: Saturday and Sunday 11:00 to 4:00 and Wednesday, 3:00 to 5:00. Admission is $2.00 for ages 2–65, $1.50 for seniors, and groups of 10 children or more, babies are free. For special programs, call 449–9144.

Los Angeles Children's Museum. 310 N. Main St., Los Angeles; 687–8800. Near downtown, City Hall, and other government buildings, this museum offers art, science, and technology exhibits where children, for once, are asked to "Please Touch." This is a learning center where children participate in such adventures as "City Streets"; they are encouraged to crawl through a mock manhole cover and discover what goes on beneath the pavement or visit a replica of Los Angeles' KNXT newsroom. There is a large "Lego" room for kids to experiment with building. Huge fabric blocks are used for construction. Art and science projects are tactile, and all exhibits are geared toward participation. Summer hours: Monday through Friday, 11:30 A.M. to 5:00 P.M.; Saturday and Sunday, 10:00 A.M. to 5:00 P.M. Winter hours (beginning in late Sept.): Wednesday and Thursday, 2:30 P.M. to 5:00 P.M.; Saturday and Sunday, 10:00 A.M. to 5:00 P.M. Summer hours are observed during school vacations. Wednesday and Thursday, free. Saturday and Sunday, admission is $2.75.

Lomita Railroad Museum. 2135 250th St., Lomita; 326–6255. Don't be surprised if you think you've gotten lost in this typical suburban neighborhood before you find the museum. Look closely, and you'll discover a replica of a turn-of-the-century Massachusetts train station. Beyond the gate, discover one of the largest collections of railroad memorabilia in the West. Climb aboard a real steam engine and take a look at the immaculate interior of the cab itself. Open Wednesday through Sunday, 10:00 A.M. to 5:00 P.M. Admission 50 cents.

Los Angeles County Museum of Natural History. 900 Exposition Blvd; 744–3411. See the skeletons of prehistoric animals, including the saber-tooth tigers, bison, mastedons, and camels, uncovered in the La Brea Tar Pits. There are also artifacts and relics of prehistoric man. In the "Hall of Gems" discover jewels in their natural forms as well as cut and polished. There's a stunning exhibit of diamonds, rubies, and sapphires. Open daily except Monday, 10:00 A.M. to 5:00 P.M. Admission: adults, $1.50 children, students and senior citizens, 75 cents.

The Museum of Rock Art. 6834 Hollywood Blvd; 463–8979 (across from Mann's Chinese Theater). This establishment started out small, but recently moved to much expanded quarters. Changing exhibits offer a glimpse into the evolution of rock music; and there are permanent 50s, 60s, 70s, and 80s galleries. An 80-seat multimedia theater also presents the "Rock and Roll Time Tunnel" every half hour. This attraction is really for kids of all ages, and it is open from 11 A.M. to 8 P.M. weekdays and 11 A.M. to midnight weekends. Closed Mondays. Admission is $3.50 for adults, $2.50 for seniors, children under 12 free.

Southwest Museum. 234 Museum Dr., Los Angeles; 221–2163. If you enter this museum from Museum Dr., it will appear as if you're entering a cave or catacombs. Enjoy the displays and niches along the walls depicting native American Indian art and artifacts from west of the Mississippi. An elevator will take you to the main floor. There is parking on the ground floor level as well. The museum houses a fine collection of clothing, tools, pottery, bows and arrows, and dolls. Children will especially enjoy an authentic tepee set up in the center room. Free. A park is conveniently located nearby for relaxation. Open Tuesday through Saturday, 11:00 A.M. to 5:00 P.M.; Sunday, 1:00 to 5:00 P.M. Adults, $1.50; senior citizens and students, $1; ages 7–18, 75¢; children 6 and under, free.

FUN AND GAMES

Bob Baker Marionette Theater. 1345 West First St.; 250–9995. Two hours of charming puppet and marionette shows delight both children and adults. Watch fairy tales come to life on stage as the brightly costumed marionettes enact the stories. Children sit close to the stage and after the show are served refreshments. As a special treat, visitors are invited backstage to see how the puppets are operated. The staff is especially patient and attentive to children and even show the workshop where the puppets and marionettes are made. Reservations are necessary. Admission: $5 for children, $6 for adults, $4 for senior citizens. Price includes performance, refreshments, and tour of the workshop area. Showtimes are 2:30 Saturday and Sunday.

Griffith Park Observatory. Atop the hill, on the south side of Griffith Park. The entrance at Los Feliz and Vermont is most convenient; 664–1191. One of the world's largest telescopes is open to the public for viewing every clear night. Exhibits display models of the planets with photographs from satellites and spacecraft. The adjoining Planetarium has dazzling daily shows that duplicate the starry sky. A guide narrates the show and points out constellations. A Laserium show is featured nightly, and other special astrology shows are offered frequently. Call the Planetarium for scheduling. The Observatory sits high above Los Angeles and from the outside decks and walkways offers a spectacular view of the city. Free. Shows: Adults, $2.25; children and seniors, $1.25.

Los Angeles Philharmonic Symphonies for Youth. Dorothy Chandler Pavilion, Music Center, 135 N. Grand Ave.; 972–0703. January and February hour-long concerts with appearances by young guest artists. Call for fees and scheduling. Summer programs in conjunction with the Hollywood Bowl called Open House. 2301 Highland Ave., Hollywood; 850–2077. Weekday mornings. $2 per person. Call for scheduling.

Santa Monica Pier. At the end of Colorado Ave., Santa Monica, jutting out into the ocean, this pier, built in 1875, holds a children's park and myriad fun and games places. Visit the arcade for old-fashioned amusement games or new electronic games. Ride on the merry-go-round, or purchase a bag of freshly fried potato chips. At the end of the pier you can rent bait and tackle to try your hand at fishing off the pier. (You don't need a license to fish off this pier.) Many eateries and refreshment stands. Roller skates can be rented from shops in front of the pier, and paved paths for rollerskaters run alongside the beach to Venice pier about three miles away. Another option is to park your family on the beach and enjoy the ocean.

Magic Mountain. Also known as Six Flags Magic Mountain, Valencia; (805) 255–4100. 260 acres of rides, shows, and amusement-park entertainment. Colossus, the world's largest roller coaster, thrills adventure seekers. (See "Theme Parks" section, below, for details.)

Travel Town. 5200 Zoo Dr., Los Angeles; 662–5874. Located on the east side of Griffith Park. A collection of airplanes, trains, and other early transportation replicas onto which the children can climb and play. The area is situated in a pleasant grassy park with ample picnic areas. A miniature train and one of Los Angeles's old trolleys take children for rides around a small track. Open Monday through Friday from 10:00 A.M. to 5:00 P.M.; and weekends from 10:00 A.M. to 6:00 P.M.

ZOOS

Los Angeles Zoo. Ventura and Golden State Fwys. intersection, Griffith Park; 666–4090, 666–5133, or 666–4650. The Los Angeles Zoo features five "continents" where the animals are grouped. A tram is available for stops at all areas. The zoo is beautifully landscaped, and areas for picnicking are available. The animals are in well-kept, spacious areas with imaginative settings for roaming or climbing. The *Children's Zoo* features a petting pen and an animal nursery. Spend a day and enjoy the zoo's newest family, koala bears from Australia housed in an area resembling their natural habitat, each with its own eucalyptus tree. (See main "Zoo" section, above, for further information.)

Marineland. 6610 Palos Verdes Dr., S., Rancho Palos Verdes; 377–1571 or 541–5663. An aquatic zoo with shows featuring killer whales, sea lions, and dolphins. This park is a combination research facility and tourist attraction. Colorful tropical fish, sea horses and other seafaring creatures reside in aquariums simulating their natural habitat. Children can romp freely in the playground-and-games area. At Sea Lion Point, view sea lions in their natural habitat. At Baja Reef visitors swim with more than 2000 varieties of fish. (Adults must accompany children for swimming.) Winter hours are Wednesday through Sunday from 10:00 A.M. to 5:00 P.M.; and summer hours are from 10:00 A.M. to 7:00 P.M. Adult admission is $9.95; senior citizens, $8.00; ages 3 to 11, $6.95; and under 3, free.

SIGHTSEEING

Catalina Island. Take the two-hour boat trip from San Pedro or Long Beach and land in port at Avalon, Catalina's main city. There is so much to do in one day that you may want to consider staying in one of the many hotels. There are tours such as the glass-bottom boat tour (make certain that it's a sunny day), a boat cruise to see the seals on Seal Rock, or the all-day inland tour spotting wild goats and buffalo and a visit to the Arabian horse ranch. There are restrictions on automobiles, but Avalon is small enough to wander about on foot. Enjoy the beach and the many shops. Rent an electric cart or walk out to the Wrigley Botanical Gardens, an extensive cactus garden, or rent a horse for a scenic ride through the hills. Be prepared to spend the day; boats arrive in the morning and do not return to the mainland until afternoon. There is also air service to the island. (See "Long Beach to San Clemente," below, for details.)

Chinatown. Between Broadway and Hill Sts., Los Angeles. Wait until dark and enjoy the colorful hanging lanterns and lighted ornate buildings; shops are open until 9:00 P.M. Stroll through the shops or have dinner in a neighborhood bistro. A great opportunity to teach children how to use chopsticks.

Grand Central Market. Hill St. between 3rd and 4th, Los Angeles. Wander through this large marketplace with over fifty stalls containing everything from fresh fruit, vegetables, dairy products, meats, fish, and eggs to exotic spices. The fixtures are still intact from the 1930s. Glass cases display noodles and legumes of every kind. The mix of customers and vendors is as colorful as the produce. Expect to hear many languages. Don't eat before you visit, for you'll find something you can't resist.

Mann's Chinese Theater. Hollywood Blvd., Los Angeles. The famous Chinese Theater with a dramatic exterior that resembles a Chinese pagoda. Stand before the footprints, handprints, and signatures of the stars engraved in the cement sidewalk in front of the theater. Every member of the family will enjoy comparing feet and hands with the cement impressions. On Hollywood Blvd. is the famous "Walk of the Stars," where golden stars with the names of the famous are imbedded in the sidewalk. The "stars" continue to the intersection of Hollywood and Vine.

NBC Studio Tour. 3000 W. Alameda Ave., Burbank; 840–4444. A backstage tour of this huge studio complex takes you through sets and the makeup and wardrobe departments. Don't be surprised if you spot a celebrity on the way to a show's taping or rehearsal. (See "Tours," above.)

Olvera St. Near Sunset and Main, Los Angeles. The first settlement in Los Angeles. You can walk down the brick street and enjoy the buildings, some of which are authentic. Others were built to replicate an authentic, bustling Mexican village. Watch colorful dancing or tortilla making; have your picture taken in a fruit cart or astride a burro. Shop to your heart's content among the bounty of Mexican merchandise. Don't be surprised to hear English only as a second language; Spanish is predominant.

Universal Studios Tour. Universal City; (818) 508–9600. This tour takes you on a tram to see sets, mock cities, special effects, and other aspects of the movie industry. Shows, which include talking birds, a Wild West fight with real stuntmen, and a trained animal show, are included with the tour. (See "Tours," above.)

THEME PARKS

Most of the area's amusement parks, including *Disneyland* and *Knott's Berry Farm,* are in and around Orange County. (See the separate chapter for Orange, below.) But the city proper does boast one large park worth checking out.

Six Flags Magic Mountain. Located in Valencia, this 260-acre park is one minute's drive west of Interstate 5 on Magic Mountain Pkwy., approximately one-half hour north of Hollywood; (818) 992–0884. Open daily, May 19 to Labor Day, from 10:00 A.M. to midnight; rest of the year open on Saturdays, Sundays, and school holidays: mid-September through October from 10:00 A.M. to 10:00 P.M.; November to Memorial Day from 10:00 A.M. to 6:00 P.M.

The roster of major rides includes the Roaring Rapids, a simulated whitewater wilderness adventure complete with whirlpools, waves, and real rapids; the Colossus, the largest dual-track wood roller coaster ever built, offering two "drops" in excess of 100 ft. and experiencing speeds up to 62 mi. per hour; the Revolution, a steel coaster with a 360°, 90-ft. vertical loop; and the Electric Rainbow, an illuminated, revolving ride in a giant circle tilting upright almost 50°.

Children can enjoy Wizard's Village, a playground of bright colors, shapes, and textures, including a punching-bag forest, a rope bridge to the Wizard's Castle, and a giant "Swiss cheese" with a maze of tunnels. Children's World is a minipark with scaled-down rides, such as the Red Baron's Airplane and the Little Sailor Ride. Reservations can be made for a child's birthday party, complete with cake, ice cream, and punch, at the Birthday House.

Other attractions of this park include a puppet theater, celebrity musical revues, Dixieland jazz, rock-and-roll concerts, and the Aqua Theater high-diving shows. Spillikin's Handcrafters Junction is a four-acre compound in which craftsmen exhibit skills and wares from blacksmithing to glassblowing.

There are many styles of food service available for dining pleasure. The Timber Mill offers hearty American food; Old El Paso's menu travels throughout Mexico; Valencia Terrace features farm-style breakfasts; and the Potato Patch serves fried chicken and fresh French fries crisped in almond oil. Also at your service are countless stands for munching hot dogs, hamburgers, cotton candy, and beverages.

Admission fee for adults is $12.95; for children under 48 inches in height the fee is $6.50; under two are admitted free. Admission includes all rides, attractions, shows, and special events. Major credit cards are accepted. From late May to early September the park is open daily; during the remainder of the year, it's open weekends and school holidays.

HISTORIC SITES. When Los Angeles celebrated its bicentennial in 1981, the event came as something of a shock to many Americans. Until then most people had assumed that Los Angeles came into being in the 1920s or thereabouts.

The city's historical heritage has not only been carefully preserved, but active restoration projects are taking place all the time. There is a great deal to be seen that pre-dates the arrival of moving pictures.

On busy Broadway in downtown Los Angeles is the amazing **Bradbury Building** (304 S. Broadway), built in 1893 and among the city's most remarkable architectural achievements. Inside the Italian Renaissance building is a Victorian world of elaborate grillwork, French-made wrought-iron railings, and decorations with Belgian marble and Mexican tile.

Also downtown is **El Pueblo de Los Angeles State Historical Park,** site of the founding of the city in 1781. It is located in the middle of today's modern city. Spread around the Old Plaza is Olvera St., which recalls the city's rich Mexican beginnings. Historical buildings include the Pelanconi House (now a restaurant), the Old Plaza Church, the Garnier Building, and the Merced, the city's first theater, which has a Bicentennial exhibit inside. Avila Adobe at 14 Olvera St., a historic house with antique furnishings, was built in 1818. Free walking tours of the area are available on an hourly basis, from 10:00 A.M. to 1:00 P.M., Tuesday through Saturday. Meet at 130 Paseo de la Plaza.

Watts Tower, 1765 E. 107th St., is the folk art legacy of an Italian immigrant tile setter, Simon Rodia. From 1920 until 1954, without helpers, he erected three cement towers embellished with bits of colored glass, broken pottery, and assorted discards. Plans are underway to stabilize and protect this unique monument, often compared to the twentieth-century architectural wonders created by Barcelona's Antonio Gaudi. Well worth a pilgrimage for art and architectural buffs (or anyone else, for that matter).

In Hollywood, the **Hollywood Studio Museum,** once known as the Lasky Barn, is directly across from the Hollywood Bowl, in the Fairfield parking lot. In December 1913, an upstart movie company rented part of a barn at Vine and Selma Ave. in what was then a quiet, rural Hollywood and began production on *The Squaw Man,* Hollywood's first feature film. The movie was completed on February 15, 1914, and the credit was given to the Jesse Lasky Play Co., which later became Paramount Studios. Sam Goldwyn was the producer and Cecil B. De Mille was the director. As the Lasky company grew, part of the barn was torn down and the remainder was used for storage. In 1926 the structure was moved from Selma and Vine to Paramount's Marathon St. lot, where it became the studio gym. In 1956 it was designated a California state landmark, and in 1980 Paramount donated it to the Hollywood Chamber of Commerce, which moved the barn to its present location. Now, aged and decrepit, the barn faces an uncertain future.

The Wiltern Theater, at Wilshire and Western (380–5005), built in 1930, is listed in the National Register of Historic Places as a striking example of Art Deco at its finest. Presently, the green terra-cotta structure is where the *Los Angeles Opera Theater* makes its home.

The **Banning Residence** in Wilmington is an interesting twenty-four-room Greek Revival mansion. In Pasadena is the Renaissance-style *Wrigley Mansion,* now home of the Pasadena Tournament of Roses Association. Free guided tours of the 18,500 sq-ft mansion at 391 S. Orange Grove Blvd. are held every Wednesday from 2:00 to 4:00 P.M., February through September. The surrounding Wrigley Gardens cover four and one-half acres and are open to the public daily. Free parking on nearby streets.

Gamble House, a noted Pasadena landmark built in 1908, is an outstanding design by Greene and Greene. It reflects a heavy Oriental influence. Also in Pasadena, the **Huntington-Sheraton Hotel,** built in 1907, features the Viennese Room containing duplicates of King Ludwig's Bavarian chadeliers. On the twenty-three acres of landscaped grounds are the Horseshow and the Japanese Gardens and the Picture Bridge. Admission free. For reservations, call the Concierge Desk, 792–0266.

Antiques are among the collection of functional fine art at the **Merle Norman Classic Beauty Collection** at Sylmar, California, which includes a collection of 100 antique, classic, and luxury automobiles; a music room filled with music boxes, mechanical instruments, a watch collection, and the Louis XV Dining Room, featuring a muraled ceiling and crystal chandelier, circa 1680. Free tours daily, Tuesday through Saturday. For tour information and reservations, call 367-1085.

MISSIONS

In 1768, when the Russian interest in Alaska was perceived to be a possible prelude to southward expansion, King Charles of Spain ordered the colonization of California. The king's decree launched the missions, which provided the seminal growth for California.

Under the astute leadership of Father Junipero Serra and Father Fermin Lausen (each founded nine missions), the gray-robed Franciscans moved slowly northward. By 1823 a chain of twenty-one missions extended 600 mi. from San Diego to Sonoma. Approximately a day's travel apart in those days (30 mi.), the missions dotted the coastal route called El Camino Real. Today US 101 parallels the historic Mission Trail, one of the state's most popular tourways.

Two of these missions are found in Los Angeles County. The first, **Mission San Fernando Rey de Espana,** is located at the north end of the San Fernando Valley in Mission Hills, 15151 San Fernando Mission Blvd.

This mission was established and named in honor of the thirteenth-century King Ferdinand III of Spain in 1797. Fifty-six Indians joined the mission to make it a self-supportive community. Soon wheat, corn, beans, and olives were grown and harvested there. In addition, the mission workshops produced metalwork, leather goods, cloth, soap, and candles. Herds of cattle, sheep, and hogs also began to prosper.

By 1833, after Mexico extended its rule over California, a civil administrator was appointed to the mission, and the priests were restricted to religious duties. The Indians began leaving, and what had been flourishing one year before became unproductive. Thirteen years later the mission, along with its properties (the entire San Fernando Valley, as we know it today), was sold for $14,000. During the next forty years, the mission buildings were neglected; settlers had stripped roofing tiles, and the adobe walls were ravaged by the weather.

Finally, in 1923, a restoration program was initiated that resulted in a recovery of the rustic elegance and the feeling of history within the mission walls.

Today, as you walk through the mission's arched corridors, you may experience *deja vu*—that feeling of having been there before—and you probably have, vicariously, through an episode of *Gunsmoke, Dragnet,* or dozens of motion picture epics. The large two-story convent building is the largest adobe structure in California today. The mission plaza consists of a grand fountain, lushly planted gardens, and a bell tower. The church's interior, especially its walls, are decorated with Indian designs and artifacts of Spanish craftsmanship depicting the mission's eighteenth-century culture. Also at the mission is a small museum and gift shop.

The Mission San Fernando Rey de Espana is open every day from 9:00 A.M. to 5:00 P.M. Admission: for adults, 75 cents; for children ages seven to fifteen, 25 cents; children under seven are admitted free.

Self-guided tours of the mission are possible, as are group tours, which can be arranged on Monday and Thursday afternoons. For information, call (818) 361–0186.

How to get there: From downtown Los Angeles, take the #5 Fwy. north approximately fifteen mi to San Fernando Mission Blvd. Exit west, and follow San Fernando Mission Blvd. one mi directly to the mission.

The other old mission, the **Mission San Gabriel Arcangel,** is located west of downtown Los Angeles in San Gabriel at 537 W. Mission Dr.

Over 200 years ago, Father Junipero Serra dedicated this mission to the great Archangel and messenger of God, Saint Gabriel. As the founders approached the mission site, they were confronted with savage Indians. In fear of battle, one of the padres produced the canvas painting *Our Lady of Sorrows.* This so impressed the Indians that they laid down their bows and arrows. This miracle produced a painting, which is on display at the mission today. Within the next fifty years, the San Gabriel Arcangel became the wealthiest of all California missions.

In 1833 the Mexican government passed the "Decree of Desecularization," and following their confiscation of the mission, it began to decline, as did the Mission San Fernando Rey. In 1855 the United States government returned the mission to the church. Unfortunately, by this time the Franciscans had departed. Not much happened until 1908, when the Claretian Fathers (the Missionary

Order of the Sons of the Immaculate Heart of Mary) took charge. In the following years much care and respect was poured into the mission.

Today Mission San Gabriel Arcangel's adobe walls preserve an era of history unchanged by the outside world. The magnificent cemetery tells the history of the mission through the people that lived, died, and were buried there. Over 6,000 Indians stricken by horrible cholera and smallpox epidemics in 1825 are buried in the cemetery.

You may walk through the grounds and admire such utilitarian spots as the soap and tallow vats, the tannery, the aqueduct, the kitchen, and the winery. The magnificent church and museum house relics reflecting the history of the padres and early visitors to San Gabriel.

And, to give visitors some sense of the scope of the California mission chains, the Court of Missions established in 1921 has models of each of the twenty-one missions still standing today. There is a gift and souvenir shop.

Hours at the museum are from 9:30 A.M. to 4:15 P.M. every day of the week. Admission is $1.00 for adults; 50¢ for children. For further information, call (818) 282–5191.

How to get there: Take Interstate 10 (San Bernardino Fwy.) from Los Angeles to New Ave. Follow New Ave. and Ramona St. north to the mission.

LIBRARIES. The *Huntington Library, Art Gallery, and Botanical Garden.* 1151 Oxford St., San Marino; (818) 792–6141 or (818) 681–6601. Formerly magnate Henry E. Huntington's estate, it became a public institution in 1928. The Art Gallery's prize collection of eighteenth-century paintings includes Gainsborough's *Blue Boy,* Lawrence's *Pinkie,* and works by Reynolds, Turner, and Blake. The library is open for scholarly research only, but it does feature a public exhibit of literary treasures, including a Gutenberg Bible, the earliest known manuscript of Chaucer's *Canterbury Tales,* a first edition of the King James' Bible, and Benjamin Franklin's original autobiography. The Botanical Garden has the world's largest cactus collection, a Japanese garden, and a camellia garden (in bloom February through April). No picnics or pets. A refreshment room is open to the public. Maps can be acquired at the main gate.

MUSEUMS. When referring to the visual arts of Los Angeles, moving pictures rather than those of canvases and sculpture come to mind. The varied collections in the county's museums and galleries have long been overshadowed by its celluloid counterpart of the movie and television industry.

From the Norton Simon Museum of Art in Pasadena, celebrated for its collection of Old Master paintings, sculpture, and tapestries, to the avant-garde exhibits of its many galleries, Los Angeles offers a broad range of art forms. (Art Galleries are covered in a separate section, below.)

The permanent collections housed at the Los Angeles County Museum of Art (LACMA), Norton Simon, and J. Paul Getty Museums can be enjoyed in a variety of architectural and landscape creations. LACMA offers a lovely garden featuring sculpture by Rodin, Calder, and Lieberman (to name a few) and the La Brea Tar Pits, imprinted by prehistoric dinosaur paws. The sleek, wood paneled halls of the Norton Simon create a wonderful environment to view art. And the Getty, the most richly endowed museum in the world, is a stately reproduction of a Roman villa set on an oceanfront estate.

Perhaps most exciting is the coming of the new Museum of Contemporary Art due to occupy a controversial modern space on an 11-acre downtown site in early 1986. For now its collection is in the colorful Temporary Contemporary nearby. (See Museum of Contemporary Art below under "Other Museums.")

The following Los Angeles museums are all in the 213 area code except where otherwise noted.

The California Museum of Science and Industry. 700 State Dr. in Exposition Park; 744–7400. This museum was vastly expanded for the Olympics. The new Aerospace Complex features a DC3, DC8, rockets and satellites plus an IMAX motion picture theater. The Taper Hall of Economics and Finance has 62 3-D exhibits, most of them computer interactive for visitors. And a new miniature winery complements McDonalds' Computer Chef exhibit of behind-the-scenes fast food cooking. The redesigned Hall of Health reveals the inner workings of the body and has a new Health for Life Arcade. Fiber optics, robotics, and high technology in 14 halls, but also the ever-popular hatchery where 150 baby chicks hatch daily for all to see. Open daily 10 A.M. to 5 P.M. Free.

Craft and Folk Art Museum. 5814 Wilshire Blvd.; 937–5544. The museum's collections include Japanese, Mexican, American, and East Indian folk art, folk textiles, Indonesian masks, and contemporary crafts. Six to eight major exhibitions are planned each year. The annual International Festival of Masks held at the end of October presents two days of performances, exhibits, food booths, and a parade of masks. The museum Library and Media Resources Center are open to the public. The Museum Shop carries displays of merchandise relating to each current exhibition as well as quality work by expert craftspeople, folk art from around the world, original postcards, and educational materials. Located on the mezzanine of the museum, overlooking the exhibitions, is the Egg and the Eye Restaurant, which serves forty exotic varieties of omelettes. Open daily, 11:00 A.M. to 5:00 P.M. Admission: adults, $1.50; students and seniors, $1; children 75¢.

The J. Paul Getty Museum. 17985 Pacific Coast Hwy., Malibu; 459–8402. Founded by oil magnate J. Paul Getty, the museum contains one of the country's finest collections of Greek and Roman antiquities in a classical building that is a recreation of a first-century Roman villa. The Main Level houses the Greek and Roman antiquities collection, which includes marble and bronze sculpture, mosaics, vases, and examples of various minor arts, such as household items. Of particular interest are the fourth-century Attic stelai (funerary monuments) and Greek and Roman portraits. The newly expanded decorative arts collection (Upper Level) features furniture, carpets, tapestries, clocks, chandeliers, and small decorative items made for the French, German, and Italian nobility, with a wealth of treasures from French royal households from Louis

XIV to Napoleon, set in period rooms. All major schools of Western art from the late thirteenth to the late nineteenth centuries are represented in the painting collection, which emphasizes Renaissance and Baroque art. The collection includes works by Masaccio, Rembrandt, Rubens, de la Tour, Van Dyck, Gainsborough, and Boucher. Newly added are Old Master drawings, medieval and Renaissance illuminated manuscripts.

The museum itself has an interesting history. Getty began collecting art in the 1930s, concentrating on the three distinct areas that are represented in the museum today: Greek and Roman antiquities, Baroque and Renaissance paintings, and eighteenth-century French decorative arts. In 1946 he purchased a large Spanish-style home on sixty-five acres of land in a canyon just north of Santa Monica, near Los Angeles. In December 1953, the J. Paul Getty Museum was officially established in part of the house to display the many art objects Getty had collected. But by the late 1960s the museum could no longer accommodate Getty's collection. He finally decided to build an entirely new museum building. Completed in 1974, this building and its gardens cover about ten acres of the total Getty property; the remaining fifty-five acres and the original house have been inherited by the museum as part of Getty's estate. Getty's estimated $1.3 billion bequest upon his death in 1976 has appreciated to $2.1 billion with the 1984 takeover by Texaco of Getty Oil.

The new museum building is a recreation of the Villa dei Papiri, a luxurious first-century Roman villa that stood on the slopes of Mount Vesuvius overlooking the Bay of Naples. Located just south of the ancient city of Herculaneum, the villa is thought to have once belonged to Lucius Calpurnius Piso, the father-in-law of Julius Caesar. The two-level, thirty-eight-gallery building and its extensive gardens (which include trees, flowers, shrubs, and herbs that might have grown 2,000 years ago at the Villa dei Papiri) provide an appropriate and harmonious setting for Getty's collection of Greek and Roman antiquities.

The museum offers concerts at 1:30 P.M. the third Thursday of most months in the upstairs Baroque Painting Gallery. Reservations are necessary. The bookstore carries art books, reproductions, calendars, and a variety of scholarly and general-interest publications. A self-service lunch is available in the indoor/outdoor Garden Tea Room. There are no tours but a docent gives 15-minute orientation talks. A weekly events brochure issued at the museum will tell about any scheduled lectures during the day. These are open to all. Open Tuesday through Sunday, year-round, 10:00 A.M. to 5:00 P.M. Closed major holidays. Free. Parking reservations are necessary. They should be made one week in advance by telephoning or writing to the museum's Reservations Office.

Hebrew Union College Skirball Museum. 3077 University at 32nd St. and Hoover St.; 749–3424. The collection comprises Judaic art, Palestinian archaeology, and anthropological material from the Negev Desert. Also in the collection are rare manuscripts, historic coins and medals, ceremonial art, ancient Israeli artifacts, and an extensive display of paintings, graphics, and sculptures. The museum offers a unique opportunity to explore Judaiism and its history and culture through esthetic and material treasures of the Jewish people. The museum itself is of architectural note because of its series of arches representative of the ten commandments. Open Tuesday through Friday, 11:00 A.M. to 4:00 P.M. and Sunday, 10:00 A.M.–5:00 P.M. with public tours at 1:00 P.M. Closed Monday and Saturday. Free.

The Huntington Art Gallery. 1151 Oxford Rd., San Marino; (818) 405–2100. On 207 acres that also include the Huntington Library (see the *Library* section) and the Huntington Botanical Gardens (see the *Garden* section), this art institution is devoted primarily to British and European art of the eighteenth and early nineteenth centuries. French furniture, decorative objects, and sculpture of the same periods are also included in the collection. The collection consists of such world-famous paintings as Gainsborough's *Blue Boy,* Lawrence's *Pinkie,* and Constable's *View on the Stour.* Added in 1984 is the Virginia Steele Scott Gallery for American Art, 1740–1930. The gallery's entry is an orientation center with information kiosks, introductory slide show, and bookstore. Open Tuesday through Sunday, 1:00 P.M. to 4:30 P.M. Reservation tickets required for Sunday only by writing to the address above (zip code 91108). For reservation information, phone (818) 405–2273. Free; voluntary parking donation, $2. Closed major holidays.

Los Angeles County Museum of Art. 5905 Wilshire Blvd.; 937–2590. The museum is a complex of three major buildings—the Ahmanson Gallery, the Frances and Armand Hammer Wing, and the Leo S. Bing Center. The four-story Ahmanson Gallery, built around a central atrium, houses a permanent collection of paintings, sculptures, graphic arts, costumes, textiles, and decorative arts from a wide range of cultures and periods, prehistoric to present plus 20th-century art. Included are works by Picasso, Rembrandt, Veronese, Dürer, Hals, de la Tour, and Homer. One of the Western world's largest collections of Indian, Nepalese, and Tibetan art is housed here. Major changing exhibitions are presented in the Frances and Armand Hammer Wing.

The Robert O. Anderson Building will be completed by fall 1986. This 75,000 sq.-ft. gallery will house 20th-century art from the museum's permanent collection. The new building will increase the museum's available exhibition space by 50 percent. Another addition (planned completion: 1986) is the Pavilion for Far Eastern Art, which will house paintings of the Edo Period (17th-18th centuries).

The Leo S. Bing Center contains the Art Rental Gallery, the Bing Theater, the Art Research Library, and the indoor/outdoor cafeteria-style Plaza Café. The museum offers the community many cultural activities, including film series (with special senior citizens matinees), concerts, lectures, tours of the collections, and student programs. The Art Research Library, with more than 75,000 volumes and an extensive collection of slides, is open for scholarly research. The Museum Shop features a selection of books, magazines, postcards, posters, antiquities, jewelry, and gifts. Open weekdays 10:00 A.M. to 5:00 P.M. and weekends 10:00 A.M. to 6:00 P.M. Closed Mondays, Thanksgiving, Christmas and New Years Day. Adults, $1.50; children, students, and senior citizens, 75¢; children under 5, free. Free admission second Tuesday of each month.

The Natural History Museum of Los Angeles County. 900 Exposition Blvd. in Exposition Park; 744–3411. The fourth largest natural history museum in the United States covers a span of history ranging from the prehistoric to the present. So many aspects of history are presented here that all couldn't possibly be absorbed in one visit. Opened in 1913, the 400,000 sq ft museum contains more than thirty-five halls and galleries displaying permanent as well as special, temporary exhibits. The main building is an attraction in itself. Spanish Renaissance in structure, the museum contains travertine columns, walls, and domes. An inlaid marble floor heightens the overall effect of magnificence. The museum is rich in its collection of prehistoric fossils, both reptile and mammal. It also houses an extensive bird and marine-life exhibit, as well as a vast display on insect life. A brilliant array of stones can be seen in the museum's *Hall of Gems and Minerals.* In addition, the museum features an elaborate taxidermy exhibit of North American and African mammals in their natural habitats. The settings are excellent replicas of the real thing.

Exhibits typifying various cultural groups include pre-Columbian artifacts and a display of crafts from the South Pacific. *The Hall of American History* presents everything from the paraphernalia of prominent historical figures to old American cars.

A gift shop features ethnic arts. Other facilities include a bookstore, free parking except during major Coliseum events, and a cafeteria. Free documentary films are shown every Saturday at 2:00 P.M., and free chamber music concerts are presented every Sunday at 2:00 P.M. Open Tuesday to Sunday, 10:00 A.M. to 5:00 P.M. Closed Monday. Admission: adults, $1.50; senior citizens, students with ID, and children from five to seventeen, 75 cents. Parking is free except during events at the Coliseum when the fee is $5.

Pacific Asia Museum. 46 N. Los Robles Dr., Pasadena; 449-ASIA. Built in the 1920s, this museum is listed in the National Register for Historic Places. Designed in the style of a Chinese imperial palace courtyard, it is highlighted by a traditional Chinese garden. The museum's collection contains a group of objects from Pacific and Asian cultures, including Australia, Japan, and China. Most of the objects are on loan from private collections and other museums; there is a constant flow of changing exhibits. A bookstore and Collectors Gallery shop sell fine art items from members' collections. Tea room for light refreshments. The extensive research library can be used by appointment only. Open Wednesday through Sunday, 12 noon to 5:00 P.M. Admission: adults $1.50; senior citizens, $1; children under 12, free.

George C. Page Museum and **La Brea Discoveries.** 5801 Wilshire Blvd.; 936–2230. A satellite of the Los Angeles County Museum of Natural History, the George C. Page Museum is located at the site of the La Brea Tar Pits formed about 35,000 years ago when deposits of oil rose to the earth's surface, collected in shallow pools, and coagulated into sticky asphalt. Animals fleeing predators stumbled into these pools and became trapped. The deposits have proved to be the richest source of Pleistocene (Ice Age) fossils in the world: Over 100 tons of fossil bones have been removed in the seventy years since excavations began there. Exhibits include reconstructed, life-size skeletons of mammals and birds whose fossils were recovered from the pits—saber-toothed cats, mammoths, wolves, sloths, eagles, and condors. Several large murals and colorful dioramas depicting the history of the Pleistocene are displayed in the well laid out museum building. The glass-enclosed Paleontological Laboratory permits observation of the ongoing cleaning, identification, and cataloging of fossils excavated from the nearby asphalt deposits. *The La Brea Story* and *Dinosaurs, the Terrible Lizards* are short documentary films shown every fifteen minutes or half hour as museum traffic requires. The Children's Concepts Exhibit displays letters and drawings sent by children who have toured this intriguing museum. Open Tuesday through Saturday, 10:00 A.M. to 5:00 P.M. Closed Mondays, Thanksgiving, Christmas and New Year's Day. Admission: adults, $1.50; children, students with ID, and senior citizens, 75 cents. Free admission the second Tuesday of each month.

Norton Simon Museum of Art. 411 W. Colorado Blvd., Pasadena near the junction of the Foothill (I-210) and Ventura (SR-134) Freeways. (818) 449–6840. One of the richest, most extensive and varied collections in Los Angeles, this is an elegant and spacious experience of art appreciation. Businessman Norton Simon reorganized the former Pasadena Museum of Modern Art in 1974 and assembled one of the world's finest collections, richest in its Rembrandts, Goyas, Degas, and Picassos—and dotted with Rodin sculptures throughout.

Rembrandt's development can be traced in three oils— *The Bearded Man in the Wide Brimmed Hat, Self Portrait,* and *Titus.* The most dramatic Goyas are two oils—*St. Jerome* and the portrait of *Dona Francisca Vicenta Chollet y Cabellero.* Down the walnut and steel staircase is the Degas gallery, enriched in 1984 with *Waiting,* a delicate study of two ballerinas, acquired jointly with the Getty Museum. Picasso's renowned *Woman with Book* highlights a comprehensive collection of his paintings, drawings, and sculptures.

Also strong are the museum's Impressionists (van Gogh, Matisse, Cezanne, Monet, Renoir, et al.) and Cubists (Braque, Gris). Older works range from Southeast Asian artworks from 100 B.C., bronze, stone and ivory sculptures from India, Cambodia, Thailand, and Nepal. On loan just until 1986 is the controversial tenth-century Indian bronze *Shivapuran Nataraja,* believed stolen and smuggled out of India but recovered and now guarded by the Indian government.

The museum's wealth of Early Renaissance, Baroque, and Rococo art works could fill an art history book. Church works by Raphael, Guariento, de Paolo, Filipino Lippi, and Lucas Cranach give way to robust Rubens maidens and Dutch landscapes, still lifes and portraits by Frans Hals, Jacob van Ruisdael and Jan Steen. And a magical Tiepolo ceiling highlights the Rococo period.

The bookstore has posters, prints and postcards. There are no dining facilities. Open Thurs.–Sun. from noon to 6:00 P.M. Admission: adults, $2; students and senior citizens, 75 cents. General admission on Sundays: $3. Admission includes free art reproduction from the collection.

Southwest Museum. 234 Museum Dr.; 221–2163. One of the oldest museums west of the Mississippi and one of the finest collections of American Indian art and artifacts, this California Mission-style museum commands a spectacular view of the city from atop Mt. Washington. Four cultural halls: California, Northwest Coast, Plains and the newly renovated Southwest Hall strong in

Navajo rugs and Pueblo pottery. Open Tuesday-Saturday, 11:00 A.M.-5:00 P.M. and Sunday, 1:00 P.M.-5:00 P.M. Admission: adults, $1.50; students and senior citizens, $1; children 7–18, 75 cents.

OTHER MUSEUMS

Kidspace. 390 South El Molino, Pasadena; 818–449–9143. A participatory museum for the younger generation, including its own television studio where kids can see themselves perform in commercials and news shows; computers; a Ranger spacecraft; grown-up occupation uniforms to try on; and the most popular, Human Habitrail, a tunnel-and-maze experience comparable to the adjacent ant colony. Open October–June on Saturday and Sunday, 11:00 A.M. –4:00 P.M., Wednesday, 3:00–5:00 P.M.; June–September on Tuesday–Sunday, 11:00 A.M.–2:00 P.M. Admission: ages 2–65, $2; senior citizens, and groups of 10 or more, $1.50.

The Los Angeles Children's Museum. 310 N. Main St. in the Los Angeles Mall; 687–8800. A large, modern museum of educational toys and children's books featuring a new Health Education Learning Project with simulated ambulance, doctor's office, and emergency room. Winter hours: Saturday and Sunday, 10:00 A.M.–5:00 P.M.; Wednesday and Thursday, 2:30–5:00 P.M. Summer hours: Monday–Friday, 11:30 A.M.–5:00 P.M.; Saturday and Sunday, 10:00 A.M.–5:00 P.M. Summer hours are observed during school vacations. Admission $2.75 for all.

Museum of Contemporary Art (MoCA). 152 N. Central at 1st St.; 382-MOCA. The only major U.S. museum in recent decades dedicated to art and culture of the last forty years. No permananet collection but continuously changing exhibitions of first-quality international art with special emphasis on West Coast artists. Now housed in a 1940s warehouse in downtown's Little Tokyo (appropriately called the Temporary Contemporary), MoCA will move into an exciting and controversial modern space at Third and Grand in early 1986, a focal point of the Bunker Hill redevelopment area. Open Mon. and Wed.–Sun., 11:00 A.M.–6:00 P.M. Admission: adults, $3; students 12–21 and senior citizens, $1.50; children under 12, free. The museum is free to all after 6 P.M.

Pasadena Historical Society and Museum. 470 W. Walnut St., Pasadena; 577–1660. Housed in the former Finnish Consulate (built in 1905) are original furnishings, antiques, and paintings owned by the Feynes–Paloheimo family. The art features works by Carl Oscar Borg, William Keith, and Benjamin Brown. Also on the premises is the Finnish Folk Art Museum in the Finlandia Gardens, with folk art and antique furnishings. Open Tuesday, Thursday, and the last Sunday of the month from 1:00 P.M. to 4:00 P.M. Admission is $2.00.

Will Rogers State Historic Park Western Art Collection. 14253 Sunset Blvd., Pacific Palisades; 454–8212. Each of the thirty-one rooms in this house once owned by the humorist Will Rogers is packed with examples of Western art, including works by Charles Bell, Charles Russell, Howard Chandler Christy, and Ed Borein. Indian crafts are also abundant here. (See the *Parks* section.) Open from 10:00 A.M.–5:00 P.M., daily. Admission: $2.00 per vehicle; 50 cents for dogs.

SPECIAL-INTEREST MUSEUMS

The California Afro-American Museum. 700 State Dr. in Exposition Park; 744–7432. Built just in time for the 1984 Olympics, its three galleries cover the visual and performing arts and the history and culture of Black Americans, with attention to Caribbean, Latin American, and African influences. Glass-enclosed sculpture court; gift shop; children's workshops every other weekend by reservation. Open daily 10:00 A.M.–5:00 P.M. Free.

Dunbar Museum of Black Culture and History. 4233 S. Central Ave., Los Angeles; 233–7168. On the site of the Dunbar Hotel (named for the poet Paul Dunbar), this was America's first hotel built by and for Black people. Dedicated as a museum in 1976, it portrays the Black experience in America. Hours: By appointment only. Free.

The Forest Lawn Museum. at 1712 S. Glendale Ave., Glendale; 254–3131. A small museum of original art and reproductions of art masterpieces. Included are works by Michelangelo, Frederic Remington, Charles Russell, and Jesse Beasley. Open 8:00 A.M. to 5:00 P.M., daily. Free but donations accepted.

Hollywood Studio Museum (originally called the Lasky Barn). In Hollywood across from the Hollywood Bowl; 874-BARN. Hollywood's first major film-company studio, where Cecil B. DeMille produced the first feature-length film, *The Squaw Man.* In 1927, the barn became Paramount Pictures, with the original company of Jesse Lasky, Cecil B. De Mille, and Samuel Goldwyn. The museum shows the origin of the motion-picture industry. Open 10:00 A.M.–4:30 P.M. daily.

Hollywood Wax Museum. 6767 Hollywood Blvd., Hollywood; 462–8860. Opened some forty years ago. Trailers of Academy Award films are shown in the Oscar Movie Theater. Open Sunday through Thursday, 10:00 A.M. to 12 midnight; Friday and Saturday, 10:00 A.M. to 2:00 A.M. Admission: adults, $5; senior citizens and service personnel, $3.50; children 6–12, $2; under 6 free with adult.

Museum of Rock Art. 6834 Hollywood Blvd. opposite Mann's Chinese Theater; 463–8979. Relocated in 1984 to greatly enlarged quarters, this four-year-old museum features rock music of note and album cover art in exhibits changing every four to six weeks. A 60-seat Video Theater shows early rock concerts, interviews and old television shows. Open 10:00 A.M.–midnight. Admission. $4.50 except children under 12—$2.

Simon Wiesenthal Center Holocaust Museum. At the Yeshiva University of Los Angeles, 9760 West Pico Blvd.; 553–9036 or 553–4478. Audio visuals, graphics, photomurals, and other exhibits portray the events of Nazi Germany from 1933 to 1945. A mechanized information center answers common questions about this period. Lectures and public outreach program. Open Monday through Thursday, 10:30 A.M. to 4:30 P.M.; Friday, 10:30 A.M. to 2:30 P.M.; Sunday, 11:00 A.M. to 4:00 P.M. Free.

Wells Fargo History Museum. 444 South Flower Street, Los Angeles; 683–7166. More than 1,000 items on display cover more than 130 years of Wells Fargo history. Old West artifacts, fine art, photographs, documents, and famous collections are arranged in five areas depicting the evolution of Wells Fargo. Hours: Monday through Friday, 9:00 A.M. to 4:00 P.M. Closed on bank holidays. Admission free.

MOVIE THEATERS. Spending two hours in a movie while visiting Los Angeles is not, as one might think, taking time out from sightseeing. Some of the most historic and beautiful theaters in the country are found here. They host first-run and revival films worth seeing if only to visit the famed movie places.

Perhaps the most celebrated movie theater in the world, *Mann's Chinese Theater,* 6925 Hollywood Blvd.; 464–8111, preserves the legend of Hollywood in cement. Formerly owned by Sid Grauman, the Chinese pagoda structure still carries out the oldest of Hollywood traditions, the hand- and foot-printing ceremony.

From Burt Reynolds to *Star Wars'* robots C3PO and R2D2, today's stars are immortalized in the spirit of Sid Grauman, who founded the theater in 1927. There are many stories about the origin of the ritual. The one most frequently circulated is that Norma Talmadge was the first to leave her impression in cement when she accidentally stepped onto the wet pavement while attending the theater's grand opening in 1927. The romantic tale is faithful only to the stuff of which Hollywood legends are made; the truth being that the imprinting rite was actually inspired by the mason who supervised the construction of the theater's forecourt.

Grauman came upon Jean W. Klossner, a French immigrant, as he put his handprint in wet cement near the marquee after he finished laying the entrance to the theater. A descendent of generations of French masons, Klossner explained that his father, grandfather, and great-grandfather had placed their handprints and signatures at the curbstone of Notre Dame in Paris to mark their contributions to civilization. Inspired by Klossner's family tradition, Grauman immediately offered the Frenchman a thirty-four-year contract to place the imprints of Hollywood's greatest stars in the secret cement mixture that Klossner had devised to stand the test of time.

Mary Pickford and Douglas Fairbanks were the first to place their hand- and footprints at the entrance to the theater at the grand opening ceremonies on May 18, 1927. Today the Chinese houses three movies and still hosts many of Hollywood's gala premieres.

Also owned by Sid Grauman was the great *Egyptian Theater* down the street at 6712 Hollywood Blvd.; 467–6167. Built before the Chinese in 1922, this theater was the site of many premieres. Now run by United Artists, the theater features a triple-screen facility for first-run movies, and the lobby maintains the ornate Egyptian decor for which it was made famous.

A contrast to Grauman's theaters is the *Cinerama Dome* on Sunset Blvd., one block west of Gower Gulch; 466–3401. This futuristic, geodesic structure was the first theater designed specifically for Cinerama in the United States. The gigantic screen and multitrack sound system create an unparalleled cinematic experience.

Movie listings are advertised daily in the Calendar section of *The Los Angeles Times* and the Style section of *The Herald Examiner.* Capsule reviews and schedules are also found in *The LA Weekly* and *LA Reader,* two free weekly publications stacked in coffee shops and book and record store entrances. The most common price of admission to first-run movies, as of this writing, is $5.00.

The less prestigious movie houses usually offer a double bill for a good price. They may not feature first-run engagements, but chances are you'll find two movies close in theme (SciFi, suspense, romance, etc.) sharing a bill at the Chinese only months before. In Hollywood: the *Fairfax 1, 2, 3,* 7907 Beverly Blvd., Fairfax, 653–3117; the *Gordon,* La Brea and Melrose, 934–2944; the *Oriental,* 7425 Sunset Blvd.; 876–0212, and *Pan Pacific,* 7554 Beverly Blvd.; 938–7070. These theaters house interesting films that you might not have felt warranted the $5.00 admission upon their release but can't be passed up for $2.50. The same bargain can be found in West Los Angeles and the Wilshire district at the *Clinton,* 526 N. Western; 461–3064; *Culver 1,2,3,* 9820 W. Washington Blvd.; 838–1893; the *Palms,* 3751 Motor; 837–7171. The *Aero* in Santa Monica on Montana at 14th St.; 395–4990, and the *Brentwood 1 and 2,* in Brentwood, 2524 Wilshire Blvd.; 829–3366, are comparable theaters found on the West side. The environment at these theaters varies from architecturally unique to not so desirable, but the price is the draw.

Los Angeles art houses bill revival, foreign films, and animation festivals on neon-decorated marquees preserved to convey the original feeling of the neighborhood movie theaters. On the West side, the *Nuart,* 11272 Santa Monica; 478–6379, the *Fox Venice,* 620 Lincoln; 396–4215, and the *Beverly Cinema,* 7165 Beverly Blvd.; 938–4038, celebrate Hollywood's greatest with mini-film festivals featuring certain directors or performers, controversial documentaries, or notable foreign films. The *Rialto Theater,* S. Pasadena, 1023 S. Fair Oaks Blvd.; 799–9567, is a richly decorated, spacious house that has not been converted into multiscreen theaters as have most large, older theaters in town. The *Vagabond Theater,* 2509 Wilshire Blvd.; 387–2171, specializes in musicals and vintage drama and comedy films. Programs change daily, though theme and foreign film festivals run one night a week over a six- to eight-week period.

In Hollywood the sixty-year-old *Vista Theater,* 4473 Sunset Dr. (Sunset Blvd. at Hillhurst Ave.); 660–6639, like other neighborhood houses, runs nostalgic double bills and special late shows of trendy films on weekends. For the past four years the *Nuart* and *Fox Venice* have been the homes of such midnight cult classics as *The Rocky Horror Picture Show, Pink Flamingos,* and *Eraserhead.*

Melnitz Hall at UCLA runs a mixture of the old, the avant-garde, and the neglected. And the true film purist should definitely check out the Los Angeles County Museum of Art's *Bing Theater,* at 5905 Wilshire Blvd.; 857–6201. It regularly runs exhaustive tributes to greats from America cinema, obtains the finest prints available, and provides well-researched program notes for all their double bills. Call for programs; admission price is $3.00. No talking or eating allowed during the films, which are presented for serious filmgoers, who prefer to watch without interruptions.

The Laemmle Theaters host the best of the latest foreign releases. *The Music Hall,* 9036 Wilshire Blvd., Beverly Hills; 274–6869 and the *Royal Theater* in West L.A., 11523 Santa Monica Blvd.; 477–5581; *Los Feliz,* 1822 N. Vermont; 664–2169; *Continental,* 5308 Melrose Ave., 461–4112; and downtown, the *Grande Fourplex,* 349 S. Figueroa St. In addition, the fourteen-theater *Cineplex* (652–7767) in the Beverly Center, 8522 Beverly Blvd., offers foreign films and first-run features.

Los Angeles is a twelve-month film festival because of its variety of theaters and unique programs. Each year the Filmex Society brings innovative and controversial films to the capital of the film industry by presenting the *Los Angeles International Film Exposition.* The nonprofit organization was founded in 1971 by a number of industry faithfuls, including director George Cukor and actress Rosalind Russell. The annual event runs in the spring, usually March and April. Main office located at 2021 N. Western Avenue. Call (213) 856–7707.

DANCE. Despite the fact that the Los Angeles Ballet went bankrupt in 1984, the L.A. dance community has taken a *grand jeté* in the past couple of years. In addition to Los Angeles's own Bella Lewitsky, yearly visiting dance companies include the Joffrey, American Ballet Theatre, Martha Graham, and Paul Taylor, to name a few. The Los Angeles Area Dance Alliance (LAADA) has provided facilities to showcase the cities' myriad of local companies.

The Music Center (135 N. Grand; 972–7211) is the western home of Robert Joffrey's bicoastal ballet company. In February and September you'll find the company dancing a full range of works from the elegant *pas de trois Monotones* to the full production of *Les Patineurs.* The yearly *Folk Dance Festival* is held in March. **The Shrine Auditorium** (649 W. Jefferson; 800–472–2272) hosts the American Ballet Theatre (ABT) in March. ABT's repertoire includes Baryshnikov's *Cinderella* and Saint Leon's classic *Coppelia.*

UCLA Center for the Arts (405 N. Hilgard; 825–9261) attracts masters of modern dance, jazz, and ballet, including Martha Graham, Bella Lewitsky, Paul Taylor, Hubbard Street Dance Company, and Bejart, along with its own UCLA Dance Company. Rush tickets priced at $5 are available on the night of the performance for full-time students and senior citizens.

Locally, LAADA (465–1100) brings to the **Pilot Theatre** (6600 Santa Monica Blvd.) a choreographer's dance exchange for local companies throughout the year. And, in June, at the **John Anson Ford** outdoor theatre (2850 Cahuenga Blvd. E.) is *Dance Kaleidoscope,* a showing of local companies on a much larger scale. At both theatres you'll find inexpensive tickets from $6 to $9.

Most dance events in Los Angeles will be listed each Sunday in the *Los Angeles Times* calendar section, and LAADA is always helpful with dance information. You can reach the LAADA at 465–1100.

The visiting dancer will find that Los Angeles has an abundance of worthwhile dance studios throughout the city. Here are a few of the major ones; they offer everything from ballet and jazz to tap and modern: The *Debbie Reynolds Studio* in the San Fernando Valley (6514 Lankershim Blvd.; 985–3193); the *Dupree Dance Academy,* Hollywood (8115 W. 3rd St.; 655–0336); the *Marinaccio School of Dance,* Hollywood (6535 Santa Monica Blvd.; 462–1816); the *Stanley Holden Dance Center,* Westwood (10521 W. Pico Blvd.; 475–1725); and *Studio A* in the Los Feliz/Silverlake area (1947 N. Hillhurst Ave.; 661–8311).

MUSIC. Los Angeles is no doubt the focus of America's contemporary music scene. Hundreds of recording studios and over twenty record companies are headquartered here. Performers and songwriters from all over the world converge on the city seeking gold-record manna in this musical mecca. As a result, the hills around Hollywood are quite literally alive with the sound of live music.

The Los Angeles Times Calendar section provides a daily listing of current as well as upcoming events, as does the Style section of *The Herald Examiner.* The *Times'* Sunday Calendar and the *Herald's* Friday Weekend sections are expanded forms that provide considerably more detail. There are also helpful listings of the wide variety of musical goings-on in southern California in *The LA Weekly, The LA Reader, Los Angeles* and *California* magazines. (All phone numbers listed, unless otherwise indicated, are in the 213 area code.)

CLASSICAL AND OPERA

After years of being regarded as a cultural invalid, Los Angeles has finally come into its own as a center for the performing arts.

The Music Center, 135 N. Grand Ave.; 972–7211, was opened less than twenty years ago and, along with the Hollywood Bowl, is the center of the city's classical music scene. The Music Center can be reached from the Hollywood Freeway (Route 101): northbound, exit on Grand Street, turn right. The Center is about a block and a half away; southbound, exit on Temple Street, turn left, then turn right on Grand Street. If traveling south on the Pasadena Freeway, exit on Hill Street, go through Chinatown, make a right on Temple, than a left on Grand.

Within the Music Center is the 3,000-seat *Dorothy Chandler Pavilion* (winter home of the Los Angeles Philharmonic and the showcase for the Los Angeles Master Chorale Group, the Los Angeles Civic Light Opera, and, in the fall, the Joffrey Ballet), the *Mark Taper Forum,* and the *Ahmanson Theater.* The Hollywood Bowl, 2301 Highland Ave. (850–2000 or 850–2060), is the Philharmonic's summer home.

Dorothy Chandler, wife of former *Los Angeles Times* publisher Norman Chandler, is the acknowledged prime mover behind the creation of the Music Center. *The Dorothy Chandler Pavilion,* opened in 1964, is noted for its outstanding acoustics, lighting, and staging capabilities. The building is rich with marble walls, sculptured columns, and crystal chandeliers. Facing the Pavilion across a reflecting pool is the 742-seat *Mark Taper Forum,* which features drama, recitals, and lectures. The 2,071-seat *Ahmanson Theater* presents musicals, ballet, and drama as well.

The Hollywood Bowl, open since 1920, is one of the world's largest natural amphitheaters. In a park surrounded by mountains, trees, and gardens, it is said to be acoustically perfect. A night at the Hollywood Bowl can be filled with fun, glamour, and romance. Summer concertgoers usually arrive early, bringing or buying picnic suppers. Picnic tables are available throughout the area, and box seat subscribers can reserve a table right in their own box. Dining styles range from eating picnic sandwiches while sprawled on a blanket to elaborate culinary feasts atop fancy tablecloths adorned with flowers, candelabras, crystal, and fine china. Restaurant dining is available on the grounds (reservations recommended). Call (213) 851–3588 for information. Concerts under the stars begin at 8:30 P.M. The seats are wooden, and so you may want to bring or rent a cushion. A convenient way to enjoy the Hollywood Bowl experience without the hassle of parking is to take one of the Park-and-Ride buses, which leave from various locations around town; call 856–5400 for information. If you're driving, there may be a short walk to the theater; wear comfortable shoes and bring a sweater. The Hollywood Bowl can be reached from the Hollywood Freeway (Route 101): northbound, exit at Highland Ave., make a right onto Highland, and a left into the Bowl; southbound, exit at Highland Ave., make a left onto Highland, and a left into the Bowl.

The Los Angeles Philharmonic, over sixty years old, puts on a powerful performance under the musical direction of its conductor, Carlo Maria Guilini. Guilini was preceded by Zubin Mehta, who conducted here from 1962 to 1978. Recognized as one of the greatest symphony orchestras in the country, the Philharmonic performs at its winter home, the Dorothy Chandler Pavilion in the Music Center, from November to April and at its summer home, the Hollywood Bowl, from July through September. Prices usually range from $6.00 to $22.00 a seat at the Chandler and from $1.00 to $27.50 at the Bowl.

The Los Angeles Civic Light Opera sponsors productions at the Dorothy Chandler Pavilion from May through October.

The Los Angeles Chamber Music Society, formed in 1977, has been growing steadily: The number of concerts has increased yearly. Members of the Los Angeles Philharmonic Orchestra are featured along with guest musicians.

Other concert halls include *The Ambassador Auditorium,* Pasadena, 300 W. Green St.; 304–6161. This theater matches the Dorothy Chandler in its elegance and tone. World-renowned soloists and groups perform here from September to May.

The Shrine Auditorium, 665 W. Jefferson Blvd.; 749–5123, was built in 1926 by the Al Malaikah Temple, and the undeniably unique decor could be termed

Basic Baghdad and Beyond. Touring companies from all over the world, along with assorted gospel and choral groups, appear here. When the silent French film epic *Napoleon* toured the country with a live orchestra a while back, its Los Angeles performances were in this one-of-a-kind, 6,400-seat theater.

The Wilshire Ebell Theater, 4401 W. Eighth St.; 939–1128, is a Renaissance-style building, Spanish in architecture and design, which was built in 1924. The Los Angeles Opera Theatre comes here as do a broad spectrum of other musical performers.

Royce Hall at UCLA; 825–9261, features internationally acclaimed performers in its 2,000-seat auditorium. The university's *Schoenberg Hall,* smaller but with wonderful acoustics, hosts a variety of concerts as well.

Wiltern Theater, at Wilshire and Western (380–5005), reopened in 1985 as a venue for the Los Angeles Opera Theater. The building was constructed in 1930, is listed in the National Register of Historic Places, and is a striking example of Art Deco in its green terra-cotta glory.

If you're looking for a complete cultural experience, don't miss the *LA Street Scene Festival;* 626–0485. Sponsored by the Joseph Schlitz Brewing Company, the event began in 1978 and is held the second week in October in the Civic Center Area. Ten square blocks around City Hall in downtown Los Angeles are closed to traffic. Stages are built, and the public is invited—for free. It is an event that features new talents (for the perusal of record company executives) and established performers, such as Chuck Berry and Helen Reddy, and veteran ensembles such as the Los Angeles Philharmonic. In addition, there are strolling Mariachi bands, soul groups, and enough ethnic food to feed a United Nations picnic.

For complete information on performances, check the listings in the aforementioned publications.

THE GREAT OUTDOORS

Located on the way in to Griffith Park, *The Greek Theater,* 2700 N. Vermont Ave.; 642–3888, offers concerts under the stars from June to October. It features everything from popular to classical music. Its Doric columns evoke the amphitheaters of ancient Greece.

The Hollywood Bowl, 2301 Highland Ave.; 856–5400, seats four times as many people as the Greek does, which means around 17,000 picnic baskets. Tucked at the base of the Hollywood Hills, it is one of the most venerable of Los Angeles's bona fide landmarks. (For more information on the Bowl, see the *Classical and Opera* section.)

ROCK

The Roxy, 9009 Sunset Blvd., 276–2222, is Los Angeles's most elegant music-industry showcase. Decorated in an Art-Deco style, this hot spot offers legitimate and performance theater as well as rock 'n' roll.

Gazzarri's, 9039 Sunset Blvd.; 273–6606, is one of the Sunset Strip's senior citizens. Teenagers frequent the club, as their parents did in the early 1960s.

Up-and-coming talent is showcased on Tuesday and Thursday nights; local bands are featured on the weekend. There are two stages and dance areas.

Doug Weston's Troubador, 9081 Santa Monica Blvd.; 276–6168, may be best known as the favorite hangout in the 1960s for many singers who helped define the Los Angeles sound: among others, Jackson Browne, Linda Ronstadt, and individual members of the Eagles before they took flight. Although the club does not now command nearly the attention it once did, it has achieved a certain landmark status.

Madame Wong's Restaurant, 900 N. Broadway in Chinatown; 624–5346, is perhaps the most exotic club in town but not the safest. In addition to housing a curious assortment of Oriental antiques, the thatched hut stage decor inherited from earlier times is best described as Early Hawaiian. There are two shows each night of state-of-the-art rock and roll. *Madame Wong's West,* 2900 Wilshire Blvd.; 829–7361 or 828–4444, offers the same musical menu in not nearly as bizarre surroundings. Madame Wong West attracts a college crowd and is tamer than the original. What it lacks in atmosphere it more than compensates for with a downstairs area that features an assortment of video games, pinball, two cocktail bars, and a disco where you can boogie to local bands.

Lingerie Club, 6507 Sunset Blvd.; 466–8557, is one of the newest and hottest spots on the circuit. Curiously enough, the building has been around for ages in variously divergent nightclub incarnations. The consensus now is that the current Lingerie identity will be around for quite a while. With a couple of bars, an upstairs lounge eminently suitable for lounging, and a spacious dance floor, the place is terrific. Shows begin at 9:00. The somewhat eclectic music it presents is a pleasing combination of rock, reggae, rhythm and blues, and New Wave.

The Country Club, 18415 Sherman Way, Reseda; (818) 881–9800, is one of the newer venues in the area. The sound is superb and it's a delight to listen to such a wide spectrum of music.

The Forum, Manchester and Prairie Ave., Inglewood; 673–1300, one of the largest indoor facilities in Los Angeles, attracts such superstar acts as the Rolling Stones, Fleetwood Mac and Michael Jackson. It is also home of Lakers basketball and Kings hockey. The *Santa Monica Civic Auditorium,* 1855 Main St.; 393–9961, former home of the Academy Awards, is the most intimate of the local concert halls, even though it can accommodate thousands of people.

Another place provoking some historical curiosity is *The Hollywood Palladium,* 6215 Sunset Blvd.; 466–4311, which has been swinging with swing music for over forty years. You can still hear big bands playing there, but now Latin dance music and New Wave bands are also featured. This is where Lawrence Welk used to perform on New Year's Eve.

The *Universal Amphitheater,* Universal City; (818) 980–9421, received a $20-million face-lift in 1982 that transformed it into a spectacular, state-of-the-art hall. A roof was put on the highly successful amphitheater, which has increased the number of shows produced annually. Pop concerts, including heavy emphasis on rock, make up 70 percent of the schedule; the remainder fall into the categories of ballet and legitimate theater. Beautiful fountains enhance the amphitheater's new look, which has to be seen to be appreciated. The capacity is 6,200, an expansion of 1,000 seats.

The Universal Amphitheater was first used in the early 1970s as part of the Universal Studios Tour where stunt shows were performed. Today the arena offers year-round scheduling of big-name talent. The new amphitheater seems to sell out quickly, despite its increase in size. Check local listings and order in advance for any acts that you really don't want to miss.

JAZZ

Los Angeles features some of the best jazz concerts around. *The Playboy Jazz Festival* is presented at the Hollywood Bowl; 850–2000, every June. It features a two-day lineup of jazz greats.

Donte's Jazz Supper Club, 4269 Lankershim Blvd.; (818) 769–1566, presents a mixture of the clearly and nearly famous. Chuck Mangione got his start here. Steak and seafood are offered at special dining tables. The show begins at 9:30 P.M. The club is closed on Sundays.

The Baked Potato, 3787 Cahuenga Blvd., West; (818) 980–1615, is so named because of the many ways they serve this particular tuber. Top jazzmen such as Tom Scott and Larry Carlton played some of their first gigs here. Shows begin at 10:00 P.M. Go early, stay late (last show at midnight). No reservations.

Marla'a Memory Lane supper club, 2323 W. Martin Luther King, Jr., Blvd.; 294–8430. Blues and jazz predominate here. Local favorites as well as top-name entertainers. Versatile dinner menu.

At My Place, 1026 Wilshire Blvd., Santa Monica; 451–8596. R&B shares the bill at this jazz joint where a 1930s style dominates. Several shows each night.

One of the real veteran jazz clubs that continually has appealing performers is the *Lighthouse* in Hermosa Beach on 30 Pier Ave.; 372–6911. Open Tuesday through Sunday, the place may look like a bit like a dive, but the music is divine.

You can find Horace Silver, Milt Jackson, and Carmen McRae at *Concerts by the Sea* at Fisherman's Wharf in Redondo Beach; 379–4998. An elegant little theater complete with chandeliers and red carpeting, the club is the top of every local jazz fan's list. The only thing bad about the place is that it's closed Monday through Wednesday.

COUNTRY AND WESTERN

Quite simply, *The Palomino,* 6907 Lankershim Blvd.; 764–4010, is *the* place. Three decades of national renown have brought everyone from Jerry Lee Lewis to Emmylou Harris here. Even if you're only remotely interested in country and western music, take this brief bit of advice: go.

McCabe's, 3101 Pico Blvd.; 828–4497, is living proof that the 1960s are not completely over. Although the emphasis is primarily on folk, you can also hear jazz, blues, and even pop music here. Doc Watson, Tom Waits, and John Fahey have passed through and return now and again, along with many other top folk folks. You can savor homemade cakes, along with herbal teas, during intermission.

STAGE. Some say that Los Angeles has become "the Broadway of the West." The scope of theater here does not really begin to compare to that of the Great White Way, but there is a uniqueness of the offerings in this vast entertainment-oriented city that is worth any visitor's while.

The growth is astounding. In 1978 only about 370 professional productions were brought to stages in Los Angeles, whereas in 1982 more than 600 were scheduled. Small theaters are blossoming all over town, and the larger houses, despite price hikes accelerating to $35.00 for a single ticket, are full more times than not.

An important aspect of Los Angeles theater to keep in mind while searching the Calendar section of *The Los Angeles Times* or *The Herald Examiner's* "Style" section for an appealing choice is that even the smallest productions might boast the biggest names in "the Business" (Los Angeles's entertainment empire). Film and television actors love to work on the stage between "big" projects as a way to refresh their talents or regenerate their creativity. Working on the stage can indeed be a more demanding exercise than working in television and film, and taking a job in the legitimate theater represents a way for these actors and actresses to get back in touch with their craft. Also, since stage work is so different from film and television work (often done piecemeal, with no sense of sequence or time), it is the perfect busman's holiday.

Those hoping for their chance in television and film are also happy to be on stage in a legitimate Los Angeles theater. It is an excellent way to be seen by those who matter in the more glitzy end of show business. Through plays and showcases many casting agents, producers, and directors find the talent that they need for their next projects. Hence a need for not only large houses—which usually mount productions that are road-company imports of established Broadway hits or, on occasion, the place where Broadway-bound material begins its initial tryout phase—but also a host of small, intimate, sometimes out-of-the-way theaters for the talent that abounds in this city.

Ticket agents operate in Los Angeles. Try Murray's Tickets at 213–234–8335; Good Time Tickets at 213–464–7383; Ticketron at 231–642–3888; Teletron at 213–410–1062; or Al Brooks at 213–626–5863.

A good showcase of free performances and events for travelers on a budget: the Los Angeles Theater Center, 1089 S. Spring Street (213–488–1122).

To give you a feel for theater in Los Angeles, the following sampling includes some of the largest houses in the area:

Mayfair Theater, 214 Santa Monica Blvd., Santa Monica; 451–0621. This charming 282-seat house is decorated in an Old World style to highlight the many live revues that are staged there. Once an opera house, the Mayfair (built in 1911) once echoed the voices of many famous European performers. Ticket prices range from $10.00 to $22.50; MC and V are accepted.

Westwood Playhouse, 10866 Le Conte Ave, Westwood; 208–6500. The basic architecture of this 498-seat house is Egyptian, with mosaics and columns decorating the walls. An acoustically superior theater. Sightlines are perfect anywhere in the house. This playhouse prefers to be known as the theater of events, where new plays are generally showcased; primarily musicals and comedies in the summer. Most productions come in from Broadway; however, two—*Perfectly Frank* and *Passionate Ladies*—went on *to* Broadway. Jason Robards and Nick Nolte both got their start at this playhouse. Ticket prices range from $17.50 to $25.00. All major credit cards are accepted.

Ahmanson Theater, 135 N. Grand Ave.; 241–9413 or 246–7165. Part of a three-theater complex (with the Dorothy Chandler Pavilion and the Mark Taper Forum), this is a modern structure made of stone and mosaic. Material presented here under direction of Robert Fryer includes both classics and new plays. The list of distinguished artists who have worked at this theater reads like a Who's Who of stage and screen. 2,071 seats. Prices for tickets range from $5.00 to $18.00, and all major credit cards are accepted.

Dorothy Chandler Pavilion, 135 N. Grand Ave.; 972–7211. Also part of the Music Center, this 3,200-seat house offers a smattering of plays in between performances of the Los Angeles Philharmonic. The theater opened in 1964. Tickets range from $15.00 to $35.00, and all major credit cards are accepted.

Mark Taper Forum, 601 W. Temple; 972–7353; charge-line, 972–7654. Also part of the three-piece Music Center complex, this house boasts 742 seats and excellent acoustics in an intimate setting. The theater, under Gordon Davidson, is committed to new works and to the development of a community of artists. Opened in 1964. Many plays, including *Children of a Lesser God,* have gone on to Broadway from the Mark Taper.

Huntington Hartford, 1615 N. Vine St., Hollywood; 462–6666; charge line, 851–9750. Centrally located in the heart of Hollywood, this house offers an intimate feeling despite its large capacity (1,038 seats). New plays, dramas, comedies, and musicals are presented here throughout the year. Tickets cost from $15.00 to $20.00; MC and V are accepted.

John Anson Ford Theater, 2580 Cahuenga Blvd.; 972–7428. This theater was built to show pilgrimage plays primarily, and the setting resembled the environment of Jerusalem. Today it is known for its Shakespeare and free summer jazz and ballet concerts. There is no general box office; fees depend on the company performing, and most summer presentations are free. Seating is 1,300.

Shubert Theater, 2020 Ave. of the Stars, Century City; 553–9000; Broadway musicals are usually on stage here in this 1,824-seat house. All major credit cards are accepted; tickets cost from $16.50 to $32.50.

Pantages, 6233 Hollywood Blvd.; 460–4411. Once the home of the Oscar telecast and big Hollywood premiers, this house is massive (2,300 seats) and splendid. Musicals direct from Broadway are usually presented here. Stars such as Yul Brynner, Mickey Rooney, Ann Miller, and most recently Sandy Duncan have appeared at the Pantages, an elaborate place that has one failing—less than perfect acoustics. Tickets run from $15.00 to $35.00. MC, V accepted.

Wilshire Theater, 8440 Wilshire Blvd., Beverly Hills; 653–4490. The interior of the Wilshire Theater, a 1,900-seat house, is decorated in Art Deco and is located in a very nice section of town; there are many restaurants in the area. Musicals from Broadway are usually the fare here. Newly renovated. Tickets range from $14.50 to $27.50. MC, V accepted.

Smaller houses are more specialized in their offerings. Here are a few:

Groundling Theater, 7307 Melrose Ave.; 934–4747. Satirical sketches are the kinds of performances that you're likely to witness here. This theater is best categorized as a comedy/improvisional house. Larraine Newman (of "*Saturday Night Live*" fame) and other comedians got their start here, which is a showcase for comics. Ticket prices range from $6.50 to $10.50.

Fountain Theater, 5060 Fountain Ave.; 669–9306 or 1525. Seating 80, this theater presents contemporary drama and comedies. Marianne Mearser and Rob Reiner both got their starts here. Most actors and actresses come here from television to do theater and then leave and go on to film work. Prices for tickets are from $7.00 to $8.00.

Japan America Theater, 244 South San Pedro, Los Angeles; 628–2725, for information; 680–3700 for the box office. This community-oriented, 880-seat theater is at the Japan Cultural Arts Center. It is home to Kabuki troupes, local Japanese koto recitals, the East West Players, and numerous children's-theater groups.

Cast Theater, 804 N. El; 462–9872. Musicals, revivals, and avant-garde improvisional pieces are done here. The production of *Working* was picked up for PBS from this house, whereas *The Hasty Heart* went on to the Ahmanson from here.

Globe Playhouse, 1107 N. Kings Rd.; 654–5623. A replica of the original Shakespeare Globe Playhouse, this theater is the only one in the world to have produced all Shakespeare's works. Most performers from Broadway come to the Globe, and then leave and go on to either film or television. Talia Shire and John Ritter got their starts here. Tickets are priced from $8.50 to $12.50.

Some other ninety-nine-seat houses (comparable to Off-Broadway) are *Cast at the Circle,* 804 N. El Centro Ave., Los Angeles; 462–0265; *Cast-at-the-Hyperion,* 1835 Hyperion Ave., Los Angeles; 661–9188; *Pilot Theater I and II,* 6600 Santa Monica Blvd., Los Angeles; 469–6600; *Hollywood Actor's Theater,* 715 N. Cahuenga Blvd., Los Angeles; 464–0300; *On the Fringe Theater,* 3709 Sunset Blvd.; 667–9556.

SHOPPING. Unlike New York, with its Fifth and Madison Avenues and Herald Square, and London, with its Bond and Oxford Streets, Los Angeles is a hodgepodge when it comes to shopping. Rodeo Drive comes to mind as the one recognizable shopping thoroughfare, but compared to the others, it is extremely short. Several cities or areas, with various shopping sections in each, exist within metropolitan Los Angeles. It can get very confusing.

For instance, you may ask someone where such and such a shop is and they may answer, "the Valley." Not much of a clue. Then they may add, "On Ventura Blvd." Still not much help since Ventura Blvd. runs for more than twenty miles from Universal City to Calabasas.

As you can see, the area covered by shopping in Los Angeles is staggering. But once you have followed some of the leads, through word-of-mouth suggestions or newspaper advertisements, you'll discover there is almost anything to be had in Los Angeles from a slew of imaginative and innovative shops in which to find them.

Beverly Hills and Rodeo Drive are the most famous in which to shop. Rodeo Drive, with the biggest name stores—and most likely, the biggest price tags, too—is similar to Fifth Avenue and Madison Avenue in New York. From Gucci to Georgette Klinger, from Cartier, Van Cleef and Arpels, to Ted Lapidus, all can be found here. What's more, the city's indigenous stores, such as Fred Joaillier, Jerry Magnin, and Bijan—probably one of the only men's boutiques in the world where you need an appointment—are mostly found in Beverly Hills. Beverly Hills is not only a great shopping experience, but it is also one of the best places for stargazing.

A star was born recently in Beverly Hills: The *Rodeo Collection,* on Rodeo Dr. between Brighton Way and Santa Monica Blvd., is the epitome of opulence and high fashion. Many famous European designers who have never had free-standing stores on the West Coast have opened their doors in this piazza-like area of marble and brass. Among them:

Cerruti is a designer known in Europe for his own fabrics. Here you'll find one of several women's franchises he has opened up worldwide. Louis Vuitton, known throughout the world for fine luggage, has a light, airy shop. Nina Ricci, with everything from accessories to evening gowns, is in a dramatic setting complete with crystal chandelier. Yves St. Laurent Pour Homme, with luggage and umbrellas, as well as his classically styled clothing, has pictures of the designer to remind you where you are shopping. Trend-setting Italian designer Gianni Versace is represented by one of the largest collections of his clothes in the U.S. Fendi is here with exquisite leather goods.

Pratesi, a new addition, has fine bed linens, with a single sheet priced as high as $900. A gallery of archaeological artifacts, Barakat, is a maze of age-old glass, sculpture, and jewelry from all over the world; according to the owner, prices range from $100 to $1 million. Ylang Ylang is a fantasyland of costume and precious jewelry; it is worth visiting just to look at the bright colors and glitter. For those who are shopping-weary, eat at Pastels, for outdoor dining, great salads, and a perfect vantage point for people-watching.

Mall shopping is so important in Los Angeles, that it is actually a sociological phenomenon. The *Beverly Center,* bounded by Beverly Blvd., La Cienega Blvd., San Vicente Blvd., and Third St., has more than 900,000 sq ft—over seven acres—and room for 200 stores. It is one of the largest shopping complexes in the Los Angeles area. Since its opening in spring 1982, the mall has catered to an upscale market taste. Many French designers—Daniel Hechter, Rodier, and others—have opened retail outlets here as have unusual American shops like By Design, and there are some interesting restaurants, such as the Tea Room–St. Petersburg, an authentic Russian restaurant with a fantastic view of the hills, Food for Thought (a restaurant/bookstore), the current rave, The Hard Rock Cafe (known, if not for its cuisine, for its fascinating decor starting with the 1959 Caddy that dives into the roof of the building above the restaurant), and the finest cineplex in Los Angeles—14 individual movie theaters.

Another shopping area, further west, that has evolved into a unique shopping area from a concept, is *Main Street, Santa Monica.* It is part of a "renewal" phase in Los Angeles in which many older neighborhoods are changing their faces; this area has been made to look like "Main Street, USA" in days past. Many of the stores and restaurants, decorated with carved wood, cut glass, and cute striped canopies, evoke a feeling that you are walking down the main street of a small western town just after the cowboys and gold miners left and the town had gained a bit of refinement. From *Willy Tiffany's Saloon* to *Main Street U.S.A.,* there is a theme—a special feeling—and it works well. This area was once well known for its large selection of antiques. Now clothing and kitchen stores and a slew of unusual galleries have come in, making this a full-service shopping area. Many of the stores carry Californian and other kinds of crafts, from original clothing to pottery and oils, and you are very likely to find items that you will see nowhere else. The Gallery of Eskimo Art and Main Street Gallery are just two of these places; and for clothes there is the Main Street Ensemble, with *very* trendy clothing, Pure Sweat, 1904 Lincoln Blvd. (396–6102), with great exercise fashions.

There are so many kinds of malls in Los Angeles that they have become an architectural as well as a social phenomenon. The new Santa Monica Place Mall is one of the best places to study the evolutionary progress of "the mall."

Next door to the new three-story enclosed mall is the old *Santa Monica Mall* —an open-air mall. This predecessor to the recent mall, which is environmentally controlled, was also innovative in its day. There are pedestrian walkways between the streets, and there is also a landscaped island. The minute you see the huge green palm tree on the side of the new building you can feel the link that this mall has with its surroundings. The light, airy atrium design allows a view of all three floors at once, and from particular points you can see the ocean in the background. *Robinson's* and *The Broadway* are the department stores.

Century City has another shopping mall, set among gleaming steel office buildings. Here, in the center of a thriving business atmosphere, is a city kind of mall—open air. Charles Jourdan shoes at I. Magnin and designer labels at Ann Taylor are for high-fashion enthusiasts. The whimsical boutique *Heaven,* with its name emblazoned on T-shirts, sweat shirts, and so on, is a great place from which to get a souvenir for someone back home. As well as the open-air mall, there is a shopping section right in the middle of the twin towers in the ABC Entertainment Center. One typical Los Angeles Store, because of the emphasis here on luxury cars, is the *Road Show,* which features antique and classic cars and all kinds of paraphernalia, books, and novelty items for any Porsche, B.M.W., Rolls Royce, and other car enthusiasts. Galleries, clothing stores such as *The City Rage,* and a *B. Dalton Bookstore* are among the other stores in this center.

Changing gears again, we move to Westwood Village, which, with the influence of the UCLA campus, is a young and lively area for shopping. On a Saturday night in the spring and summer the stores are open late; there is a movie line around every corner; cars and people cruise; and the whole place looks like a scene from *Animal House.* It is great fun, and many of the stores are open as late as 11:00 P.M.

The recent arrival of pedicabs—bicycle-carts—in Westwood adds to the merriment. At about $6 an hour, they aren't a bad deal.

One particularly unique little shopping area in Westwood is the *Contempo Westwood Center,* at 10886 Le Conte Ave., right across the street from the UCLA campus. A certificate of Historical Preservation and Restoration is the building's claim to fame, and there is a photographic display of the history of the area.

Westwood has often been compared to New York's Greenwich Village. As in New York's "Village," you are likely to see anything while strolling down the streets of Westwood Village. You may see a mime marrying two passersby or a tap-dancing twelve year old.

Farmers Market at Fairfax and Third is the historical shopping area of Los Angeles. It is near the top of every list of tourist attractions. Originally it was an open field where farmers went to sell their crops; now it is a huge shopping area with some of the best produce for miles around. There are other wares and a few restaurants offered as well.

Hollywood and West Hollywood are two shopping areas that depict special aspects of the Southern California life-style. In Hollywood it is the star and dazzle style that goes along with the show business industry. This sparkle is especially apparent in Hollywood, on Sunset Blvd.—or the Sunset Strip. The stores here and on Hollywood and Santa Monica Blvds. offer ultrahigh fashion as well as intriguing furnishings and antiques. The male shopper has more innovative stores to chose from here than perhaps anywhere in the city.

West Hollywood, especially on Melrose Avenue, is where young shoppers should try their luck as should those who appreciate vintage styles in clothing and furnishings. This is definitely one of the "hottest" shopping areas in Los Angeles; part of its attraction is the blend of different kinds of stores. It is on this boulevard of flashing neon that you'll find the latest trends in New Wave and whatever's next in style. The mile-and-a-half of intriguing, one-of-a-kind shops and bistros, which stretches from a few blocks west of La Brea to a few blocks west of Crescent Heights, has become to L.A. what the West Village has long been to New York City. Some samples: *Art Deco L.A. Antiques,* (7300 Melrose) is full of lacquered furniture, porcelain radios, neon clocks, and juke-boxes; *From Italy* (7320 Melrose) has super furniture and furnishings that combine a youthful Italian look with fresh California zest (they ship worldwide); *Off the Wall* (7325 Melrose) claims a specialization in "antiques and weird stuff." At *Fantasies Come True* (2408 Melrose), "When You Wish Upon a Star" plays from the tapedeck as you enter this store packed with Walt Disney memorabilia.

Also in this area is the Blue Whale: the *Pacific Design Center,* a building that's hard to miss. A huge blue edifice on the corner of Melrose Ave. and San Vicente Blvd., this center houses everything from furniture to window coverings, from fixtures to accessories. More of the same kinds of design stores can be found on Robertson Avenue.

Downtown Los Angeles, with its impressive renovation project in the Bunker Hill area, is undergoing a dramatic face-lifting. In the past few years downtown has become a recognizable force in the art world. Like New York City's SoHo section, there are converted lofts and galleries everywhere between Figueroa and Mateo Sts., on Los Angeles Street, in the ARCO Center, and all over this area. On any weekend you can stroll through this area and probably find a show opening or two offering wine and cheese and good art viewing.

Many up-and-coming artists—the new breed of "young Turks"—hang around and show their art in this section. There is a renegade atmosphere that usually develops in an art-oriented urban area. There is also a great deal of innovative contemporary art worth seeing and buying. Also downtown is the clothing district—the *California Mart* at 110 East 9th St. On the last Friday of each month the wholesale showrooms are open to the public for great bargains on sample items.

Downtown also affords the visitor to Los Angeles a great view of the many ethnic influences that make up the city. On Olvera St., one of the oldest streets in Los Angeles, you may visit the *Avila Adobe,* the well-preserved home that stood in Los Angele's original town square. Lining this pedestrian alley, stores offer handmade crafts and foods from Mexico.

Little Tokyo is the largest Japanese shopping district in the country. Japanese businesses started coming here in 1884, and this section has been going strong ever since. The evolution has filled Little Tokyo with an interesting mix of Japanese architecture interspersed with the usual American urban architecture.

Japanese tradition is still very strong here, and the important festivals, which are all celebrated in community fashion, offer a good way for the visitor to get a glimpse into this intriguing culture. The stores in Little Tokyo offer the most modern of Japanese merchandise. All are representative of the delicate Oriental touch. Clothing, jewelry, home furnishings, and other kinds of stores offer an unlimited variety from which to choose. For instance, *Matsuzakaya* is the first American branch of the oldest department store in Japan (founded in 1611). Typical of a department store, it features china to watches, ladies' and men's clothing, and much more. This is just one store in Weller Court—on Weller St. between First and Second St., near the New Otani Hotel and Garden. The Weller Court area is representative of what Tokyo looks like today.

Leaving downtown and traveling as far west as possible, you will find quite a bit of shopping in the beach communities. The Pacific Palisades has chic, and expensive stores, such as *Jona* for women's clothing and fashion consultation. Farther down the coast are Santa Monica, Venice, and Marina del Rey. Santa Monica has particularly good shopping on Main St. and the Santa Monica Place Mall. Another great shopping area in Santa Monica is Montana Ave. With *Brenda Himmel* for stationery and gifts, *Weathervane I* and *II* for women's and men's clothing, and *Lisa Norman* for the finest lingerie, this short strip of shopping—from about 11th St. to 23rd—is chock full of possibilities.

Venice is second only to Melrose Avenue as the punk or New Wave headquarters of Los Angeles, and shopping reflects this style. West Washington St. is the place to shop for unusual items in Venice; *Choux Sale,* with vintage shoes and clothing, is only one of the shops to explore. In the Marina, on Admiralty Wy., *Blondie's,* with a selection of cute, punk clothing for women, typifies this style. *Mudra Naturals,* on Washington Ave. near the beach, with earthy natural cottons that reflect a beach look, is quite different. *Kroma,* in Venice, has some eye-catching stained-glass art. The glass is coated by means of a special chemical process and turns different colors as the light hits it; it is a treat to see. Such items sell from about $30.00 to $5,000.

The South Bay communities of Redondo Beach, Manhattan Beach, and Hermosa Beach also contain a variety of shops on their respective shopping streets. In Redondo the shopping is good in the Kings Harbor section. Other streets for shopping include Pacific Coast Hwy., Torrance Blvd., and Catalina Ave. (There is no real "downtown" in Redondo.) Hermosa has its pier and Hermosa Ave. with shops; and the "strand," which is connected to the pier, is another shopping attraction. In Manhattan Beach, the Manhattan Village Mall, on Sepulveda at Rosecrans, has stores such as *Pappagallo,* the popular women's shoe and clothing store. *Del Amo Fashion Center,* at 3525 Carson, in Torrance, is said to be the world's largest shopping mall. It has 350 stores and 2.4 million square feet of space.

The Valley, which was briefly mentioned, is a great place to shop, but it is important to get your bearings and directions straight before you set out. It is a sprawling area. The Valley refers to the San Fernando Valley, which is north of Los Angeles; but there is a lot more "out there." East of Los Angeles is the San Gabriel Valley and nearby are Pasadena, Glendale, and dozens of other communities.

There are hundreds of shopping areas within this section; but there are some, in the Valley especially, that stand out. Ventura Blvd., which runs through many different cities—Universal City, Sherman Oaks, Topanga—has shops scattered along the way to Calabasas.

Well-known shops such as *Importique* in Encino, with contemporary sportswear at reasonable prices, and the *1900's Company,* with great reproductions of American antiques, are spread out among newer shops. At least one shop is opening each week in this thriving area.

In addition to Ventura Blvd. and other shopping streets, the Valley has a surprising number of malls. The Sherman Oaks Galleria is the newest. This is an upper-market mall featuring such stores as *Crabtree and Evelyn,* the famous English store, with delightful perfumes and beauty items; the *Casual Gourmet,* with everything for the kitchen; and *Martin Lawrence* for art; it offers a good selection of Dali and Rockwell originals. The atrium-style mall with glass elevators has about 120 stores anchored by the May Company and Robinson's.

Other malls in the Valley and in other outlying areas include the *Woodland Hills Promenade,* the *Topanga Canyon Mall,* the *May Company Plaza* in North Hollywood, the *Town and Country Shopping Center and Plaza de Oro* in Encino, and the *Glendale Galleria.*

Pasadena—east of Hollywood—is a refreshing older community in the midst of all these modern shopping areas. Pasadena has a wide range of shops to chose from. Many are in the crafts and gifts area. *Los Angeles* Magazine (February

1982) called Pasadena " . . . a place where time seems to move a little slower and people smile as they pass each other on the street. It's relaxed. It's classy. It's even colorful. And across the board, it's a good deal less expensive than comparable areas of Southern California."

One of the stores that expresses this friendly feeling is *The Gold Company* on East Green St. The proprietor/designer Karen McGrary is a marvel who has a special gift for designing jewelry in unusual combinations—a tourmaline crystal with a peach-colored pearl—and other striking pairings. The *Holly Street Bazaar,* on Holly St, is a cooperative effort offering separate booths containing such items as plastic costume jewelry, beaded lamp shades, and chenille bedspreads. Then there is *Four Quarters,* with gifts for the host or hostess.

MEN'S AND WOMEN'S CLOTHING

In Beverly Hills are some of the country's most traditional, classic, and expensive men's and women's clothing stores, as well as some of the trendiest. *Camp Beverly Hills* is in the latter category. Located at 9640 Santa Monica Blvd., this is more than just a clothing store; it is an institution. The motto of the store (and not *all* stores have mottos) is: "Survival clothing for the most modern age"; this is where you will find the most recent in chic uniforms—fatigues, sailor's pants and tops, and painter's pants—in dozens of colors, all piled high. There are also socks, sunglasses. sweat shirts, T-shirts, and an extensive collection of cards. Camp Beverly Hills T-shirts and sweat shirts make great souvenirs and presents for people back home. The *Rec Center* (9388 Little Santa Monica) looks like the inside of a swimming pool, circa 1940. It's a lot of fun shopping for casual women's wear with changing rooms resembling locker rooms in health spas.

Changing gears swiftly, we turn to *Celine,* 333 N. Rodeo Dr., one of the most posh names in international circles. Fine Old World craftsmanship and classic design are the key concepts at this store. Luggage, shoes, and accessories, as well as traditionally tailored clothes of the finest fabrics, are featured.

Have you heard of the book *Scruples? Giorgio,* Beverly Hills, at 273 N. Rodeo Dr., is the setting for this famous novel. One does not merely shop at Giorgio's; one also refreshes oneself at the stunning Oak Bar that separates the men's and women's clothes. A Beverly Hills landmark, Giorgio's is one of the stores that dresses the stars. Available are the best in American and European clothing, as well as superbly fashioned accessories and footwear.

At 9699 Wilshire Blvd., *Jaeger International Shop* is one of the best known first-class British clothiers. A complete line of cashmere and woolen separates is available in traditionally designed fashions.

The *Lanvin Boutique,* 362 N. Rodeo Dr., is a big name in French *haute couture;* the full line of Lanvin fashions for men and women is featured here along with toiletries and gift items. The staff speak several languages and even takes foreign currency. *Theodore* and *Theodore Man* are two more impressive clothing stores at 453 N. Rodeo Dr. These stores offer trendy items in fabulous fabrics. Everything is done with a real eye for color. The *Leather Club* at 9526 Santa Monica Blvd has the best pants, jackets, skirts, and other items in leather and suede from French, Italian, and Spanish designers.

Carroll and Company, 466 N. Rodeo Dr., Beverly Hills, has been one of the finest clothing stores in Los Angeles for more than thirty-two years. Carroll and Company offers only the best in design, fabric, and fit.

On Melrose Ave. are other upbeat clothing stores, including the ever-popular *Fred Segal* at 8100 Melrose. Fred Segal has a reputation for providing the most innovative of styling in men's and women's clothing. Featured are many designers and manufacturers, including New Man, Ralph Lauren, and Calvin Klein, to name only a few. Children's clothing, accessories, and shoes are also stocked at the Melrose store. *Harrari,* at 8463 Melrose and at 1015 Ocean Front Walk in Venice, has very unusual styles, "clothes with a sense of humor," as they say in their ads.

If you are interested in vintage clothes for men and women, try *Pinnacle Vintage* at 28925 W. Pacific Coast Hwy. in Malibu, across from the pier. The huge collection consists of clothing spanning the years from the 1890s through the 1960s, and the prices are reasonable. Avant-garde and punk clothing for men and women can be found at the *Main Street Ensemble* at 2803 Main Street in Santa Monica. This small shop is chock full of new designs.

In Westwood is *Chanin's* at 1030 Westwood Blvd., for the best in casual wear. The UCLA influence can be seen in the youthful and fun fashions featured here. *Gary's and Company,* at 4728 Admiralty Way in Marina del Rey, brings us back to the classics. A preppie's dream, Gary's has men's and women's fashions by Ralph Lauren and Southwick and shoes by Cole Haan, to name only a few of the lines. Gary's does alterations and tapers shirts for free—if you don't mind a bit of a wait.

Raffles, a Clothing Collection, at 17554 Ventura Blvd. in Encino, is one of the Valley's most extensive stores. It is a treat for the eye to see so many interesting fashions for men and women in one place. There are accessories and shoes here as well, and the staff offers wardrobe-coordination advice.

Echelon is another store that carries many lines, some better known in Europe than in this country. Located in the Courtyard, 550 Deep Valley Dr., Rolling Hills Estate, this boutique carries La Squadra, J.P.G., Mario Valentino shoes, Soo Young Lee, Crash, Christian Dior, and other lines.

North Beach Leather, through its nine stores in the Los Angeles area, offers limited-edition leather designs for discriminating men and women. Classic designs and more trendy styles fill the racks, and there is something for everyone in the finest of leathers and suedes.

Maxfield Bleu, 9091 Santa Monica Ave. in West Hollywood, is a haunt of some of the most famous Hollywood residents. The store stocks the most recent European and American designer clothing. This is good place to see what is "in," even if you can't afford it.

WOMEN'S CLOTHING

The Beverly Center features French designers' outlets including *Philippe Salvet, Daniel Hechter,* and *Rodier Paris.* In the same tradition is *Laise Adzer,* at 8583 Melrose Ave. in the Beverly Center, and at Century City. This Moroccan designer makes free-flowing clothes in the most luxurious natural fabrics. Only pure vegetable dyes are used to make the luscious colors. This store, including its mosque-like design, is a real treat, as is her new store in the Century City Shopping Center.

Back to Beverly Hills for women's clothing. We start out at *Jag,* 9612 Brighton Way. At the forefront of the jeans revolution a few years ago, this store still has a good selection of well-styled jeans as well as other clothing. The *Right Bank Clothing Company and Tea Room* at 301 N. Rodeo has some of the highest quality, best designed, and highest priced clothing in town.

Alan Austin and Company offers traditional clothing in a wide selection of fabrics and colors. The store, located at 9533 Brighton Way, manufactures its own designs, so you can have your clothing made to order. *Lady Battaglia* is the women's version of the men's store; at 456 N. Rodeo, this store, like its counterpart, offers the most beautiful clothing from Italy.

Matthews, 309 Rodeo Dr., is run by Ruth Matthews. She has a good eye for fashion, which can be seen in the collection of clothing available in her store. Everything is well coordinated to provide you with "a look."

Ann Taylor, at 357 N. Camden Dr. and at several other locations around Los Angeles, offers the epitome of the young executive look for women; there is also a good selection of more casual clothing. Featuring such designers as Carol Horn and Perry Ellis, the store also carries a full line of Joan and David shoes.

Melons, Ltd., 8750 Melrose Ave., and *Melons, Ltd.,* 8739 Melrose Ave., are two of the newest and hottest stores on this street. They have a wide selection of innovative designs from young designers. The store and its owners have received much attention from the Los Angeles press since its opening because of their impressive clothing selection.

Ellene Warren, 8590 Melrose Ave., offers its own original designs for women. One recent ad showed an unusual minidress with a print featuring musical notes—only one of many unusual designs you are likely to find on any given visit to this store. *Cowboys and Poodles Vintage Clothing,* 7379 Melrose Ave., attracts tourists from all over the world. Their collection of unused vintage clothes from the 1950s to the 1960s is worth a look; they also make some of their own designs.

Blondie's, 4732 Admiralty Way in the Marina, is full of punk and nearly punk styles. The owner Lynette Nagel, a blond, hence the name, searches the mart for the unusual, resulting in a selection of out-of-the-ordinary casual clothing. *Jona,* 12532 Ventura Blvd. in Studio City and at 1013 Swathmore Ave. in Pacific Palisades, is billed as a wardrobe-consultation service and store in one. They will outfit you from head to toe, using precisely the right style to enhance your personal look and tastes. They have a great selection of clothing from which to choose.

Also in the Valley, at 12642 Ventura Blvd., are *Van Tassell* for complete wardrobe counseling and the *Klassy Lady Boutique,* at 17064 Ventura Blvd.

Ferouchi, at 518 Wilshire Blvd., in Santa Monica, has designer clothing that changes with the seasons; among labels featured are DD Dominick, Nancy Heller, and Terryl De Vino. *Nancee G.,* 943 Westwood Blvd., offers a great blend of domestic and European fashions. It has active sportwear as well as more dressy clothing by Leon Max and Marithe and Francois Girbaud among others.

More punk fashions can be found at *Domo,* 107 Washington Ave. in the Marina, also on 2817 Main in Santa Monica. This store carries the latest in punk fashions and accessories; there is an impressive selection of swimwear as well. Down the street, at 22½ Washington Ave., *Mudra Naturals* manufactures its own line of natural cotton, beachy clothing. Bright yellows, reds, and blues are the colors for this line of simple, well-styled skirts, pants, jackets, and tops of all kinds.

Nana, at 126 Broadway in Santa Monica, is another trendy store offering some of the most current of contemporary fashions. They claim that they have the best collection of tights and socks in town; and they also have jeans and swimwear. English T-shirts, magazines, and records will please the Anglophiles.

Weathervane II, 1209 Montana Ave., Santa Monica, is a large, bright shop. The friendly staff makes browsing among the beautiful fashions even more fun. Classic styles are mixed with the offbeat, and all are of the finest quality and best fabrics. Across the street, at 1134 Montana Ave., *Lisa Norman Lingerie, Etc.,* is almost too good to be true. This modern, elegant store houses one of the largest collections of high-quality lingerie from Europe and the United States. It concentrates on all natural fibers—silk and cotton—and designs its own items as well. Bins of bikinis, fine and expensive silk stockings, slips, camisoles, robes, and at-home clothes are only some of the items carried by Lisa Norman. *Trashy Lingerie,* at 402 N. La Cienega Blvd. in West Hollywood, has just what the name suggests. This is a place for the more daring; it carries sexy black-and-red garter belts and such.

Johnathan for Women, 1707 S. Catalina Ave. in Redondo Beach, carries loungewear and dancewear as well as some of the most beautiful imported lingerie from Europe, the Orient, and South America. *The Old Soft Shoe,* at 1242 Hermosa Ave., is a resale shop with "almost new," pampered designer clothing.

Hats are the thing at *Brown's Hats,* at 68A N. Venice Blvd. in Venice. Straight from London, this store has nothing but hats in all shapes and sizes—berets, bowlers, large floppy hats, and small pillboxes.

Holly's Harp, 8605 Sunset Blvd., and 950 Cahuenga, is among the most "in" stores in Los Angeles. Holly's creates fashions for many of the well-known people of the world. Five lines are created each year, and she also carries a selection of items from other designers.

MEN'S CLOTHING

One men's clothing store that has generated quite a bit of publicity is *Bijan,* at 420 N. Rodeo Dr. The store's shopping is by appointment only. It has made a splash by offering a line of bulletproof clothing. Bijan claims that many Arabian sheiks and other royalty shop here along with some of the wealthiest men in the United States. The most expensive and well-made clothing is available; many of the styles are designed especially for Bijan; they contain the best in leathers, cashmeres, silks, and other natural materials.

Abercrombie and Fitch, at 9429 Wilshire Blvd. and at the Beverly Center, is listed under men's clothing because it has been traditionally known for its fine men's clothing and sportswear. But there is also a great deal more available—women's clothing, accessories, and sporting equipment. The most elegant of sports clothes for safaris as well as tennis are stocked, in keeping with Abercrombie's ninety-year old tradition.

Battaglia, 306 N. Rodeo, features the richest of Italian fashions in the most luxurious silks, wools, cottons, and cashmeres. Accessories, shoes, and men's apparel are shown in stylish surroundings. *Cecil Gee* came to 346 N. Rodeo Dr. directly from London's Bond St.; this shop is one of the most well-respected English shops. Cecil Gee offers the best in styling and materials, and shopping here will expose you to the amenities that go with English life; you can relax and have tea or a drink while the staff takes care of you.

Cyril's, 370 N. Beverly Dr., features fine clothing in the latest European styles. This elegant store carries such labels as Valentino, Cerruti, and Michale Axel. *Jerry Magnin,* at 323 N. Rodeo Dr., has one of the best reputations as a gentleman's clothier in the city. One of the largest men's stores, Magnin's has a large selection of dressy and traditional styles as well as casual styles. Shoes and accessories are also in good supply.

Mr. Guy, 369 N. Rodeo Dr., is known and well respected throughout the country. Mr. Guy offers tasteful and well-made clothing; all the needs of the well-dressed man can be obtained under one roof. *W. D. Silk* in the Century City Shopping Center is another fine name in menswear. "Low key" and good taste are watchwords here; there is nothing trendy about this store. Everything is classic: Aquascutum suits, Cole Haan shoes, and other respected labels are stocked.

Brooks Brothers, a men's tradition since 1818, is located at 530 W. 7th St., downtown. The store's reputation is worldwide, and deservedly so, for its own line of pure cotton shirts, suits, and neckwear. You cannot go wrong with these classically styled clothes. Business cases and other furnishings for the executive complete the Brooks Brothers profile.

Preferred Stock, 1914 Wilshire Blvd. in Santa Monica, is a new shop that offers the best that you can buy for your money. Their credo is that great fashion ought to be of good value as well as good looking. Their buyers scour the markets for merchandise that is just right. They offer the best in natural fabrics

—cotton, wool, silk, linen, and tweed; and they create wearable fashions out of these fabrics. The staff is friendly and gives customers personal attention.

CHILDREN'S CLOTHING

Auntie Barbara's, 202 S. Beverly Blvd., Beverly Hills, keeps the kids busy while their mothers shop. The children play with various toys and the mothers survey the most recent designs in domestic and imported children's clothing.

Nanny, (131 N. La Cienega in the Beverly Center and 186 N. Canon Blvd. in Beverly Hills) has beautiful one-of-a-kind clothes and shoes imported from France, Greece, and Italy for infants to size 14. Good for nursery furnishings, shower gifts, and toys to take home to the little ones. At Bonwit Teller is *Bambola Children's Boutique,* with beautiful clothes imported from all over the world for infants to teens. *Adelaine, Boutique d'Enfants,* 350 N. Canon Dr. in Beverly Hills, has an irresistible collection of children's clothing from France, Italy, Germany, Israel, Denmark, England, and Sweden.

Pixie Town, at 400 N. Beverly Dr., Beverly Hills, has been dressing children for thirty years. Everything from baby's clothes and accessories to impeccably designed clothing for boys and girls is available at this pleasant shop.

JEWELRY

The large chain jewelers such as Slavick's, Weisfields, and Zales are well represented at shopping areas and malls throughout the Southland. But there are also a number of individual jewelers of note. Whether you want posh and expensive or more artsy-craftsy jewelry, there is a store for all tastes. *Tiffany and Company,* at the Beverly Wilshire Hotel in Beverly Hills, hardly needs an introduction. Bearing the finest of reputations for the finest of jewelry, this store is a bit smaller than one might expect, but it is still full of the most well designed, most expensive jewels to be found. *Cartier* recently opened its doors at 370 N. Rodeo; and *Van Cleef and Arpels* has a large store one block west.

Perhaps the most prestigious jewelry store in Beverly Hills (or Los Angeles, for that matter) is *Fred Joaillier.* This is one of the classiest jewelry stores in the country, and the store at 401 N. Rodeo was the first U.S. branch of this famous Paris store. They design many of their own pieces and have a leather boutique as well.

Pepi, at Fred Segal, 8100 Melrose, is a California-based jewelry designer who has made quite a name for herself throughout the country. With modern designs and a real flair for style, her collection is worth a look. *Shanes Jewelers,* in Westwood at 1015 Broxton, is a more youth-oriented jewelry store geared to the large number of college students in the area. They specialize in earrings, chains, and watches.

Another name in California jewelry is the well-known *Morgan and Company Jewelers,* at 1131 Glendon in Westwood, and *Morgan on Main,* at 2721 Main St. in Santa Monica. Here estate jewelry and well designed, high-quality jewels are featured. *Denton Fine Jewelers,* at 11696 San Vicente Blvd. in Brentwood, and 15231 Sunset Blvd. in Pacific Palisades, offers the finest in rings, watches, and other jewelry. A small classic collection is offered in fashionable and comfortable surroundings.

Another store geared to younger tastes is *Fashionable Affordables,* 103 W. Washington Ave., Marina del Rey. Thin gold bracelets and chains are featured, and the prices are right; you can pick up a bracelet for less than $40.00.

Norman and Company, at 11640 San Vicente Blvd., is a light, airy, modern store with classic as well as more innovative jewelry. High price tags and very high quality are key words here. *The Gold Company,* at 951 E. Green St. in Pasadena, carries one-of-a-kind designs by Karen McGrary, proprietor-designer. Such combinations as tourmaline crystals and pearls are made by McGrary, who has a real flair for jewelry design. She will be happy to work with individual customers who have loose stones or want a piece of jewelry that is way out of the ordinary. She also has a line of more conventional pieces.

GIFTS AND STATIONERY

Many shops that do not fit into any other category fit here. Los Angeles has an abundance of individual gift stores with just the right present for someone at home: Here are a few:

Brenda Himmel, Fine Stationery and Gifts, at 1126 Montana Ave, Santa Monica, is a paper lover's heaven. Offering stationery, blank books, address books, and gift items, this store has an added attraction: the helpful and knowledgeable owner—Brenda Himmel. *Discovery, A Gift Boutique,* at 3835 Cross Creek Rd., No. 21, The Country Mart, Malibu, has a good selection of handicrafts from the United States and around the world. Accessories, jewelry, cards, and stationery are all available here. At 9634 Santa Monica Blvd., Beverly Hills, *Marshall Todd's Glass Menagerie* has a whimsical collection of glass from all over the world. Animals and limited-edition sculptures, as well as other decorative and useful glass pieces, are featured.

Richard–Ginori, 9555 Santa Monica Blvd., Beverly Hills, has been manufacturing fine china in Europe since 1735. This store, in addition to having a large stock of china, has *objets d'art* and other decorative items. *Geary's North,* 437 N. Beverly Dr., Beverly Hills, has been a well-respected name in Los Angeles for years. *Geary's*—the more traditional sister store down the street—carries china, silver, and crystal, whereas this store carries a hodgepodge of items—graphics, ceramic dishes, stuffed pillows, and other unusual gifts.

Homeworks, 2913 Main St. in Santa Monica, is a great place to go when you want to buy something but you are not quite sure what. From pens and address books to a great selection of housewares, this store is chock full of high tech merchandise. It also carries a whole line of Braun items—clocks, scales, and so on. Also on Main St., at 2801, is the recently expanded *Bobbi Leonard.* Packed with furniture, novelty items, and accessories such as fans, lacquer boxes, and silk flowers, this store is a fantasy land of things for the home.

The Rainbow, 434 N. Camden Dr., Beverly Hills, is a wonderful store filled with unusual gift items; all the profits go to a treatment center for children with cancer. A variety of toys, stationery, gifts, quilts, and more is carried.

SPORTING GOODS AND SPORTS CLOTHING

With the emphasis on health and fitness so much a part of the way of life in Southern California, it would follow that there are many stores in this category. Because new stores in this field pop up all the time, here is just a smattering:

Oshman's sporting goods stores, with many locations in the Los Angeles area, are virtual supermarkets for sporting goods; from baseballs to volleyball nets, these stores have whatever you need to keep fit.

Big 5, a sporting-goods store with a loyal following, also has branches in various areas.

Smith's Sporting Goods has stores in the Marina, West Los Angeles, and the Pacific Palisades. With many brand names such as Adidas, Nike, K-Swiss, Head, and more, this is another one-stop place to shop for sports items. *Phidippides Sports* call themselves, "your aerobic sports center," and all the personnel at the stores in Marina del Rey, Rolling Hills Estates, and Manhattan Beach are very well versed in athletic footwear. They can help you with any specific need and know what kinds of shoes you will need for the specific sport you participate in.

The Dance Center of London, with locations in Pasadena, Westwood, and Beverly Hills, is one of the best places for women's athletic and dance clothing. They have tremendous stocks of fashionable and colorful warm-up suits, leotards, and other dancewear. Price tags are a bit hefty; but this is the place to go when you want something that you won't see everyone else wearing.

ANTIQUES

As a relatively young city, compared to those on the East Coast, Los Angeles has a surprisingly good selection of antique stores. Probably the most popular and one of the best priced collections of antiques can be found at the *Antique Guild,* 8800 Venice Blvd. Here, amid three acres of showrooms, is a full stock of English, Danish, French, and Italian furniture, clocks, jewelry, and other collectibles. Other countries are often represented as well in this collection that spans several eras of antiques. The Guild carries books on antiques and small items such as glass and china. A group of buyers is employed by the store to acquire the best buys in Europe. Dealers and decorators, along with retail buyers, shop here so you can be assured that you will be getting a good buy.

Cricket Antiques, 2025 Pacific Ave., Venice, is a surprisingly elegant establishment for such a casual beach community. But herein is the attraction of shopping in Venice: It offers the unusual as well as the unexpected. This shop specializes in French and English items from the seventeenth through the nineteenth centuries. In addition to furniture there are dishes and whimsical accessories such as a life-sized, colorful carousel horse.

At *Harvey's,* 7365 Melrose, West Hollywood, 857–1991, you'll find everything from Victorian through fifties-era designer pieces, specializing in the latter. Rattan—possibly the largest selection in the world—is in one room and deco furniture in the other.

Both *King's Arts and Antiques,* 529–531 N. La Cienega, and *Y. C. King and Sons,* 308 N. Rodeo Dr., have fine selections of Oriental antiques, including cloisonne, porcelain, jade, and semiprecious stones. Architectural antiques and cash registers constitute the fare at *The Vintage Cash Register and Scale Company,* Sherman Oaks, 13448 Ventura Blvd. Brass cash registers of all kinds are displayed with antique scales and architectural fixtures and accessories. Brass ceiling fixtures, bank teller cages, and slot machines provide only a sampling of the unusual items stocked.

ART GALLERIES

Although large in number, the art galleries of Los Angeles are as spread out as the city itself. The highest concentration, however, exists in Hollywood and West Hollywood; the galleries in the newer areas of downtown and Venice are developing and may perhaps overtake the Hollywood galleries in importance in the future. The downtown gallery scene, in particular, is coming more and more into prominence because it offers a cheaper area in which to open a business simply for art's sake.

Most Los Angeles galleries offer Southern California art; others include a smattering of international works.

The following is a selected tour of galleries throughout the city. For further general information, contact the Los Angeles Convention and Visitors Bureau, or, for current information about showings, consult either local Los Angeles papers, such as *LA Weekly* and the *LA Reader,* or *The Los Angeles Times* and *Herald Examiner.*

With more galleries popping up all the time, the downtown art scene there is especially important.

The *ARCO Center for Visual Arts* is located on Level B of the ARCO Plaza, 505 S. Flower St., one of the largest subterranean shopping centers in the country; it contains more than sixty shops and restaurants. This particular gallery specializes in current photography; and the exhibits change regularly.

LA Artcore, 652 Mateo St., embodies an interesting concept as well as some of the best Los Angeles art. Its literature describes it this way: "LA Artcore is a nonprofit public benefit corporation established to further professional opportunities for artists and to bring art into the lives of the general public." But beyond this, LA Artcore is a active gallery: "We focus on bringing new artists to light in the Los Angeles area," notes gallery president Julie Belnick. The gallery shows predominately contemporary paintings and sculptures; besides the Los Angeles influence, they often have other kinds of exhibits—contemporary Korean drawings, for example.

A long-time fixture in the Los Angeles art world is the *Ankrum Gallery,* 657 N. La Cienega Blvd. This gallery shows abstract and figurative contemporary art and emphasizes California artists. Sculpture is also shown on a decked balcony upstairs.

Galerie Helene, 8232 W. 3rd St., is unique in that it specializes in primitive and naive art by American and European artists. *Z Gallerie,* with many locations—Santa Monica, Sherman Oaks, Redondo Beach, Malibu, Encino, and Marina del Rey—is a poster gallery that specializes in big, bright, contemporary graphics. Some of the artists represented include Brian Davis, Steven Kenny, James Paul Brown, Jerry Schurr, Marcus Vailevsky, Edward Hopper, and Robert Weil. It also carries Filmex posters and photographs by Ansel Adams and Richard Avedon. This chain offers reasonably priced art at its best.

In Beverly Hills, at 399 N. Rodeo Dr., *Wally Findlay Galleries* is *the* place for contemporary art. This gallery has been in business for over 100 years and carries all genres by American and European artists. The *Speaker Gallery,* 9025 Santa Monica Blvd., West Hollywood, often has unusual exhibits.

In addition to fine-art galleries, there are many crafts galleries around Los Angeles. The *Main Street Gallery,* 2803 Main St., Santa Monica, has an interesting collection. Japanese folk art, featuring porcelain, scrolls, and masks, among many other crafts, is offered. In Brentwood, at 11981 San Vicente Blvd., the *del Mano Gallery* carries contemporary American crafts. Jewelry, ceramics, blown glass, wearable art, fiberworks, woodworks, and more are available here at a wide range of prices—from $2.00 to $2,000.

Freehand, 8413 W. Third Street, 655–2607, is a gallery shop featuring contemporary American crafts, mostly by California artists. As the renaissance of crafts in America in the last 50 years comes to a heyday, this particular showplace is a valuable source for contemporary works by area artisans.

Wounded Knee Indian Gallery, 2413 Wilshire Blvd., has old and new Indian crafts. From pottery to rugs to graphics and beadwork, a multitude is offered from many nations, including the Navajo and the Hopi. Another such gallery, *The Gallery of Eskimo Art,* is located at 2665 Main St. in Santa Monica.

The Silver Man Gallery, 11740 San Vicente, Brentwood, features an extensive collection of American Indian jewelry and folk art and a potpourri of authentic gift items from the world over.

Last, but certainly not least, is *Sherwood Gallery* in the Santa Monica Place Mall (and in Laguna Beach). This gallery is a fantasy land of soft sculptures—a grandmother, kids, and even a flasher equipped with a raincoat—all stand waiting to be snatched up and taken home. Traditional graphics and other types of nonhuman soft sculpture, such as flowers and palm trees, are also shown. This gallery is especially fun during the holidays; and it is always enlightening just to watch kids' faces as they enter.

The following is a list of smaller galleries by area. Phone numbers are included, since it is often necessary to make an appointment at these places.

West Hollywood/Hollywood. *Gemini Graphics Editions Limited,* 8365 Melrose Ave.; 651–0513. Limited edition graphics and small sculptures. The shows change as the graphics are published. Established names offer their work here. *Flow Ace Gallery,* 8373 Melrose Ave.; 658–6980. Exhibits in this three-room gallery change every four to six weeks. Artists include Sam Francis, Robert Rauschenberg, Mark Di Suvero, and Edward Ruscha. Also on Melrose, at number 7220, is *Wild Blue* (939–8434), a contemporary gallery of ceramics, paintings, photographs, and jewelry designed largely by Californians. Crisp, clean setting is appropriate for the colorful and sometimes humorous art pieces sold within. *Los Angeles Institute of Contemporary Art* (LAICA), 2020 S. Robertson Blvd.; 559–5033. This nonprofit museum was founded in 1973 to provide alternatives to visual arts from its laboratory for new art. Everything in the gallery, including international installations, along with paintings and sculpture, is related to video. *Janus Gallery,* 8000 Melrose; 658–6084. Skylights show off paintings, sculpture, and contemporary ceramics created by both West and East Coast artists. *170 S. La Brea Galleries* (contains Jan Baum Gallery; 932–0170; Roy Boyd Gallery; 938–2328; and Prints and Art of Japan; 933–8382). Located in an old apartment building that has been renovated and now contains the galleries, plus an outstanding bookstore (*Art Works,* one of Los Angeles' best for art books). *Municipal Art Gallery,* 4800 Hollywood Blvd., Barnsdall Park, Los Feliz; 485–4581. This city-owned gallery contains two separate spaces filled with work by Southern California artists. Exhibits change once a month. Admissionis 50 cents; Free tours at 2:00 P.M. A gift shop and a bookshop are on the premises.

Downtown. *Cirrus,* at 542 S. Alameda St. (680–3473), features sculpted works and contemporary paintings by local artists. *Los Angeles Contemporary Exhibitions* (LACE), 240 S. Broadway, third floor; 620–0104. Painting, sculpture, and performance pieces are highlighted in this converted loft space. Also, an art periodical library. The entire concept leans toward the avant-garde. *Stella Polaris Gallery,* 445 S. Beverly Dr., Beverly Hills; 553–4400. This is one of the city's most unusual galleries; filled with international contemporary paintings, drawings, and graphics and focuses on one-person shows.

Beach Area (Venice/Santa Monica). *Los Angeles Louver Galleries,* 77 Market St. and 55 N. Venice Blvd., Venice; 822–4955. Across the street from the West Beach Café serving French cuisine in the European style, this gallery offers European and American contemporary art with an emphasis on English works. Claims to hold the country's largest collection of graphic arts outside New York City. *Tortue Gallery,* 2917 Santa Monica Blvd., Santa Monica; 828–8878. Features contemporary American art with an emphasis on California painting, sculpture, and drawings. Exhibits change once a month.

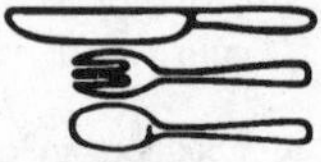

DINING OUT. It wasn't too many years ago that Los Angeles was considered a gastronomic wasteland; if you were in a restaurant and were served a steak the way you ordered it, you were considered a lucky individual. Ethnic restaurants were a rarity, and it was the general consensus that New York was the only city where you could literally eat your way around the world.

In the last decade, there has been a tremendous growth in the restaurant industry of Los Angeles. Chinese restaurants now include Szechuan, Hunan, Cantonese, and Mandarin restaurants, categorized by the region of the country, not just the country as a whole. Italian restaurants also became specialized and now serve either northern or southern Italian cuisine. There grew to be representation of other countries as well: Hungary, Jordan, Israel, Ethiopia, Morocco, Spain, Germany, and Jamaica. Ethnic bistros, offering home-style food at budget prices, are now in every corner of the city.

French restaurants have also undergone growth. The classic dishes alone, such as coq au vin or boeuf bourgignon, no longer satisfied a curious and more sophisticated clientele. When nouvelle cuisine became the vogue, French restaurants in Los Angeles, such as Ma Maison and L'Orangerie, offered this cuisine on their menu at practically the same time as the rage hit Paris. Here, too, Franco-Japanese meals first caught on, which combines the finery of French food with appetizing Japanese flair.

Other restaurants have recently blossomed that tout the California and the New America cuisine. This emphasis on fresh, local foodstuff, usually prepared by grilling, is evident at L.A. Nicola in Las Feliz and Bernie's in Westwood, as well as at many other eateries.

Most of Los Angeles's most distinguished restaurants are within the borders of Hollywood and West Los Angeles, incorporating part of Los Angeles proper, Beverly Hills, and West Hollywood. Such notable restaurants as the Palm, Spago, Ma Maison, and Le St. Germain, all lie within this area, as do hundreds of ethnic cafés. Chinatown offers the highest concentration of Chinese restaurants; Little Tokyo, Japanese restaurants; Little Korea, Korean restaurants. The Fairfax district specializes in Israeli and Jewish-style cafés.

For budget dining, ethnic restaurants offer the best value for your dollar and generally provide warm hospitality in a "Momma–Poppa" family-style operation. Many restaurants offer "early-bird dinners" between the hours of 5:00 P.M. and 6:30 P.M., when you can dine at reduced cost; but it's best to phone ahead to be certain.

In a city well noted for its entertainment industry and celebrities, it is to be expected that there will be many very expensive restaurants that cater to "beautiful people." The Bistro, Ma Maison, Spago, La Serre at lunch, Jimmy's, and many more restaurants offer haute cuisine dining experiences in elegant surroundings with a clientele to match. It's not uncommon to see a plethora of famous faces at these bistros. There's no need to feel intimidated about making a reservation at one of the star-studded restaurants; if you dress appropriately and are prepared to spend money, in nine out of ten cases you'll be treated kindly. If your pocketbook does not match your curiosity, you can have lunch instead of dinner, save 10 to 20 percent of the bill, and still have the same exciting experience.

Dining out at Sunday brunch is a trend in Los Angeles. Traditionally this late morning/early afternoon meal includes breakfast fare as well as light luncheon dishes, either as a buffet or as a sit-down repast. Eggs Benedict, crepes, quiches, and salads are usual brunch items. Several Los Angeles hotel dining rooms offer spectacular brunches, featuring everything from eggs and crepes to crab legs and roast beef. The Westwood Marquis, the Sheraton Universal, and the Century Plaza hotels offer outstanding buffet brunches. The offering at the Fine Affair in Bel Air—an airy restaurant filled with lush greenery, trellises, and mirrors—is representative of a chic California brunch. It serves French/California-style entrees on dainty flowered china. Brunch has become so popular that many Los Angeles restaurants are beginning to offer a Saturday brunch besides the traditional Sunday one.

The most popular evening dining hours are between 7:00 P.M. and 9:00 P.M.; Friday and Saturday nights are the busiest. Always make a reservation to be certain of getting a table and always check the dress code as well. Many restaurants are closed on Sunday and/or Monday nights.

Price categories are approximate and generally are set for a three-course meal—appetizer, entree, and dessert—per person. The price does *not* include cocktails, wine, tax, tip, or gratuities. Fifteen percent is the expected tip, 20 percent for very fine service or for a dinner at the city's most expensive restaurants, where dining is an evening's experience. An *expensive* dinner runs $30 and up. A *moderate* meal usually costs between $12 and $30 per person. An *inexpensive* dinner runs under $12.

Credit cards are accepted at most restaurants, but inexpensive specialty or ethnic restaurants usually accept cash only. Restaurants' acceptance of credit cards appears at the end of each of the following listings according to the following abbreviations:

AE - American Express
CB - Carte Blanche
DC - Diner's Club
MC - Master Card
V - Visa

If a listing indicates "No CB," for example, that means the restaurant accepts all credit cards but Carte Blanche.

Restaurants are categorized first by location and then by ethnicity. Sections are broken down within each cuisine according to its price category; entries are in alphabetical order within the price category. Before we begin our formal listings, here are a few notes on additional dining spots that do not fit into our regular categories.

Fast food. Internationally operated restaurants such as *McDonald's, Burger King,* and *Kentucky Fried Chicken* proliferate in Los Angeles. The White or Yellow Pages of the telephone directory will give you the location of one in your vicinity. *Cassell's* and *Fatburgers* in Los Angeles, *Fat Jack's* in Studio City, and *The Apple Pan* in West Los Angeles offer the best hamburgers at fast-food prices. *Pink's Famous Chili Dogs* is indeed the most famous hotdog stand in the city, and *Tail of the Pup* is one hotdog stand that is actually shaped like a hotdog. Mexican taco stands, much like pizza stands in New York, are in abundance. Soft-shell tacos, enchiladas, tostadas, and burritos are popular, inexpensive snacks and are generally freshly prepared. It's hit or miss, but *King Taco* in East Los Angeles, *Burrito King, Campos,* and *Lucie's,* all chains in Los Angeles, offer superior products.

Chains. Several moderately priced chain restaurants, notably *Victoria Station, Charley Brown's, the Velvet Turtle* and *the Hungry Tiger,* all successful in the steak/seafood genre. The *Sizzler* chain steakhouses are inexpensive steak-and-salad-bar restaurants that cater to families.

Twenty-four hour and late-dining stops. There are a few restaurants open twenty-four hours, besides coffee-shop chains such as *Denny's. Vickman's* (1228 E. 8th St.) in downtown Los Angeles opens at 3:00 A.M. to serve fresh pies and Danishes, eggs, and simple American fare. *The Pantry* (877 S. Figueroa) and the *Pacific Dining Car* (1310 W. 6th St.), also located downtown, serve steaks, eggs, and other hearty items twenty-four hours a day. *Roscoe's House of Chicken and Waffles* (1514 N. Gower, in Hollywood) stays open until 3:00 A.M. It serves excellent fresh waffles, crispy fried chicken, and homemade biscuits. *DuPars* is a chain of coffee shops that stays open until the wee hours of the morning and all night at some locations. The shops bake their own pies, cakes, and doughnuts on the premises and use fresh and natural ingredients.

Desserts. Ice cream parlors and chocolate-chip cookie stores are located throughout the city; there is a section for those with sweet tooths at the end of this *Dining Out* section.

LOS ANGELES

African

Walia Ethiopian Cuisine. *Inexpensive.* 5881 W. Pico Blvd., Los Angeles; 933–1215. A restaurant with thatched walls, African-print tablecloths, and walls covered with African woven baskets, mirrors bordered with shells, and Ethiopian travel posters. Dishes are served communal-style; one eats with the aid of *injera,* the Ethiopian flat bread. *Sambusas* are crispy meat-filled turnovers, and entrees include spicy stewed beef in red pepper sauce, chicken stew, raw chopped beef with hot pepper and spicy butter, and a combination vegetable platter. Best to order a combination plate to sample a variety of foods. Try the honey wine; it's homemade with raisins, hops, and honey. It tastes like nectar from the gods. Dinner Tuesday through Sunday. V, Mc.

American

Pacific Dining Car. *Expensive-Moderate.* 1310 W. 6th St., Los Angeles; 483–6000. One of Los Angeles's oldest restaurants. Great wine list with low prices. Known for steaks that are aged on the premises and charbroiled. Also good is the boned saddle of lamb and abalone steak. Desserts include a superior cheesecake, hot apple pie, and excellent ice cream. Open 24 hours daily. Valet parking. MC, V.

Lawry's California Center. *Moderate.* 570 West Ave. 26, Los Angeles; 225–2491. One of the most romantic restaurants in the city, with completely alfresco dining. Open May through October only. You'll dine outdoors at tables strategically placed throughout lush gardens of palms and tropical plants. Strolling mariachis serenade. Dinners are charbroiled New York steak, fresh swordfish, salmon, or hickory-smoked chicken. All dinners include salad, corn on the cob, sour cream tortilla casserole, fresh steamed vegetables, and hot herb bread. Strolling through the landscaped gardens is a must, either pre- or postdinner. Located near Dodger Stadium. Lunch daily; dinner Wednesday through Sunday. Reservations accepted for six or more only. AE, MC, V at dinner only.

Maurice's Snack and Chat. *Moderate.* 5349 W. Pico Blvd., Los Angeles; 931–3877. A tiny, popular soul-food restaurant. Friendly service. The menu features short ribs, smothered pork chops, pan-fried fish, and liver and onions. Black-eyed peas, greens, and candied yams are up to par. Save room for fresh coconut cake; it's worth it. Lunch Monday through Friday; dinner daily. No credit cards.

The New York Company. *Moderate.* 2470 Fletcher Dr., Los Angeles; 665–1115. Despite the out-of-the-way location, this restaurant/saloon, depicting the urban hustle and bustle of New York, creates an unusual ambience. The cuisine is Continental/American and features spinach salad, salmon mousse, prime New York steak, fresh fish, and Provimi veal. It draws an eclectic crowd, particularly in the adjoining bar that has an elaborate video-and-sound system projecting occasional entertainment. Lunch daily except Saturday and dinner daily. All major credit cards.

O'Shaughnessy's. *Moderate.* Arco Plaza, 515 S. Flower St., Los Angeles; 629–2565. Located on the "C" level of a modern shopping plaza, this restaurant, stressing the West, features the cuisine of the United States. Appetizers include homemade rabbit pâté and melon with spiced Kentucky ham. Seafood selections take advantage of Lake Superior whitefish, Pacific red snapper, and California sand dabs. Buffalo steak and buffalo stew, as well as roast saddle of rabbit, are highlighted menu items. Less adventurous souls can stick to chicken teriyaki or a T-bone steak. Chocolate fondue laced with Kirsch will please everyone. Unusual coffees with assorted liqueurs. Located close to the downtown Music Center; special dinners before curtain call. Lunch Monday through Friday; dinner Monday through Saturday. Validated parking. AE, DC, V.

Tam O'Shanter Inn. *Moderate.* 2980 Los Feliz Blvd., Los Angeles; 664–0228. The warm ambience of a Scottish inn. The menu features excellent prime rib with the same creamy horseradish sauce as Lawry's Prime Rib. Specials of the day. Lunch menu features sandwiches, salads, omelettes, and fish and chips. Great cole slaw with the interesting addition of chopped peanuts. Recent remodeling includes an upgraded menu. You can count on the success of the Lawry's chain to keep up this restaurant's high standards of cuisine and service. Lunch weekdays, sandwich bar on weekends for lunch. Dinner daily. No CB.

The Egg and the Eye. *Moderate* 5814 Wilshire Blvd., Los Angeles; 933–5596. A luncheon restaurant featuring dozens of varieties of omelettes and homemade desserts. Across from the Los Angeles County Art Museum. Crafts and folk art, which fit right into the cultural mood lingering from a visit to the museum, are exhibited. Lunch Tuesday through Sunday; dinner Friday and Saturday. All major credit cards.

Phillippe's Original Sandwich Shop. *Inexpensive.* 1001 N. Alameda St., Los Angeles; 628–3781. A 76-year-old cafeteria close to Union Station. Giant haunches of meat rest on a long counter where they are sliced into thick and juicy roast-beef sandwiches. Stew, soup, salads, and chili are also on the menu, but the sandwiches are the real draw. Dining is communal; everyone eats together at long tables. Coffee is still 10 cents a cup! Breakfast, lunch, and dinner daily until 10 P.M. No reservations, no credit cards.

Vickman's. *Inexpensive.* 1228 E. Eighth St., Los Angeles; 622–3852. All the action starts here at the improbable hour of 3:00 A.M. when this restaurant opens its doors. It's located by the downtown produce mart, and its customers are truck drivers, delivery men, and insomniacs. The fare is plain and wholesome

American food, including an excellent assortment of freshly baked goods. The strawberry pie is not to be missed, and the Danishes are sheer heaven. Ham, omelettes, poached salmon, and stuffed pork chops are satisfying. Monday through Friday, from 3:00 A.M. to 3:00 P.M.; Saturday, 3:00 A.M. to 1:00 P.M. No reservations, no credit cards.

Chinese

Lew Mitchell's Orient Express. *Moderate.* 5400 Wilshire Blvd., Los Angeles; 935–6000. This is no ordinary neighborhood Chinese restaurant. It's chic and sophisticated, with bentwood chairs, a plethora of potted palms, and ivy covered trellises in the windows. In other words, no one will throw you your chopsticks here. Specialties include sesame beef, thin sliced steak glazed with honey and sesame seeds, tea-smoked duck, beggar's chicken, and Peking duck (the latter requiring 24-hour notice). Szechuan dishes are predominant, but Mandarin cooking is featured as well. For the timid there is even a Western-style menu, which boasts a New York steak, mahi mahi, and squab. The dessert menu is eclectic; you can order the traditional lychee fruit or go for an Italian tartufo, a rich ice cream, or cheesecake with raspberry sauce. "Something for everybody" should be their motto. Closed Sunday. AE, V, MC. Lunch and dinner.

Shanghai Winter Garden. *Moderate.* 5651 Wilshire Blvd., Los Angeles; 934–0505. A reliable Oriental restaurant consistently serving Shanghai and Szechuan cuisine prepared authentically. Hot and sour soup is excellent, and the eight-precious duck is not to be overlooked. Kindly service. Open daily, lunch and dinner. Valet parking. All major credit cards.

The Twin Dragon. *Moderate-Inexpensive.* 8597 W. Pico Blvd., Los Angeles; 655–9805. One of top Los Angeles restaurants for Peking, Shanghai, and Szechuan cooking. Shrimp toast and hot and sour soup here are superior; the mu-shu pork and spicy chicken excel. Lunch; dinner daily. No CB.

Chinese Friends Restaurant. *Inexpensive.* 984 N. Broadway, Los Angeles; 626–1837. This restaurant may be minuscule, but the dishes it serves are bold and fiery. The Hunan style of cooking is predominant, and at lunch there is a multitude of tasty noodle dishes. Lunch and dinner daily. MC, V.

Chung Mee Café. *Inexpensive.* 207 Ord St., Los Angeles; 628–5026. Forget the nonexistent decor and concentrate on the excellently prepared Cantonese food. Specialties include steamed pork with fruit peel, oysters, and fried squab. The rice and soup are thrown in at no charge. Dinner daily. Open until 3:00 A.M. No credit cards.

Mandarin Shanghai Restaurant. *Inexpensive.* 970 N. Broadway, Los Angeles; 625–1195. Located in the Mandarin Plaza (#114), this Shanghai restaurant uses authentic ingredients not always available in this country. Golden fried yellow fish, meats and vegetables simmered in an earthen pot, and shrimps with chives are excellent choices. Lunch and dinner daily. AE, MC, V.

Mon Kee Live Fish and Seafood Restaurant. *Inexpensive.* 679 N. Spring St., Los Angeles; 628–6717. A large, complex menu with extensive seafood offerings.

Bare decor, but the fish just can't be beat. Lunch and dinner daily. All major credit cards.

New Moon. *Inexpensive.* 912 S. San Pedro St., Los Angeles; 622–1091. A Cantonese restaurant located close to the downtown garment district. Steak cubes, shredded chicken salad, lemon chicken, and crystal shrimp. Full bar. Lunch and dinner daily. All major credit cards.

Continental

The Betsy. *Expensive.* 1001 N. Vermont; 662–2116. Combining Art Deco with subtle Oriental tones, the Betsy dishes up creative French fare. An appetizer of flan with morels, fresh asparagus with chervil, and coquilles St. Jacques with oysters are a few of the specialties. Lunch, Monday through Friday; dinner, Monday through Saturday. Valet parking. All major credit cards.

Ravel. *Expensive.* 333 S. Figueroa St.; 617–1133. Located inside the new Sheraton Grande hotel, this bistro is named for the famed composer. Decorated with etched glass and miniature trees, Ravel features such creative fare as curried consomme of duck, prawns with Pernod, and roast quail with cashews. Lunch, Monday through Friday; dinner daily. Valet parking. All major credit cards.

Scandia. *Expensive.* 9040 Sunset Blvd., Los Angeles; 278–3555 or 272–9521. This elegant Scandinavian/Continental restaurant has long been a fixture on the Sunset Strip and has been the winner of numerous awards for many years. Different rooms have different themes, from the flowery garden atmosphere of the Belle Terrasse to the Danish Room, with copper utensils decorating the walls. Tables are beautifully and formally appointed, and fresh flowers are everywhere. Hors d'oeuvres include shrimps in dill, miniature pancakes flavored with aquavit and served with sour cream and Danish caviar, and the best gravlax you could hope to try. Entrees feature sauteed spring chicken, saddle of lamb, veal Oskar and kalldolmar, white cabbage filled with veal and pork stuffing. All tables get baskets of excellent assorted fresh breads, including the noted parmesan-crusted pumpernickel bread. A cold, creamy kiwi fruit souffle and Danish rum pudding top the dessert list. From 10:30 P.M. to 1:00 A.M., late night dining with a lighter menu is featured. Jackets required for men. Lunch Tuesday through Sunday; dinner Tuesday through Sunday. Sunday brunch. Valet parking. All major credit cards.

Seventh Street Bistro. *Expensive.* 815 W. 7th St.; 627–1242. Inside the historic Fine Arts Building is this casual, yet elegant restaurant. Classical French cuisine: John Dory with lime-ginger sauce, lobster with anise and sweet garlic, and squab with cabbage and port wine. Lunch, Monday through Friday; dinner, Monday through Saturday. Valet parking. All major credit cards.

Tower. *Expensive.* 1150 S. Olive St., Los Angeles; 746–1554. Offering one of the best views of the city, this restaurant is located on the 32nd floor of an office building in downtown Los Angeles. You'll have to take two elevators to get there; the last one is the private one that takes you to the top of the building and has its own elevator operator for restaurant clientele. The view at night stretches as far as the eye can see, and it is breathtaking. The Continental/French cuisine features classical dishes: coq au vin, duckling with turnips, sole with pine nuts, and Lyonnaise sausages. Service is very proper, and the tables are well-appointed. Lunch Monday through Friday; dinner daily except Sunday. All major credit cards. Valet parking.

The Cove. *Moderate.* 3191 W. 7th St., Los Angeles; 388–0361. A Continental restaurant with a European flair. One walks downstairs to enter a cozy room with dark booths and flocked wallpaper. Soft lamps illuminate the tables. The dinner menu is extensive and features everything from steaks, chops, and seafood to wiener schnitzel, sauerbraten, and boneless squab. Desserts include cherries jubilee, crepes Suzette, and a German chocolate cake with cherries made on the premises. Valet parking. Lunch Monday through Firday; dinner Monday through Saturday. Closed Sunday. All major credit cards.

Delicatessen

Canter's. *Inexpensive.* 419 N. Fairfax Ave., Los Angeles; 651–2030. The most renowned Los Angeles deli, located in the Fairfax district close to Farmers Market. The food is not what it used to be, but the name attracts customers on a continual basis. A hangout for entertainers late at night. Near the entrance is a display case filled with home-baked desserts. The waitresses are known to mother customers. Open twenty-four hours. No credit cards.

French

Bernard's. *Expensive.* Biltmore Hotel, 515 S. Olive St., Los Angeles; 624–0183. A renowned Los Angeles restaurant often overlooked owing to its downtown location. The emphasis is on seafood, but there are also such marvels as veal rib eye with marinated corn and roasted squab on country bread. Maine lobster in red wine sauce and red snapper braised in beer exemplify this bistro's creativity. Lunch weekdays, dinner Monday through Saturday. Valet parking. All major credit cards.

François. *Expensive.* 555 S. Flower St., Los Angeles; 680–2727. Close to the Music Center and located on the C-level in the underground shopping area of ARCO Plaza. The dining room is handsome, restrained dignity. A creative hors d'oeuvre is baked oysters on a bed of creamed spinach. Pepper steak in a Cognac sauce is superb. Also served are turkey breast Oklahoma, sea bass with lemon sauce, and chicken breast stuffed with crab meat. There are always fresh fish and daily specials, as well as special pre-theater dinners at bargain prices. Lunch Monday through Friday; dinner daily except Sunday. All major credit cards.

Le Dome. *Expensive.* 8720 Sunset Blvd., Los Angeles; 659–6919. An elegant French restaurant with a round bar that attracts a show- and music-business crowd. Country French cuisine, including blood sausage, smoked meats, and headcheese, is featured. Fragrant, fresh fruit desserts. Lunch Monday through Saturday; dinner Monday through Saturday. Valet parking. All major credit cards.

L'Ermitage. *Expensive.* 730 N. La Cienaga Blvd.; 652–5840. One of LA's most refined French restaurants. Brought to great heights by its late owner, Jean Bertranou, L'Ermitage's beautiful ambience is complimented by such entrees as breast of chicken with goose liver and port wine, and sauteed veal loin with green apples. Creativity reigns in chef Michel Blanchet's capable kitchen. Valet parking. Dinner Monday through Saturday. All major credit cards.

L'Orangerie. *Expensive.* 903 N. La Cienega Blvd., Los Angeles; 652–9770. One of Los Angeles's most renowned French restaurants, though it caters largely to a Beverly Hills crowd. The restaurant, with a dining room and a bar that face a formal courtyard, was built along architecturally classic lines. The tables are beautifully appointed. The very French menu includes eggs with caviar, terrine of duck with pistachio, medallions of veal in a three-mustard sauce, and chicken with shallots. Elaborate, freshly prepared desserts include chocolate charlotte and a hot apple tart served with a pitcher of heavy whipped cream. Valet parking. Dinner daily. Jackets for men are required. All major credit cards.

Le Chardonnay. *Expensive-Moderate.* 8284 Melrose Ave.; 655–8880. Billed as a French bistro/rotisserie, this restaurant offers many grilled dishes as well as those cooked on a spit. Roast duck with thyme, sauteed liver with glazed shallots, and beef ragout lure many patrons. Booked almost every night, Le Chardonnay is a new mecca for celebrities. Lunch, Monday through Friday; dinner, Monday through Saturday. All major credit cards.

Ma Maison. *Expensive.* 8368 Melrose Ave., Los Angeles; 655–1991. Los Angeles's most star-studded restaurant, in a converted bungalow under a canvas roof. This restaurant is so chic that its phone number is unlisted. Rows of Mercedes and Rolls Royces fill the parking lot. Owner Patrick Terrail is the suave, ever-present host. The cuisine matches the glamour of the clientele. Only the best and the freshest ingredients are chosen for the French-style menu. Excellent wine list. Excellent for people watching. Lunch and dinner Monday through Saturday. All major credit cards.

Entourage. *Expensive-Moderate.* 8450 W. Third St., Los Angeles; 653–1079. This chic French restaurant, located next door to a major recording studio, draws many famous recording artists. Beautiful decor, particularly the sky-lighted garden room in the rear. The menu highlights duckling in pear sauce and trout stuffed with a mousseline in a Cognac-cream sauce. All sauces are silken and rich, and the poultry, fish, and produce are very fresh. Try the escargot wrapped in puff pastry and cloaked with a creamy sauce. Desserts, particularly the chocolate mousse cake topped with shavings of white chocolate, are extra rich. Valet parking. Lunch Monday through Friday; dinner Monday through Saturday. All major credit cards.

La Toque. *Expensive-Moderate.* 8171 Sunset Blvd., Los Angeles; 656–7515. An intimate French bistro with a flair for the unusual. Owner Ken Frank is so creative in the kitchen that he changes his menu daily according to the best of fresh ingredients he sees at the markets. Sauces are silken understatements, and each plate arrives at the table with appeal to both the eye and the senses. Service is kindly, not stuffy. Always fresh fish, excellent soups. Heavy use of native

California fish and vegetables. An experience. Valet parking. Dinner Monday through Saturday. All major credit cards.

Greek

Constadina's. *Inexpensive.* 540 S. Vermont Ave., Los Angeles; 388–9478. A restaurant with a schizophrenic personality. By day it's an American coffee shop. By night it is transformed into a Greek restaurant and nightclub. The menu features chicken baked with lemon and oregano, roast leg of lamb, grape leaves, and fresh fried calamari. Expert Greek dancing, and you're invited to join in. Comfortable atmosphere; many booths. Dinner Tuesday through Saturday. Limited lunch menu, Monday through Friday. All major credit cards.

Health

Golden Temple of Conscious Cookery. *Inexpensive.* 7910 W. 3rd St., Los Angeles; 655–1891. A vegetarian restaurant with lofty principles. The menu is international in scope, and the food is generally prepared well. Close to Farmers Market and CBS. Many salads; eggplant parmigiana is a specialty. Nightly specials. Lunch Monday through Saturday; dinner Monday through Saturday. MC, V.

Hungarian

Budapest Hungarian Restaurant. *Moderate.* 432 N. Fairfax Ave., Los Angeles; 655–0111. Close to Farmers Market and CBS. A small neighborhood restaurant that caters to an older Jewish and European clientele. Seltzer is served instead of water. Beef goulash, roast goose (in season), stuffed cabbage, and strudel are specialties. The food is not great, but you get bountiful portions, honestly prepared, at low prices, and you can't beat the ambience. Dinner daily; brunch Sunday. All major credit cards.

Indian

Gitanjali India Restaurant. *Moderate.* 414 N. La Cienega Blvd., Los Angeles; 657–2117. Authentic decor in this northern Indian restaurant. Tandoori chicken and marinated tikka dishes. The large menu includes beef, fish, and vegetarian entrees. Attentive service. Wine, beer. Lunch, Monday through Friday; dinner daily. No CB.

Italian

Adriano's Ristorante. *Expensive.* 2930 Beverly Glen Circle, Los Angeles; 475–9807. One of Los Angeles's most distinctive Northern Italian restaurants. The decor is sophisticated; it includes an outdoor patio surrounded by greenery adorned with twinkling lights. Indoors are an intimate bar and a chic dining room with peach-colored walls, green carpeting, and a lot of walnut wood trim. Pastas are all made on the premises. Gnocchi with pesto is good, but even better is the fettuccine Tre 'P'—fettuccine with prosciutto, peas, and grated parmesan combined with a silken, creamy sauce. Roast duck with olives, a casserole of rabbit with polenta, and many veal dishes complete a discriminating menu. Desserts include fresh berries with cream and fragole gratinate, a velvety custard with ice cream, and marinated strawberries baked in a caramel crust. Good wine list. Attentive service provided by both captains and waiters. Lunch Tuesday through Saturday; dinner Tuesday through Sunday. Sunday brunch. AE, V, MC.

Giuseppei! *Expensive.* 8256 Beverly Blvd., Los Angeles; 653–8025. Very California looking, with chic decor and a plethora of plants. Calamari with marinara sauce is fine, and so is the porterhouse steak, which is well marinated in olive oil and herbs. The best of all is the gnocchi Genovese, a plate of the lightest most tender gnocchi ever in a smooth and fragrant pesto sauce. Classic souffles and fresh pastries. Lunch Monday through Friday; dinner, Monday through Saturday. Valet parking. All major credit cards.

Rex Il Ristorante. *Expensive.* 617 S. Olive St., Los Angeles; 627–2300. One of Los Angeles's most respected restaurateurs, Mauro Vincenti, opened this architectural masterpiece featuring sophisticated "nuova cucina" (the new cuisine) Italian dining. The decor features imported French oak, rich carpeting, Italian marble, and a burgundy color scheme, all creating an Art Deco ambience. Every dish is prepared from fresh ingredients. Ice cream, pasta, and bread are made on the premises. All dishes are prepared in copperware only. The wine cellar features over 300 labels of Italian, French, and California wines. An experience. Valet parking. Lunch Monday through Friday; dinner Monday through Saturday. All major credit cards.

Dan Tana's. *Expensive-Moderate.* 9071 Santa Monica Blvd., Los Angeles; 275–9444. Located close to the Troubadour nightclub; good for celebrity spotting. Cioppino, chicken Florentine with spinach and cheese, and veal rollatini are good here. Valet parking. Dinner daily. All major credit cards.

Alberto's. *Moderate.* 8826 Melrose Ave., Los Angeles; 278–2770. Despite the elegance of this restaurant's appointments, it still has a comfortable neighborhood bistro appeal. Clams oregenata and mozzarella marinara excel as appetizers. and the chicken pappagallo and most veal dishes here can't be beat. Distinctive service. The cheesecake is so rich and creamy that it makes other cheesecakes taste like cardboard. Valet parking. Dinner daily. All major credit cards.

La Strada. *Moderate.* 3000 Los Feliz Blvd., Los Angeles; 664–2955. The Italian food is good, but it's even better combined with the opera and musical comedy offered. Have you ever tried *La Boheme* with fettuccine? Sometimes there are costumes and scenery, other times singers will serenade you at your table. Veal, fresh fish, daily specials. Valet parking. Dinner Tuesday through Sunday. All major credit cards.

Virgilio's. *Moderate.* 2611 S. La Cienega Blvd., Los Angeles; 559–8532. A sleek Italian restaurant with a wide variety of pastas. Featured are spaghettini with black olives, garlic, and capers; fettuccine; mostacciole; linguini; lasagna. An elaborate chicken preparation is the Pollo Alla Romana, chicken sauteed with crabmeat, asparagus, and bearnaise sauce. Veal, beef, and sweetbreads round out a well-planned menu. Desserts include Champagne sherbet, souffles, and fresh berries. A delightful after-dinner drink is the Italian coffee spiked with Frangelico. Lunch Monday through Friday; dinner daily. All major credit cards.

Japanese

Eigiku. *Moderate.* 314 E. 1st. St., Los Angeles; 629–3029. Popular downtown Japanese restaurant. Efficient service. Nigiri, tekka, and inari sushi. Full bar. Dinner daily except Sunday. All major credit cards.

Lyon. *Moderate.* 3360 West First St., Los Angeles; 381–5040. A unique restaurant serving a blend of French and Japanese cuisine. Although it's counter service only, the dishes are sophisticated. Rack of lamb in mint sauce, chicken in red wine, snow peas, and teriyaki marinades accent the menu. Soups are prepared daily from stock pot. Stark Oriental decor. Limited wines. The desserts are homemade and include cranberry ice with custard sauce and cheesecake with cranberry custard. Reservations required. Lunch, Tueday through Friday; dinner, Tuesday through Saturday. MC, V at dinner only.

Ichiban Café. *Inexpensive.* 108 S. San Pedro St., Los Angeles; 622–4453. A tiny downtown bistro catering mostly to Japanese customers. Small sushi bar; table service for tempura, oshinko maki, and nigiri. *Sake,* wine, and beer. Lunch and dinner daily, except Wednesday. MC, V.

Mexican

Antonio's Restaurant. *Moderate-Inexpensive.* 7472 Melrose Ave., Los Angeles; 655–0480. The usual Mexican fare, with the addition of more complex specialties. Jicama salad with fresh exotic fruits and chicken with an intriguing mole sauce excel. Authentic ropa vieja. Mariachi music Wednesday through Sunday. Lunch, dinner daily. Valet parking at night only. AE, MC, V.

El Cholo. *Inexpensive.* 1121 S. Western Ave., Los Angeles; 734–2773. Attentive service, a huge menu, and giant portions characterize this comfortable Mexican restaurant. Great for families, starving artists, and virtually everyone who thinks spending a lot of money to eat out is a ridiculous thing to do. Lunch and dinner daily. AE, MC, V.

El Coyote Spanish Café. *Inexpensive.* 7312 Beverly Blvd., Los Angeles; 939–7766. Spartan Mexican decor. Smiling waitresses bring you warm, fresh tortillas the moment you sit down. Traditional Mexican fare: enchiladas, burritos, tostadas, and so on. Lunch and dinner daily. MC, V.

El Tepeyac. *Inexpensive.* 812 N. Evergreen Ave., East L.A.; 267–8668. Home of the largest burritos in town. You'll leave stuffed from this Mexican restaurant that offers a plain, kitchen-like ambiance and patio, as well as indoor dining. Open Monday and Wednesday–Friday for lunch and dinner; closed Tuesdays. Cash only.

The Gardens of Taxco. *Inexpensive.* 11135 N. Harper Ave., Los Angeles; 654–1746. Mexican food is most popular in Los Angeles, and this restaurant represents the best of Mexico City cuisine. Margaritas, sangria, and Mexican beer will quench your thirst. The quesadillas are splendid, the chicken mole is terrific, and there are at least ten desserts to choose from, including flan and bananas in a creamy custard. Dinner daily, except Monday. AE, MC, V.

Russian

Mischa's. *Moderate.* 7561 Sunset Blvd., Los Angeles; 874–3467. This Russian cabaret restaurant is always alive with the energy of its performers and the enthusiasm of the clientele. The food is in the classical Russian vein and includes chicken Czar Alexander, with a cream sauce accented by mushrooms and cucumbers, a smooth beef Stroganoff, and fresh fish and veal specialties. Fine wine list; many varieties of vodka. Dinner daily. All major credit cards.

Gorky's. *Moderate–Inexpensive.* 536 Eighth St., L.A.; 627–4060. Russian avant-garde restaurant with an art school cafeteria atmosphere. Blues and jazz most evenings; a hang-out for downtown artists and blue-collar workers. Kasha, borscht, and piroshkis appear on the menu with espresso, wine, and beer. Local art on the high walls. Open Monday through Thursday, 7 A.M. to 1 A.M. 24 hrs. on Friday and Saturday. Cash only.

Seafood

The Fishmarket. *Expensive-Moderate.* 9229 Sunset Blvd., Los Angeles; 550–1544. An elegant seafood restaurant popular for fresh fish flown in from Hawaii. Ulua, ono, mahi mahi, and opaka-paka are featured menu items. You can expect to find fresh catfish, fresh salmon, and abalone—suggested entree selections. Fresh oysters Rockefeller, fresh cherrystone clams, and fresh Blue Point oysters are also popular. Fresh berries are always available; if not in season, they're flown in. Comfortable soft lighted booths and competent service. Lunch, dinner daily. All major credit cards.

South American

Caché. *Moderate.* 2395 Glendale Blvd.; 660–6154. The menu here roams from the Caribbean to South America and Spain. Romantic dinner music is performed nightly and the elegant decor includes crystal table lamps and rich, burgundy fabric walls. Paella is primo, although Cuban-style steak is also popular. Lunch, dinner daily except Monday. All major credit cards.

El Dorado. *Inexpensive.* 4273 Beverly Blvd., Los Angeles; 660–7746. A tiny bistro serving Colombian food. Flank steak with sauce, blood sausage, bean soup with fried pork skin, and beef tripe soup are all highlighted on the menu. All dishes are unusual and well prepared. Lunch and dinner daily. Beer and wine only. All major credit cards.

Spanish

La Masia. *Moderate.* 9077 Santa Monica Blvd.; Los Angeles; 273–7066. An intimate restaurant with warm ambience. Excellent paella and Spanish-style bouillabaisse. Dinners include salad, vegetables, and rice in the price. A guitar player entertains on weekends. Usually very busy; be sure to make reservations. Dinner daily, except Monday. All major credit cards.

Thai/Southeast Asian

Siam Orchid. *Moderate.* Beverly Center, 8500 Beverly Blvd., Los Angeles; 652–6000. A fortune was spent to build this restaurant out of imported teakwood and carved teak doors. Cascades of Thai lanterns and silk panels add to its authenticity. The kitchen staff, imported from Thailand, prepare stuffed omelets and vegetable soup, glass-noodle salad and roast-duck red curry among many items on the lengthy menu. Lunch and dinner daily. All major credit cards.

Saigon Flavor Restaurant. *Inexpensive.* 1044 S. Fairfax Ave., Los Angeles; 935–1564. A top Vietnamese restaurant; spacious, comfortable booths with friendly service. The seafood specialties are best represented by salted rock crab, crab claws wrapped in shrimp, and shrimp balls on sugar cane. Wine, beer. Lunch and dinner daily except Tuesday. All major credit cards.

Siamese Princess. *Inexpensive.* 8048 W. Third St., Los Angeles; 653–2643. A great restaurant for those unfamiliar with Thai food; explanations are written in detail below each featured dish. Strips of beef marinated in coconut milk and spices are charbroiled and served with cucumber relish and a dip of curried peanut butter. Coconut-chicken soup and orange sour soup are other offerings. Quenelles of sea bass in mussel shells and sauteed stuffed squid are even more exotic. Lunch, Monday through Friday; dinner daily. All major credit cards.

Tepparod Tea House. *Inexpensive.* 4645 Melbourne Ave., Los Feliz; 669–9117. One of the most successful Thai restaurants in Los Angeles. Try the minced pork soup, fried beef sauteed in oyster oil, or the Siamese greens with chicken. Wine, beer. Lunch and dinner daily. No credit cards.

GLENDALE/PASADENA
(Area code 818)

Continental

Maldonado's. *Moderate.* 1202 E. Green St., Pasadena; (818) 796–1126. A musical restaurant, Maldonado's features haute cuisine with a side order of opera, musical comedy, and other cabaret entertainment. Appetizers include escargots and a salad of crisp spinach and romaine tossed with crumbled Roquefort. There are always several specials, as well as duckling with sauce Grand Marnier and a kiwi fruit garnish, medallions of lamb sauteed with thyme sauce and artichoke hearts, and an honorable chicken Marengo. Fine wine list. Lunch Tuesday through Friday; dinner daily except Monday. All major credit cards.

Phoenicia. *Moderate.* 343 N. Central Ave., Glendale; 956–7800. Ara Kalfayan and his wife Silva are the two loveliest restaurant owners in town. They go out of their way to make each guest feel at home while dining. Silva goes downtown to the flower market and creates beautiful flower arrangements for each table. Ara is Lebanese, Silva is Russian, and their chef is Swiss, so it's a veritable United Nations in the kitchen. Salmon mousse with Champagne sauce is a smooth and satisfying hors d'oeuvre, as is the mozzarella marinara and the pheasant pâté. Salads are arranged artistically, with fresh spinach, bacon, herbs, and walnuts or hearts of palm with shrimp. Chicken baked in clay is a specialty that has brought the Kalfayans much acclaim. It has to be specially ordered; the chicken is marinated before it is baked and brought tableside, where the clay is then cracked—all the juices are sealed in and the fragrance perfumes the room. Roast quail stuffed with apples and grapes, shish kebab, and veal with avocado, tomatoes, and cheese round out a well-planned menu. The service is impeccable, and the wine list is extraordinary. Lunch Monday through Friday; dinner daily, except Monday. All major credit cards.

HOLLYWOOD/LOS FELIZ/WEST HOLLYWOOD

American

Morton's. *Expensive.* 8800 Melrose Ave., West Hollywood; 276–5205. This trendy spot bases its success on grilled chicken, fish, and steaks. Usually crowded with celebrities and Beautiful People. Dinner Monday through Saturday. AE, MC, V.

The Palm. *Expensive.* 9001 Santa Monica Blvd., West Hollywood; 550–8811. One branch of a successful national chain. Sawdust on the floors, caricatures on the walls, and a high noise level. It is not uncommon to see celebrities here. The steaks are the best in the city. The lobsters are enormous, usually five pounds and over, but they can be shared. Cheesecake is flown in from New York, and it's thick, creamy, and very, very rich. The fried onions can't be beat. Entrees are served with hunks of sourdough and pumpernickle bread. New York-style waiters, brash but kindly. Valet parking. Lunch Monday through Friday; dinner daily. All major credit cards.

Greenblatt's. *Moderate-Inexpensive.* 8017 Sunset Blvd., Hollywood; 656–0606. A favored deli with the show-biz crowd. Enormous wine selection. Fat sandwiches of pastrami, corned beef, and roast beef are popular. Smoked ribs and ham. Takeout or sit down, but you order at the counter. Catering. Breakfast, lunch, and dinner daily. No reservations. Wines to go only. MC, V.

Roscoe's House of Chicken and Waffles. *Moderate-Inexpensive.* 1514 N. Gower St., Hollywood; 466–7453. A tasty soul-food restaurant that serves mostly breakfast, no matter what time of day. There are hot and fresh biscuits, sinfully smothered chicken livers, and feathery-light waffles made from Roscoe's own mix. Chicken, "fried to the bone," is done properly, and it's served in various combinations with eggs or waffles. Open daily, except Monday, for breakfast, lunch, and dinner. Usually open until 3:00 A.M. No credit cards.

The Hard Rock Café. *Inexpensive.* 8600 Beverly Blvd., West Hollywood; 276–7605. This fifties-style café has a vintage '59 Cadillac jetting out of the roof, *Happy Days*' Fonzie's leather jacket hangs on the wall—as does Elvis's motor cycle—and the waitresses are dressed in appropriate threads of the era. The American menu consists of burgers, baby back ribs basted in watermelon barbecue sauce, and apple pie. The restaurant's message? Rock 'n' roll is here to stay. Fast becoming an L.A. landmark. Open daily, lunch and dinner. V, MC, AE.

Lillian's. *Inexpensive.* 962 N. Cahuenga Blvd., Hollywood; 462–0435. A casual storefront restaurant where just about everything is homemade. The soups, straight from a stockpot, are rich, and dinners include just about every course but the kitchen sink. Lunch Monday through Friday. No credit cards.

California/Continental

Spago. *Moderate.* 1114 Horn Ave. just off Sunset Strip, West Hollywood; 652–4025. Owner Wolfgang Puck is the "golden chef" of Los Angeles, and this California-style restaurant has helped make Puck shine all the more. It's innovative, creative, and unique, and the menu features produce, poultry, and seafood native to California. Wood-burning ovens cook your meals right in the dining room as a bit of a show. Many unusual combinations of pizza: Did you ever have lox and cream cheese on pizza before? There are also Santa Barbara shrimp, California goat cheese, homemade duck sausage, and pastas with seafood. Ravioli may be filled with lobster, and the fresh fish is served strict and pure, grilled with butter only. The restaurant, decorated in a beige color scheme, has small tables and ice cream parlor chairs and fine art on the walls. You'll see rows of Rolls Royces and Mercedes in the parking lot; this is a restaurant patronized by the elite—great for celebrity spotting. Interesting wine list. The pastry chef prepares flaky tarts, cakes, and other pastries, many with fresh fruit and liqueurs. Valet parking. Dinner nightly. All major credit cards.

Chinese

The Mandarette. *Moderate–Inexpensive.* 8386 Beverly Blvd., W. Hollywood; 655–6115. Casual, simple, and contemporary, there's a big surprise in store for those who saunter in to this diner-like café near the Beverly Center: It's great! The service is friendly and Chinese home cooking is at its best in an unlikely part of town. Try the clams in black bean sauce, 1,000-year-old eggs or steamed pork-filled dumplings. Ask for the fresh vegetables of the day and don't miss the onion pancakes. Lunch, Monday through Friday; dinner daily. MC, V.

Chin Chin. *Moderate–Inexpensive.* 8618 Sunset Blvd., Hollywood; 652–1818. High-tech decor in the midst of the Sunset Strip. Eat indoors or out in this great people-watching area. Order the shredded chicken salad or Cantonese duck. Beer, wine. Lunch and dinner, Monday through Saturday. MC, V.

Continental

Trumps. *Expensive.* 8764 Melrose Ave., West Hollywood; 855–1480. Contemporary decor marks this chic and popular Los Angeles restaurant featuring an eclectic Continental menu. Weekday tea is most popular, almost overtaking the lunch hour; Sherry, tea, and assorted tea sandwiches and scones are offered. This kitchen is always inventive, and the food will not disappoint. Lunch Monday through Saturday; tea Monday through Saturday from 3:30 P.M. to 6:00 P.M.; dinner Monday through Saturday. Valet parking. Patio dining. AE, MC, V.

L.A. Nicola. *Expensive–Moderate.* 4326 Sunset Blvd., Hollywood; 660–7217. Nouvelle friendly cuisine served in a very lively atmosphere where owner Larry Nicola makes everyone feel welcome. Changing menu filled with imagination plus old favorites like potato skin appetizers and one of the best Greek salads to be found in the city. The full bar, newly opened, has a fresh look and is a favorite hangout for the upscale clientele. Around the corner from ABC Studios. Features an airy outdoor café. Closed Sundays. Lunch (except Saturday) and dinner. All major credit cards.

Pierre's Los Feliz Inn. *Expensive–Moderate.* 2138 Hillhurst Ave., Hollywood/Los Feliz; 663–8001. An emphasis on fresh fish and vegetables. Wild game gets special treatment here. Cozy, neighborhood Old World ambience. Close to Dodger Stadium, Griffith Park, and the zoo. Lunch Monday through Friday, dinner daily. Valet parking. All major credit cards.

English

The Cock 'n Bull. *Moderate.* 9170 Sunset Blvd., West Hollywood; 273–0081. The British pub atmosphere draws many stray Englishmen. Long a fixture on the Sunset Strip, this restaurant features prime rib, steak-and-kidney pie, and other stalwart entrees. Sunday brunch consists of a proper plate of eggs, sausage, finnan haddie, chicken, and fruit. Service is kindly, and although it's buffet service for your entree and vegetables, soup, salad, or Welsh rarebit are served at the table. Valet parking. Lunch Monday through Friday; dinner daily; Sunday brunch. AE, MC, V.

Oscar's. *Moderate.* 8210 Sunset Blvd., Los Angeles; 654–3457. A restaurant with a salute to English cooking—and Art-Deco decor. Starters or appetizers include angels on horseback (oysters wrapped in bacon, baked, and served on toast points) and potted shrimp. Entrees featured are chicken parsley pie, quiche, pasta primavera, steak-and-kidney pie, and "bangers and mash"—pork sausages and mashed potatoes with onion gravy. There is always trifle for dessert. You have the option of dining in the jazz room, where soft combos or nostalgia singers perform. Valet parking. Dinner theater Saturday night, British vaudeville. Lunch Monday through Friday; dinner daily. AE, MC, V.

Franco/Japanese

La Petite Chaya. *Expensive.* 1930 Hillhurst Ave., Hollywood/Los Feliz; 665–5991. Freshly done and highly touted restaurant serving the newest in-vogue cuisine. French-trained Japanese chef is very imaginative, service is impeccable, and decor is simple, yet elegant. Enclosed porch makes for a very romantic dining spot. Near ABC Studios. Lunch Monday through Friday; dinner daily. Closed Sunday. Valet parking. Full bar. All major credit cards.

French

Le St. Germain. *Expensive.* 5955 Melrose Ave., Hollywood; 467–1108. A serene restaurant, decidedly French and decidedly chic. One of the restaurants to see and "be seen" in. The menu is elegant, and the specials of the day are always the best. The service is impeccable. The presentation of the plates is a joy to behold. The surroundings are formal despite a casual ambience. Salmon with a sorrel cream sauce and roast chicken in a Champagne sauce are noted entrees. Fresh berry fruit tarts are the best bet for dessert. Lunch Monday through Friday; dinner Monday through Saturday. No CB.

Greek

Athenian Gardens. *Moderate-Inexpensive.* 1835 N. Cahuenga Blvd., Hollywood; 469–7038. Long a fixture in Hollywood. The menu features moussaka, roast lamb, dolmades, and pastitsio. Greek music and dancing. Dinner Tuesday through Sunday. Valet parking. AE, MC, V.

Health

Old World. *Inexpensive.* 8782 Sunset Blvd., West Hollywood; 652–2520. Also at 1019 Westwood Blvd., Westwood; 208–4033; and 216 N. Beverly Dr., Beverly Hills; 274–7695. The West Hollywood location is the original. All the Old World restaurants feature health-oriented cuisine, including superior hamburgers, Belgian waffles, and homemade soups. Their vegetable platters and vegetarian burgers are not only healthy for you, but they also taste good, too. Breakfast, lunch, and dinner daily. AE, DC, MC, V.

Indian

Bengal Tiger. *Inexpensive.* 1710 N. Las Palmas Ave., Hollywood; 469–1991. This tiny Indian and Pakistani restaurant consistently prepares authentic cuisine from its corner of the world. Mulligatawny soup is a spicy specialty, and curries will be prepared just as hot as you can stand them. Appetizers include *samosas,* the deep-fried pastry pockets filled with meat or vegetables and dipped into a sweet and hot murky sauce. Breads are truly delights; the *poori,* deep-fried puffed wheat bread, and *parathas,* flaky layered, crisp bread stuffed with potatoes or vegetables, are some of the best prepared Indian breads in the city. Wine, beer. Lunch and dinner daily. AE, MC, V.

Bombay Curry. *Inexpensive.* 7617 Sunset Blvd., Hollywood; 876–2799. A simple, Indian-style café featuring traditional Indian cuisine. Specialties include lamb Madras and chicken birani. Entrees come with samosas, mulligatawny soup, rice, chutney, and custard pudding or baklava. Lunch and dinner daily, except Tuesday. MC, V.

Paru. *Inexpensive.* 5140 Sunset Blvd., Hollywood; 661–7600. Southern Indian cuisine that is vegetarian: A lot of rice dishes, lentil soup, and poori bread stuffed with potatoes and curry. Homemade yogurt. Good *lassis,* the yogurt drinks that are flavored with rosewater. Lunch, dinner daily, except Monday. Wine, beer. MC, V.

Israeli

Shula and Esther. *Inexpensive.* 519 N. Fairfax Ave., West Hollywood; 852–9154. You could break out in the hora over the good food of this Israeli café. There is a great appetizer plate with a fiery Turkish salad and rich hummus and tahina. Shaslik and schnitzel are quite authentic, and there is also moussaka. No ambience, but a neighborhood hangout for a young Israeli crowd. Breakfast, lunch, and dinner daily. No credit cards.

Tel Aviv Café. *Inexpensive.* 509½ N. Fairfax Ave., West Hollywood; 653–7031. Fine Israeli cuisine in a restaurant that lacks atmosphere. But the clientele is colorful enough, and the steam tables are laden with delicious moussaka, kebabs, and stuffed peppers. There is hot pita bread and the usual Middle Eastern salads. Counter seats only: you will be served quickly, and you can't beat the prices. Lunch and dinner daily, except Sunday. No credit cards.

Italian

Bono's. *Expensive.* 8478 Melrose Ave., West Hollywood; 651–1842. Entertainer Sonny Bono is at the helm of this trendy and celebrity-filled bistro. Antipasto, pasta, and Italian-style seafood. Crowded and noisy. Come for the scene rather than the food and you'll not be disappointed. Valet parking. Lunch, dinner daily. AE, MC, V.

Angeli. *Moderate.* 7274 Melrose Ave., W. Hollywood; 936–9086. Upscale pizzeria's pesto pie with fresh garlic and onions strives to rival Spago fare. Atmosphere definitely 1980s with tiny, dough sculptures lining the walls. Closed Monday but open from 11 A.M. to midnight all other days. Make reservations if possible, it's popular. AE, MC, V.

Japanese

Imperial Gardens. *Expensive-Moderate.* 8225 Sunset Blvd., West Hollywood; 656–1750. A gathering spot for entertainment industry sushi freaks as well as restaurateurs who come here on their nights off. Different dining rooms feature tempura, teriyaki, and shabu-shabu. Tatami room. Valet parking. Dinner daily. All major credit cards.

Restaurant Katzu. *Moderate.* 1972 N. Hillhurst Ave., Los Feliz; 665–1891. This new entry into the sushi bar/restaurant market is indeed refreshing. A stark hi-tech interior and exterior (no sign indicates that there's a restaurant inside) provides a great showplace for some of the city's most imaginative sushi. Owner/designer/sushi-chef Katzu never compromises on his own tastes; hence all sushi orders are authentic. (No California Roll sushi at Katzu's place.) Richly designed plates and cups in a modern motif mix well with the highly technological chemistry equipment that is used to mix the sauces that must accompany sushi. Wine and beer. Lunch from 11:30 A.M. to 2:00 P.M.; dinner from 5:30 to 10:00 P.M. Closed Sunday. MC, V.

Yamashiro. *Moderate.* 1999 N. Sycamore Ave., Hollywood; 466–5125. This beautiful restaurant in the hills of Hollywood resembles an Oriental palace set amid acres of flowering gardens. At night the view is mind-boggling; you can see almost to the ocean. The menu is Japanese, but there are also Continental offerings such as steak, veal, and fish. The food tends to be uneven; best advice is to order hors d'oeuvres and drinks and enjoy the view. Valet parking. Lunch Monday through Friday; dinner daily. AE, MC, V.

Yoriki. *Inexpensive.* 4057 W. Third St.; 388–8983. Featured here is Kushikatsu, a chef's selection of fresh foods that are lightly breaded and deep-fried on a skewer. Contests are often held here as to how many of these delights patrons can down. Those with adventurous palates should try the turtle soup. Lunch, Monday through Friday; dinner, Monday through Saturday. MC, V.

Mexican

La Casita. *Inexpensive.* 6611 Hollywood Blvd., Hollywood; 464–9480. Salvadorian and Mexican cuisine. Steaks, fried fresh fish, and black beans and rice. Wine and beer only. Lunch and dinner daily. No credit cards.

El Conquistador. *Inexpensive.* 3701 Sunset Blvd., Hollywood/Silverlake; 666–5136. Standard Mexican and Cal-Mex cuisine, generally well prepared. Patio dining. Lunch and dinner daily. No CB.

Lucy's El Adobe. *Inexpensive.* 5536 Melrose Ave., Hollywood; 462–9421. An intimate Mexican restaurant that is a music-industry hangout. Reportedly was a rendezvous for Governor Jerry Brown and his ex-girlfriend Linda Ronstadt. Arroz con pollo, enchiladas rancheros, and enchiladas verdes are specialties. Lunch and dinner Monday through Saturday. MC, V.

Moroccan

Dar Maghreb. *Expensive-Moderate.* 7651 Sunset Blvd., Hollywood; 876–7651. A posh Moroccan restaurant with authentic decor. Dine on low benches piled high with cushions, and eat off communal plates set atop ivory-inlaid tables. There is a dramatic interior courtyard with a fountain. Hand-painted tiles, Moroccan rugs, and costumed waiters. Dinners include a choice of chicken, pigeon, lamb, or rabbit. Hands are washed in rose-scented water. *B'stilla,* couscous, mint tea, fruit and nuts, and baklava are all included in the dinner price. Dinner daily. Valet parking. MC, V.

Moun of Tunis. *Moderate.* 7445½ Sunset Blvd., Hollywood; 874–3333. Like your neighborhood casbah. Enter through an arched door leading to small rooms with cushioned benches and round, low tables. Waiters and waitresses are dressed in traditional garb. There are several choices of full-course meals: *b'stilla* is wonderful, as is the lemon chicken with almonds, which literally falls apart in your fingers because it's so moist. A mixed salad plate includes a couple of hot salads; be prepared to breathe fire. Belly dancing nightly. All major credit cards.

El Morocco. *Moderate–Inexpensive.* 8222 Santa Monica Blvd., W. Hollywood; 654–9550. A home-style Moroccan restaurant that offers a full seven-course feast at reasonable prices. Daily specials include stuffed prunes, spicey halibut, and chicken with Jerusalem artichokes. BYOB. Open Monday through Saturday. MC, V.

South American

Chile Lindo. *Inexpensive.* 5237 Sunset Blvd., Hollywood; 667–9973. Home style Chilean food. Dinners include a hearty homemade soup. Highlights of the menu are the *corvina* (Peruvian fish and rice) and the *lomo con ensalada Chilena* (steak with an onion and tomato salad). Beer and Chilean wine by the glass. Weekend entertainment features live Latino music to an enthusiastic audience. Lunch and dinner daily, except Thursday. MC, V.

Thai

Tommy Tang's. *Moderate.* 7473 Melrose Ave., Hollywood. This trendy Thai bistro caters to the entertainment industry with a punkish flair. Thai cuisine has an American flavor. Try the spicy bbq chicken, squid with mint leaves and chili, and *mee krob.* Sushi bar. Upbeat, eclectic atmosphere. Lunch Monday through Friday, dinner daily, closed Sunday. MC, V, AE.

Chao Praya. *Inexpensive.* Corner Yucca and Vine at 6307 Yucca, Hollywood; 464–9652. This earthy restaurant is set smack in the middle of Hollywood, cater-cornered from the Capital Records Building. The delicious Thai cuisine is served in newly decorated surroundings. Highlights: beef and pork *stay, mee krob,* barbecued and garlic chicken dishes. Generous portions. Lunch, dinner; daily. All major credit cards.

Jitlada. *Inexpensive.* 5233½ Sunset Blvd., Hollywood; 667–9809. In a small shopping center. Specialties include *mee krob,* lemon grass, and prawn soup. Wonderful curries. Lunch and dinner, Tuesday through Sunday. DC, MC, V.

BEVERLY HILLS/CENTURY CITY

American

En Brochette. *Expensive-Moderate.* 9018 Burton Way, Beverly Hills; 276–9990. Two outdoor dining patios, one facing Burton Way where you can watch the shoppers, and the other on the side, gazebo-style. Strolling musicians play classical music. Appetizers include quiche, broiled mushrooms, and guacamole. The featured entrees are skewered beef and chicken and fish served with assorted dipping sauces. Mousse pies for dessert. Lunch and dinner daily. Valet parking. All major credit cards.

Gingerman. *Moderate.* 369 Bedford Dr., Beverly Hills; 273–7585. Patrick O'Neil and Carroll O'Connor own this sleek establishment that is both a pub and a restaurant. The bar area, packed at "happy hour" and into the evening, has become a singles meeting place. The restaurant produces fine fare. Burgers, salads, and omelettes are always right, and there is always a selection of fresh fish. Lunch and dinner daily. Sunday brunch. Valet parking. AE, MC, V.

The Grill. *Moderate.* 9560 Dayton Way, Beverly Hills; 276–0615. Traditional but trendy, the menu here stresses meats and seafood cooked over oak and charcoal. Such American staples as short ribs, rice pudding, and apple pie are some of patrons' favorites. Lots of celebrities hob nob in elegant booths. Lunch, dinner, Monday through Saturday. AE, DC, MC, V.

Lawry's the Prime Rib. *Moderate.* 55 N. La Cienega Blvd., Beverly Hills; 652–2827. The leading restaurant in Los Angeles for prime ribs. Silver carts are wheeled to your table, where your individual slice of beef is hand carved. Each dinner is served with a salad that is spun on a bed of ice and tossed with Lawry's French dressing. The creamed horseradish sauce, slightly spicy and slightly sweet, is one of the best. Yorkshire pudding, a bit bland, accompanies the dinner. A separate dessert menu, with fresh Hawaiian pineapple, chocolate pecan pie, and a chocolate fantasy cake that is indeed fantastic, is featured. Dinner daily. All major credit cards.

Lawry's Westside Broiler. *Moderate.* 116 N. La Cienega Blvd., Beverly Hills; 655–8686. A well-designed, casual restaurant with an elegant flair. Steaks are the specialty, and they are thick, tender, and charbroiled. There are some creative appetizers, such as mussels in escargot butter with pistachios. Broiled Indonesian shrimp and chicken tempura are also available for noncarnivores. Their vegetables taste very fresh, as does a creative assortment of desserts. Young, eager—if inexperienced—waiters. Lunch Monday through Friday; dinner nightly. Valet parking. AE, MC, V.

R.J.'s the Rib Joint. *Moderate.* 252 N. Beverly Dr., Beverly Hills; 274–RIBS. A unique restaurant serving bountiful quality food in a relaxed and casual atmosphere. Its "Green Grocery Salad Bar" is tops in the city. An ice-cold cast-iron skillet is your salad plate, and you'll choose from several varieties of lettuce or exotic raw vegetables served with homemade dressings and homemade croutons. Cut your own hunk of bread to take to the table. Ribs are the specialty, and they're generally tender and slightly sweet. Sunday brunch includes the salad bar and a smoked fish platter brought to your table, as well as such items as zucchini bread and fried bagels (fried bagels?). Desserts are slices of cake so big that one slice can easily feed four hungry adults. Valet parking. Lunch Monday through Saturday; dinner daily; Sunday brunch. MC, V.

Larry Parker's Beverly Hills Diner. *Moderate–Inexpensive.* 2065 Beverly Drive, B.H.; 274–5655. Eclectic menu consisting of Mexican, American, and Oriental specialties. Ribs, chicken, fish, salads, fresh croissants, espresso. Jukebox plays music 24 hours. No dress code here and a fun place for families as well as singles. AE, DC, MC, V.

Nate 'n Al's. *Moderate-Inexpensive.* 414 N. Beverly Dr., Beverly Hills; 274–0101. A home away from home for deli lovers from New York. Some of the best smoked salmon (lox) in town. Fat sandwiches and freshly squeezed orange juice. The potato pancakes are crisp, and the blintzes are good enough to make you plump. Known as a show-biz haunt for deli eaters. Breakfast, lunch, and dinner daily. No reservations. DC, CB.

Chinese

The Mandarin. *Moderate.* 430 N. Camden Dr., Beverly Hills; 272–0267. A sister restaurant of the successful Mandarin in San Francisco. Blue and green tile floors, orange carpeting, and rooms filled with much greenery and gracious antiques. The table settings are elegant, and the waiters are quite competent. Beggar's chicken is a specialty, and their Szechuan shrimp is a delight. Mongolian firepot is featured; guests can cook their own meats, seafood, and vegetables or let the chef do it instead. Good California wine list. Lunch Monday through Friday; dinner daily. Valet parking. All major credit cards.

Monkey West. *Moderate.* 170 N. La Cienega Blvd., Beverly Hills; 652–4188. Mandarin Chinese cuisine in an elegant atmosphere. The ceilings are covered with hanging silk lanterns; the walls are oak paneled and feature illuminated silk screens. On each table rests a vase with a single bud rose—positively romantic. The menu features hot braised Mandarin lobster, sweet and sour cubed fish, Szechuan spicy shrimp, pineapple duckling, and chicken with pinenuts. Peking duck is superior here, as are the many *dim sum* appetizers. Gracious service for a relaxing dining experience. Lunch and dinner daily. All major credit cards.

Yangtze. *Moderate.* 262 S. Beverly Dr., Beverly Hills; 859–2580. Szechuan and Mandarin dishes in an elegant but unpretentious presentation. Known for Da Chien chicken. Great desserts: Almond jello, pina colada and mango ice cream. Open for Lunch Monday through Staurday; dinner daily. DC, MC, V.

Continental

The Coterie. *Expensive.* The Beverly Hills Hotel, 9641 Sunset Blvd., Beverly Hills; 276–2251. Cozy booths, attentive captains and waiters, and a motif of browns and bronze characterize this restaurant. The Continental menu highlights filet mignon Coterie, a thick filet cloaked with crispy fried onion strands and sauteed mushrooms. Also popular are lamb sauteed au jus and seasoned with fresh rosemary, veal with sliced apples and apple brandy, and, as an appetizer, a scallop mousse with a watercress sauce. There are souffles on the menu, but the rolling pastry cart stars freshly baked tarts and cakes. A popular dessert is the coconut mousse topped with strawberries and then flambéed. Noted wine cellar. Dinner daily. All major credit cards.

L'Escoffier. *Inexpensive.* Beverly Hilton Hotel, 9876 Wilshire Blvd., Beverly Hills; 274–7777. An elegant penthouse restaurant with a superb view of the city. An impressive mural of inlaid mosiac, featuring all the signs of the zodiac, covers one wall. Dining is in the tradition of the famed "King of Chefs," Auguste Escoffier, who is renowned for his classical French cuisine. Dancing to an orchestra every night but Monday. Jacket and tie required for men. Dinner Monday through Saturday. Validated parking. All major credit cards.

Jimmy's. *Expensive.* 201 S. Moreno Dr., Beverly Hills; 879–2394. A serene and sophisticated restaurant with a country club-like atmosphere. Cold lobster salad is a delight at lunch; veal piccata is excellently light. The French–Continental menu is well-constructed, with an emphasis on the nouvelle. Lunchtime is very hectic, and service can be harried then. Dinner is a more relaxing experience. Lunch Monday through Friday; dinner daily except Sunday. Valet parking. All major credit cards.

The Vineyard. *Expensive.* Century Plaza Hotel, 2025 Avenue of the Stars, Century City; 277–2000. A dedication to the choicest, freshest ingredients, with a presentation of artistically arranged plates, makes the Vineyard one of Los Angeles's finest restaurants. It is a bit of a well-kept secret, for it is buried within a hotel, and hotels were not associated with fine dining in this city until recently. Appetizers include smoked breast of goose and pâté of wild game with a lingonberry sauce. Daily specials. Regular entrees feature quail with wild rice stuffing and saddle of lamb prepared with chutney, almonds, English mustard, and garlic. Lunch Monday through Friday. All major credit cards.

Andre's of Beverly Hills. *Moderate.* 8635 Wilshire Blvd., Beverly Hills; 657–2446. Also at 6332 Fairfax Ave., Los Angeles; 935–1246. Despite the fancy title, this Continental restaurant is truly a bargain. Portions are enormous, and you'll get complete dinners expertly prepared. You'll begin with an appetizer plate filled with assorted salads and pâté, then soup or salad, your entree, and dessert. Lunch Tuesday through Friday; dinner daily, except Monday. All major credit cards.

Bistango. *Moderate.* 133 N. La Cienega Blvd., Beverly Hills; 652–7788. A chic eaterie devoted to French/International fare. Specialties include roasted squab, red snapper in Pinot Noir, and pasta with caviar. Lunch, dinner daily. All major credit cards.

Trader Vic's. *Moderate.* 9876 Wilshire Blvd., Beverly Hills; 276–6345. Located in the Beverly Hilton Hotel. Not really Continental, the tropical South Sea Island decor is highlighted by much greenery and wicker chairs and an enormous selection of tropical drinks with such names as Dr. Funk's Son and Missionary's Downfall. The Menu is Polynesian, some Continental and Chinese, including barbecued meats prepared in Chinese clay ovens. The appetizers are renowned, and the clay ovens produce juicy, succulent meats. Valet parking. Dinner daily. All major credit cards, including the Hilton.

French

Antonie's of Beverly Hills. *Expensive.* 50 N. La Cienege, B.H.; 274–2449. Sit down to a feast fit for a king, right down to the buckwheat crêpes with caviar—Beluga no less—and sour cream. Lovely salads like Belgium endives with pears, walnuts, blue D'aruvergne, vinaigrette, and sage. Quail in muscatel sauce just one gem on a long list of imaginative entrees. Piano salon. Jackets required. Lunch, Monday through Friday; dinner, Monday through Saturday; Sunday brunch. All major credit cards.

Italian

La Scala. *Expensive.* 9455 Santa Monica Blvd., Beverly Hills; 275-0579. One of Los Angeles's trend setters in bringing fine Italian cuisine to this city; an elegant northern Italian restaurant decorated Florentine-style with a series of intimate dining areas. Elaborate Italian pottery filled with large bouquets of flowers has been placed throughout the rooms. A smartly dressed Beverly Hills crowd. Specialties include smoked Scottish salmon, zuppa all' Ortolana, fettuccine Leon, calf's liver all' Veneziana, and homemade ice cream. The luncheon menu includes light salads and omelettes as well as veal, pasta, and seafood. Valet parking. Lunch Monday through Friday; dinner daily except Sunday. AE, MC, V.

Harry's Bar. *Moderate.* In the ABC Entertainment Center near the Shubert Theater, 2020 Avenue of the Stars, Century City; 277–2333. Fashioned after the world-famous restaurant in Florence, Italy. A charming room with warmth and excellent service. The specialties are veal dishes and fettucine Alfredo. Closed on Sundays for lunch. AE, MC, V.

La Scala Boutique. *Moderate.* 475 N. Beverly Dr., Beverly Hills; 550–8288. A less formal and smaller version of La Scala (above). Large glass windows afford terrific people watching, especially of Beverly Hills shoppers. There are cartoons of celebrities on the walls. Specialties include prosciutto and melon, linguini and clams, veal and peppers, and whitefish alla Casalinga. The luncheon menu has salads, sandwiches, and omelettes. Lunch daily except Sunday; dinner daily except Sunday. All major credit cards.

Japanese

Benihana of Tokyo. *Moderate.* 38 N. La Cienega Blvd., Beverly Hills; 659–1511. Also at 14160 Panay Wy., Marina del Rey; 821–0888. Also at 16226 Ventura Blvd., Encino; 788–7121. One of a chain of restaurants that feature American food prepared Japanese-style by chefs who flash their knives about much like samurai. The tables are round and group together several customers, whether they know each other or not. Chefs stand in the cutout center of the table, where they stir-fry your dinner before your eyes in dramatic fashion on a grill set in the table. Steaks, seafood, and vegetables; good quality maintained. Efficient service. Valet parking. All major credit cards.

Mexican

Acapulco. *Inexpensive.* 134 N. La Cienega Blvd., Beverly Hills; 652–5344. Also at 1109 Glendon Ave., Westwood; 208–3884. One chain restaurant that does not compromise its standards. Gracious Mexican hacienda-style decor and an eighteen-page menu. Friendly service. Their crabmeat enchiladas are really special. Lunch and dinner daily. AE, MC, V.

SAN FERNANDO VALLEY
(Area Code 818)
American

The Beef 'n' Barrel. *Moderate.* 8920 Tampa Ave., Northridge; 885–1055. A value restaurant serving quality food at reasonable prices. There are five dining rooms, each with its own fireplace. Dinners include an above-average salad bar and your own iron kettle of homemade soup. Prime rib, a tender cut served in natural juices with a side of slightly sweet creamy horseradish sauce, is a specialty. Teriyaki sirloin is also of good quality, and there are various combinations of surf and turf (seafood and beef). There is a children's menu. Desserts, not made on the premises, generally consist of mousse pies. A creative variety of mixed drinks highlights liqueur and ice cream. Twilight economy dinners are served between 5:00 P.M. and 6:30 P.M. Lunch Monday through Friday; Sunday brunch; dinner nightly. AE, MC, V.

Diamonds the Rib Place. *Moderate.* 20022 Ventura Blvd., Woodland Hills; 818–710–8900. Very American restaurant offers baby-back ribs; onion rings; and large, juicy steaks. No reservations necessary. Open for lunch and dinner, Sunday through Thursday. CB, DC, MC, V.

Victoria Station. *Moderate.* 3850 Lankershim Blvd., North Hollywood; 760–0714. Located atop the Universal Studios hill, this chain restaurant has been built to resemble a British railway station. Much memorabilia graces the walls, and you'll feel as if you're dining in a railroad car. The service is young, cheerful, and efficient. Quality top sirloin and good teriyaki steak; gooey, cheesy baked potato skins provide a perfect appetizer. Their ribs are a wee bit greasy but have a nice smoky flavor. There is a great children's menu charging very reasonable prices. Dinners come with soup of the day or a pleasant salad bar and whole-grain bread. Lemon sorbets in minicones provide a refreshing touch. No matter what age you are, don't leave without trying the peanut butter pie. It's a nutty peanut butter filling frozen into a graham cracker crust with whipped cream on top and chocolate hot fudge sauce on the side; sinful. Good value here. Consult the phone directory for other locations. Lunch, dinner daily. All major credit cards.

Dr. Hogly Wogly's Tyler Texas Barbeque. *Moderate-Inexpensive.* 8136 Sepulveda Blvd., Van Nuys; 782–2480. The best barbecue restaurant in the San Fernando Valley. Succulent, lean and tender, smoky ribs are brought to your table. Beef ribs and spareribs are equally good; there are also sliced beef and pork and links. Pick the baked beans; they've been simmered for hours, and they're thick, smoky, and slightly sweet with maple syrup. Pecan pie here is just okay; the sweet potato pie fares better. Lunch and dinner daily. No credit cards.

The Melting Pot. *Moderate-Inexpensive.* 16348 Ventura Blvd., Encino; 995–6500. An all-purpose café, equally suitable for breakfast, lunch, or dinner. Computer games and televisions tuned in to soap operas amuse in the waiting area/lounge. The restaurant is decorated with antique mirrors and lush hanging plants. Tables are heavy oak, and the lighting shines through Tiffany-style lamps. The menu moves from salads, such as Chinese chicken, to omelettes, freshly baked waffles, and mushroom burgers. Mexican-style appetizers, terrific taquitos de Machos. Desserts are baked on the premises. Chocolate mousse cake, honey date nut cake, and warm pistachio cake with French vanilla ice cream are hard to pass up. Lunch and dinner daily. Sunday brunch. AE, MC, V.

Womphopper's Wagon Works. *Moderate-Inexpensive.* 100 Universal City Plaza, Universal City; 508–3939. A great place to bring the family. MCA built this restaurant adjacent to the Universal Studios Tour and created a legend to go with it. C. L. Womphopper is supposed to have been a wagon salesman who did a lot of wheeling and dealing in the Old West. It cost close to $4 million to build Womphopper's; it is made out of authentic barnwood to resemble an 1880s wagon factory. The restaurant is divided into nine rooms, each with a different theme. Antique lighting fixtures, hooked rugs, and velvet draperies fill the rooms. Buffalo-meat chili is a must to try; it's robust, hearty and rich with spices. There are many barbecued items as well as steaks, salad plates, and sandwiches, on the menu. Their ribs, in a sweet and smoky sauce, are meaty and tender. Hot apple cobbler is made on the premises, and it has a buttery flaky top crust. Country-and-western entertainment after 9:00 P.M. Breakfast during the summer only. Lunch and dinner daily. All major credit cards.

Art's Delicatessen. *Inexpensive.* 12224 Ventura Blvd., Studio City; 769–9808 or 762–1221. One of the best Jewish-style delicatessens in the city. The sandwiches are mammoth and are made from some of the best corned beef, pastrami, and other cold cuts around. Matzoh-ball soup and sweet-and-sour cabbage soup are specialties. Good chopped chicken liver. Beer. Breakfast, lunch, and dinner Tuesday through Sunday. No credit cards.

Barron's. *Inexpensive.* 4130 W. Burbank Blvd., Burbank; 846–0043. This is a momma–poppa restaurant where the love in the kitchen shows up on your plate. The decor is virtually nonexistent; the place is more like a coffee shop. But the Barrons have brought in their own antique collection of Depression glass and fine china and proudly display them by the front door, which adds warmth and charm. Dinners include soup or salad, baked, mashed, or French fried potatoes, vegetables, bread and butter, beverage, and a choice of home baked desserts. Entrees include roast turkey, baked chicken, roast beef, and roast pork. At this restaurant no one walks out the door hungry. Soups are made daily in a giant stock pot, and desserts are light-as-a-feather marble cakes and pies. The whole family participates in this operation, and it shows. Open weekdays for breakfast, lunch, and dinner. No credit cards.

Hampton's. *Inexpensive.* 4301 Riverside Dr., Burbank; 845–3009. Also at 1342 N. Highland Ave., Los Angeles; 469–1090. A casual café-style restaurant with anything and everything you'd ever want to put on a hamburger—and then some. Would you believe a peanut butter and jelly burger? Only in California! Thick and juicy hamburgers, the meat ground fresh daily. Lunch Monday through Friday, dinner daily in Burbank. Lunch and dinner daily in Los Angeles. Reservations requested for six or more. Valet parking. MC, V.

Paty's. *Inexpensive.* 10001 Riverside Dr., Toluca Lake; 760–9164. Paty's is a place to dine and star gaze and not have to mortgage your home to pay the bill. It's located close to NBC, Warner Brothers, and the Disney Studio, and so you're liable to see top series stars, producers, and even the gaffers dining here. This is an all-American style upgraded coffee shop with a comfortable, eclectic decor. Breakfasts are charming; the omelettes are plump, and the biscuits are homemade and served with high-quality jam. Lunches and dinners include Swiss steak and a hearty beef stew that is served in a hollowed-out loaf of home baked bread. Roast turkey is served with dressing and a moist and sweet loaf of home-baked nut or raisin bread. All desserts are worth saving room for; they're made on the premises and taste sinfully butter rich. New Orleans bread pudding with a hot brandy sauce is popular, and the Danishes are gigantic. Breakfast, lunch, and dinner daily. No credit cards.

Chinese

Fung Lum. *Moderate.* Universal Studios, Universal City; 760–4603. Located in the Universal Studios complex, this ornate Chinese restaurant cost millions to build. It's a replica of a Chinese palace, and the interior design includes handcarved, painted, and embroidered panels, rosewood and teak furniture, and breathtaking, handwoven carpeting. The menu is long and primarily Cantonese. Best to come here in a large group where you can taste a multitude of courses. The minced squab in lettuce leaves is wonderful. Open daily for lunch and dinner. No reservations. AE, MC, V.

Continental

Camille's. *Expensive-Moderate.* 13573 Ventura Blvd., Sherman Oaks; 995–1660. One of the most romantic restaurants in the Valley. Rose-colored walls, an eclectic assortment of antique mirrors and paintings, trailing plants, and a lot of lattice work provide a sentimental Art Deco–Victorian ambience. Here is one restaurant where the cuisine is as charming as the decor. Chef/co-owner Peter Schawalder is Swiss; his creations are individualistic as well as poetic in presentation. Entrees are often garnished with carrot stars, olives hold enoki mushrooms, and strawberries are sculptured into blossoming roses. Entrees include sauteed whitefish and grapefruit, veal steak with mushroom puree, and roasted duckling with apple and chestnut puree. The soup of the day is always fresh, and their desserts are worth giving up a diet for. Lunch, Tuesday through Friday; dinner, Tuesday through Saturday. All major credit cards.

Four Stages Restaurant. *Moderate.* Sheraton–Universal Hotel; 3838 Lankershim Blvd., Universal City; 980–1212. Imagination takes precedent in a restaurant where the decor carries out the theme of the neighboring movie studio. There are four authentic movie sets, including a western saloon, a medieval castle, and a courtyard in India. The menu is Continental and well prepared. Best is the Sunday brunch, which is an elegant buffet that includes crab legs and caviar as well as many hot and cold entrees. Sunday brunch; dinner daily. All major credit cards.

Europa. *Moderate-Inexpensive.* 14929 Magnolia Blvd., Sherman Oaks; 501–9175. The menu here roams the world. Great goulash, terrific teriyaki—even great matzoh ball soup. Tiny and casual; reservations are a must as this is a community favorite. Lunch, dinner daily. MC, V.

French

La Serre. *Expensive.* 12969 Ventura Blvd., Studio City; 990–0500. Undoubtedly the most beautiful restaurant in the San Fernando Valley. The rooms are lattice divided, the floors are brick, and there are fresh flowers and lush greenery everywhere you look. It's a bit like dining in a greenhouse. At lunchtime celebrities flock here in droves, for it is near the Universal, Warner, and Disney studios. Julie Andrews, Lorne Greene, Walter Matthau, and Michael Caine have all been spotted lunching at La Serre. The cuisine is very French and very nouvelle, and it's all served on the finest china with sparkling crystal and silverware. Captains and waiters are most attentive. Valet parking. Lunch Monday through Friday; dinner Monday through Saturday. AE, MC, V.

Aux Delices. *Expensive-Moderate.* 15466 Ventura Blvd., Sherman Oaks; 783–3007. Although this French restaurant is small, it has a decidedly reserved ambience. Its food is superior to most restaurants in the Valley. A mousse of scallops with cream and Cognac is soft, rich, and delicate—an outstanding appetizer. Escargots, onion soup, and duck pâté are equally pleasing. Baked jumbo shrimp with paprika, Cognac, and cream is a gustatory delight. Sauces are always silken and sophisticated without being overwhelming. Other entrees include veal with apples, cider, cream, and Calvados and sweetbreads sauteed in a truffle sauce with goose liver pâté. The bouillabaisse is one of the best in Los Angeles. Specials daily. Good wine list, heavy on French wines. Desserts include the traditional mousse and creme caramel, but the freshly baked, flaky tarts filled with custard and fresh fruit should not be overlooked. This touch of Paris in Sherman Oaks will please even the most discriminating diner. Dinner daily, except Monday. All major credit cards.

Le Café. *Moderate.* 14633 Ventura Blvd., Sherman Oaks; 986–2662. This high-tech café/restaurant provides fine food in a relaxing ambience. Small tables fill one large room with walls papered from French newspapers. The menu, running the gamut from ratatouille omelettes and salad Nicoise to filet mignon in blue cheese sauce and shrimp in a saffron cream sauce, is brasserie-style. Fresh fish is always a wise choice, and the spinach canneloni is hard to beat.

Le Café serves Haagen Dazs ice cream; the owner's homemade cheesecake is definitely the best. Lunch, dinner daily. All major credit cards.

Wine Bistro. *Moderate.* 11915 Ventura Blvd., Studio City; 766–6233. A cheerful wine bar with an extensive blackboard menu. The airy decor features butcher block and a lot of plants. Several daily offerings of different California and French wines and Champagnes by the glass. Filet of sole Veronique, salmon with mustard sauce, and daily cream soups are always refreshing and tasty. A giant brass espresso maker produces vibrant cups of cappuccino and espresso. Desserts, usually fruit tarts, are made on the premises. A partially open kitchen provides entertainment, for you can watch the chefs scurry about. Valet parking. Lunch, dinner daily, except Sunday. All major credit cards.

Epicurean Express. *Moderate-Inexpensive.* 19014 Ventura Blvd., Tarzana; 996–7977. One of the newer and most unique concepts in fast-food gourmet dining. There are only a few tables in this country-French-style restaurant that predominantly features food to go. There's an open kitchen, and chef/owner Joe Donahue is a joy to behold as he madly yet efficiently dashes from pot to pan. Within fifteen minutes, you can be enjoying prime milk-fed veal flamed in Madeira wine and simmered with wild mushrooms and fresh cream. There are always daily specials, and the fresh pastas are not to be missed. Also good is the roast duck that is brushed with rosemary and served with a sauce of the day. There are Cobb salad, spinach salad, or a shellfish salad for those with lighter appetites. One popular dish is the brie-and-almond sandwich: brie cheese melted onto French bread and topped with toasted almonds. Desserts are melt-in-your-mouth pastries and cakes, all baked on the premises. Lunch and dinner daily, except Sunday (dinner only) and Monday (lunch only). MC, V.

German

The Weinstube. *Moderate.* 17739 Sherman Way, Reseda; 345–1994. German food is traditionally supposed to be heavy, but this German restaurant is a happy surprise. Yes, there are smoked pork chops and wiener schnitzel on the menu, but there is also a light entree of veal medallions sauteed in butter and white wine with herbs out of the chef's garden. Also light yet bursting with flavor is a roast loin of milk-fed veal served with imported wild mushrooms. Other dishes include sauerbraten, Chinook salmon poached in a white wine/herb sauce, and roast goose stuffed with apples, potatoes, and goose liver in season. Charming decor; waitresses are garbed in traditional costumes. Cozy booths, softly lighted. Lunch Tuesday through Friday; dinner daily, except Monday. AE, MC, V.

Greek

Great Greek. *Moderate.* 13362 Ventura Blvd., Sherman Oaks; 818/905-5250. This joint is jumping with Greek music and Old World dancing where everyone joins in. Food a delight: Loukaniki, Greek sausages; butter-fried calamari; and two kinds of shish kabob. Valet parking. Open seven days, lunch and dinner. All major credit cards.

The Greek Market. *Moderate-Inexpensive.* 9034 Tampa Ave., Northridge; 349–9689. Zorba the Greek himself would love the authentic Greek cuisine served here. Appetizers include the zesty tarmosalata, a salty Greek caviar made with carp roe. Tiropitas, cheese filled phyllo-dough pastries, and fried squid and octopus in red wine sauce are other appetizer selections. Leg of lamb is roasted with cloves of whole garlic, black pepper, and lemon juice, and the moussaka, with its layers of eggplant and ground lamb cloaked in a thick rich bechamel sauce, will not disappoint. All entrees come with the vegetable of the day, rice pilaf, and pita bread. Desserts are made on the premises, and the baklava—layers of phyllo dough and nuts drenched in honey syrup—is luscious. Dancing to live Greek music. If you drink enough ouzo, you might want to throw a plate or two! Lunch and dinner daily, except Sunday. MC, V.

Health

The Good Earth. *Moderate-Inexpensive.* 17212 Ventura Blvd., Encino; 986–9990; also, 1002 Westwood Blvd., Westwood; 208–8215; 23397 Mulholland Dr., Woodland Hills; 888–6300. Eating healthfully does not have to mean eating a diet of alfalfa sprouts and wheat germ. The menus of this health-oriented chain feature whole-grain breads, desserts baked with honey, and entrees heavy on fruit and vegetables rather than meat. Even the decor, with earth-tone walls and furnishings and macramé and wicker baskets on the walls, is earthy. Breakfast items feature turkey sausages, ten-grain sourdough pancakes, and a choice of omelettes. Vegetarian burgers, curried chicken, and Zhivago's beef Stroganoff are superior. Their yogurt cream pie tastes almost like cheesecake, but the carrot cake is a little heavy, probably because of the whole-grain flour content. Breakfast, lunch, and dinner daily. MC, V.

Chez Natural. *Inexpensive.* 11838 Ventura Blvd., Studio City; 763–1044. It's not easy to find gourmet health food, especially in a restaurant that has an attractive ambience as well as a creative menu. A dinner at Chez Natural includes a fruit cup or soup or salad, lightly steamed fresh vegetables, and homemade, stone-ground whole-grain rolls with sweet butter. Vegetables Chez Natural consists of a popular plate of steamed vegetables on a bed of brown rice covered with melted cheese and sliced almonds. Another successful entree is the breast of chicken (organic, of course) that's boned and stuffed with a blend of pine nuts, cheese, and herbs and then covered with a golden brown nut sauce. There are a lot of California-style salads, omelettes, and quiches on the menu as well. Considering that they contain carob and honey instead of chocolate and sugar, the desserts are superior. It's no Snickers bar, but the Carob Caress is the healthful way to junk-food heaven. Open daily for lunch and dinner. All major credit cards.

Italian

Matta's Ristorante. *Moderate.* 21733 Ventura Blvd., Woodland Hills; 704–9191. Everything is soft here. The lighting is soft, the music is soft, and even the waiters speak softly. Very relaxing. This Italian restaurant has a great house salad that includes red cabbage, romaine lettuce, artichoke hearts, hearts of palm, and fresh mushrooms and will make you forget every iceberg lettuce salad you've ever endured. The homemade dressing is a smooth and creamy vinaigrette that is enlivened with fresh herbs. Cucumbered sole is a fresh filet cloaked in a delicate cream sauce that contains the essence of fresh cucumbers; slices of cucumber garnish the fish. Other unusual dishes include chicken with Mandarin orange wedges and green grapes, veal with brandy and water chestnuts, and veal with prosciutto and provolone wrapped around jumbo scampi. Desserts are made on the premises; the chocolate mousse is not to be missed. Lunch Monday through Friday; dinner daily. All major credit cards.

Japanese

Hatsuhana. *Moderate-Expensive.* 17167 Ventura Blvd., Encino; 789–8287. Plenty of flash at this trendy Japanese restaurant, right down to the rolling sushi bar. High-tech space with a good measure of Japanese influence. Fresh, fresh fish imported from around the world. Try the Hatsuhana special, a combination of sushi and sashimi, salmon teriyaki, tempura, and half a lobster. Parking lot. Lunch and dinner daily. All major credit cards.

Teru Sushi. *Moderate.* 11940 Ventura Blvd., Studio City; 763–6201. Entertainment-industry clientele feast on some of the best sushi in town here at a bar where the chefs put on a show. The freshest fish is served. Table service features traditional Japanese fare, especially a tender teriyaki. Lunch Monday through Friday; dinner daily. All major credit cards.

Domo. *Moderate-Inexpensive.* 11680 Ventura Blvd., Studio City; 761–6151. A Japanese restaurant tucked into a small neighborhood shopping center. Japanese kites hang from high-beamed ceilings. Two levels; the tatami room is on the top one. There is a small bar. Dinners come with soup, salad, and rice. Teriyaki and tofu steak are both wise choices. Lunch Tuesday through Friday; dinner Tuesday through Sunday. All major credit cards.

Moroccan

Marrakesh. *Moderate.* 13003 Ventura Blvd., Studio City; 788–6354. A maze of intimate rooms, much like a Moroccan home. Soft lighting, cushioned benches, and communal plates of *b'stilla,* salads, couscous, and lamb, as well as fish, chicken, or rabbit, are ceremoniously served. The servers are traditionally garbed in robes and will wash your hands and attend you most graciously. It's comfortable, casual, and most unusual. Dinner daily. Valet parking. All major credit cards.

Swiss

St. Moritz. *Moderate.* 11720 Ventura Blvd., Studio City; 980–1122. There aren't too many Swiss restaurants in Los Angeles, but St. Moritz qualifies as one of the best. It's styled a bit like a Swiss chalet, with cozy booths and an Alpine mural on the wall. Ask to sit on the enclosed patio that offers a pretty garden view and a replica of a potbellied stove in the center of the room. Appetizers include a shrimp dish with dill and pernod and a light cannelloni prepared à la Swiss. The salad Neuchatel consists of a heaping plate of Bibb lettuce with sweet bay shrimp and an unusual yogurt-dill dressing. Entrees include the traditional wiener schnitzel and the not-so-traditional shrimp sauteed with almonds, mushrooms, and romaine lettuce. Chicken in a tarragon cream sauce is always a favorite. Some desserts are not made on the premises, but they are purchased from a top Los Angeles bakery. Lunch Tuesday through Friday; dinner Tuesday through Sunday. AE, MC, V.

Thai

Anajuh Thai. *Inexpensive.* 14704 Ventura Blvd., Sherman Oaks; 501–4201. When you walk into this restaurant you might become confused: the walls are baby blue, graceful ferns separate the tables, and each table is appointed with gleaming silver. But despite the tasteful Western decor, you'll still get treated to inexpensive Thai food. Start with the regal barbecue spareribs. It's lick-your-fingers time because these ribs are smoothly coated in a dark reddish-brown sauce that's slightly sweet and slightly spicy. *Tom yum kai* is an intriguing soup that blends chunks of white meat chicken with mushrooms and that exotic Thai herb, lemon grass. There's a lot of curry on the menu, as well as a satisfying rendition of *mee krob,* the popular, sweet and crisp rice noodle dish. Service is kindly. Lunch Tuesday through Friday; dinner daily except Monday. AE, MC, V.

WEST LOS ANGELES/WESTWOOD/SANTA MONICA

American

The Corkscrew. *Moderate.* 11647 San Vicente Blvd., Brentwood; 826–5501. A comfortable neighborhood restaurant featuring steaks, prime rib, and old-fashioned chicken and dumplings. One of the city's best salad bars includes a superior gazpacho soup with assorted toppings. Daily homey specials such as short ribs, lamb shanks, and English-style pot roast. Baked potatoes are à la carte, but they are huge. Crispy onion rings accompany steak orders but can also be ordered à la carte. Booths and tables, low lighting. Lunch Monday through Friday; dinner daily. All major credit cards.

Junior's. *Moderate-Inexpensive.* 2379 Westwood Blvd., W. Los Angeles; 475–5771. It may not be New York, but Angelenos take their delis seriously. The menu is vast, and all sandwiches are jumbo. A pickle barrel is placed on each table, just as in the old days. Open daily for breakfast, lunch, and dinner. MC, V.

Caribbean

Act I. *Inexpensive.* 2921 S. La Cienega Blvd., Culver City; 558–9314. A touch of the Caribbean in Los Angeles, this Jamaican restaurant features Jamaica's gastronomic specialty, curried goat. There are also Jamaican-style chicken, red snapper, and exotic desserts. Lunch, dinner, Tuesday through Saturday. No credit cards.

Kitty's. *Inexpensive.* 10924 W. Pico, W. L.A.; 470–1255. Go Caribbean at this Jamaican eatery where the homeland is advertised on posters on the wall. Curried goat is on the menu, as are oxtail stew and changing specials. Lunch weekdays; dinner daily except Sunday.

Chinese

Chinois on Main. *Moderate.* 2709 Main St., Santa Monica; 392–3037. An inspirational restaurant, both in decor and menu. Wolfgang Puck's and Barbara Lazaroff's Chinese/French/California cuisine. Lunch, Wednesday through Friday; dinner daily. Valet parking. Reservations a must. AE, MC, V.

Continental

The Dynasty. *Expensive.* 930 Hilgard Ave., Westwood; 208–8765. Located in the elegant Westwood Marquis Hotel. The dramatic decor features Chinese artifacts and artwork by Erté. The menu is Continental; entrees include foie gras, smoked salmon, and escargots. House specialties are lobster Newburg, veal Marsala, calf's liver, veal Oscar, and thick grilled lamb chops. Fine, reasonably priced wine list. Dinner nightly. All major credit cards.

Bon-Appetit. *Moderate* 1601 Broxton Ave., Westwood; 208–3830. Jazz permeates this romantic eatery on Friday and Saturday evenings. It's located in the heart of the village where the favorites are Duck l'Orange and boneless breast of chicken sautéed with artichokes and mushrooms. Fresh seafood daily. Quiches, sandwiches, and salads for lunch. Full bar. Open Monday through Saturday.

Cutters. *Moderate.* 2425 Colorado Ave., Santa Monica; 453–3588. Termed "unstructured eating," the menu allows diners to order a couple of starters rather than a complete dinner. Orzo pasta salad, Olympia oysters, and Korean short ribs are some of the offerings. Lunch, dinner daily. AE, MC, V.

French

Les Anges. *Expensive.* 14809 Pacific Coast Hwy., Santa Monica; 454–1331. Minimalist decor; superlative French cuisine. Famed for Mort du Chocolat torte. Dinner Wednesday through Sunday. AE, MC, V.

Au Chambertin. *Expensive.* 708 W. Pico Blvd., Santa Monica; 392–8738. A formal and chic dining room decorated to reflect impeccable taste. Owned by a Vietnamese family who lend a touch of Oriental artistry to haute French cuisine featuring fresh seafood, veal, filet mignon with herbs, pheasant, and Grand Marnier souffles, in the *nouvelle* slant. Dinner Monday through Saturday. Valet parking. CB, MC, V.

Camelions. *Expensive.* 246 26th St., Santa Monica; 395–0746. Classic French cuisine with emphasis on simple, fresh flavors. Intimate dining room; soft colors, lighting. Lunch Tuesday through Saturday; dinner Tuesday through Sunday. All major credit cards.

Le Cellier. *Moderate.* 2628 Wilshire Blvd., Santa Monica; 828–1585. Moderate priced but high-quality French food. The ambience is that of a fashionable country inn with soft lighting and French paintings. Dinners include soup and salad. The appetizer list is standard, but the chef comes up with unusual monthly specials that focus on regional French cuisine. Breast of mallard duck with green peppercorn and loin of lamb with crushed pepper, pears, and cabbage are special entrees. Le Cellier's bouillabaisse is always popular, as are its souffles and its rolling dessert cart. Valet parking. Dinner daily, except Monday. All major credit cards.

Café Reni. *Inexpensive.* 2226 Wilshire Blvd., Santa Monica; 829–5303. It's hard to believe that there is any French restaurant you can dine in well and not pay a bill equal to the price of a plane ticket to Paris. But this intimate French café is genuinely inexpensive. There is a fresh soup of the day; entrees all come with crusty French bread. Choose between beef Bourguignon, sand dabs, chicken Florentine, or a creamy blend of crab, shrimp, and other fish. There are always fresh specials listed on the blackboard. The wine list is small. Beer. Lunch Monday through Friday; dinner daily. Sunday brunch. All major credit cards.

Chez Puce. *Inexpensive.* 318 Santa Monica Blvd., Santa Monica; 393–4454. Some of the best crepes in the city. Many assorted fillings, or you can just have the crepes plain with melted butter. There are dessert crepes and pizza too. Beer and wine. Lunch and dinner Monday through Saturday. MC, V.

Pioneer Boulangerie. *Inexpensive.* 2012 S. Main St., Santa Monica; 399–1405. Close to the ocean, this treasure of a restaurant serves strictly fresh, strictly homemade soups and breads of the French persuasion. There are several soups to choose from daily, as well as hearty stews. French baguettes are made on the premises, and you can buy loaves to take home. Occasionally Pioneer offers some Basque specialties. Lunch and dinner daily. MC, V.

Greek

Skorpios. *Inexpensive.* 1133 Westwood Blvd., Westwood; 208–3480. Mostly a takeout stand, but some tables. Good, home-prepared Greek cooking: souvlaki, gyros, psari, mezedhes, assorted appetizers, and falafel. Lunch and dinner daily. No credit cards.

Health

Meyera. *Inexpensive.* 3009 Main St., Santa Monica; 399–1010. An attractive and cozy health food restaurant; vegetarian cuisine. The breads and pastries are freshly baked. Creative menu. Wine, beer. Days and hours fluctuate dramatically so call to check. MC, V.

Indian

Gypsy's. *Inexpensive.* 1215 4th St., Santa Monica; 451–2841. A tiny Indian restaurant specializing in Eastern Indian cuisine. Homemade chutneys, nice use of spices. Lamb korma and chicken Hyderabad are specialties. Wine, beer. Dinner Tuesday through Sunday. DC, MC, V.

Canard de Bombay. *Moderate.* 476 S. San Vicente Blvd., W. L.A.; 852–0095. Elegant ambiance sets the stage for English-style Indian food. More than 130 curries made to order, ranging from extremely mild to extremely hot. Lunch Thursday through Friday; dinner daily. All major credit cards.

Italian

Valentino. *Expensive.* 3115 Pico Blvd., Santa Monica; 829–4313. Noted as one of Los Angeles's finest restaurants, with an extensive and exciting Italian menu. Chicken in clay, mussels in brandy, osso buco, and fine pastas are a delight. Crema fritta (fried cream) is a splendid dessert with a cup of espresso. Admirable wine list. Attentive service; the tables are well appointed. Valet parking. Dinner daily except Sunday. All major credit cards.

Donatello's Ristorante. *Expensive-Moderate.* 11712 San Vicente Blvd., Brentwood; 820–9719. An intimate European-style bistro featuring northern Italian cuisine. Its long, complex menu includes such appetizers as a galantine of chicken, veal, ham and truffles, vitello tonnato, and every salad you can think of from spinach to roasted green peppers. Their mozzarella marinara is a must; the tomato sauce captures all the essence of fresh ripe tomatoes. They offer many soups besides stracciatella and minestrone. The pasta list is long; try rigatoni with eggplant, string beans and cream, or tortelloni stuffed with veal and vegetables. Risottos, veal, fish, and beef dishes featured. Red snapper wrapped in parchment in a cream and porcini mushroom sauce is a delight. Desserts include two varieties of ice cream, hard and soft, both homemade. Banana sorbet is smooth and rich in flavor. Lunch Monday through Friday; dinner Monday through Saturday. All major credit cards.

Marquis West. *Expensive-Moderate.* 3110 Santa Monica Blvd., Santa Monica; 828–4567. A warm northern-Italian restaurant, too elegant to be called a neighborhood bistro, yet that feeling of hospitality is ever present. Comfortable booths, soft lighting, thick carpeting, and friendly waiters prevail. Appetizers include mussels marinara, a satisfying mozzarella marinara, and a fine shrimp cocktail. Entrees feature fresh fish in a variety of styles, a big bowl of calamari, frog legs, and linguine al pesto (basil). Tripolino and tartufo are special desserts of rich ice cream and dark, sweet chocolate. Espresso, cappuccino. Valet parking. Lunch Monday through Friday; dinner daily. All major credit cards.

Verdi. *Expensive-Moderate.* 1519 Wilshire Blvd., Santa Monica; 393–0706. A unique restaurant with a novel concept—opera while you dine. An excellent ensemble performs arias from several operas, though an occasional Broadway tune is included. The dining room is high-tech; painted murals on the walls depict famous opera scenes. The menu is northern Italian with home-baked sweets. There is a fine antipasto plate and a careful selection of pastas. There are shrimp scampi, veal with cream and mushrooms, and an excellent broiled piece of swordfish marinated with olive oils and herbs. Valet parking. Dinner nightly, except Monday. AE, MC, V.

Anna's. *Moderate.* 10929 West Pico Blvd., W. Los Angeles; 474–0102. Also at 15300 Ventura Blvd., Sherman Oaks; (818) 787-ANNA. Unsophisticated Roman cuisine is the specialty of these sister Italian restaurants. The Los Angeles restaurant features comfortable booths and typical southern Italian ambience. The newer Sherman Oaks restaurant has its main dining room centered on a gazebo. Within and surrounding the gazebo are individual booths, each with its own awning marked for a different Italian city. Portions, featuring linguine, spaghetti, fettuccine, and cannelloni—all at inexpensive prices—are generous. Slightly more expensive are the veal dishes prepared in a variety of styles and the American-style steaks. Desserts include homemade ricotta cheesecake, and on Saturday night you can try the zuppa inglese. Lunch weekdays; dinner daily; Sunday brunch. All major credit cards.

Pontevecchio. *Moderate.* 2518 Wilshire Blvd., Santa Monica; 829–1112. An intimate, warm northern-Italian restaurant, decorated with antiques and plants. Appetizers include mussels marinara, scampi, and a splendid antipasto. Besides the traditional minestrone soup, Roman stracciatella is offered. Pastas are fresh and include vermicelli with red pesto, spaghetti with tomato, cream, and fresh basil, and linguine with shellfish in a white wine-tomato sauce. The veal is milkfed white veal and is prepared with lemon and butter, sage, and prosciutto or in an osso bucco Milanese. Desserts, made on the premises, are impressive. A perky demitasse of espresso is the perfect accompaniment. Service is attentive. Lunch Monday through Friday; dinner daily. AE, MC, V.

Japanese

Asuka. *Moderate.* 1266 Westwood Blvd., Westwood; 474–7412. One of the largest sushi bars in Los Angeles, offering many varieties. Squeamish customers (and you know who you are) may opt for their good tempura, sukiyaki, or teppanyaki. Lunch Monday through Friday; dinner daily. AE, MC, V.

Hiro Sushi. *Moderate.* 1621 Wilshire Blvd., Santa Monica; 395–3570. The waiting area features video games. As you would expect, Hiro offers an excellent variety of sushi. Again, for those with timid palates, teriyaki and sukiyaki are also featured. Lunch Sunday, Monday, Wednesday through Friday; dinner daily except Tuesday. MC, V.

Mexican

Verita's La Cantina. *Moderate.* 10323 Santa Monica Blvd., W. Los Angeles; 277–3362. A little shopping center strangely named New England Village is the home of this charming Mexican restaurant with fireplaces and cozy decor. The cooking is Sonora-style, and the menu includes sea bass baked in a corn husk, liver marinated in tequila, and rack of lamb with *salsa borracha* (drunk sauce). Good omelettes, good mole dishes. Occasional mariachi music. Lunch Monday through Saturday; dinner Monday through Saturday. Valet parking. All major credit cards.

Macho's. *Inexpensive.* 939 Broxton Ave., Westwood; 208–8050. Located in the heart of Westwood Village. You don't have to be macho to like the enchiladas, tacos, or the carne en serappi here. AE, MC, V.

Sagebrush Cantina. *Inexpensive.* 9523 Culver Blvd., Culver City; 836–5321. Also at 23527 Calabasas Rd., Calabasas; 888–6062. Always popular as a singles' meeting place for the young set, this restaurant offers pleasant Mexican-style fare as well as steaks, seafood, barbecued chicken, and ribs. Usually a wait for tables, especially on the weekends. Lunch and dinner Monday through Friday in Culver City; Tuesday through Sunday in Calabasas. MC, V.

Middle Eastern

Beach Café. *Inexpensive.* 304 Santa Monica Blvd., Santa Monica; 394–8448. Middle Eastern food in a sparkling clean restaurant with excellent service. The steak kebab is tender and is made from filet mignon; lamb simmered with kidney beans and spinach makes a hearty and rich stew. Yogurt soup is accented with cilantro, and all entrees come with hot Persian bread and butter. Lunch and dinner daily. MC, V.

Moroccan

Koutoubia. *Expensive-Moderate.* 2116 Westwood Blvd., Westwood; 475–0729. A touch of Morocco in Westwood. You'll eat with your hands from communal plates on ornate brass tables. The "Wedding Feast" is a romantic, leisurely multicourse dinner featuring soup, salad, *b'stilla,* lemon chicken, and couscous. Waiters will frequently pour water from samovar-style pitchers over your hands to cleanse them. Dishes can be ordered à la carte as well. Dinner daily, except Sunday. All major credit cards.

Seafood

Famous Enterprise Fish Company. *Moderate.* 174 Kinney, Santa Monica; 392–8366. A popular and crowded restaurant serving fresh fish broiled over mesquite charcoal and prepared in an open kitchen. Nautical atmosphere, friendly service. Lunch and dinner daily. No reservations. AE, MC, V.

The **Pelican** Restaurants. *Moderate.* A chain of seafood restaurants specializing in charbroiled fresh fish. Not for indecisive folks; there's usually a choice of twenty varieties. Expertly broiled, your catch of the sea comes with fresh, crisp vegetables and potato chunks, lightly fried. There is excellent sourdough bread with dinner, as well as green salad or chowder. Nautical decor, casual service. Lunch Monday through Friday; dinner daily. MC, V. Located at: 1717 Ocean Ave., Santa Monica; 451–0818; 2720 Main St., Santa Monica; 392–5711; 1715 Pacific Ave., Venice Beach; 392–3933; 3801 Highland, Manhattan Beach; 545–6563; 8232 Sepulveda Blvd., Van Nuys; 988–6334; 24454 Calabasas Rd., Calabasas; 710–1550.

The Captain. *Inexpensive.* 1028 Swarthmore Ave., Pacific Palisades; 459–7571. Fresh flowers are on each table, and the walls are covered with murals of the seashore. Fresh seafood is the specialty, but there are also chicken, Swedish meatloaf, a vegetarian platter, and steak. Soup or salad and hot bread are included with each entree. Lunch and dinner daily. No AE.

Spanish

Toledo Restaurant. *Moderate.* 11613 Santa Monica Blvd., West Los Angeles; 477–2400. Castillian cuisine; paella, callos a la Madrilena, garlic soup, and gazpacho are specialties. Wine and beer only. Lunch Tuesday through Friday; dinner Tuesday through Sunday. AE, MC, V.

Thai

Thai Pepper Restaurant. *Inexpensive.* 11480 Lindbrook Dr., Westwood; 208–9140. Authentic ambience and gracious service at this bistro located close to the heart of Westwood. *Mee krob,* beef satay, Thai spring rolls, and ginger chicken are specialties. Lunch Monday through Saturday; dinner daily. MC, V.

BEACHES

Gladstone's 4 Fish. *Moderate.* 17300 Pacific Coast Hwy., Pacific Palisades; GL-4-FISH. This restaurant is located right on the ocean; fresh fish broiled over mesquite charcoal is their specialty. Huge tanks hold live lobster and crab. There are always daily specials, and cioppino and sashimi are also on the menu. All dinners include green salad or chowder, coleslaw, sourdough bread, and a choice of rice, potatoes, or vegetables. Save room for the Works, a gigantic slice of cake loaded with mounds of ice cream, fresh fruit, hot fudge sauce, candies, and whipped cream. After this dessert, go straight to the dentist. Casual nautical decor, slightly noisy because it's always packed. Breakfast, lunch, and dinner daily. All major credit cards.

Sausalito South. *Moderate.* 3280 N. Sepulveda Blvd., Manhattan Beach; 546–4507. A perfectly decorated restaurant despite its being so close to the sea. There is a lot of greenery and wood with an airy, open flair plus a lot of fresh fish on the menu and a mean Ramos Fizz. A friendly, relaxed atmosphere. Congenial service. Dinner daily. AE, MC, V.

AIRPORT/MARINA DEL REY

Continental

Le Gourmet. *Expensive.* Sheraton Plaza La Reina Hotel, 6101 W. Century Blvd., Los Angeles; 642–1111. This dining room lifts hotel food out of its usual doldrums. The decor is dark green velvety walls with brass accents, etched glass dividers, and peach-tinted mirrors. No dish is precooked. Everything is seared on a flattop stove at superhigh heat. All sauces are naturally reduced. Exciting hors d'oeuvres include quail with julienne of zucchini and potatoes, sashimi with hazelnut oil, and pigeon with truffles. The salads, such as sweetbreads, langostino, or fish salad with Japanese eggplant, are unusual. Entrees include sliced breast of duck with marrow, snapper with black pepper, and quail with prunes. Dinner Monday through Saturday. All major credit cards.

Fiasco. *Moderate.* 4451 Admiralty Way; 823–6395. Popular Marina eaterie with an ocean view and an accent on seafood. Good steaks, prime rib, grilled fish of the day. Generous portions. Always busy. Noisy bar with plenty of action. Lunch Monday–Friday; dinner daily. All major credit cards.

T. J. Peppercorn's. *Moderate.* Hyatt Hotel at Los Angeles International Airport; 6225 W. Century Blvd., Inglewood; 670–9000. A comfortable hotel dining room noted for its excellent duck, prepared rotisserie-style. Also steaks, fresh fish, and veal Oscar. The salad and dessert bars offer a multitude of items. Lunch Monday through Friday; dinner daily. All major credit cards.

Indian

Akbar. *Moderate.* 590 Washington St., Marina del Rey; 822–4116. An intimate dining room featuring mulligatawny soup, vindaloo, curries, and a real Tandoori oven. Akbar's homemade desserts excel. There is soft Indian music in the background. Lunch Monday through Saturday; dinner daily. No AE.

Mexican

Baja Cantina. *Moderate.* 311 Washington St., Marina del Rey; 821–2250. Also at 23410 Civic Center Way, Malibu; 456-2021. Lighthearted Mexican food in a high-energy restaurant. The names of the dishes are whimsical, but don't let that scare you; the preparation is careful and sophisticated. Monday night is all-you-can-eat taco night. Tuesday night has whole Maine lobster as a special, and every night there is a wonderful choice of exotic drinks. Brunch is a real bargain, with a selection of eight egg dishes, Champagne, tortillas, and fresh fruit. Relaxed decor with unusual antiques. Lunch and dinner daily. Sunday brunch. AE, MC, V.

LONG BEACH/SAN PEDRO

Continental

Delius. *Expensive-Moderate.* 3550 Long Beach Blvd., Long Beach; 426–0694. Close to the *Queen Mary.* The price-fixed Continental menu starts with Champagne and includes soup, an appetizer, entree, vegetables, dessert, and coffee. Dinner Tuesday through Saturday. Reservations a must. No credit cards.

Greek

Papadakis Taverna. *Moderate-Inexpensive.* 301 W. 6th St., San Pedro; 548–1186. A kick-up-your-heels Greek taverna. Waiters, cooks, and customers all join in for song and dance up and down the aisles. Their moussaka, pastitsio, and tiropitas will not disappoint. Greek wines. Always a daily special, anything from stuffed eggplant to squid or red snapper Greek style. There are baskets of ferns and prints of the Acropolis on the walls. This is the most authentic Greek restaurant in Los Angeles. Dinner daily. MC, V.

Yugoslavian

Paragon Inn. *Moderate.* 660 W. 7th St., San Pedro; 831–2200. Yugoslavian specialties. Located close to the harbor and Ports O'Call Village, Paragon offers shish kebab, sarma, musaka, leg of lamb, fresh fish, and strudel. Yugoslav folk dancing. Wine and beer. Dinner Tuesday through Sunday. CB, MC, V.

DESSERT. Despite the rumor that Los Angelenos are preoccupied with slim and trim bodies, there is no lack of dessert parlors in this city.

When the craving for sweets strikes after the midnight hour, there is nothing to fear, for *DuPar's* is open until the wee hours of the morning throughout the city. These chain restaurants have in-house bakeries that whip up assorted varieties of buttery Danishes, pies, cakes, and doughnuts. They also brew a strong cup of coffee guaranteed to keep you awake for the drive back to your hotel.

It's natural to assume that in a city with such a moderate climate, ice-cream parlors would abound. *Häagen-Dazs,* offering a superb, rich, hand-packed ice cream in a multitude of flavors, with a choice of freshly prepared fudge and nut toppings, is the king of the chains. *Baskin-Robbins* is a California tradition; they are known for creating 101 different flavors of ice cream. Here's your chance to try bubble-gum flavored ice cream or blueberry cheesecake ice cream from among a rainbow of assorted tastes and colors. *Swenson's* is another popular Los Angeles chain offering a variety of flavors guaranteed to please the true ice-cream connoisseur. All the above chains have various outlets throughout the city.

Bennett's Ice Cream, located in Farmers Market in Los Angeles, has splendid fresh ice cream, ice-cream cakes, and fountain service.

San Fernando Valley visitors need only trek to Encino to discover *Robb's Ice Cream Co.,* 17621 Ventura Blvd., Encino; 784–0867. This intimate parlor features over thirty-five flavors of ice cream, including cinafee (cinnamon and coffee) and banaffee (banana and coffee). A true hedonist will add some M&M and Reese's candy toppings.

The Beverly Hills Hotel, 9641 Sunset Blvd., Beverly Hills; 276–2251. Not usually thought of as a place in which to eat dessert, but its downstairs fountain shop makes a wicked chocolate milk shake—rich, thick, cold, and very chocolaty.

C. C. Brown's Hot Fudge Shoppe, 7007 Hollywood Blvd., Hollywood; 464–9726, is an ice-cream legend in Los Angeles. This Hollywood landmark is renowned for its excellent hot fudge sundaes. Judy Garland was once a waitress here.

Michel Richard, 310 S. Robertson, Los Angeles; 275–5707. This charming bistro is representative of many city cafés specializing in pastries and espresso. A bakery as well, Michel Richard's offers the crème de la crème of fine baking, with tiny tables for enjoying the confections on the premises. Also at 12321 Ventura Blvd., Studio City; 508–9977.

La Fondue Bourguignonne, 13354 Ventura Blvd., Sherman Oaks; 501–0181. This restaurant, specializing in fondue, will, on special order, serve that wonder of wonders, chocolate dessert fondue. Chilled fresh fruits in season, along with marshmallows, are skewered onto long forks and dipped into a pot of warm, fudgy chocolate. If that wasn't heaven enough, you then get to dip the finished product into a bowl of freshly whipped heavy cream. Open 5:00 P.M. to 8:00 P.M. Closed Mondays.

Miss Grace Lemon Cakes, 443 S. Robertson Blvd., Beverly Hills; 274–2879; also at 16571 Ventura Blvd., Encino; 995–1976. Fabulous cakes to go, made with the freshest, prime ingredients. Their lemon cake is filled with the essence of so many lemons that it will make your mouth pucker with joy. Also chocolate fudge, banana, and carrot cakes as well as chocolate chip cookies.

Freshly baked chocolate-chip cookies have been the rage of Los Angeles cookie eaters for some time. *Famous Amos* started the trend, and many other entrepreneurs have entered the race. Famous Amos, at 7181 Sunset Blvd., Hollywood; 851–6777, still has the original store with which its multimillion dollar business started. Most major shopping malls feature chocolate-chip cookie emporiums, such as the *Original Chocolate Chip Cookie Company, Mrs. Fields,* and *David's,* a successful New York cookie company, featuring cookies made with Lindt's imported bittersweet chocolate. David's is located at the Broadway Department Store, Century City.

If you're lucky and it's the spring or summer months, you'll find carts with peddlers selling the latest sweet creation: ice creamwiches. These sinful desserts have chocolate-chip cookie outer shells and ice-cream fillings. They're usually located in the Beverly Hills and Century City areas as well as across from the Los Angeles County Art Museum.

COFFEEHOUSES AND CAFÉS. Grabbing a quick bite while touring Los Angeles shouldn't be passed off as purely a functional stop. From the uniformity of a hamburger chain to the more particular ambience of a neighborhood café, eating and running (or eating and driving) is part of the Los Angeles experience.

For only cents more than such familiar places as Burger King or Taco Bell, travelers can explore the many walk-up, drive-in, and takeout stands featuring "chili on everything," a California speciality.

The original *Tommy's Hamburgers* near the USC campus (2575 Beverly at Rampart) is a Los Angeles tradition where you'll find students and other devotees scooping up the famous double-chili cheeseburger. Many locations, two in the Valley: in Burbank, 1310 N. San Fernando Blvd., and in Van Nuys, 6180 Van Nuys Blvd. in Van Nuys.

Although it is a professed imitation, try *Tom's #5,* 1544 La Cienega, and *Tom's #5* in Santa Monica at 1906 Ocean Ave. (an easy walk from the Ocean Ave. entrance to Santa Monica Beach at the end of Pico Blvd.) These stands, like Tommy's, satisfy by providing chili on everything for a good price. Open twenty-four hours; tables provided for traffic watching.

Pink's (at Melrose and La Brea) serves a celebrated chili-cheesedog. A favorite for even the most discerning gourmet, Pink's guarantees a full stomach.

A novel setting is *Carney's,* 8351 W. Sunset Blvd. in West Hollywood, and also in Studio City at 12601 Ventura Blvd., between Coldwater Canyon and Whitset. Some of the best hamburgers in town are served from these converted railroad cars. The Hollywood booths face well-lighted Sunset Strip.

Also boasting the best burgers around is *Fat Jack's* on Ventura Blvd. in Studio City, located west of Universal Studios, a five-minute drive away.

For a more upbeat, contemporary eating experience, Los Angeles offers a number of fine cafés with no set minimum. *Downtown L.A. Cafe,* 418 E. First St., downtown (680–0445), is where artists and theater-goers go for innovative salads and wine by the glass. Make reservations if you're planning to try out the café after theater; otherwise it's probably safe to just drop in. Open Monday through Friday, 11 A.M. to 11 P.M.; 11 A.M. to 7 P.M. Saturday and Sunday. Sunday brunch, 11 A.M. to 7 P.M. MC, V. *Café Beverly Hills* (9725 Wilshire Blvd. at La Cienega; 273–6397), open twenty-four hours a day, is a favorite late-night haunt. The cuisine is straight coffee shop, though beer and wine are served. Prices range to $7.00. Cash only. Parking.

Also competing as the best patio in the West Hollywood area is the enclosed tree-planted area at *Joe Allen,* 8706 W. 3rd St.; 274–7144. The New York theatrical decor features the same checked tablecloths and blackboard menus found at namesake restaurants located in New York, Paris, London, and Toronto. Though reservations are accepted, there is usually a wait, well passed at the lively bar. Daily 11:30 A.M.–2:00 A.M. Price range: $5.00–$15.00 à la carte. MC, V, AE.

El Coyote Spanish Café, 7312 Beverly Blvd.; 939–7766, cannot be beat for its inexpensive Mexican food and festive decor. Costumed waitresses are friendly; the service is great. Daily 11:00 A.M.–10:00 P.M. MC, V. A town favorite, so expect a wait.

Where Melrose Ave. begins at Doheny Dr. on the edge of Beverly Hills, so does the real Los Angeles café life. A newcomer worth a look is *Starlight Café* (655–0955) at 7505 Melrose Ave.; 655–1310. An upbeat place, it is equipped with music and disc jockey and some refreshingly updated luncheonette fare, with pizza as a specialty. Sunday through Thursday, noon on (until 3:00 A.M. Friday and Saturday). All major credit cards. The large bay windows of *Café Figaro,* 9010 Melrose; 274–7664, reveal comfortable coffeehouse surroundings. The healthful food is popular with students and entertainment-industry aspirants. Monday–Thursday 11:30 A.M.–2:00 A.M., Friday and Saturday until 3:00 A.M., Sunday 4:00 P.M.–2:00 A.M. Reservations.

Cucina, 7381 Melrose (653–8333), is a black-and-white showplace for great —not to mention authentic—northern Italian cuisine. Elegant yet understated. Open Monday–Saturday, 11:30 A.M. to midnight; Sunday 5 P.M.–midnight.

At *Cafe 50s,* 838 Lincoln Blvd. in Venice (399–1955), fifties photos, old advertisements, and movie posters adorn the walls. Blintzes are to die for and the Leave It To Beaver omelet is a treat. Music boxes play tunes for a nickle at each table. Open Sunday–Thursday, 7 A.M. to 11 P.M.; Friday and Saturday until 1 A.M. No reservations; cash only.

A number of French cafés can be found in Los Angeles. The authentic music and Continental waiters at *La Poubelle,* 5909 Franklin, Hollywood; 462–9264, give it a true café atmosphere. Chef's specialties are crepes, quiches, and omelettes, all homemade with fresh ingredients. Reservations. Daily 5:30 P.M.–11:30 P.M. MC, V.

Michel Richard (310 S. Robertson; 275–5707) sets tables just outside the busy baker/restaurant, giving it the most "sidewalk feeling" within Los Angeles. Croissants and coffees are enough for a substantial lunch, though a small menu is offered. The clientele is largely French. (Also in the San Fernando Valley, 12321 Ventura Blvd., Studio City; 508–9977.) MC, V.

Downtown, *Café de Paris* (821 S. Spring opposite Cal Mart; 623–7308) is a tiny hole in the wall offering a big French experience. The freshly baked goods and coffee provide a quick shopping respite. The prices are more than reasonable. Monday–Friday, 8:00 A.M.–4:00 P.M.

Clifton's Cafeteria has six restaurants in the Los Angeles area, but the downtown location (515 W. 7th St. at Olive) has persevered in a Los Angeles landmark building where much of the 1920s decor has been maintained. The fourth generation family-owned-and-operated business serves family-style recipes. Monday–Friday, 7:00 A.M.–3:30 P.M. $3.50 luncheon, $4.50 dinner.

Open twenty-four hours for the past fifty-five years, the *Original Pantry,* 977 S. Figueroa; 972–9272, offers big helpings, strictly of the meat-and-potatoes kind. Though it is always crowded, you can't go wrong here.

The Westside is Los Angeles's best part of town for strolling and café lounging. In Beverly Hills try *Café Rodeo* (360 N. Rodeo Dr.; 273–0300), well worth the $3.50 minimum for its Continental cuisine and stargazing on the famous drive where many celebrities stop for lunch. There is usually a wait for patio dining. Reservations are suggested for dinner. All major credit cards. Daily 7:00 A.M.–midnight. Valet parking.

Caffé Roma (350 N. Canon Dr., 274–7834) offers an outdoor dining experience, while inside blond wood and tiling serves as the setting for tiny pizzas and Italian wines. AE, DC, MC.

Nearby is *Santo Pietros* at 2954 Beverly Glen Circle, Bel Air; 474–4349. This country Italian café features chopped-antipasto salad, light pastas, pizza, beer, and wine. Desserts are great. Try the pistachio cake. It's definitely a place to see and be seen.

The café/cafeteria style at *Café Casino* (9595 Wilshire, Beverly Hills; 274–0201, and in two other locations at 1299 Ocean Ave., Santa Monica; 394–1135, and in Westwood at 1135 Gayley Ave.; 208–1010) allows for slightly lower prices in this normally high-density eating district. The proprietors are French, as are the fresh croissants, pâtés, salads, and hot entrees. Choose what you like, and carry your tray to the shaded umbrella patio, or take out a fresh pastry from the bakery counter and window shop. Open seven days, 7:00 A.M.–10:00 P.M. MC, V.

Thirty varieties of the town's finest cheesecake are found at the *Cheesecake Factory* (364 N. Beverly Dr., Beverly Hills; 278–7270). The $3.00 minimum is easily spent on one of their unique flavors: amaretto, peanut butter, and marble, to name a few, and a cup of steaming espresso. Otherwise, the full menu and salad bar may be enjoyed in the casual, pleasant atmosphere. Monday–Thursday 11:00 A.M.–11:00 P.M., Friday and Saturday 11:00 A.M.–12:30 A.M., Sunday 11:00 A.M.–10:00 P.M.

The contemporary *Cadillac Café,* 359 N. La Cienega Blvd.; 657–4762, is a frequent eating spot for such celebrities as Teri Garr and Steve Martin. The diverse menu features the freshest of salads. Open Monday through Friday, 11:30 A.M. to midnight, Saturday and Sunday, 10:00 A.M. to midnight.

The more ethnic coffee shop cuisine is *Junior's Deli/Restaurant,* 2379 Westwood Blvd.; 475–5771. Always busy, their Jewish cooking is unrivaled on the Westside. Daily 6:30 A.M. to 11:30 P.M. MC, V.

The Hamburger Hamlet, 10943 Weyburn Ave.; 208–8980, serves plump and juicy hamburgers. Lobster bisque and overloaded omelettes are also specialties. Several locations. All major credit cards. Monday–Thursday, 11:30 A.M.–9:00 P.M. Friday–Saturday 11:00 A.M.–11:00 P.M.

D. B. Levy's (10936 Lindbrook Ave.; 208–3773) features 164 sandwiches (at last count), 27 ice-cream creations, homemade soups, and a variety of cheesecakes. The upper level is bright and airy. All major credit cards. Monday–Thursday, 11:30 A.M.–12:00 P.M., Friday and Saturday, 11:00 A.M.–2:00 A.M., Sunday 11:00 A.M.–11:00 P.M. AE, MC, V.

In West Los Angeles French–California cuisine is served at the *Bicycle Shop Café* (12217 Wilshire Blvd.; 826–7831). Antique bicycles are set among plants and waterfalls. Excellent for after-theater and movie dining. Cary Grant is a frequent customer for their authentic French onion soup. Weekends a fabulous brunch. No minimum, lunch about $7.00, $10.00 for dinner. Daily 11:00 A.M. –midnight. MC, V.

Get ready for a flash from the past at the *Hardrock Café* 8614 Beverly Blvd., on the ground floor of the Beverly Center shopping mall; 276–7605. Waitresses are known to break into a 50s dance routine in the middle of taking your order.

The most frequented outdoor café in Venice is *The Sidewalk Café* (1401 Ocean Front Walk; 399–5547). From any seat in the patio, diners are treated to the famous Venice charades. Mimes, magicians, acrobats, and roller-skating dancers glide by the busy café. An ocean view, too. Omelettes, salads, and sandwiches. Expect a wait! Daily 8:00 A.M.–1.00 A.M. V, MC.

The Dandelion Café (636 Venice Blvd.) is best known for its omelettes. Vegetable chili and homemade sherry trifle at reasonable prices are also specialties. Tuesday–Sunday 8:00 A.M.–4:00 P.M. No credit cards. Easy parking.

Figtree's Café, 429 Ocean Front Walk; 396–5559, is a warm and friendly natural-foods coffeehouse with vegetarian and espresso specialties. $2.50 minimum on weekends. Parking on Rose Ave. lot.

The Rose (220 Rose Ave., 399–0711) serves an elegant dinner and luncheon menu, but the coffee shop serves croissants and fruit tarts without the $6.00 minimum. Monday–Saturday 8:00 A.M.–11:00 P.M., Sunday 9:00 A.M.–5:00 P.M. MC, V.

In Pasadena don't miss *The Espresso Bar,* 34 S. Raymond Ave.; 356–9095. High vaulted ceilings, Persian rugs, and a fireplace create a unique European café atmosphere. Interesting salads and soups are the specialties. Tuesday through Saturday a Continental breakfast is served, 8:00 A.M.–11:00 A.M., lunch 11:30 A.M.–4:00 P.M. Dinner is served Tuesday through Saturday 7:00 P.M. –10:30 P.M., but open until 2:00 A.M. for espresso, cappuccino, and pastries. Monday night there is jazz in the alcove; wonderful acoustics.

NIGHTLIFE. Nightlife in Los Angeles has come to mean anything from catching a comedy act at the Comedy Store to frenetic disco dancing at Chippendales or dreamily listening to a sultry chanteuse at Chez Nora's. This city offers a potpourri of specialized entertainment, not only in the hub of the city but also in the outlying suburban communities.

Despite the diversity of entertainment and the high energy level of the nightlife crowd, Los Angeles nightclubs are not known for keeping their doors open until the wee hours of the morning. This is an early-to-bed city, and it's not unusual to hear the call for "last drinks" at 1:30 A.M. It's safe to say that by 2:00 A.M., most jazz, rock, and disco clubs are closed for the night. Afterhours clubs are few and far between. Perhaps it's because of the temperate climate and the sports orientation of the city. Most Angelenos want to be on the tennis court or out jogging by 9:00 A.M., and so a late night social life is often out of the question.

The accent in this city is on trendy rock clubs, smooth country-and-Western establishments, intimate jazz spots, and laugh-a-minute comedy clubs. City residents generally do not gravitate toward hotels for nighttime entertainment, but you can discover there a quiet evening of soft piano or harp music, often accompanied by sentimental vocalists, for a refreshing change of pace.

The Sunset Strip, running from West Hollywood to Beverly Hills, offers a wide assortment of nighttime diversions. Comedy stores, restaurants with piano bars, cocktail lounges, and hard-rock clubs proliferate.

Westwood, home of UCLA, is a college town, and this section of Los Angeles comes alive at night with rock and new-wave discos and clubs playing the canned and live music. It's one of the few areas in Los Angeles with a true neighborhood spirit. You'll see people of all ages strolling its streets at night, and you can feel the excitement and energy in the air. On the other hand, downtown Los Angeles is generally not the place to be at night. Other than the Dorothy Chandler Pavilion for concerts and theater, downtown night life is virtually nonexistent.

Dress codes vary depending on the establishment you choose to visit. Jackets are expected at the more traditional night entertainment spots, such as cabarets and hotels. Discos are generally quite casual, although some prohibit the wearing of blue jeans. New-wave and punk-rock clubs are the most casual of all—almost anything goes there! The rule of thumb is to phone ahead and check the dress code, but, on the whole, Los Angeles is oriented toward casual wear.

The following night spots are divided according to their orientation: jazz; folk/pop/rock; cabaret; disco/dancing; country; hotel rooms and piano bars; and comedy/magic. Consult *Los Angeles* and *California* magazines for up-to-the-minute listings. The Sunday *Los Angeles Times* Calendar section, the free *Los Angeles Weekly,* and *Los Angeles Reader* also provide wide listings.

Don't think that the suburbs of this city have no night life. Some of Los Angeles's best jazz, discos, and comedy clubs are scattered throughout the San Fernando and San Gabriel valleys. For example, the Baked Potato in Studio City offers dynamic jazz, and the Palomino Club in North Hollywood boasts nationally recognized country-and-western performers.

With a little exploration you will discover that "the City of Angels" can easily bring out a bit of the devil in you.

Key to credit card information following each listing:
AE = American Express
CB = Carte Blanche
DC = Diners Club
MC = MasterCard
V = Visa

Expensive is a charge of $10.00 or more per person; *Moderate* is $5.00–$9.00. *Inexpensive* refers to places where the cover and/or minimum totals less than $5.00. On weekend nights, cover charges at most establishments are usually a few dollars higher than on weeknights.

JAZZ

Concerts by the Sea. 100 Fisherman's Wharf, Redondo Beach; 379–4998. One of Los Angeles's most popular jazz clubs. Many name acts, including Lionel Hampton, Jimmy Smith, and Ramsey Lewis. A wide variety of jazz artists featured. Three shows nightly. Valet parking available. Thursday through Sunday. *Expensive.* MC, V.

Nucleus Nuance. 7267 Melrose Ave., Hollywood; 939–8666. This Art Deco restaurant features vintage jazz Friday and Saturday from 10:00 P.M. on. *Moderate to Expensive.* All major credit cards.

Donte's. 4269 Lankershim Blvd., North Hollywood; (818) 769–1566. A comfortable room featuring a variety of jazz entertainment, including top-name big bands. Many studio musicians and talk-show orchestra members sit in on shows. The dinner menu includes many Continental specialties. Closed Sunday. *Moderate.* All major credit cards.

Jazz Safari. 1119 Queen's Highway, Long Beach; 436–9341. Contemporary jazz fills this club. Junglelike decor: There are ceramic tigers and lions, huge trees, and a forty-gallon fish tank filled with exotic fish. International hamburgers, steak, and scampi are the dining specialties. Open seven days. *Moderate.* All major credit cards.

Le Café. 14633 Ventura Blvd., Sherman Oaks; 986–2662. The Room Upstairs is of high-tech design and features mellow jazz. It's an intimate room; many vocalists, including owner Lois Boileau, are presented. Three shows nightly, Thursday through Saturday. Downstairs is a dynamic restaurant-café offering everything from onion soup to the best fresh duck in town. *Moderate.* AE, MC, V.

Memory Lane. 2323 W. Martin Luther King Jr. Blvd., Los Angeles; 294–8430. Now owned by comedy star Marla Gibbs of "The Jeffersons" fame. Newly remodeled, the club seats 275. This room pops with blues, jazz, and easy listening. Kenny Burrell and Ernie Andrews play here from time to time. A new menu includes roast prime rib of beef and Alaskan King Crab Legs. *Moderate.* AE, CB, DC.

One for L.A. 3707 W. Cahuenga, N. Hollywood; 509–9066. Local jazz favorites seven nights a week. Light food and a full bar. Cover varies; usually *Inexpensive.* MC, V.

The Baked Potato. 3787 Cahuenga Blvd., west, North Hollywood; (818) 980–1615. A tiny club where they pack you in like sardines to hear a powerhouse of jazz. The featured item on the menu is, of course, baked potatoes; they're jumbo and stuffed with everything from steak to vegetables. This intimate, intelligent jazz club usually features Don Randi and Quest, Wednesday through Saturday. *Inexpensive.* MC, V.

Carmelo's. 4449 Van Nuys Blvd., Sherman Oaks; 995–9532, and 784–3268. An intimate club seating no more than 100 people. Dixieland and straightforward jazz is featured. Sarah Vaughan is known to "sit in" on occasion. Dinner can be ordered; Italian and Continental cuisine. *Inexpensive.* AE, MC, V.

Coffee Emporium. 4345 Glencoe Ave., Marina del Rey; 823–4446. This earthy coffeehouse features jazz quartets and quintets on Friday and Saturday evenings from 8:30 P.M. to midnight. It's full of green plants, fresh flowers on oak tables, and a giant espresso machine that brews several varieties of imported coffees. Pastries and cheesecake are specialties. Generally standing room only; come early. Cover on Fridays and Saturdays. MC, V.

Comeback Inn. 1633 W. Washington Blvd., Venice; 396–7255. A showcase for original music. "Fusion," jazz blended with funk, pop, ethnic, and electronic music, is strong here. From April through November are featured outdoor concerts. A European-style bistro with a bohemian flair. The club serves strict vegetarian cuisine. Entertainment nightly and weekend afternoons. *Inexpensive.* AE, MC, V.

Flying Jib. 17237 Ventura Blvd., Encino; 986–2598. A large room, separate from their Continental-style restaurant. Progressive jazz is highlighted. Munch on potato skins and egg rolls during sets. Open seven days. *Inexpensive.* AE, MC, V.

The Lighthouse. 30 Pier Ave., Hermosa Beach; 372–6911 and 376–9833. One of Los Angeles's finest. A broad spectrum of jazz from progressive to big band. Jam sessions often on weekends. Freddie Hubbard, Woody Herman, and Jimmy Witherspoon have all played here. The decor is of wood, brass, and brick, with a lot of plants. Dine on fettucini, assorted appetizers, or steaks while hearing the sounds. *No cover.* MC, V with a $5.00 minimum.

The Money Tree. 10149 Riverside Dr., Toluca Lake; 766–9891 and 766–8348. A restaurant-jazz club featuring assorted vocalists and small combos. Studio musicians often sit in. Open seven days. *No cover, no minimum.* MC, V.

FOLK/POP/ROCK

The Palace. 1735 N. Vine St., Hollywood; 462–3000 or 462–6031. The in spot for the upwardly mobile. It's plush Art Deco—truely a palace—and boasts live entertainment, a fabulous sound system, full bar and dining upstairs in the L'Élysée Matignon restaurant. Patrons dress to kill. *Expensive.* Tickets available at Ticketron or at the Palace box office. AE, V, MC.

Radiotron. 715 S. Park View St., Los Angeles; 480–9562. Danceable funk, D.J.s spin contemporary tunes. All ages and no booze. *Moderate.* Cover is $5.

McCabe's Guitar Shop. 3101 Pico Blvd., Santa Monica; 828–4497. Folk, acoustic rock, bluegrass, and soul in an intimate concert-hall setting. Coffee, herb tea, apple juice, and homemade sweets are served during intermission. Friday through Sunday only. *Expensive to Moderate.* All major credit cards.

The Roxy. 9009 Sunset Blvd., West Hollywood; 276–2222. The premier Los Angeles rock club. Classy and comfortable, this intimate club now also offers performance art as well as theatrical productions. Many famous Los Angeles groups got their start here as opening acts. *Expensive to Moderate.* No credit cards.

The Central. 8852 Sunset Blvd., West Hollywood; 855–9183. A musician's hangout. Road crews, pop-act managers, and famous guitarists alike come to hear live music in the pop, soul, and jazz-fusion genres. Many celebrity musicians attend the Tuesday night jam sessions. *Moderate.* No credit cards.

Club Lingerie. 6507 Sunset Blvd., Hollywood; 466–8557. This exciting Art Deco night spot features everything from reggae to big-band music. Drink prices are fair, and the door varies according to the attraction. *Moderate.* No credit cards.

Gazzari's. 9039 Sunset Blvd., West Hollywood; 273–6606. A Sunset Strip landmark. Pure rock and roll with a 19- early 20's age group. Dress is casual. *Moderate.* No credit cards.

Madame Wong's Restaurant. 949 Sun Mun Way, Los Angeles; 624–5346. A young crowd; new-wave fanatics. Two shows nightly. Also Madame Wong's West, 2900 Wilshire Blvd., Santa Monica; 829–7361. *Moderate.*

Perkins Palace. 129 N. Raymond Ave., Pasadena; 796–7001. Rock-and-roll concerts, Friday and Saturday only. Up-and-coming talent as well as some name acts. *Moderate.*

At My Place. 1026 Wilshire Blvd., Santa Monica; 451–8596. One of the new LA clubs, this year-old enterprise features a provocative blend of jazz/fusion, pop, and rhythm-and-blues music acts. Comedy performers open the weekend shows, and on Sunday afternoons you can enjoy a 20-piece ensemble playing big-band music. Some of the culinary specialties include quiche and potato skins. There is also a full bar. *Moderate.* V, MC.

Banjo Café. 2906 Lincoln Blvd., Santa Monica; 392–5716. Dixieland, folk, and jazz music are featured. An intimate, casual club with inexpensive, quality food. *Inexpensive* cover for nondiners. MC, V.

Club 88. 11784 Pico Blvd., West Los Angeles; 479–6923. Rock and roll nightly. *Inexpensive.*

Pier 52. 52 Pier Ave., Hermosa Beach; 376–1629. From Tuesday through Sunday there are live dance bands playing pure rock and roll and Top 40s. Monday night is saved for top bands, including new wave and heavy metal. *Inexpensive.* No credit cards.

Sasch. 11345 Ventura Blvd., Studio City; (818) 769–5555. A live band plays Top 40s for the twenty-one to thirty-five age group. Anything goes for dress. *Inexpensive.* All major credit cards.

Sunset Saloon. 1 Washington St., Venice; 396–5914. This club draws a beach crowd with primarily rock and roll entertainment. *Inexpensive.* MC, V with $5.00 minimum.

The Troubador. 9081 Santa Monica Blvd., West Hollywood; 276–1158. In the early 1970s this was one of the hottest clubs in town for major talent. Business then became shaky for a few years as the music industry changed its focus; but now it's rolling again, this time with up-and-coming talent. The adjoining bar is a great place to see and be seen. *Inexpensive.* No credit cards.

Twenty Grand West. 5812 Overhill Dr., Los Angeles; 296–3195. This reggae club draws many a homesick Jamaican. Jamaican food is another strong plus here. *No cover.* No credit cards.

CABARET

Playboy Club. ABC Entertainment Center, 2020 Ave. of the Stars, Century City; 277–2777. If you want to fork over $35.00 for instant membership, you've got instant admittance to Playboy clubs all over the country. You may bring an unlimited number of guests. Bunnies will provide the drinks; the likes of Lainie Kazan and other chanteuses will provide the entertainment. Disco in the Living Room. Closed Sunday. *Expensive to Moderate,* depending on whether you are a member. All major credit cards.

Studio One Backlot. 652 N. La Peer, West Hollywood; 659–0472. An elegant, classy night spot featuring excellent musical acts, singers, comedians, and dancers. Closed Sunday through Tuesday. *Expensive to Moderate.* AE, MC, V.

Hop Singh's. 4110 Lincoln Blvd., Marina del Rey; 822–4008. Intimate and innovative. Jazz, rock, folk, and comedy—what more could you want? Closed Monday and Tuesday. *Moderate.* All major credit cards.

L.A. Cabaret. 17271 Ventura Blvd., Encino; 501–3737. This new night spot features a variety of comedy acts on weekends and on Wednesday. Often, famous entertainers will make surprise appearances. *Moderate.* AE, V, MC.

La Cage aux Folles. 643 N. La Cienega Blvd., West Hollywood; 657–1091. A cabaret supper club that has a unique angle: female impersonators who do impressions of famous female stars such as Liza Minnelli or Barbra Streisand. The ambience, with a shocking-pink and stark-blue color scheme, resembles a European bistro of forty years ago. An unusual fun nightspot. There is an extensive French–Continental menu. *Moderate* cover charge for diners; *Expensive* for nondiners. AE, DC, MC, V.

Gio's Cabaret. 7574 Sunset Blvd., Hollywood; 876–1120. An eclectic variety of talented Los Angeles artists perform here. One night will feature comedians; another night it's big-band time or jazz quartets or aspiring theatrical talent performing Broadway vignettes. The cabaret menu features sandwiches, calamari fritti (fried squid), and mozzarella marinara. The adjoining restaurant specializes in Brazilian cuisine. *Moderate to Inexpensive.* All major credit cards.

DISCO/DANCING

Chippendale's. 3739 Overland Ave., West Los Angeles; 202–8850. A popular Los Angeles disco, well-known for its male exotic dancers–waiters who strip down to G-strings for women only from Wednesday through Sunday at the 8:30 P.M. shows. On Tuesday night it's rock videos, and every night it's disco, disco, disco. Loud punk, funk, and new-wave music spills out the doors and into the street. Not for the timid or prudish. The cover varies; usually *Expensive.* Occasional free night for ladies. AE, DC, MC, V.

Osko's Disco. 333 S. La Cienega Blvd., Los Angeles; 652–9333. A leading Los Angeles disco. This multilevel club was featured in the disco film *Thank God It's Friday.* There are female mud wrestlers and male exotic dancers as well as the latest disco singles. *Moderate* cover. All major credit cards.

The Speakeasy. 8531 Santa Monica Blvd., West Hollywood; 657–4777. A softly lighted disco with the latest of disco music pounding the room. Soul-type music predominates. A well-dressed crowd; people really get up and boggie seriously. Cover *Moderate.* MC, V in bar only.

Tennessee Gin and Cotton Co. 19710 Ventura Blvd., Woodland Hills; (818) 347–4044. Two dance floors; one is a disco, and the other has a live rock or Top 40s band for a classy over-twenty-one crowd. Casual but neat dress. *Moderate.* Closed Monday. AE, MC, V.

Circus Disco. 6648 Lexington Ave., Hollywood; 462–1291. Gay owned and operated, this disco features funk and rock, with new wave exclusively on Thursday nights, all played over a large-scale quadrophonic sound system. Open nightly. *Moderate to Inexpensive.* No credit cards.

Le Hot Club. 15910 Ventura Blvd., Encino; 986–7034. The San Fernando Valley's most chic club. A lot of backgammon tables and a well-dressed crowd of all ages. Music is played by a D.J. with a deference toward all disco factions. *Moderate to Inexpensive.* Closed Monday. AE, MC, V.

Annabelle's. 1700 Pacific Coast Hwy., Redondo Beach; 316–1434. It's jazz until 9:00 P.M., and then disco is king—seven nights a week. *No cover charge.* MC, V.

Beverly Cavern Discotheque. 4289 Beverly Blvd., Los Angeles; 662–6035. Disco and backgammon is popular here. Oldies as well as the latest in disco and rock and roll predominate. *Inexpensive.* No credit cards.

Coconut Traszer. 8177 Sunset Blvd., Los Angeles; 654–4773. Disco dancing, great barbecue menu, and killer drinks make for lively fun. Caters to the 18–25-year-old crowd. After hours. D.J.s spin hot forties danceables. Friday and Saturday, $2.00 cover; no cover on Tuesday.

Filthy McNasty's. 11700 Victory Blvd., North Hollywood; 769–2220. McNasty is almost a Hollywood landmark himself, having held court on the Sunset Strip for countless years. He has since moved to the San Fernando Valley for another wild and crazy club. Proceed at your own risk. There is female mud wrestling for male oglers and male exotic dancers for female oglers. Live and canned music. After hours Friday and Saturday until 4:00 A.M. Some nights long-time entrepreneur McNasty himself gets up on stage.

Le Chic. 1717 Silverlake Blvd., Los Angeles; 666–2885. A mixture of Latino, funk, and pop disco. The crowd is of all ages. Backgammon is a popular game between dances. Free disco lessons on Wednesday and Sunday. *Inexpensive.* MC, V.

Odyssey I. 8471 Beverly Blvd., West Hollywood; 658–8106. Rock nightly until 4:00 A.M., Friday and Saturday until 5:00 A.M. Pool table and pinball machines. *Inexpensive.* No credit cards.

Playboy Club. ABC Entertainment Center, 2020 Ave. of the Stars, Century City; 277–2777. An instant key costs $25.00 and includes unlimited guests. Disco in the Living Room from 9:00 P.M. until 2:00 A.M. *Moderate.* All major credit cards.

The Stop. 12446 Moorpark St., Studio City; 761–8686. Hard rock-and-roll disco; young, for a twenties crowd. *No cover.* MC, V.

Studio One. 652 N. LaPeer Dr., West Hollywood; 659–0471. Known as Los Angeles's largest disco, it hosts a predominately gay crowd. Dancing nightly. *Inexpensive.* No credit cards.

The Tapestry. 10177 Reseda Blvd., Northridge; 993–7071. Progressive disco with the very latest of pure disco music. The records that play here are straight from New York of record distributors. The crowd is eighteen to twenty-five. Sunday is New-Wave night. *Inexpensive.* Closed Monday. MC, V.

COUNTRY

Little Nashville Club. 13350 Sherman Way, North Hollywood; 764–0420. Country–Western entertainment and dancing nightly. Free dance lessons Wednesday and Saturday. *No cover; two-drink minimum.* MC, V.

The Palomino. 6907 Lankershim Blvd., North Hollywood; 764–4010. There is occasionally a wild crowd at this premier country showcase in Los Angeles.

Good old boys and hip cowboys meet here, and everybody has a good time. The cover varies between *Moderate and Inexpensive.* All major credit cards.

Womphopper's Wagon Works. 100 Universal City Plaza, Universal City; 508–3939. Live country-Western entertainment at this unique restaurant built out of barnwood, in an authentic Western motif with painstaking attention to details. Dancing nightly. Full bar. Try the buffalo-meat chili. All major credit cards.

HOTEL ROOMS AND PIANO BARS

Alberto's Ristorante. 8826 Melrose Ave., Los Angeles; 278–2770. This piano bar draws a neighborhood crowd, generally over forty and well-to-do. Excellent Italian food as well. All major credit cards.

Bel-Air Sands Hotel. 11461 Sunset Blvd., Bel Air; 476–6571. The Bimini Bar features a singer–pianist who performs songs of the 1940s, 1950s, and 1960s. All major credit cards.

Beverly Hills Hotel. 9641 Sunset Blvd., Beverly Hills; 276–2251. There is late supper and after-theater piano entertainment in the Polo Lounge nightly. This stately old hotel is a celebrity mecca. All major credit cards.

Century Plaza Hotel. 2025 Ave. of the Stars, Century City; 227–2000. The Lobby Lounge features piano music nightly. All major credit cards.

Hotel Bel Air. 701 Stone Canyon Rd., Bel Air; 472–1211. Entertainment Tuesday through Sunday, alternating between a pianist and a vocalist. This is one of Los Angeles's most famous hotels. All major credit cards.

Hyatt Regency. 711 S. Hope St., Los Angeles; 683–1234. There is a good piano lounge in this spectacularly designed hotel. All major credit cards.

Hyatt Wilshire. 3515 Wilshire Blvd., Los Angeles; 381–7411. There is entertainment in the Café Carnival Lounge. All major credit cards.

Los Angeles Marriott. 5855 W. Century Blvd., Los Angeles; 641–5700. The Hangar Room on the top floor of the hotel offers a panoramic view of the city and especially of the arrival and departure of planes at the Los Angeles International Airport. It's a romantic place to go for a drink and soft piano music accompanied by a soothing vocalist. Both standard and contemporary songs are featured. All major credit cards.

The New Otani Hotel and Garden. 120 S. Los Angeles St., Los Angeles; 629–1200. The Genji Bar of this Japanese-style hotel offers a sentimental vocalist. All major credit cards.

Sheraton–Universal Hotel. 30 Universal City Plaza, North Hollywood; 980–1212. Soft combos perform in the Portuguese Bar. The hotel is convenient to restaurants and the entertainment complex in Universal City. All major credit cards.

Simply Blues. 6290 Sunset Blvd., Hollywood; 466–5239. This has an action-filled bar area; a lot of people crowd into the bar and listen to the soft piano music. All major credit cards.

Smoke House. 4420 Lakeside Dr., Burbank; 845–3731. There is a lounge room with assorted entertainment separate from the restaurant. Many musical acts of the 1950s are featured. All major credit cards.

Sportsmen's Lodge Restaurant. 12833 Ventura Blvd., Studio City; 984–0202. There is a pianist in the lounge connected to the lovely Sportsmen's Lodge Hotel. The setting, with brooks and swan-filled ponds, is pretty. All major credit cards.

S. S. Princess Louise Restaurant. Berth 94, Port of Los Angeles, San Pedro; 831–2341. This ship sails to nowhere but stays afloat with a piano bar and a good restaurant. Enjoy a romantic view of the ocean and the incoming ships. If you get carried away, you can get married at the ship's chapel. All major credit cards.

Tony Roma's. 9404 Brighton Way, Beverly Hills; 278–1207. There is piano entertainment in the lounge nightly. The restaurant is known for moderate-priced but tasty ribs. MC, V.

Westin Bonaventure Hotel. 5th and Figueroa St., Los Angeles; 624–1000. In the Lobby Court there is music nightly. Another room, Top of Five, features two pianists in a revolving lounge, offering breathtaking sights of the whole city. All major credit cards.

Westwood Marquis. 930 Hilgard Ave., Westwood; 208–8765. The Westwood Lounge of this chic hotel offers cozy settees, soft lights, and a piano or a harp player. Occasional vocals. Very relaxing. All major credit cards.

COMEDY AND MAGIC

Comedy Store. 8433 Sunset Blvd., Hollywood; 656–6225. Los Angeles's premier comedy showcase for over a decade. Many famous comedians, such as Robin Williams and Steve Martin, try out routines here. The cover varies; usually *Moderate.* MC, V.

The Improvisation. 8162 Melrose Ave., West Hollywood; 651–2583. The Improv is a transplanted New York establishment: eighteen years in the Big Apple, now seven in the Big Orange. Comedy is showcased here, with some vocalists. The Improv was the proving ground for Liza Minelli and Richard Pryor, among others. *Moderate.* MC, V accepted for food and drinks only, not for the cover.

Merlin McFly Magical Bar and Grill. 2702 Main St., Santa Monica; 392–8468. This is one bar where you might see double, and it may not be because of the drinks: magical illusions are featured nightly until midnight. Ladies, watch out for the powder room; lights will dim there, and you'll see a Houdini-like figure with a crystal ball in the mirror. *No cover.* All major credit cards.

The New Ice House Comedy Showroom. 24 N. Mentor Ave., Pasadena; 681–1923. Three-act shows here feature comedians and magicians from Las Vegas as well as from television shows. *Moderate;* special bargain prices include show and dinner. MC, V.

Comedy and Magic Club. 1018 Hermosa Ave., Hermosa Beach; 372–2626. This beachfront club features many magicians and comedians seen on television and in Las Vegas. The Unknown Comic, Elayne Boosler, and Pat Paulsen have all played here. Closed Monday. Tuesday is Ladies' Night, Wednesday is Men's Night. Reservations are suggested. The menu features light American fare and many appetizers. *Moderate to Inexpensive,* depending on the featured act. MC, V.

Bert's Deli-Smoker. 14513 Ventura Blvd., Sherman Oaks; (818) 990–8650. Sawdust on the floor, big brisket sandwiches—and lots of laughs. This deli turns into a comedy club Thursday through Saturday evenings. Local favorites as well as those trying to get established are featured. *Inexpensive.* MC, V.

L.A. Connection. 13442 Ventura Blvd., Sherman Oaks; (818) 784–1868. Comedy revues and improvisation in a theater setting. *Inexpensive.* Reservations suggested on Saturday and Sunday. No credit cards.

The Laugh Factory. 8001 Sunset Blvd., Hollywood; 656–8860. A variety of comedy acts and improvisation. Closed Sunday. No age limit. Food, drink. *Inexpensive.*

Groundlings Theater. 7307 Melrose Ave., Hollywood; 934–9700. Original skits, music, improvisation with each player contributing his/her own flavor to this most hysterical performance. *Inexpensive to Moderate.* MC, V.

CASINOS. In the late 1930s the famed gambling ship *Rex,* anchored just outside the three-mile limit, catered to Los Angelenos looking for the occasional brief fling with Lady Luck. Each night tuxedoed men and gowned ladies took a motor launch out to the ship for an evening of gaming—blackjack, roulette, craps, or poker. Readers of Raymond Chandler's *Farewell, My Lovely* will recognize the scene.

Today the *Rex* is only a memory perpetuated largely through a restaurant in downtown Los Angeles that bears its name and Art Deco motif. Anyone who lusts for the thrill of "bones" dancing across green felt has to hop a jet to Las Vegas; it's just an hour away.

Poker players, though, don't have to make that trek. Just fifteen miles south of the Los Angeles civic center is the community of Gardena, home of six combination card rooms, restaurants, and cocktail lounges. These are not full gaming casinos, and there are no attached hotels. Although California law now prohibits gambling, Gardena had enacted an ordinance years ago allowing operators to run draw-poker, low-ball, and pan card games.

The six card rooms are fairly standardized, even though the decor varies and limits on maximum bets differ. A card room, for example, can have no more than thirty-five tables. Typically a poker table has eight seats and a designated limit on bets. The minimum bet is $1.00 before the draw and $2.00 after the draw and no limits on the number of raises. Some tables have a "house" dealer; the card room collects a fee, ranging from $1.00 up to $24.00 an hour in the $100–$200 games, from the players every half hour.

Gardena card rooms are open twenty-four hours a day, and you can play as long as your cash and stamina hold out. It is not uncommon to see women in their seventies playing twenty-four hours straight. Card rooms also have surprisingly good food in their restaurants at reasonable prices. Law requires that the bar be separate and outside the building. Usually these bars are unimaginative and rarely offer entertainment, but they are a welcome oasis for someone who thirsts for a gin and tonic after a grueling six hours at the table. You can't have a drink brought to your table.

Don't expect headline entertainers (there is no entertainment other than the excitement of winning a fat pot) and craps, "21," roulette, baccarat, and slot machines are banned. Yet even without the glitter and some of the more alluring games, Gardena is a great break for the $2.00 or $2,000 bettor. All area codes are 213.

The Horseshoe Club. 14305 S. Vermont, Gardena 90247; 323–7520. One of the most famous of the Gardena card rooms, it has $1.00–$2.00 games in poker, low ball, and a special "jackpot" card game. No pan. Co-owner Tom Parks has put in two large-screen TVs so players can watch sporting events between games. The Horseshoe Restaurant serves a hefty New York Steak for $13.90. The Kings Inn bar is nothing special.

The New Gardena Club. 15046 S. Western Ave., Gardena, 90247; 323–7301. General manager George Ursich claims to have the hottest card action and best restaurant in Gardena. The menu is an amazing combination of Oriental, Mexican, and Continental fare. The filet mignon in orange sauce is only $8.95. The Four Queens cocktail lounge serves $1.75 drinks, and the coffee shop runs breakfast specials from 3:00 A.M. to noon for $1.95. The New Gardena also offers Pan, a combination of gin rummy and poker, where a player wins depending on certain melds. Players can also buy chips and charge them to a Visa or Master Card credit card.

The Eldorado Club. 15411 S. Vermont Ave., Gardena, 90247; 323–2800. This is the high rollers club, and the only card room with a $100–$200 limit game going nonstop. That means that your first bet can be up to $100, and after the draw (cards from the dealer), the maximum bet is $200. With eight players and no limits on the number of times players can raise, pots can easily double or triple. "I've seen $40,000 winners and $40,000 losers," says general manager Peter Ackoury. The food at bargain prices is superb. A lavish luncheon buffet costs $6.00; at night more food is piled on, and the price is bumped up a buck to $7.00. One third of the tables have house dealers. Establish credit and you can cash checks easily, but no credit cards are accepted for chips. The Eldorado Room bar has one of Gardena's only one-man musical shows, nightly 9:00 P.M. to 2:00 A.M.

Normandie Club. 1045 W. Rosecrans, Gardena 90249; 515–1466. This is Gardena's newest club, a European-style card room that opened in October 1980. Most of the table games are $40.00–$80.00 stakes, but some are lower. New players are welcomed. Instruction is offered free by staffers. The Candlelight Room has full Italian dinners at less than $10.00 and the chef is accomplished.

BARS. Despite its well-publicized penchant for hedonism, Los Angeles, unlike New York City, Chicago, and San Francisco, is not a saloon town. The practiced art of pubcrawling—barhopping with old friends or in quest of new ones—has never flourished in Los Angeles mainly because the city has few real neighborhoods and plenty of freeways. Your favorite Mexican cantina may be in Marina del Rey, or the premier Irish pub may be in Pasadena, more than 25 miles away.

Even though the sheer sprawl has stunted the growth of a true saloon society, do not conclude that the Women's Christian Temperance Union (WCTU) rules Los Angeles. Far from it. There are hundreds of great cozy bars, lively pubs, and festive watering holes to quench your thirst for conversation and fine spirits. They are simply not confined to a particular neighborhood. Nor are they dominated by regulars or cliques that often, though unintentionally, give first-time visitors the cold shoulder.

The Los Angeleno, in short, has no real loyalty to any libational hangout. He or she is adventuresome, willing to crisscross the city to try an authentic Piña Colada, or share some suds with a pal at a bar that just opened. The Angeleno is fickle and forever searching for the new spiritual experience, the newest, most "in" bar. Unlike New Yorkers, the Angeleno will not adopt a single saloon as his own home base from which to wander to other saloons to meet and greet his pals. Angelenos are too nomadic.

But that is changing. The price of gasoline and the trend toward close-in living are spawning a new breed of saloongoer. In a town that has lured legions of New Yorkers, Chicagoans, other Midwesterners, and Texans—not to mention Europeans, Asians, and now South Americans—there is a new sociology springing up in saloons. People are getting acquainted not just for the proverbial one-night stand but to form conversational communities of interest. At 5:00 P.M., the cocktail hour, Rive Gauche in Sherman Oaks is as lively as Henry Africa's in San Francisco or Charley O's in Manhattan, but the prices are about $1.00 a drink less, and the proprietors lay out a near-bacchanalian buffet.

The message here is that you as a visitor will still have to venture out on freeway forays to find the bar that you feel most comfortable in. We've compiled a compendium of cantinas, a slice of the saloon scene, but it is by no means complete. Space does not permit a larger listing.

Yet before you begin this expedition, keep these guidelines in mind:

South Bay bars and any place near the water have younger, hipper, more hedonistic crowds. Depending on the establishment, this is more or less the Endless Summer scene. Rugby shirts and cutoffs are commonplace. Oceans of beer flow, and the talk is largely about volleyball, beach parties, real estate syndications, and sports cars.

Westside thirst parlors are typically more trendy. Designer jeans and silk chemises. Again, the open-neck shirt is perfectly acceptable and casual-chic is the watchword. Generally most pub patrons here opt for white wine (French, preferably, if sold by the glass), and the conversation ranges from shrewd investments to the most "in" restaurant. Fighting to be taken seriously as gourmets, West Los Angelenos are now tracking the careers of young European chefs, just as culture buffs follow symphony conductors.

In West Hollywood and Hollywood environs, the attire is even more relaxed: young directors in jogging suits; out-of-work actors in racquetball attire—tense on the inside, laid back on the outside. Here bars buzz with the intoxicating talk of "deals," as in "three-picture deals," "development deals," "book deals," "album deals." Deals are the lifeblood of the entertainment industry. The libational nectars are often European in their roots—Kir (cream de cassis and white wine), Campari, Dubonnet on the rocks, premium Scotch on the rocks, or imported beers and wines. Never rush; that's uncool, and never neck crane if Rod Stewart slides in the front door. Also uncool. Everyone is expected to act as if, "Hey, doesn't he always come in here?" In fact, autograph hounding in Los Angeles bars and bistros is discouraged by owner-managers who are thrilled whenever celebs choose to frequent their places and don't want them to be bothered.

Pasadena pubs, once fiercely conservative, have loosened and livened up. But the attire is still traditional—button-down shirts, rep ties, blue blazer—or decidedly preppy—women in corduroy and chino or tailored skirts and suits; men in Polo shirts or sweaters. The three-piece suit is a sartorial staple. Conversation spans the spectrum from business and wise investments to politics, football, and alumni gossip.

The downtown bars are generally a bastion for bankers, brokers, and other business folk, including a burgeoning brigade of import-export executives. Two- and three-piece suits are de rigeur, and the conversation is usually expansionary, as in company acquisitions and conquering global markets. Whiskies (Scotch and Canadian but little American bourbon) are popular, and the dry martini is worshipped. Vodka drinkers have largely switched to wine, and liqueurs are popular during the cocktail hour. Even though California brandy is delicious, the preference is for Cognac.

Naturally, these are generalities, but they are solid ones. As for specific advice, the best wisdom we can offer is to monitor your intake of spirits if you're driving. California has enacted some very tough laws to rid its streets and freeways of intoxicated motorists. Although the laws have yet to be tested in the courts as of this writing, a first-time offender who has more than a 0.1 percent blood-alcohol reading is supposed to get twenty-four hours in jail and a stiff fine. So beware.

Otherwise, welcome to Los Angeles and "Bottoms up!"

DOWNTOWN

Downtown Los Angeles, once a deserted ghost town after dusk, is enjoying a renaissance as a dining, drinking, and socializing center for Angelenos who thirst for the excitement of a city at night. Not exactly a chic complex of bistros and bars, downtown is nevertheless now honeycombed with libational retreats often unfamiliar even to locals. A little exploration will yield a treasure chest of cantinas and cocktail lounges that is sure to delight any visitor who heretofore harbored the notion that Beverly Hills and the Westside are the only places to imbibe.

For starters we recommend what may be Los Angeles's biggest surprise, the five-story Romanesque-style *Variety Arts Theater* at 940 S. Figueroa. Inside this cavernous structure is near nonstop entertainment: vaudevillians, singers, magicians, and comics—plus the fourth-floor W. C. Fields Bar, rescued from a San Pedro waterfront saloon. Enjoy Fields's favorite "martoonie" (a martini with a kumquat), and dance to the dreamy sounds of Art Deco and his orchestra. Kick back with a cool one in Tin Pan Alley, or just wander through fifty years of showbiz memories. Admission is $5.00 at night, free during the day.

A mile north, west of the Harbor Freeway, the venerable *Pacific Dining Car* at 1310 W. 6th has a large bar open 24 hours that serves gourmet hors d'oeuvres nightly at no charge. Choose from beef tartar, paté, stuffed mushrooms, and husky drinks mixed only with premium liquors. A Los Angeles landmark. Beneath the ARCO Towers at 515 S. Flower, *O'Shaughnessy's* may not be the most authentic Irish pub, but it's one of the most popular. Sample a Bailey's Irish Cream and milk on the rocks to soothe your ulcer. Several streets east, the sleek *Grand Avenue Bar* in the Biltmore Hotel, opposite Pershing Square, serves —and rocks—until 2:00 A.M. Bring money. For serenity amid gothic splendor, the Biltmore's *Lobby Bar* is cheery and cozy. Its perfect Manhattans are renowned among downtowners. Sake or a bottle of brewed-in-Japan Kirin beer at the nearby Bonaventure Hotel's *Inagiku* restaurant bar has become a tradition. But for a sweeping view of the city, hop up to the Bonaventure's *Top of the Five* after 11:00 P.M., and share a Cognac with a friend while the rotating bar takes you on a leisurely 360-degree trip. Sweet music, too. Not to be outdone, *Angel's Flight,* atop the Hyatt Regency Hotel, 711 S. Hope, is remote and romantic, and it also rotates while you dance cheek to cheek or simply soak up the city lights and expertly mixed cocktails.

Sports buffs shouldn't miss the bar at *Little Joe's,* 900 N. Broadway, across the street from Chinatown. Prices are cheap, the pour is stiff, and the big-screen TV is always tuned to the hottest game. Los Angeles Dodger manager Tommy Lasorda is a regular these days. Bulbous-nosed comic W. C. Fields frequented the bar in the 1930s. The unpretentious bar at *Nikola's,* 1449 W. Sunset Blvd., a ten-minute drive east of downtown, draws Dodger players, sportswriters, and die-hard fans alike. Prices are twenty years behind the times. The bartenders have photographic memories; once they learn your name, they never forget it. Put them to the test. A bit farther east, virtually unknown to tourists, *Taix Les Freres,* 1911 W. Sunset, will uncork a bottle of good French wine without busting your budget. In the heart of downtown *Casey's Bar,* 613 S. Grand, is probably the area's most popular pub. If you can't strike up a conversation there, join a monastery. Frothy Irish coffees are the specialties. Despite the din, there are plenty of corners for quiet conversation.

Even though downtown Los Angeles is landlocked, you can venture off on a voyage of sorts. *Rex,* on the ground floor of the historic Oviatt Building, 617 S. Olive, radiates the Art-Deco ambience of a 1930s cruise liner. Essentially a fine restaurant, it is an elegant escape, if only for an hour-long cocktail break. Sip slowly and enjoy.

Itching to swap yarns with the world-weary, or looking for a political debate? The gaudy, gabby *Redwood House* is the hangout for the Los Angeles press corps. Reporters from *The Los Angeles Times* and United Press International pack this place at 316 W. Second St. after 5:00 P.M. to postmortem the day's big stories or to drink their lunch if they're working nightside.

RESTAURANT ROW

Once partly lined with saloons where scantily clad, leg-gartered women swung from the ceiling, La Cienega Blvd. is now bereft of pubs per se. Today the bars are part of the boulevard's restaurants and are usually small alcoves off dining rooms, more European than Californian. The bar at *L'Ermitage,* generally considered one of the five best restaurants in Los Angeles, at 730 N. La Cienega, is intimate, personable, and staffed by a mixologist who takes his time when concocting a cool one. Across the street and down the block is Lou Paciocco's *La Cage Aux Folles,* 643 N. La Cienega, a saucy saloon and cabaret featuring female impersonators romping through an ever-changing revue. The bar is Paris circa 1920, the drinks are a bit steep, and the barkeeps talk your ear off. You can sip and not be pressured to stay for the show. *385 North,* located at 385 N. La Cienega, is a contemporary, warm setting. Piano bar Friday and Saturday evenings. *Ma Maison,* 8368 Melrose, around the corner, is mainly a restaurant, but drop in after 2:00 P.M. or at the cocktail hour, and slip into a Campari and soda or a Kir (white wine and creme de cassis). Host Patrick Terrail has set up a small bar for such intimate imbibing. Or have drinks at a table in the covered patio and while away the afternoon with a friend. Back on the boulevard, the *Tail of the Cock* bar, 477 S. La Cienega, is courtly, comfy, and thoroughly calming. Leather booths ring the room, a pianist takes requests during the cocktail hour, and the gratis munchies compare with canapes offered at an East Hampton garden party. Stout drinks and hearty conversation.

MID-WILSHIRE

Wilshire Blvd. is the umbilical cord linking downtown to Beverly Hills, Santa Monica, and the Pacific Ocean. It's lined with good (some great) bars. *HMS Bounty,* 3357 Wilshire, is an apres-work business person's watering hole; very clubby, very gabby. Premium brands are in the well; order a Scotch and soda or a bourbon and water and rest assured that you'll get a good drink. Across the street, the *Palm Bar* in the Ambassador Hotel, 3400 Wilshire Blvd., is a nostalgia-filled nook off the lobby. Walter Winchell hung out here. Dustin Hoffman rendezvoused with Mrs. Robinson here in the hit film *The Graduate.* Drink here in dignity, and soak up eighty years of elegance. Less pretentious, for it has been a businessman's bar for more than four decades, is the *Bull 'n Bush,* 3450 W. 6th St. Nothing fancy; just a heritage of hefty drinks at fair prices and customers who chat up a storm with total strangers—a rarity today. For a frothy strawberry margarita or some other potent south-of-the-border potable, the *Red Onion* at 3580 Wilshire is a classic cantina, though a chain operation. Packed during happy hour, a throbbing disco later in the evening. *Taylor's Prime Steaks,* 3361 W. 8th St., is known for its thick slabs of aged prime beef. Any sports buff who loves verbally to replay great moments of big games should belly up to Tex Taylor's; there's always one USC Trojan booster on a bar stool. Superb Bloody Marys there, too. Farther West, two of Los Angeles's best Irish pubs, both off Wilshire, can be found. *Tom Bergin's,* 840 S. Fairfax, is plastered with Day-Glo shamrocks perpetuating the names of thousands of the patrons who have passed through the door. The long rectangular bar is well stocked with friendly folks twenty-one to sixty-five. The Irish coffees here aren't imaginative, but they're strong. A few blocks north, *Molly Malone's,* 575 S. Fairfax, is your real Irish pub. Gaelic music on weekends, Harp beer all the time, and a hamburger that is a feast in itself. Small and cozy. Ask for Angela; she'll make you feel you're in Ireland.

BEVERLY HILLS

Ten years ago you would never have found a corner saloon in Beverly Hills. Too déclassé. But as the world citizenry flocked to this enclave of wealth, they brought with them the customs of the leisurely rich. Add to that the growing affluence of Los Angelenos who had made killings in real estate, television, screenwriting, or stocks. You'll find now that this small city is riddled with libational refuges from the rat race.

Chrystie's Bar at 8442 Wilshire Blvd. is smack-dab in the middle of an obvious location: Chrystie's Restaurant, right in front of the Wilshire Theater. The bar, catering to the needs of the after-work bunch, quenches the thirst with everything from Ale to Zombies, and soothes the eye with its Art Deco style.

If you're looking for a new drink, check out *R. J.'s* at 252 N. Beverly Dr. Behind the oak bar and beyond the brass rail is literally a library of liquor—800 bottles stacked to the ceiling. Barkeeps shinny up a ladder to fill your request. R. J.'s is a hoot. Dip into the barrel of unshelled peanuts, listen to the piano player pound out his favorite ditty, elbow-bend at the bar with a brace of new buddies. Women can enjoy R. J.'s and not be hassled. For an old-style New York saloon, try *The Ginger Man,* fondly known as "Archie's Place" 369 N. Bedford Dr., since it's co-owned by actor Carroll O'Connor. Tile floored, with green shades over small tables, this is the stand-up-and-rap haunt of young execs, lovely women, and O'Connor's pals such as Sammy Davis Jr. On a per square foot basis, the compact bar at the *Rangoon Racquet Club,* 9474 Little Santa Monica Blvd., may be Beverly Hills' busiest. The house special is a Pimm's Cup served by snappy regimental bartenders. Once you commandeer a stool, don't budge or it will disappear. A block away, the *Saloon* has reopened as an American pub with tudor tendencies and a 50-foot bar for lively people watching. *La Scala,* 9455 Santa Monica Blvd., has a quaint bar, but the treasure here is the wine cellar with its immense selection of California and European vintages. Pick one out downstairs; enjoy it upstairs. La Scala is honeycombed with celebrities nightly. At the *Café Swiss* bar, 450 N. Rodeo Dr., the crowd is older and mellower, more self-assured: agents and business managers, chic shopkeepers unwinding with pedigree spirits generously poured. A pricier version is the *El Padrino Room* of the Beverly Wilshire Hotel, 9500 Wilshire. Sink into comfortable chairs as attentive waitresses fill your requests. The ambience is one of casual elegance, but you pay for it. A couple of miles away, the *Polo Lounge* of the Beverly Hills Hotel, 9641 Sunset, no longer attracts the superstars and the gossip columnists (Howard Hughes drank here in his prerecluse days when he lived in one of the hotel bungalows). But the room, with its deep forest green decor and tiny bar, has lost none of its cachet. The drinks are made slowly and courteously, and only premium mixers are used. Farther west and past the gated entrance to one of Los Angeles's most exclusive neighborhoods, the bar at the *Bel Air Hotel* is the ultimate hideaway favored by industrialists and producers among others. The banquettes are comfortable. Deferential waiters serve skillfully mixed potables while a piano player works his keyboard magic; everything is soothing, never obtrusive. Back down in Beverly Hills, *Trader Vic's* bar, in the Beverly Hilton Hotel, 9876 Wilshire Blvd., is an opulent version of Don the Beachcombers. Demon rum is poured freely here. After all, Vic invented the Mai Tai, Scorpion, and—probably his most popular creation of all—Tiki Puka Puka, a potent blend of dark rum, orange, and lime. Most exotic drinks are around $4.00 a glass.

CENTURY CITY

Nestled within this sprawling complex of towering office buildings and luxury condominiums, once the back lot of 20th Century Fox, are several good bars and saloons. But do not expect aged wood and venerable barkeeps. Century City is too new to have a heritage. It does have *Harry's Bar & American Grill,* a reasonably authentic version of the famed Florence bar and grill that Hemingway and other rogues of the pen frequented. Sandwiched inside the tri-level ABC Entertainment Center, 2020 Ave. of the Stars, Harry's Bar is unrivaled, from our viewpoint at least, for its potent cappuccino. Across the mall, the *Avenue Saloon* is a central place to meet friends for cocktails before or after the show at the Shubert Theater: warm decor and exceptionally generous drinks, but the bartenders are generally chilly.

WESTWOOD/WESTSIDE

Before the franchisers and mall builders arrived, Westwood Village was your basic quaint college town (something out of a sleepy Midwest hamlet), the front door to UCLA. Now it is still an university town, but it's also a popular hangout for kids of all ages. Order your first drink at *Yesterday's,* 1056 Westwood Blvd., and sit amid three quarters of a million dollars worth of antiques. There's a small bar downstairs, and upstairs is a veranda bar, where you can leisurely sip on a banana daiquiri and listen to a guitarist and other music makers. Two blocks north, inside a tree shaded courtyard, the bantam sized bar at *Stratton's,* 10886 Le Conte, is for stool sitters only. Essentially, this is a restaurant that looks like the inside of an 11th-century castle. The bartenders are unusually loquacious and the drinks imaginative and strong—but prices are semisteep. For free meatballs the size of baseballs, we recommend *Monty's* atop an office building at 1100 Glendon. Pull up a stool and look out over a lush residential neighborhood and beyond to Beverly Hills. Or plop in a comfy couch. A two-piece combo plays from midweek on. Across the street is the *Acapulco,* 1109 Glendon. The Acapulco was once an Irish pub, and the conviviality lives on. There is a good assortment of Mexican beers. A sumptuous spread of nachos, tacquitos, and quesadillas are laid out nightly, and there is an endless supply of free freshly popped popcorn. Dollar for dollar, though, the most inviting bar in Los Angeles could well be inside the *Westwood Marquis Hotel,* 930 Hilgard. A one-time UCLA dorm, this European-style hostelry has turned its bar into a giant living room with pillow-soft sofas, coffee tables, a harpist and a pianist nightly, and silk gowned waitresses serving canapes on sterling silver trays. Favored by chief executive officers, entertainers, and visiting royalty (it's away from the hoopola of Hollywood and Beverly Hills), it is known for its fine French wines served by the glass and its expertly crafted drinks. Another bar that has adopted the homey look is the *Hungry Tiger's* step down saloon, 936 Westwood Blvd. The look evokes the library and playroom of a turn-of-the-century home. Arrive at happy hour, and save half a dollar a drink; feast on hot hors d'oeurves and cheddar cheese. The best bargain in Westwood during happy hour is the elfin size bar (five stools, four small tables) in the *Old World,* 1019 Westwood Blvd. A glass of wine is 75 cents, mixed drinks are $1.25. They've held the prices at that level for 1½ years.

Moving west: The bar stashed inside the *Bel Air Sands Hotel,* 11461 Sunset, is for lovers and anyone who wants to avoid the madding crowds. Sit on the patio out by the pool as the sun sets or inside at night when the piano music starts. Munchies go with the music, and the drinks are hearty. The reigning singles bar and disco is a place called, of all things, *Hamburger Hamlet,* 11648 San Vicente. For some unfathomable reason, this has become the Westside's hottest meet um 'n mate um bar, so don't walk in looking for solitude. A funky version of the traditional fern bar is the *San Francisco Saloon,* 11501 W. Pico Blvd. This is thrift store chic ambience, but the crowd is adventurous, and there are always rabid chess and backgammon players at their boards. The bar provides the boards. Only premium brand liquors (Beefeaters, Jack Daniels, J&B Scotch) are poured in the drinks. A real gritty Mexican cantina is several blocks east at 11751 Pico. Known as *The Talpa,* it has Coors on tap, chips and salsa on the bar, and a color TV on at all times. You know the food is first rate because most of the patrons are Hispanic. A favorite of budget-conscious journalists.

SANTA MONICA AND THE BEACHES

Santa Monica may be the most globally cosmopolitan city in Southern California. The British, for example, love its cool weather and its proximity to the ocean. Not surprisingly then, there are some authentic British pubs in this charming seaside community. Try *Ye Olde King's Head* at 116 Santa Monica Blvd. for a pint of bitters and a fast game of darts. Appropriately seedy and reeking of brew, it nevertheless is stocked with Brits eager to hear or dispense news from the home front. From there it's a short crawl to *Ye Old Mucky Duck,* 1810 Ocean, where co-owners Frank Green (from Scotland) and Maureen Morrison (from Liverpool) serve up draught Watney's, Guinness, and Bass, plus genuine Scotch eggs and Cornish pastries. *Cheerio's* at 1828 Ocean is more a country inn than pure pub. One feels as if he (or she) is in Nottingham or Yorkshire. Lovely, attentive waitresses purvey powerful potables. Delightful.

Beach bums, barristers, sailors, and superstars (the likes of Warren Beatty, Julie Christie, Ali McGraw) pack themselves nightly into *Chez Jay,* a shack of a saloon at 1657 Ocean that has endured for thirty years. Actor/balloonist Jay Fiondello and his mother Alice have a following of loyalists that includes California Governor Jerry Brown. There are superb food and drink at fair prices. Along revitalized Main Street, the tiny bar in the *Galley Steak House* is recommended for nostalgics who want to see Santa Monica circa 1940. Once located at the end of the Santa Monica pier, the Galley, 2442 Main, is thick with nautical mementos and people who appreciate the siren song of the sea, not to mention zesty Bloody Marys. *Merlin McFly's,* 2702 Main is a stained-glass filled Victorian pub with a roving magician who does close-up magic that is as dazzling as the drinks. Pure escape. The secret here is the Chinese chicken salad; a mountain of it on a plate is less than $5.25. Try it with a McFlying Saucer—Amaretto, cream de cocoa, and cream, blended. For a saloon that looks as if it has been trashed rather than decorated, the *Oar House* shouldn't be missed. Located at 2941 Main, it has motorcycles and carriages hanging from the dust covered ceiling. The fact is that something old has been glued or nailed to every square inch of the place. Drinks are downright cheap. This sawdust-on-the-floor joint jumps nightly until 2:00 A.M., seven days a week.

MARINA DEL REY/VENICE

If you play the ponies, you'll love turtle racing, a parking lot grand prix that is a fixture at *Brennan's,* 4089 Lincoln Blvd. This Irish pub's big open bar makes conversation easy and the powerful drinks make it lively. Down the street a bit, *Casablanca,* 220 Lincoln, sounds as if it should be a Bogey bar. Instead, it is a Mexican bar and grill featuring a woman pounding and cooking tortillas right before your eyes. Order a fresh, hot one, slather it with butter, and wash it down with a cerveza. Cook it again, Maria. For swashbuckling saloongoers, we recommend the *Black Whale,* 3016 Washington Blvd. Plenty of mates ready to swing rum with you. Or sample a little tequila and tonic for a summertime cooler (it's always summer in Los Angeles) at the *Baja Cantina,* 311 Washington St. Beach women love this bar. Fair prices, too. *West Beach Cafe* at 60 N. Venice Blvd. is a very popular night spot. The bar is often crowded with Westside yuppies and has a changing contemporary art show. Valet parking and no cover.

Inside the marina, the bar at *Fiasco,* 4451 Admiralty Way, draws yachting types and aspiring commodores. The platters of munchies are piled high at cocktail hour, and no one rushes you. A real kick back bar. Nearby the *Warehouse,* 4499 Admiralty Way, has streams stocked with fish, a bar stocked with tourists, and a buffet brunch renowned in these parts. Ex-cinematographer Burt Hixon collected tropical drink recipes on his South Seas forays and whips up one of the most sinfully rich Pina Coladas this side of Samoa. Popular, so get there early. There is also *Don the Beachcomber* in the Marina, 13530 Bali Way, but it's not as comfortable as its half-century old Hollywood counterpart. Even the Marina locals often overlook the intimate *Flagship Lounge* in the Marina International Hotel, 4200 Admiralty Way. Dark and cozy, it is a great place to play footsies with a friend. The piano bar alternates with a guitarist. Parking is free. For pubcrawlers who want to save their energy, the *Red Onion,* 4215 Admiralty Way, has a three-hour happy hour (4:00–7:00 P.M.) during the week and thirty-one flavors of margaritas. Underneath is *Pearl's Harbor,* a wild bar and disco operated by the Red Onion folks. Don't forget *TGI Friday's,* 13470 Maxella Ave., the consummate "meet market."

AIRPORT AND SOUTH BAY

The airport has half a dozen hotels vying for the business traveler and his or her expense account, but only one has an outstanding bar—the Hyatt LAX. It's called the *Park at the Top,* 6225 W. Century, and sits twelve stories in the air, providing a sweeping 330 degree view of the airport. This is one you cannot overlook. Each night a mini-Las Vegaslike buffet is served free. Jazz starts at 5:00 P.M. and goes nonstop till midnight. The drinks are robust. Try a Grand Cafe a La Park (Grand Marnier with cream de banana). South of the Airport, at Rosecrans and Sepulveda, Barnabey's Hotel is the home of *Rosie's Pub,* a turn of the century theme bar packed with 19th-century antiques, floor-to-ceiling bookcases, and a forest of ferns. Watney's is on tap. Rosie's Bombay Bomb, a Pina Colada made with Bombay gin, is the specialty.

In Manhattan Beach, the second-story bar at *Orville and Wilbur's,* 401 W. Rosecrans, has a spectacular view of the Pacific, and behind the bar are aspiring actresses who don't know how to pour skimpy drinks. You can eat lunch at the bar. The clientele is an eclectic mix of surfers, business folks, and rugby shirted beach rats who live for sunny days and volleyball. A real sundown place.

HOLLYWOOD

The bar and saloon scene in the film capital of the world is no longer the raucous, gin soaked setting that Zelda and Scott Fitzgerald, Errol Flynn, Robert Benchley, and even Sinatra and Burton adored. The great Sunset Strip nightclubs—the Mocambo, Ciro's, Trocadero, Interlude—are gone. The barhopping ritual of the 1940s, crawling down Sunset in a top-down '47 Chrysler convertible in quest of the next Cuba Libre, has been replaced by cruisers who clog that boulevard and others the moment the sun sets. But for the patron of the libational arts who has fond memories of Hollywood past or who might like briefly to relive yesteryear, there are some oases that should be visited.

The bar at *Musso and Franks,* 6667 Hollywood Blvd., once hosted film studio moguls and two-dollar-a-day extras alike. Today the Rob Roys are just as smooth and the clientele just as eclectic. No-nonsense bartenders will give you an oral history of the boulevard; just ask. Overlooking Hollywood is *Yamashiro's,* a Japanese restaurant at 1999 N. Sycamore Ave. A lovely tradition is to meet there at sunset for cocktails on the terrace and gaze down on the city. Or take your drink and wander through the gardens.

Ask around among your friends beforehand to find out whether any are members of the *Magic Castle.* It's the private club for magicians and others and right next door to Yamashiro. As a guest of a member, you'll still pay the $5.00 admission at the door, but once you utter the magic words "open sesame" to a blinking owl, a bookcase slides back to reveal a secret panel and a three-level celebration of the magical arts. Watch out for the first bar stool on the left; perch on it and you get this sinking feeling.

Holiday Inns are not exactly known for their imaginative cocktail lounges, but *Windows on Hollywood,* atop the city's Holiday Inn at 1755 N. Highland, is a pub with a panoramic view. Late afternoon is the best time to imbibe. Try their Tequila Sunrise at sunset. Hollywood *is* the city of celluloid and song, and to spot the heavyweights in the film and record business, motor over to *Martoni's,* 1523 Cahuenga, the venerable Italian restaurant launched decades ago by Frank Sinatra's former valet. The cozy bar is packed nightly with agents, studio musicians, and stars on the ascent, all feasting on free pizza, meatballs, and other delicacies dished out to guests around the 5:00 P.M. happy hour. Zesty conversation. *The China Club* at 8338 W. 3rd recently was refurbished to its Art Deco best. This is a meeting spot for the beautiful people, where special events are scheduled for changing contemporary art exhibits, poetry readings, and musical entertainment.

Nucleus Nuance, 7267 Melrose Ave., in the heart of the Melrose Avenue experience, offers vintage wines, a variety of mixed imbibements, and earfuls of music of the '30s and '40s performed live at night in an adjacent room. For stargazers who appreciate chatty bartenders and frugally priced drinks, *Nickodell,* 5507 Melrose, next door to Paramount Studios, is a must. You're apt to see some familiar faces who appear on many popular sitcoms. The TV is always tuned to the hottest sporting event. Nickodell may have the most talented mixologists in town. A few doors down, *Vine Street Bar & Grill,* 1610 N. Vine, re-creates the glamour of Duke Ellington's swingtime '40s. Nostalgic sounds of the Ink Spots and Herb Jeffries float through the Art Deco-style bar. A bit south (and very near the Los Angeles border), the bar attached to the nifty *Fellini's* restaurant, 6810 Melrose Ave., is a cozy *cantina* packed with a young, hip crowd. Good spirits and suds list, including Taddy porter, hearty English brew for discriminating quaffers. *L.A. Nicola Bar* at 4326 Sunset Blvd. (next door to L.A. Nicola Restaurant), is decorated with a modern touch almost reaching New Wave status, and is a friendly place—thanks to Larry Nicola's warming presence. The clientele is usually a mix of business and "biz" folk, who take full advantage of the close proximity to ABC Studios.

WEST HOLLYWOOD

Carlos and Charlie's, 8240 W. Sunset, is a slick Los Angeles version of the funky cantinas found throughout Mexico under a variety of names (Carlos O'Brian's in Puerto Vallarta, for instance). A beautiful-people hangout complete with tasty hors d'oeurves and steep prices. Big with the record industry crowd. *El Privado,* upstairs, is a throbbing disco. Farther west, at 8720 W. Sunset, is *LeDome's* circular bar offering $3.00 drinks and French "house" wine. It draws the likes of rocker Rod Stewart and actors Michael Caine and Richard (*American Gigolo*) Gere. The best time to visit is after 11:00 P.M., when it *really* starts to jump. Owners Eddie and Michel are usually there nightly. One big fault: the bartenders are aloof and the service ranges from prompt to indifferent. Far friendlier and not as congested is the bar at *Trumps,* 8764 Melrose. Sink into soft sofas, and sip a tall gin and tonic. Moderate to expensive drink prices, but the European ambience—clean, contemporary design—makes you feel like a jet setter. Across the street, *Morton's,* 8800 Melrose Ave., has a small bar (the place is mainly a restaurant) but a big-name clientele. Look hard and you might see the latest James Bond or Jacquie Bissett. Skip, the bartender, keeps up a lively rap with patrons. Another late-night haunt is *Dan Tana's,* 9071 Santa Monica; again, mainly a restaurant but blessed with a busy bar. Ask Michael, the bartender, to whip up a Gibson Special (cappuccino laced with a generous shot of Napoleon Cognac), named after top record-industry press agent Bob Gibson.

New Yorkers will feel right at home in West Hollywood. The Los Angeles version of the Big Apple's venerable *Palm Restaurant,* 9001 Santa Monica Blvd., is big among Hollywood lawyers, agents, and luminaries such as Farrah Fawcett and Ryan O'Neal (there is always a crowd of tabloid papparazzi milling around out front). But the stellar attraction is Frosty, the bartender, who spins yarns and pours stiff drinks for those who perch on the five bar stools. From there, pubcrawlers can move over to *Joe Allen's,* the Los Angeles clone of the New York saloon of the same name, at 8706 W. Third. The crowd is a mix of showbiz, interior design, and advertising types. The bartenders are young and not too personable. Walk a block west and you're at *Kathy Gallagher's,* a casual-chic bar and bistro that catches the Joe Allen overflow. You'll find a congenial crowd of ex-New Yorkers reminiscing about the excitement of Manhattan, but then they'd never have their year-round tans or wear their open-neck shirts if they still lived and worked there. You can't miss Kathy; she's a former fashion model. A block away, at 8715 Beverly Blvd., *Dominick's* is a virtually unknown, secluded bar and grill frequented by Hollywood heavies, Jack Lemmon, Johnny Carson, and his producer Freddie De Cordova, among others. With wood paneling, traditional pictures, and a staff that's courteous, never obsequious, Dominick's bar is great for a before-dinner dry martini or late evening Cognac and cigars. One of the most comfortable and hospitable thirst parlors in West Hollywood remains the *Cock 'n Bull* at 9170 W. Sunset. A landmark on the strip, it opened in the late 1930s, gained fame as the home of the Moscow Mule (vodka and ginger beer in an iced copper mug), and was the chosen hideaway pub for stars and studio execs for decades. Even today the bar is filled with character actors whose faces are instantly recognizable, though their names may mean nothing to you. You can always find a partner here for a chess game. Cock and Bull may have the best buffet lunch in Los Angeles. Several blocks east, *Scandia* remains quiet, dignified, and tranquilizing. The house special is a Danish Mary—tomato juice and Aquavit, wickedly spiced. Walk in tired and come out a Viking. Celebrity watching is a polished art at *Spago,* 8795 W. Sunset. The tiny bar tucked away inside this ultrachic bistro is immensely popular; consider yourself fortunate if you can stake out a bar stool. The host/chef is Wolfgang Puck, a charming, chatty chap.

PASADENA

Pasadena is the closest thing in Los Angeles to a traditional Eastern or Midwestern city. Famed worldwide for the Rose Bowl game and the New Year's Day Rose Parade, it also boasts some of the friendliest bars and pubs in southern California. First stop for any first timer should be *Monahan's Pub,* 110 S. Lake Ave., where host Peter Monahan whips up a frothy Irish coffee and cheery conversation. Single women can comfortably perch on a bar stool in this warm, woodsy setting and not be hassled. Why? Many of the patrons are off-duty police who favor it because best-selling author and ex-cop Joe Wambaugh elbow-bends there regularly. A few blocks south is the *Chronicle,* 897 Granite Dr., essentially a restaurant and the site of a congenial horseshoe-shaped bar stocked with preppies in their mid thirties and their families. You feel as if you're drinking in an old turn-of-the-century mansion. Friendly bartenders and generous drinks.

Pasadena's best hideaway bar is the *Tap Room* of the Huntington Sheraton Hotel, tucked away in this graceful hostelry and a popular retreat for more than fifty years. Debs and dowagers alike, plus business folks, nibble on thick roast beef sandwiches and drink cold beers. One of the bartenders has been there twenty-seven years. Comfortable captains chairs and tables, rich woods, munchies in the afternoon. Pasadena politicos and business leaders flock after work to *Fanny's,* a turn-of-the-century Victorian bar, the lower level of the Pasadena Hilton, 150 S. Los Robles. Visit during the 4:30–7:00 P.M. "happy hour" for free hors d'oeuvres and relatively cheap drinks. Fernando presides over the bustling bar. If you feel like dancing, shoot upstairs to *Slick's,* the top floor speakeasy/disco. No little old ladies from Pasadena here; action central.

A mellow saloon steeped in history is *Josephina's,* 110 E. Holly, festooned with fresh ferns, fly fans, and antiques. You can dine and drink on a budget in this restored relic of Pasadena's past. Or try *Maldonado's* tiny European-style bar attached to one of Pasadena's finest restaurants at 1202 E. Green. Perch on a bar stool, order a glass of French wine, and enjoy live opera and Broadway show tunes. No Muzak here. For a fast game of darts and a pint of Watney's or Courage, check out the *John Bull* in Old Pasadena, a British pub that looks as if it is straight out of London. Proprietress Delyse Sharp is always on the premises giving the latest news of the mother country. At 103 S. Fair Oaks.

Apres-work unwinding spots include *Beckham Place,* 77 W. Walnut, a rather fancy "Olde English" pub known for its huge drinks, free roast beef sandwiches, and wingback chairs around a roaring fire. Packed with engineers and science buffs; the conversation is heady, the serving wenches friendly. *Vinchenzo's,* 901 E. Del Mar, is said to be the reigning Pasadena semisingles bar, especially on Friday night. Get there early for thick margaritas and gratis finger foods.

SAN FERNANDO VALLEY

The San Fernando Valley, once known for acres of tract houses supplanting fields of orange trees, is rapidly becoming a sophisticated suburban bedroom community, especially the southern (closer to Ventura Blvd.) slice of this 1.2-million-person mini-megalopolis. Commuters traverse the Ventura Freeway east to west and often stop off to dine and drink at a potpourri of French, Italian, Asian, and trendy American bistros. Some are old favorites; others are daring discoveries. In Calabassas, a one-time stagecoach stop complete with a hanging tree, the *Sagebrush Cantina* (23527 Calabassas Rd.), is an indoor-outdoor saloon, sort of the Valley version of the Via Veneto café scene. Motorcycle hippies mix comfortably with computer moguls and showbiz folk including a platoon of stunt people. Margaritas fetch a buck during happy hour; so do house drinks and beer. Great for table hopping. Country-pop entertainment nightly. For sophisticated saloonophiles and civilized conversationalists, the venerable *Tail o' the Cock* restaurant in Studio City (12950 Ventura) has a discreet, dark-paneled pub and piano bar. Vested bartenders pour healthy drinks and spin fascinating yarns of the Valley from a simpler era. Favored by film and TV producers and actors. *Houlihans,* 17150 Ventura Blvd., Encino, is one of the better antique-crammed, fern-filled "meet market" bar-restaurants proffering less-than-a-dollar beer, wine, and single mixed drinks in the late afternoon and early evening. Stick around at night and boogie in the disco. Plenty of people and fun.

NORTH ALONG THE COAST

Malibu

Twenty-seven miles of picturesque beaches and mountain peaks ranging over 2,000 feet are the essence of the colony of Malibu, just up the coast from Los Angeles, a spectacular sight from sunrise to sunset. The canyons and summits of the Santa Monica Mountains provide not only an amazing background for the sea but also countless opportunities for adventure and exploration.

Hikers, horseback riders, and bicyclists will be pleased at the number of trails available throughout the area, Malibu Creek Park, Topanga State Park, and Point Mugu State Park among them. Camping and picnic sites abound within the area as well. For the less ambitious, a drive along any of the major canyon roads provides unforgettable views of Santa Monica Bay and the mountains on one side and the San Fernando Valley on the other.

But Malibu pays a price for its beauty: This exquisite topography is susceptible to natural disasters. The last few years has taken a real toll on the Pacific Coast Highway and the houses lining it; it is not unusual to see bulldozers and other heavy equipment rebuilding what heavy rainstorms and slides have torn down. For miles, from Santa Monica to Malibu proper, danger signs warn travelers of slide areas. The Malibu Pier, originally built in 1903 and reconstructed in 1946, has been one of the areas hardest hit in recent times, and much of it was totally destroyed. The first phase of reconstruction has been completed, allowing limited access. Mountain and canyon areas are prone to fires during dry summer months. Caution is advisable with matches and fires, and these are banned in many places. Despite these natural drawbacks, many of the affluent call this home. With houses ranging from about $250,000 for a modest beach bungalow, to over $350,000,000 for a beach-view mansion, a great number of celebrities live here. Many have a city home and a beach home, and the Malibu Beach Colony is the setting for many of these beach cottages. Since 1926, movie stars have come here to get away from the hubbub of the city. Among the celebrities living in Malibu now are Barbra Streisand, Larry (J.R.) Hagman, Neil Diamond, and Johnny Carson.

The History

Malibu's recorded history begins with the ancient Chumash Indians who lived on the crescent shaped coast. Grass-covered huts and wooden canoes specked the landscape then, and the Channel Islands seemed like a distant land. Through the years, goods, tools, and crafts found from this era have shown this tribe to be one of the most advanced in California.

Point Dume, in the northern part of Malibu, was named in 1794 by George Vancouver, the English explorer. Even after this discovery Malibu remained fairly isolated until 1802, when José Bartoleme Tapia was given permission by the Commandant of the Garrison at Santa Barbara to let his livestock graze on what was then called the Topanga-Malibu-Sequit Rancho. This land became the focus of many lawsuits through the years with many people laying claim to it. In 1887 Frederick Hastings Rindge, a wealthy man from the East, bought the rancho and worked for the rest of his life to keep its natural beauty and isolation intact.

At this point there were no roads leading to Malibu, and horseback, boat, and, later, horse-drawn wagons, were the only way to get there. In 1904 the Southern Pacific Railroad tried to build a route into the area, but when Rindge found out that he could stop them by building his own, that is what he did. This 20-mile standard gauge railroad was used until the late 1920s.

Rindge died in 1905, and his widow May K. Rindge maintained and improved the ranch for more than 20 years. By this time it was considered one of the most valuable single real estate holdings in the United States.

After many more battles to prevent construction of a road through the ranch, the Roosevelt Highway was finally built; it was opened to traffic in 1928. In 1929 Mrs. Rindge started to build a great house overlooking the sea in Malibu Canyon. She established a pottery plant and imported European artisans to make artistic tile for the "castle." The house was never finished, and in 1942 the land and uncompleted building were sold to the Franciscan Order for the Serra Retreat.

In 1952, several years after Mrs. Rindge's death, her daughter, Rhoda R. Adamson, took control of the ranch, and under her able direction the area prospered. She constructed a Moorish-Spanish house at Vacquero Point, and this house is now open for view as part of the Malibu Lagoon Museum.

It is Malibu's ambiance, its sheltered geography, that has given it such an appeal. And that feeling of refuge and nature at its wildest is still part of its immense attraction.

The Malibu Beaches

Most of the beaches in Malibu are privately owned by those who live there, but coastal accessways every few miles allow visitors to stroll along the beaches, perhaps even relax and take a swim, and get a close-up of the houses and their occupants. However, there are no lifeguards or restrooms around, so water sports are not recommended.

Malibu's reputation as a surfer's paradise, stemming from the old Beach Boys songs and Frankie Avalon movies, is just a small but noticeable part of what Malibu really is. Several public beaches stretch along the Malibu coast, providing the type of sun and fun that everyone across the country once dreamed about. The four most popular of these beaches are Topanga Canyon Beach, Malibu Surfrider Beach, Zuma Beach, and Leo Carillo State Beach. All offer swimming and limited areas for surfing, both body and board. Surfrider attracts board-riders from around the world in September, when the annual International Surfing Contest takes place. During this time waves reach from three to five feet. Zuma Beach is the largest of the four, running over three miles long. Leo Carillo Beach has some rocky caves to explore, as well as camping facilities right on the beach. Lifeguards and restrooms are also provided. Easy parking make Zuma and Leo Carillo more convenient than the others, where unloading your vehicle can be a big problem.

Fishing, boating, and scuba diving are also everywhere to be found in Malibu. Boats can be rented at Paradise Cove or at the Malibu pier. Sport fishing boats leave the pier twice daily. From March through August, when these small fish come up on the beach to spawn, searching for grunion is a favorite sport in Malibu.

To add to all its natural attractions, Malibu also offers a variety of cultural experiences. The J. Paul Getty Museum, located on the Pacific Coast Hwy., one mile north of Sunset Boulevard, houses fine collections of Greek and Roman antiquities as well as Renaissance and Baroque paintings. The museum also features decorative arts made for Frenchmen from Louis XIV to Napolean. The building itself is modeled on an ancient Roman country house called the Villa dei Papiri, located outside the city of Herculaneum. The villa, destroyed during the eruption of Vesuvius in A.D. 79, was discovered in the 18th century. Getty decided to model his building on this classic. The museum itself contains one of the most important private art collections in the United States.

Another of Malibu's cultural havens in Pepperdine University where, along with other intellectual opportunities, various programs in art and music are offered. High-caliber concerts and shows are frequently presented there.

Restaurants along the Malibu coast offer wonderful food in a perfect setting. Ranging in price from moderate to expensive, most of the colony's restaurants are situated right on the beach. Malibu is a favorite dinner spot for residents and visitors alike.

PRACTICAL INFORMATION FOR MALIBU

HOW TO GET THERE AND HOW TO GET AROUND. By car. Most of the cities from Malibu north to Cambria can be reached directly via the Pacific Coast Hwy. (Route 1), one of the country's most scenic highways. If you are entering Malibu from the north, Hwy. 101 meets Rte. 1 near Ventura. The exit to each city or community from there on is clearly marked. All major car rental firms are here; check the Yellow Pages for phone numbers.

By bus. Greyhound Bus Lines and Great American Stage Lines travel between Oxnard and Los Angeles on eight round trips each day. RTD bus #474 will get you from Los Angeles to and around Malibu. Call 626–4455 for information.

TELEPHONES. The area code for Malibu is 213. You do not need to dial the area code if it is the same as the one from which you are calling. Information (known as directory assistance) is 411. When dialing a long-distance number you must dial the number 1 (one) *before* you dial the area code and the number itself. An operator will assist you with person-to-person, credit card, and collect calls if you dial 0 first. Pay telephones start at 20 cents.

HOTELS AND MOTELS. Sleeping accommodations along the coast, although very lovely, are not as plentiful as you would find south of Los Angeles. Therefore, it's a good idea to plan ahead, especially during the high seasons of the spring, summer (in particular), and fall. Many of the hotels and motels are oceanside, and many operate swimming pools. Many establishments have seasonal rates, so during winter months you can often find a bargain. Some of the more exclusive properties require a certain length of stay during their busy season—three days must often be booked in the summer. To be on the safe side, be sure to call well ahead of your intended visit.

The following is a **selection** of hotels and motels in the area. Price categories for double-occupancy rooms in this region are: *Deluxe,* $60.00 and up; *Expensive,* $50.00–$59.00; *Moderate,* $40.00–$49.00; *Inexpensive,* $40.00 and under. For a more complete explanation of categories, refer to the *Facts At Your Fingertips* section at the front of this book.

Casa Malibu. *Deluxe.* 22752 W. Pacific Coast Hwy; 456–2219. Located right on the ocean, this property contains twenty-one units, eight of which are on the sand. Low winter rates.

Shangri-La Hotel. *Deluxe–Expensive.* 1301 Ocean Ave.; 394–2791. Streamlined modern in its design, this hotel is extremely quaint and charming. Movie stars frequent this property. Surrounded by garden patios, the hotel offers complimentary breakfasts; and there are laundry facilities and free parking. 58 rooms.

Tonga Lei Motor Hotel. *Expensive.* 22878 Pacific Coast Hwy; 456–6444. A nine-unit motel right on the sand. Polynesian-style architecture. V, MC, AE.

Malibu Surfer Motel. *Moderate.* 22541 W. Pacific Coast Hwy; 456–6169. Across the street from the beach, in a nice section of Malibu. 16 units.

Malibu Riviera Motel. *Moderate–Inexpensive.* 28920 Pacific Coast Hwy.; 457–9503. Color TV, health spa, and sundeck, Located between Malibu Beach and Point Dume in the heart of the beach community. Free parking for guests. 15 rooms.

Malibu Shore Hotel. *Inexpensive.* 23033 Pacific Coast Hwy; 456–6559. Moments from the beach, the hotel is easily spotted because of its Spanish design. Color TV, laundry. Spanish is spoken. Plenty of free parking. 18 rooms.

TOURIST INFORMATION. In Malibu the Chamber of Commerce is located at 22235 Pacific Coast Hwy., 90265; (213) 456–9025. Hours: Monday to Friday, 9 A.M. to 4 P.M. For road conditions, call the the Malibu Sheriff's Station at 456–6652 and ask for the message center.

SEASONAL EVENTS. Many events in the area are scheduled at the last moment, preventing us from including them. One of the best ways to find out about such happenings is to check local papers such as the *Malibu Times* and the *Surfside News.*

March through August. A favorite California pastime, *grunion hunting* takes place on Malibu beaches during the high tide of these months. The small fish come to spawn, and just around sundown is the best time to hunt them.

July. Usually held on the fourth Sunday of the month is the *Malibu Summer Festival.* Fine arts and handmade crafts are shown. There is entertainment, including face painting for the kids. Malibu Civic Center. For information call 456–9025.

September. Surfrider Beach is the site of the annual *International Surfing Contest,* which attracts surfers from all over the world. Winners go on to other national and international competitions.

PARKS. *Malibu Creek Park,* 28754 Mulholland Dr., 991–1827, has an entrance off Malibu Canyon. The park has 4,000 acres and includes a lake, ageless oaks, chapparal, and volcanic rock. Excellent hiking possibilities.

Point Magu State Park, across from Leo Carillo State Beach, 457–5538. Close to 70 miles of trails are accessible here amid lovely trees and canyons. Camping facilities are on site; reservations are needed.

Topanga State Park, off Topanga Canyon Rd., at 20825 Entrada Rd., 455–2465, offers hiking and self-guided trails. Beautiful ocean views can be seen from the peaks. The park covers 9,000 acres.

BEACHES. Malibu's 27 miles of beach are definitely its largest attraction. Many of the beaches are private, but it is legal to be on a beach if there is public access. The best bet is to try to go to public beaches where there are usually lifeguard stands, health facilities, and concession stands. See also the Los Angeles "Beaches" section.

Starting north of Malibu, *County Line Beach* is partially in Ventura County; it is good for surfing.

Leo Carillo State Beach is very active and has caves to explore. Swimming, scuba diving, snorkeling, and body surfing are all good in this area.

Zuma Beach is the largest of the Malibu beaches. It is five miles long and an excellent family recreation area.

Paradise Cove is a private beach at Point Dume. With its red sandstone cliffs and clean sandy beach, it is worth the $3 entrance fee.

Corral Beach is a small area near Pepperdine University. It is usually less crowded than other beaches during the height of the season.

Surfrider Beach, near the pier, is world famous for offering some of the best surfing in Southern California.

Las Tunas Beach is a good surf-fishing location.

Topanga Canyon Beach is near the illustrious Getty Museum and is good for swimming and fishing.

PARTICIPANT SPORTS. Water sports. The Pacific is really too cool for swimming except during the summer, but other activities, such as grunion hunting, keep sports fanatics busy along the coastal waters.

Surfing. Surfing has become a big sport in California in recent years. There are more than seventy-five beaches between Cambria and Los Angeles. For exciting observation or participation in the skills of surfing and the "surfing scene," head out to the beaches bright and early (best time is between 6:00 and 9:00 A.M.). Expert surfers follow the tide and swell conditions in choosing their beach. See also "Beaches," above. For surfing lessons and rentals, check the Yellow Pages; also check establishments that offer windsurfing lessons and rentals, listed below.

Fishing. The Malibu Pier will eventually be back intact for pier fishers. Full-day and half-day boats are available for rental at Paradise Cove. Surf fishing is also popular.

Hiking. The Zuma-Dune Trail to Paradise Cove is a four-mile beach hike. It travels along the western part of Zuma Beach, over the Point Dume Headlands for spectacular coastal views, and then comes down near Paradise Cove. Park your car near the end of Zuma Beach, on Pacific Coast Hwy., take the sandy trail up the sandstone cliffs to the top of Point Dume, keep toward the edge of the bluffs until you see the trail that descends to the east side of the beach; a short walk on the beach then brings you to Paradise Cove.

Malibu Creek State Park, Topanga State Park, and Point Magu State Park are also all excellent for hiking.

Windsurfing. For those daring souls who would like to learn, lessons and rentals are available at *Zuma Jay* (456–8044); and *Natural Progression* (456–6302).

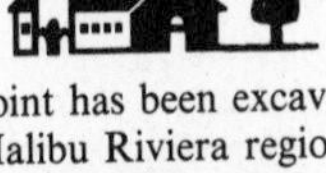

HISTORICAL SITES. *Point Dume,* located at the tip of a now-residential area jutting into the ocean, was named in honor of Father Dumetz, one of the Franciscan fathers at the Ventura Mission, in 1794. The once-jagged point has been excavated for building purposes. Point Dume is located in the Malibu Riviera region.

The Malibu Chamber of Commerce has a visitors' map, which locates several historic sites. Included are: a *Chumash Indian Village site* supposedly visited by

Cabrillo during his voyage along the coast in 1542; the *engine house* of the Rindge railroad; the *Decker Elementary School,* which is the first schoolhouse in Malibu; *site of the Rindge castle;* and the old *Malibu Courthouse* building.

MUSEUMS. *The J. Paul Getty Museum,* 17985 Pacific Coast Hwy.; 459–8402. Precisely modeled on an ancient Roman villa, the Villa dei Papiri, once situated in the old city of Herculaneum. The villa was destroyed in A.D. 79 when Mount Vesuvius erupted. In making his decision to replicate the villa, Getty didn't miss a thing. Everything (from the colonnades and the frescoes to the gardens) resembles the original. The museum itself is one of the most important in the country as far as private art collections are concerned. Greek and Roman antiquities, fine Rennaisance and Baroque paintings, and decorative arts from eighteenth- and nineteenth-century France abound within the museum.

Hours: Tuesday through Sunday; 10:00 A.M. to 5:00 P.M. Free but reservations are recommended for parking. (For more details on the J. Paul Getty Museum, see Los Angeles "Practical Information," *Museums.*)

The Malibu Lagoon Museum, 23200 Pacific Coast Hwy.; 456–8432. The 10-room Adamson Beach Home is one of the finest examples of Spanish-Moorish architecture in the country. It contains rooms of world-famous Malibu Tile from the Malibu Potteries, hand-carved teakwood doors, hand-painted murals, molded ceilings, hand-wrought filagree ironwork, and lead-framed bottle glass windows. The adjoining museum contains a collection of artifacts, rare photographs, maps, documents, and publications that recall the colorful history of Malibu from the days of the Chumash Indians through the Spanish California culture, the genteel days of the Rindge and Adamson families, and the growth years leading to the present. Call for hours. Tuesday, Thursday, and Saturday morning tours can be arranged.

STAGE. The *Smothers Theater* at Pepperdine University offers several different productions a year, including an annual Christmas concert and performances by the Santa Barbara Ballet. For information call 456–4522.

SHOPPING. Shopping in Malibu is rustic and beachy, with a good selection of unique stores from which to choose. The *Malibu Center* is a shopping area at 23410 Civic Center Way. *Johnnie's General Store,* as the name suggests, offers everything from handmade wooden toys to candy and teas. *Karenina* has stunning imported women's fashions. *Charlotte's Web* has toys and games. *Books and Company* has a wide selection of regional historical books as well as general reading material.

Next door, the *Malibu Country Mart* is a very low-key shopping area with a playground in the middle for kids. The popular Hollywood store, *Fred Segal,* has a huge outpost here with trendy fashions for men and women. Especially interesting is the "laundromat" boutique section, complete with washing machines, laundry baskets, and detergent around for effect.

The *Tidepool Gallery,* at 22761 W. Pacific Coast Hwy., is one of the area's best stores offering seashells and ocean-inspired art work.

DINING OUT. Price ranges are as follows (per person, with no wine or tip included; for more information see "Facts at Your Fingertips"): *Expensive,* $25.00 and up; *Moderate,* $10.00–$25.00; *Inexpensive,* below $10.00.

La Scala Malibu. *Expensive.* 3835 Cross Creek Rd; 456–1979. The tables are arranged informally for relaxed dining by the beach. There is an enclosed patio with a decorated Florentine tile floor. Specialties include roasted red peppers, gazpacho, rigatoni "Malibu," and pollo al forno. Excellent wine list. Cappuccino and espresso; light desserts. Dinner reservations only. Lunch, Tuesday through Friday; dinner, daily except Monday. AE, MC, V.

Sandcastle Restaurant. 28128 W. Pacific Coast Hwy. in Paradise Cove; 457–2503. *Expensive to Moderate.* Situated right on the sand, this restaurant offers excellent seafood and Continental cuisine. Open daily for breakfast, lunch, and dinner. Major credit cards.

Alice's Restaurant. 23000 Pacific Coast Hwy; 456–6646. *Moderate.* This popular restaurant, at the base of the Malibu pier, offers organic American food complete with an ocean view. During happy hour, Monday through Friday from 4:00 P.M. to 6:00 P.M., special alcoholic concoctions are $1.25, and there is a free buffet. Open seven days. MC, V.

Beaurivage Restaurant. 26025 Pacific Coast Hwy; 456–5733. *Moderate.* Mediterranean cuisine. Beautiful spot overlooks ocean, with outdoor patio and garden complete with fountain. Sunday brunch. Lunch and dinner daily. All major credit cards.

The Chart House. 18412 Pacific Coast Hwy; 454–9321. *Moderate.* Features steak and lobster in a rustic setting on the ocean. Reservations are necessary, especially on the weekends. Prices range from $8.45 a dinner to $17.95 for lobster. All major credit cards.

Moonshadows. 20356 Pacific Coast Hwy.; 456–3010. *Moderate.* Steak and seafood are specialties in this restaurant. A lot of wood and hanging plants give the restaurant a rustic yet elegant look. Prices for dinner range from $8.95 to $19.95. Located right on the beach. Reservations recommended. AE, DC, MC, V.

Nantucket Light. 22706 Pacific Coast Hwy.; 456–3105. *Moderate.* Offers ocean-view dining. The fare is basically seafood. Salad bar. Reservations recommended. All major credit cards.

NIGHTLIFE. The largest concentration of nightlife activities in the area is of course in nearby Los Angeles, but for a special, sophisticated Western evening, try the *Calamigos Ranch;* (818) 889–6280. This former cattle ranch offers the "starlight round-up" complete with hayrides, music, and moonlit lakes. Popular with a citified clientele, aged 25–45, who yearn to "kick up their heels" from time to time. Reservations necessary.

SOUTH OF LOS ANGELES

Anaheim/Orange County

Along 42 miles of sun-drenched southern California coastline, between the counties of Los Angeles and San Diego, Orange County extends some 25 miles inland across rolling farmland, strawberry fields, and orange groves. At the eastern end lie the canyons and largely uninhabited mountain wilderness of the Santa Ana Mountains. The county's population of nearly two million is contained primarily in the cities in the northwest corner and along the coast. This section of our guide covers the northwestern and central parts, not the coast or the east.

In the 1600s, the Spaniards discovered this area—now known as Orange County—and colonized it, basking in the new-found land rich with ranching and farming possibilities. Land was not parceled out in small units, but rather divided into six rambling ranches, where oranges, walnuts, strawberries, and flowers flourished in the lush valley between the ocean and the mountains.

The original land grants have changed hands, of course, but most of the land parcels have remained intact, never having been subdivided by the individual owners. In fact, three quarters of Orange County is privately owned by a few landholders, with most of the industrial and urban growth having been achieved on leased land—a peculiarity in the United States indigenous to Orange County.

Anaheim

Once a part of these Spanish land grants, Anaheim—or "the home by the river"—was named by early German settlers who bought the land for two dollars an acre in the mid-1800s. German colonists immigrated to the region to grow grapes and seek their fortunes producing wine. In fact, for many years, Anaheim was the state's wine capital. But in the 1880s, blight completely wiped out the vineyards, ending the new wine industry.

Undaunted, colonists looked to their citrus crops, which were perfectly suited to the area's climate. Extensive groves were planted and a prosperous orange industry was soon developed. The years that followed were a time of ever increasing expansion and development for the young city of Anaheim.

Then, in 1955, Walt Disney opened the doors of his magic kingdom, Disneyland; tourism came to the area, forever changing the face of Anaheim and Orange County.

Anaheim is a prime world-class visitor destination today. It is the headquarters of almost all the area amusement parks: besides Disneyland, there are Knott's Berry Farm and attractions such as Six Flags' Movieland Wax Museum. In fact, this city has the unusual distinction of being able to claim two of the three most popular amusement parks in the nation. Anaheim's world-famous Disneyland, visited by more than ten million each year is, of course, first, followed in third place by Knott's Berry Farm, host annually to nearly five million people (Florida's Disney World is number two).

Disneyland

At Disneyland, visitors will find the fruits of Walt Disney's dream; this fantasy-maker had hopes of creating the "happiest place on earth," and there are literally millions who agree that he did just that. From the entrance into Main Street, a typical turn-of-the-century American thoroughfare, the various "lands" of Disneyland—Tomorrowland, Frontierland, Fantasyland, Adventureland—open up.

Tomorrowland offers a glimpse into the future as a monorail whisks passengers around the park, giving them an unhindered view of the many attractions. On a miniature reproduction of the freeways of the future, scale automobiles can be driven. Other forms of transportation include a sky ride and a rocket trip to the moon. Space Mountain is a fast-paced journey hurtling through space.

Fantasyland has Pinocchio's Daring Journey, a new character ride; ocean waves and a fly-through waterfall are elements of the Peter Pan Flight; and logs turn into crocodiles in Snow White's Scary Adventures.

Sporting a new snowcap and with a new bobsled, the Matterhorn is for the brave, who careen through snowstorms, fog, icy caverns, and an encounter with the Abominable Snowman.

In Frontierland, visitors can step back into America's yesteryear. Passengers experience Wild West adventures in southwestern terrain, complete with mining tunnels, caverns, earthquakes, and avalanches. One of Disneyland's newest rides, Big Thunder Mountain, a runaway mine train, whips down a spine-tingling roller-coaster track as it travels along twisting mountain paths. The sternwheeler *Mark Train* and the sailing vessel *Columbia* take passengers aboard to explore the rivers of America and the popular Tom Sawyer's Island. Ride on rafts, just as

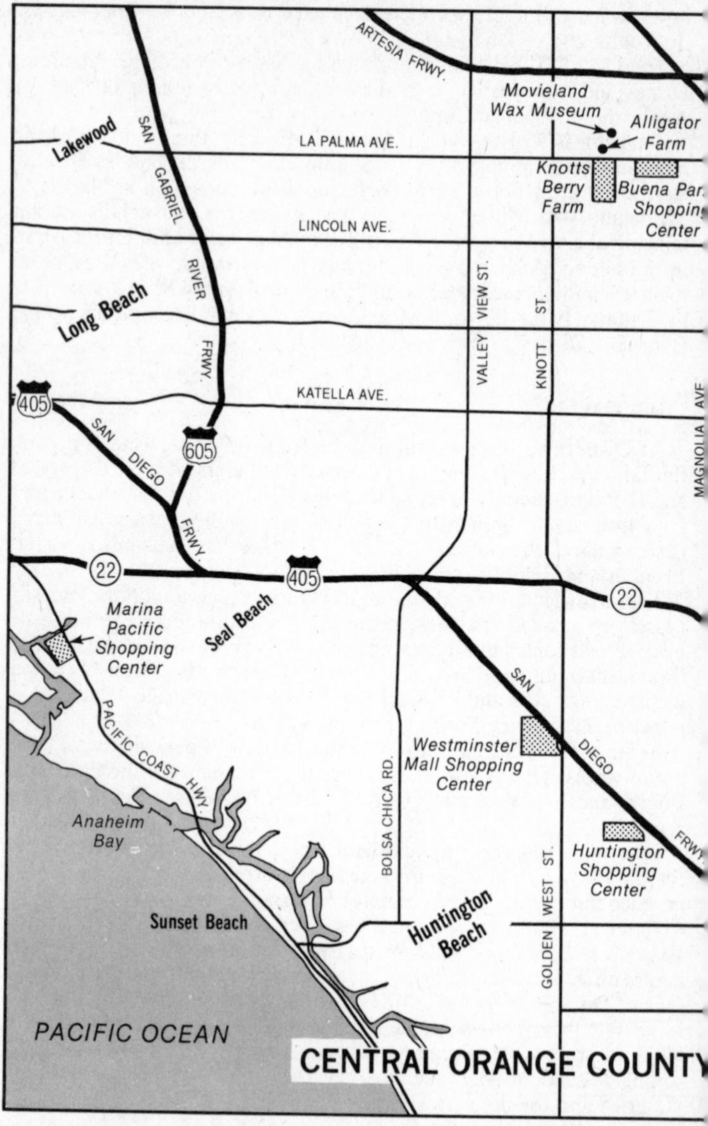
ARTESIA FRWY.
Movieland Wax Museum
Alligator Farm
Lakewood
SAN GABRIEL RIVER FRWY.
LA PALMA AVE.
Knotts Berry Farm
Buena Par. Shoppin Center
LINCOLN AVE.
Long Beach
VALLEY VIEW ST.
KNOTT ST.
KATELLA AVE.
MAGNOLIA AVE
405
SAN DIEGO FRWY.
605
22
405
22
Seal Beach
Marina Pacific Shopping Center
SAN DIEGO FRWY
Westminster Mall Shopping Center
PACIFIC COAST HWY.
BOLSA CHICA RD.
Anaheim Bay
Huntington Shopping Center
GOLDEN WEST ST.
Sunset Beach
Huntington Beach
PACIFIC OCEAN
CENTRAL ORANGE COUNTY

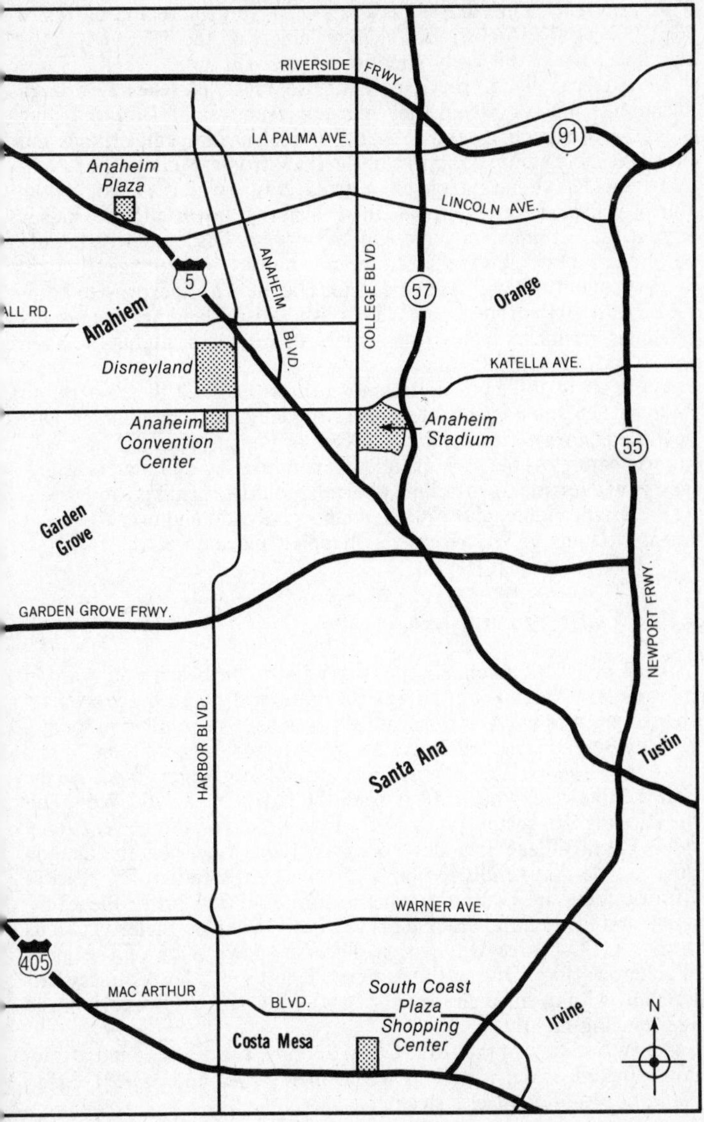
RIVERSIDE FRWY.
LA PALMA AVE.
91
Anaheim Plaza
LINCOLN AVE.
ANAHEIM BLVD.
COLLEGE BLVD.
5
57
Orange
ALL RD.
Anaheim
Disneyland
KATELLA AVE.
Anaheim Convention Center
Anaheim Stadium
55
Garden Grove
GARDEN GROVE FRWY.
NEWPORT FRWY.
HARBOR BLVD.
Santa Ana
Tustin
WARNER AVE.
405
MAC ARTHUR BLVD.
South Coast Plaza Shopping Center
Irvine
N
Costa Mesa

Tom and Huck Finn did, or seek out caves to explore and burros to ride. During the summer season, entertainers on the dock and on the two boats cruise this early American western lagoon.

In Adventureland, the Jungle Cruise takes passengers through swamplike jungles, where they must be ever watchful for snapping alligators or crocodiles. Jungle sounds screech as rampaging rhinos and other menacing animals appear in the thick tropical foliage. For every swashbuckler, young and old alike, an adventure with the Pirates of the Caribbean satisfies the renegade in all. Another favorite for the kids is a climb into a tremendous tree, similar to one in Disney's Swiss Family Robinson movie. This tree has *three* tree houses to rummage through.

Throughout the park are curio shops, some with inexpensive keepsakes, some with exquisite mementos. And Disneyland has restaurants of all descriptions, ranging from expensive full-course dining rooms to snack and refreshment stands.

There seems to be no end to enjoyment in this vast theme park, no matter when you come; winter (open weekends only) or summer, Disneyland is always fresh and clean. One of the surprising, if not well-known features, is the park's spotless reputation. Everything in Disneyland is wholesome (no drinking of alcohol on the premises) and everywhere bright, polite, cheerful attendants give each and every visitor a warm welcome to Walt Disney's "happiest place on earth!"

Knott's Berry Farm

A ten-acre fruit patch, Knott's Berry Farm, on Beach Boulevard in Buena Park, began entertaining visitors several decades ago as a re-created ghost town. Additions and expansions have resulted in today's Knott's Berry Farm, a 150-acre complex, featuring more than 20 restaurants, 40 shops, and 100 rides and attractions. Among them are the Calico Mine ride, which brings back the flavor of the Old West, and the Roaring '20s section, with its old-time airfield and some very zippy rides. Fiesta Village, includes a Soapbox Races ride, plus the Dragon Boat, a ride that recalls the days of Viking exploration. For fearless visitors, there are two attractions unsurpassed for thrills: the Corkscrew and Sky Jump parachute rides. For those who prefer vicarious thrills, a 180-degree Omnivision Theater shows films of the more treacherous rides. During the summer, Knott's also hosts an ice-skating show with talented performers. In addition, there is live rock music and dancing nightly.

A new addition to the park, Camp Snoopy, has 30 rides and attractions. Included are: a mule-powered merry-go-round, a Red Baron plane ride, and a wheeler steamboat.

Because of Knott's Berry Farm, Disneyland, and other area attractions—not to mention the city's proximity to many popular nearby beaches—Anaheim has become a natural site for conventions of all description. More than 650,000 delegates travel there annually to meet in the newly expanded Anaheim Convention Center, an ultramodern facility with 35 spacious meeting rooms and an arena that easily seats more than 9,000.

More visitors than ever, from all over the world, visited this area for the 1984 summer Olympics, and Orange County geared up with new hotels, restaurants, and attractions. Raging Waters, an aquatic recreation park and the 15,000-seat Pacific Amphitheater at the Orange County Fairgrounds are among the additions. South Coast Metro, which includes South Coast Plaza shopping center, is fast becoming urbanized, offering visitors high-caliber shopping as well as cultural additions such as the Noguchi Sculpture Gardens in Koll Center and the Orange County Performing Arts Center. The Center, with a projected cost of $53 million, is slated for a 1986 opening.

Annual festivals in major Orange County cities feature almost everything, from local arts-and-crafts exhibits to the area's own special brand of attractions. Most of Orange County's cities—Anaheim, Orange, Fullerton, Santa Ana, and Garden Grove—are undergoing restoration of their original turn-of-the century downtown buildings.

Restaurants in the area have begun to rival those of more populated Los Angeles, with every type of cuisine imaginable. Shopping in the County is also quite distinct; nearly every community has a shopping area, whether it be an enclosed mall, a boardwalk village, or a collection of more sophisticated international shops. With all of these offerings, Orange County continues to beckon visitors to its vacation wonderland, promising them all sorts of adventures.

PRACTICAL INFORMATION FOR ORANGE COUNTY

HOW TO GET THERE. By air. Some 35 miles from downtown Anaheim, Los Angeles International Airport (LAX) is easily accessible by ground transportation from the Orange County area. LAX can be reached from any point in the United States; the airport is serviced by more airlines than any other in the world.

The John Wayne Orange County Airport is 14 miles south from centrally located Anaheim, with daily local flights from San Diego, Los Angeles, Denver, Salt Lake City, Seattle, Phoenix, and other major cities. The airport services American, Air Cal, Frontier, Golden West, Imperial, Pacific Southwest Airlines (PSA), Republic, and Western.

Fullerton Municipal Airport, one of the busiest in California for general aviation, offers a number of charter flights. Long Beach Airport is about 20 minutes from Anaheim and is served by American, PSA, United, Jet America, and Alaska.

By bus. Bus service is offered from LAX and Anaheim every 30 minutes and frequently between the John Wayne Airport and Anaheim by Airport Service. Call toll free: (800) 962–1975; and within CA (800) 962–1976; local, (714) 776–9210 or (213) 723–4636.

By train. Amtrak offers six departures daily from Los Angeles, south to San Diego, with stops in Fullerton, Santa Ana, San Clemente, and San Juan Capistrano. Fullerton or Santa Ana stops are convenient and easily accessible from Anaheim.

By car. Interstate Highways 5 and 405 travel north-south through the county, intersecting with Highways 22, 55, and 91, which travel east to the mountains and west to the beaches. U.S. 5 goes directly south to San Diego.

TELEPHONES. In 1982 Orange County was split into two area codes, 714 and 619. The majority of numbers in this section are in the central and coastal areas of the county, 714; the 619 code covers the eastern and southern area of the county. If in doubt, check with the operator. You do not need to dial the area code if it is the same as the one from which you are calling, although you must dial "1" (one) for some city-to-city calls. Information (known as directory assistance) is 411. When direct-dialing a long-distance number from anywhere in Orange County, you must dial the number "1" (one) *before* you dial the area code and the number itself. An operator will assist you on person-to-person, credit card, and collect calls if you dial "0" first. Pay telephones start at 20 cents.

CLIMATE. Orange County boasts a year-round temperate climate ranging from a low of 45 degrees in the winter to a high of 79 degrees in the summer. Average annual rainfall is 15 inches, which includes some April showers. Come early fall, the Santana (or Santa Ana) Winds invade the area, causing September and the first part of October to be the hottest and most uncomfortable months of the year. These winds, which Californians have come to know as the cause of their Indian Summer, create a very dry and windy climate—and inevitably take a turn for the better, making the end of October and November a most attractive time to visit Orange County.

Because temperatures in this area tend to drop dramatically in the evening, a sweater or light overcoat is recommended.

HOTELS & MOTELS. Orange County's overnight facilities are plentiful, especially with Anaheim's recent convention industry boom. More than ten million worldwide visitors annually come to the Anaheim/Orange County area seeking adventure at Disneyland and other attractions. You are likely to find accommodations easily adaptable to any budget, from the elaborate to the bargain. Take note: Even though more than 16,000 rooms are available, reservations are necessary year-round. Based on double occupancy, price categories are as follows: *Super Deluxe,* $75 and up; *Deluxe,* $60–$75; *Expensive,* $42–$60; *Moderate,* $30–$42; and *Inexpensive,* $18–$30. Listings are divided by price range category. For more details, see the "Facts at Your Fingertips" section.

ANAHEIM

Super Deluxe

Anaheim Hilton and Tower. 777 Convention Way; (714) 750–4321. Newly opened in May 1984, this hotel is the area's largest facility. The $200 million, 15-story building has 1,600 rooms with three restaurants; lounges; shops; meeting and banquet space. Recreational facilities include indoor pool, outdoor pool, health club, spa, and sundeck.

Emerald of Anaheim. 1717 South West St.; (714) 999–0900; (800) 821–8976 (outside CA); (800) 321–8976 (in CA). Completed in summer 1984, this hotel has 508 rooms and is geared toward the business traveler. Three fine restaurants, including a Japanese one; swimming pool, sundeck, Jacuzzi.

Deluxe

Disneyland Hotel. 1150 West Cerritos Ave.; (714) 778–6600. Connected to Disneyland by monorail, this 1,100-room hotel is actually a 60-acre resort. Choose accommodations in one of the tropical villages, or perch in the spacious towers. Shop at the waterfront bazaar, with ports-of-call shops specializing in

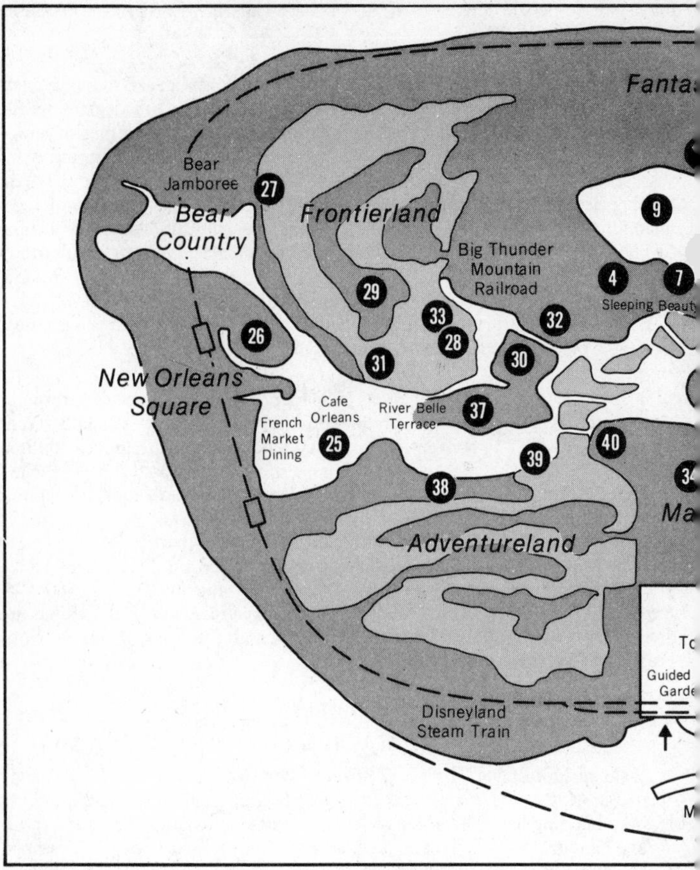

Fantasyland

1) Motor Boat Cruise
2) "It's A Small World"
3) Mr. Toad's Wild Ride
4) Fantasyland Autopia
5) Matterhorn Bobsleds
6) Storybook Land
7) Snow White's Adventures
8) Mad Tea Party
9) Dumbo Flying Elephants
10) Casey Jr. Circus Train
11) King Arthur Carrousel
12) Peter Pan Flight
13) Alice in Wonderland

Tomorrowland

14) Skyway to Fantasyland
15) America the Beautiful
16) People Mover
17) America Sings
18) Rocket Jets
19) Submarine Voyage
20) Tomorrowland Monorail
21) Mission to Mars
22) Tomorrowland Autopia
23) Adventure Thru Inner Space
24) Space Mountain

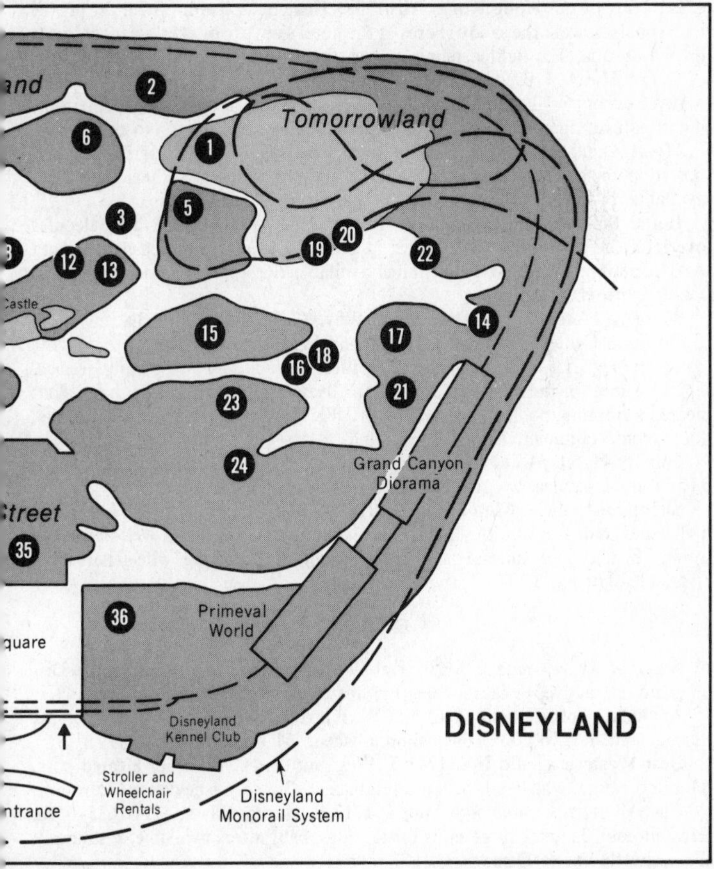

New Orleans Square

25) Pirates of the Caribbean
26) Haunted Mansion

Frontierland

27) Explorer Canoes
28) Columbia Sailing Ship
29) Tom Sawyer's Island
30) Golden Horseshoe
31) Keel Boats and Tom Sawyer Rafts
32) Shooting Gallery
33) Mark Twain Steamboat

Main Street

34) Penny Arcade
35) Main Street Cinema
36) The Walt Disney Story and "Great Moments With Mr. Lincoln"

Adventureland

37) Big Game Shoot
38) Swiss Family Tree House
39) Jungle Cruise
40) Enchanted Tiki Room

exotic wares from Hong Kong, Australia, Mexico, or Tahiti. Swim in one of three pools or walk the sandy shores of the hotel's cove. For exercise, pedal-boat on the marina. Ten lighted tennis courts, fourteen (yes!) restaurants.

Grand Hotel. 7 Freedman Way; (714) 772-7777. Adjacent to Disneyland with a free shuttle. Boutiques and gift shop keep guests happy. Special entertainment features dinner theater. Dining room, coffee shop, pool. No pets.

Hyatt Anaheim. 1700 S. Harbor Blvd.; (714) 772–5900. Near Disneyland; heated pool, suites available, restaurant and discotheque. Wheelchair units available. No pets.

Inn at the Park. 1855 S. Harbor Blvd.; (714) 750–1811. Private balconies overlook the man-made Matterhorn at Disneyland and the God-made Santa Ana Mountains. Heated pool. Suites available. Restaurant and coffee shop; lounge with entertainment.

Marriott Hotel. 700 W. Convention Way.; (714) 750–8000. Adjacent to the Convention Center, two blocks from Disneyland, this new hotel caters to the convention visitor with its outstanding meeting facilities and quality service. Special suites for the busy executive or the lively family. Gift shops, hair salon, heated swimming pool, elegant dining in *JW's,* plus two additional restaurants, lounge entertainment. 1050 rooms.

Quality Hotel. 616 Convention Way; (714) 750–3131. Close to Disneyland; heated pool, saunas, bar, restaurant; suites available. 285 rooms.

Sheraton-Anaheim Motor Hotel. 1015 W. Ball Rd.; (714) 778–1700. Close to Disneyland, free shuttle. This Tudor-style motel has large, well-decorated rooms, heated pool; suites available; restaurant, bar, dancing; wheelchair units available. 370 rooms.

Expensive

Anaheim TraveLodge. 1166 W. Katella Ave.; (714) 774–7817. Close to Disneyland, attractive; restaurant nearby; heated pool. 57 rooms.

Anaheim Aloha TraveLodge. 505 W. Katella Ave.; (714) 774–8710. Near Disneyland; heated pool; coffee shop adjacent. 51 rooms.

Best Western Apollo Inn. 1741 S. West St.; (714) 772–9750. Heated pool, laundry, sauna, whirlpool; restaurant adjacent. Bus to Disneyland. 135 rooms.

Best Western Cosmic Age Lodge. 1717 S. Harbor Blvd.; (714) 635–6550. Heated pool, Jacuzzi, large units for families, babysitters available, restaurant. Free shuttle bus to Disneyland. 156 rooms.

Best Western Space Age Lodge. 1176 Katella Ave.; (714) 776–0140. Heated pool, restaurant; shopping center adjacent. Laundry, beauty salon, barber shop, family accommodations, babysitting available, pets accepted; free shuttle to Disneyland. 100 rooms.

Best Western Galaxy Motel. 1735 S. Harbor Blvd.; (714) 772–1520. Heated pool; restaurant adjacent; laundry, large family suites; free shuttle to Disneyland. 93 rooms.

Best Western Inn of Tomorrow. 1110 W. Katella Ave.; (714) 778–1880. Unique garden of topiary trees, heated pool, sauna and Jacuzzi, laundry, over 800 works of art, restaurant. 290 units.

Conestoga Inn TraveLodge. 1240 S. Walnut.; (714) 535–0300. Heated pool, Jacuzzi, suites, restaurant, and coffee shop, bar. 255 rooms.

Anaheim Holiday Inn. 1850 S. Harbor Blvd.; (714) 750–2801. Heated pool, laundry, Jacuzzi, suites, dining room, coffee shop, cocktails, entertainment. 313 rooms available.

Moderate

Admiral's Cove Motel. 1028 W. Ball Road; (714) 774–1650. Heated pool, sauna, Jacuzzi, spacious rooms, large family units available, two efficiency apts.; restaurant opposite. 61 rooms.

Akua Best Western Motor Hotel. 1018 E. Orangethorpe Ave.; (714) 871–2830. Heated pool, four two-room units. 63 rooms.

Alamo Motor Lodge. 1140 W. Katella Ave.; (714) 635–8070. Heated pool, no pets. 50 rooms.

Alpine Motel. 715 W. Katella Ave.; (714) 535–2186. Heated pool, steam baths, family units available; restaurant; substantial rate reductions September to May. Across the street from the Anaheim Convention Center. 41 rooms.

Anaheim Friendship Inn. 426 W. Ball Road; (714) 774–3882. Small heated pool, laundry, Jacuzzi, four efficiency apts. Restaurant adjacent. 33 rooms.

Anaheim Park Motor Inn. 915 S. West Street; (714) 778–0350. Heated pool, Jacuzzi. Lower winter rates. 114 rooms.

Best Western Stardust Holiday Motel. 1057 W. Ball Road; (714) 774–7600. Heated pool; restaurant adjacent. 104 rooms.

Cavalier Motor Lodge. 11811 Harbor Blvd.; (714) 750–1000. Heated pool, jacuzzi. 93 rooms.

Concord Inn. 1111 S. Harbor Blvd.; (714) 533–8830. Heated pool, Jacuzzi, one large kitchen unit. Free bus to Disneyland. 82 rooms.

Harbor Inn TraveLodge. 2171 S. Harbor Blvd.; (714) 750–3100. Heated pool, Jacuzzi; coffee shop adjacent. Deluxe rooms with kitchenettes available. 128 rooms.

Jolly Roger Inn Hotel. 640 W. Katella; (714) 772–7621. Two heated pools, Jacuzzi; suites available, one suite with private pool. Restaurant, coffee shop, dancing, entertainment; beauty salon, dress shop, liquor and sundries shop; free shuttle to Disneyland. 180 rooms.

Eden Rock Kona Kai Motel. 1820 S. West St.; (714) 971–5506. Heated pool, aqua-slide; family suites with kitchenettes available; restaurant adjacent. 30 rooms.

Lamplighter Motel. 1759 S. West St.; (714) 774–2136. Heated pool, refrigerators, family units, laundry; restaurant adjacent; shopping center nearby. Free morning coffee. Low rates Labor Day to May 22. 55 units.

Magic Lamp Motel. 1030 W. Katella; (714) 772–7242. Heated pool, laundry, 15 efficiency apartments available; restaurant adjacent. Lower winter rates. 78 rooms.

Park Vue Motel. 1570 S. Harbor Blvd.; (714) 772–5721. Heated pool, family units, kitchen apartments, laundry, sundeck, restaurant. Lower winter rates. 90 rooms.

Penny Sleeper Inn. 1441 S. Manchester Ave.; (714) 991–8100. Heated pool, laundry, game room. 206 rooms.

Saga Motel. 1650 S. Harbor Blvd.; (714) 772–0440. Heated pool, laundry, Jacuzzi; coffee shop adjacent. Lower winter rate; AAA discount prices. 102 rooms.

Sandman Anaheim. 921 S. Harbor Blvd.; (714) 956–5730. Heated pool; coffee shop adjacent. No pets. 93 rooms.

The Sands Motel. 1520 S. Harbor Blvd.; (714) 774–1324. Heated pool, family units. 32 rooms.

Inexpensive

Ana-Lin Motel. 2123 W. Lincoln Ave.; (714) 535–8446. Midway between Disneyland and Knott's Berry Farm. Heated pool, no pets; three efficiency apartments; restaurants and shopping nearby. Lower winter rates. 23 rooms.

Anchor Motel. 1358 E. Lincoln Ave.; (714) 533–3972. Heated pool, some refrigerators. 20 rooms.

Ha' Penny Inn. 2630 W. Lincoln Ave.; (714) 821–3690. All suites with kitchenettes, heated pool; free shuttles from Amtrak station and airport. 127 units.

Mecca Motel. 1544 S. Harbor Blvd.; (714) 533–4581. Two heated pools, laundry; efficiency apartments available. Restaurant adjacent. Lower winter rates. 96 rooms.

Polynesian Motel. 641 S. Brookhurst Street; (714) 778–6892. Heated pool; efficiency units available; coffee shop nearby; low winter rates. 28 rooms.

BUENA PARK

Deluxe

Buena Park Hotel and Convention Center. 7675 Crescent Ave.; (714) 995–1111. Heated pool, suites; dining room and coffee shop, cocktails, entertainment. 320 rooms.

Holiday Inn Plaza Hotel. 7000 Beach Blvd.; (714) 522–7000. Heated pool, laundry, Jacuzzi, kennels, suites, dining room, lounge, room service, bar entertainment. 250 units.

Expensive

Buena Park TraveLodge. 7640 Beach Blvd.; (714) 522–8461. Heated pool, pets allowed; kitchenettes and family units available. Restaurant across the street. 68 rooms.

Moderate

Buena Park Quality Inn. 7555 Beach Blvd.; (714) 522–7360. Heated pool, sauna, Jacuzzi, current movies; restaurant nearby. 200 rooms.

Farm De Ville Friendship Inn. 7800 Crescent Ave.; (714) 527–2201. Two heated pools, sauna, suites, efficiency apts., laundry. Coffee shop close by. 130 rooms.

Inexpensive

Capri Motel. 7860 Beach Blvd.; (714) 522–7221. 400 feet to Knott's Berry Farm. Heated pool, kitchenettes, family units. Restaurant adjacent. 70 rooms.

Covered Wagon Motel. 7830 Crescent Ave.; (714) 995–0033. Heated pool, family units. Opposite southern entrance to Knott's Berry Farm. 20 rooms.

Gaslite Motel. 7777 Beach Blvd.; (714) 522–8441. Pool, laundry, kitchenettes; coffee shop nearby. 77 rooms.

Siesta International Motel. 7930 Beach Blvd.; (714) 522–2422. Heated pool, 40 efficiency units, family units, some refrigerators, laundry; coffee shop adjacent. 80 rooms.

COSTA MESA

The Westin South Coast Plaza. *Super Deluxe.* 666 Anton Blvd.; (714) 540–2500. The Westin South Coast Plaza Hotel is a modern 400-room hotel with a variety of sports facilities. Volleyball, shuffleboard, putting green, swimming pool, and tennis courts are all on the grounds. There is an additional restaurant, three bars, and live entertainment nightly. A special weekend plan is available—everything, including the room, is up to 50% less than the regular rates.

FULLERTON

Willow Tree Lodge. *Moderate.* 1015 S. Harbor Blvd.; (714) 871–5430. Heated pool, family units available. 61 rooms.

IRVINE

Irvine Marriott. *Super Deluxe.* 1800 Von Karman; (714) 851–1100. This brand-new hotel, the third Marriott property in Orange County, has 501 guest rooms. Indoor-outdoor swimming pool, lighted tennis courts, game rooms. Restaurants, lounge, entertainment. AE, CB, DC, MC, V.

The Registry Hotel. *Super Deluxe.* 18800 MacArthur Blvd.; (714) 752–8777. Accessibility is a main feature of this hotel. It is right across from the John Wayne Orange County Airport, four miles from the ocean, and 15 to 20 minutes from Disneyland. The 300-room hotel has a swimming pool, tennis courts, a Jacuzzi, and complimentary coffee and *Wall Street Journal* are offered. Le Chardonnay offers gourmet dining, the Gazebo is open from 6:00 A.M. to 2:00 A.M. daily for lighter fare, and for entertainment and dancing there is the Saloon. Pool and tennis. Special weekend packages. Complimentary limousine service from the airport.

Airporter Inn Hotel. *Deluxe–Expensive.* 18700 MacArthur Blvd.; (714) 833–2770. Heated pool, dining room, cocktails, entertainment, suites, one room with private pool. Opposite John Wayne Orange County Airport. 215 rooms.

ORANGE

Doubletree Hotel. *Super Deluxe.* 100 The City Dr.; (714) 634–4500. This new hotel has 460 rooms, a concierge floor, two restaurants, and a lounge. Geared toward the business traveler with versatile meeting and banquet rooms. Lighted tennis courts, heated pool spa.

Best Western El Camino. *Moderate.* 3191 N. Tustin Ave.; (714) 998-0360. Centrally located about twenty minutes from Disneyland or Knott's Berry Farm. Heated pool, efficiency apts., steam baths, Jacuzzi. 56 rooms.

El Matador Motel. *Moderate.* 1300 E. Katella Ave.; (714) 639–2500. Small pool; restaurant close to hotel. 29 rooms.

SANTA ANA

Howard Johnson Hotel. *Expensive.* 1600 E. First St.; (714) 835–3051. Heated pool, sauna, Jacuzzi, restaurant and coffee shop. 150 rooms.

El Cortez Inn. *Moderate.* 1503 E. First St.; (714) 835–2585. Heated pool; coffee shop nearby. 60 rooms.

Orange Tree Motel. *Moderate.* 2720 N. Grand Ave.; (714) 997–2330. Small pool; restaurant adjacent. 48 rooms.

Vagabond Lodge. *Moderate.* 1519 E. First St.; (714) 547–9426. Pool, children's playground, coffee shop, family units. 52 rooms.

TRABUCO CANYON

Coto de Caza. *Super Deluxe.* 22000 Plano Trabuco Rd.; (714) 586–0761. This resort community is at the base of the Saddleback Mountains. The 5,000-acre valley served as the site for the Modern Pentathlon during the 1984 Olympics. Available in the complex are swimming pool, whirlpool, gym, tennis, bowling, horseback riding, billiards, racquetball, dining facilities, and shops.

HOW TO GET AROUND. By car. Avis, Budget, and Hertz have offices at both Los Angeles International Airport and John Wayne County Airport.

By taxi. Taxis are available, as are limousine services offering full transportation from all airports, harbor areas, and other locations on request. *Luxe Livery Service,* toll-free in California (800) 422–4267 or from other areas (800) 854–8171; *Green Flag Airport Shuttle,* (714) 991–5660.

By bus. *Continental Trailways* and *Greyhound* operate out of the central bus terminal in Los Angeles, servicing major cities in Orange County. There are convenient shuttle buses and comfortable air-conditioned motor coaches traveling from both airports to designated stops and hotels in Orange County. *Airport Service Motor Coach,* (714) 776–9210. *Air Link,* (714) 635–1390.

Locally, the Orange County Transit District operates buses daily throughout the county; call (714) 636–RIDE for route information.

TOURIST INFORMATION SERVICES. Most cities in Orange County have Chamber-of-Commerce bureaus. These organizations are more than happy to assist out-of-town guests.

In Anaheim, contact the *Anaheim Area Visitor and Convention Bureau,* 800 W. Katella Ave., Anaheim, CA 92803; (714) 999–8999. The Automobile Club of Southern California, for members only, provides maps, brochures, booklets, and information on many special events, fishing, hunting, and camping. The Anaheim Automobile Club of Southern California is located at 150 W. Vermont Ave., Anaheim; (714) 774–2392.

In Buena Park, stop by the *Buena Park Visitor's Bureau* at 6696 Beach Blvd. for information on the immediate area. Maps, restaurant guides, hotel brochures and more. Call (714) 994–1511.

SEASONAL EVENTS. The events listed are for inland Orange County only. For coastal events, of which there are many, please refer to the "Long Beach to San Clemente" section.

April–September. Major league *baseball season,* with season opener the California Angels vs. the Los Angeles Dodgers at Anaheim Stadium.

April. *A Night in Fullerton,* an annual festival featuring arts, crafts, shows, and exhibits.

May. Memorial Day Weekend. Annual *Strawberry Festival* celebrates the annual harvest of strawberries; Garden Grove.

July–August. *Orange Country Fair,* Fairgrounds, Costa Mesa.

August–December. *National Football League* season, with the Los Angeles Rams at home in Anaheim Stadium.

September. Labor Day Weekend. *International Street Fair,* a festival featuring different international foods and art; at Orange Circle in the city of Orange.

TOURS. Special sightseeing tours operate daily out of Anaheim to such varied places as Universal Studios, the many beach areas, Six Flags' Magic Mountain, Catalina Island, Hollywood, San Juan Capistrano Mission, San Diego, RMS *Queen Mary,* and Mexico and Las Vegas. Contact the Anaheim Area Visitor Bureau for information.

In Anaheim, a free *Fun Bus* tours the area from hotels to amusement sights several times daily, leaving its own terminal at 304 Katella Way in Anaheim. Fun Bus tour routes include Disneyland, the Anaheim Convention Center, Anaheim Stadium, Knott's Berry Farm, Movieland Wax Museum, and the Buena Park Shopping Center. For information on hotel pickups, call (714) 635–1390. *The City Shopper* offers visits to the Crystal Cathedral, the City Shopping Center in Orange, and local hotels. Only $1 one way; children under 5 free.

SPECIAL-INTEREST TOURS. Tucker Wildlife Preserve, in Modjeska Canyon, is 17 miles southeast of the city of Orange, a pleasant drive through rolling hills and farmland. At live-oak-lined Modjeska Canyon, you'll find a bird watcher's haven (or heaven), nestled in the foothills of the Santa Ana Mountains. The preserve features more than 50 bird species, most of which are migratory. Colorful resident hummingbirds are plentiful and delightful to watch. An observation porch aids in sighting and an attendant is available daily for help in identification.

PARKS. The foothills of the Santa Ana Mountains offer several excellent, conveniently located recreation areas; the best two are:

The *Irvine Regional Park,* once a part of the Mexican land grant, Rancho Lomas de Santiago, that belonged to the Yorba family. In 1876, James Irvine bought the ranch to raise sheep. The area has always been a popular picnic site. Now the vast park—located seven miles east of Orange—boasts 477 acres of picnic grounds, a boating lagoon, hiking trails, an amphitheater, a small petting zoo, and pony stables.

Irvine Lake Park. About 15 miles southeast of Orange, on the Santiago Reservoir, this recreational lake sports boating and swimming.

CAMPING. Camping is limited in the inland Orange County area. The coastline, however, has abundant and excellent camping sites. (Please refer to the Long Beach to San Clemente section.) A few lovely campsites, however, are available in the Santa Ana Mountains. These are full-service, state-owned campsites, offering showers, stoves, tables, drinking water, and toilets.

Trabuco Canyon. O'Neill Regional Park offers camping among live oaks in the Cleveland National Forest, with 350 campsites available; 13 full-service rest rooms throughout. Trailer space available.

Featherly Regional Park. Up Santa Ana Canyon, this park has more than 200 campsites, trailer spaces available, and ample restrooms throughout.

For further information on camping and campsites, contact the California State Department of Parks and Recreation, P.O. Box 2390, Sacramento 95811, or call (213) 620–3342 or (619) 427–5133.

RV parks are abundant in Orange County. Here is a partial listing: *Anaheim Vacation Park* (311 N. Beach Blvd.); *KOA Campground* (1221 S. West St., Anaheim); *Orangeland RV Park* (1600 W. Struck Ave., Orange); *Tratel Garden Grove Trailer Park* (13190 Harbor Blvd., Garden Grove); *Travelers World RV Park* (333 W. Ball Rd., Anaheim); *Vacationland RV Park* (1343 S. West St., Anaheim).

CHILDREN'S ACTIVITIES. Orange County is a family paradise with more family-oriented activities in a single area than anywhere else in the United States.

Disneyland, 1313 Harbor Blvd., Anaheim; 999–4565. 27 miles southeast of downtown Los Angeles via Santa Ana Freeway. This "Magic Kingdom," the late Walt Disney's legacy to the Southland's amusement and entertainment world, now boasts of seven lands of Fantasy—about $200,-000,000 worth of magic. Ride mules or space ships, but plan at least a six-hour visit starting on Main Street with its turn-of-the-century nostalgia. (For a fuller description, see the Orange County introductory section, above).

Disneyland is the center of an immense vacation playground that includes Knott's Berry Farm, Movieland Wax Museum and Palace of Living Art, and Anaheim Stadium.

Admission to Disneyland is $14 for adults and $9 for children from 3 to 12. For information, call (714) 999–4565. Hours are as follows: Monday through Friday, 10:00 A.M. to 7:00 P.M.; Saturday, 9:00 A.M. to 12 midnight; and Sunday, from 9:00 A.M. to 6:00 P.M.—except during the summer when from June 19th until the middle of September the park stays open from 9:00 A.M. to 12 midnight during the week, and 9:00 A.M. to 1:00 A.M. on weekends.

How to get there from Los Angeles: Take the #5 Freeway south or the San Diego #405 Freeway south to #5 north to Harbor Blvd. Disneyland will be on the right side of the boulevard.

Knott's Berry Farm, 8039 Beach Blvd., Buena Park; 952–9400. A family fun place with an atmosphere of the Old West and Gold Rush eras. Visitors pan for gold, ride ore cars, stagecoaches, a narrow-gauge railroad, burros, and eat finger-lickin' chicken dinners. 180-degree omnivision theater, showing films of thrill rides. Ice-skating show, live rock music and dancing in the summer.

Admission is $10.95; $8.95 for children; parking is free. Summer hours are Sunday through Friday, 9:00 A.M. to midnight; Saturday, 9:00 A.M. to 1:00 A.M. Winter hours are weekends from 10:00 A.M. to 9:00 P.M. and weekdays from 10:00 A.M. to 6:00 P.M. Closed Wednesdays and Thursdays during the winter except for holiday and vacation periods. Also closed Christmas Day. American Express, Visa, and MasterCard accepted.

To get there: Take the #5 to #91 East to Beach Blvd; turn right to La Palma and Beach.

Lion Country Safari, 8800 Irvine Center Drive, Laguna Hills; (714) 837–1200. If you think a wildebeest is a mythical creature from Shakespeare or early Arthurian tales, you're in for a surprise. This African wildlife preserve features not only lions, rhinos, cheetahs, zebras, and giraffes, but such interesting and exotic creatures as the oryx, gazelle, eland, gnu, aoudad, and, yes, the wildebeest. Take an hour and drive through this 500-acre mini-African veldt watching the uncaged animals roam.

Admission is $7.25 for adults; $4.50 for children. Open every day, 9:45 A.M. to 5:00 P.M. May 1 to October 30. In winter open until 3:30 P.M.

How to get there from Los Angeles: Take the San Diego Freeway #405 south to Irvine Center Drive, turn right.

Movieland Wax Museum and Palace of Living Art, 7711 Beach Blvd., Buena Park.; (714) 522–1154. Inside a modern, white building with elegant gold trim are more than 200 wax figures depicting famous and infamous movie and television stars of all eras. This 20-year-old shrine to these memorable personalities, both living and dead, show off our favorite characters in interesting ways. Walk through the original set of Doctor Zhivago or stroll down the Yellow Brick Road with Dorothy and the Tin Man. Strike a pose with John Wayne or flirt with *Happy Days'* The Fonz. A new attraction, the Black Box, takes visitors through lifelike scenes from *Halloween, Alien,* and *Altered States.*

Admission is $7.95 for adults; $5.95 for children 4–11, and children under four are admitted free. Open daily, 8:00 A.M. to 9:00 P.M. (summer); 10:00 A.M. to 10:00 P.M. the rest of the year. Hours frequently change so call before visiting.

How to get there from Los Angeles: Take the #5 Freeway south and exit right on Knott Ave. Turn left on Orange Thorpe Ave. and right on Beach Blvd.

Raging Waters, 150 East Puddingstone Rd., San Dimas; (714) 592–6453. The newest addition to Orange County's theme parks, this 30-acre attraction has water slides, the Wave Pool with waves breaking on a sandy beach, and a splash pool for "little dippers." Lifeguards are on duty. Open 10:00 A.M. to 10:00 P.M., June through August; from 10:00 A.M. to 7:00 P.M., starting in September. Admission is $8.50 for adults; $7.00 for children 4 to 11; younger than 4, free; $5.00 for seniors. After 5:00 P.M. admission is $5.00 for adults. Season passes and group rates are available.

Santa's Village is a special attraction for kids; Santa Claus is always in residence and the Rainbow Man and Lollypop Lady entertain each day. Located in a pine forest in the San Bernardino Mountains, the atmosphere is just right for a year-round winter. Rides and an Alice-in-Wonderland Maze keep children happy all day—along with the candy shop and restaurants. Open daily, 10:00 A.M. to 5:00 P.M. mid-June through mid-September, and mid-November through December (weather permitting). Closed March through May. Open weekends and holidays, from 10:00 A.M. to 5:00 P.M. the rest of the year.

Admission with unlimited rides costs $5 for ages 17 and over, $3 for those 65 or older, free for kids two and under.

How to get there from Los Angeles: take the San Bernardino Fwy. (10) east all the way to San Bernardino and route 215 north; take 215 north approximately 4 miles. When the road divides, stay in the right lane and follow signs toward mountain resorts. At Waterman Ave., Hwy. 18, turn left and stay on Hwy. 18 for about 25 miles. Santa's Village is on the left. For more information, call (714) 337–2481.

For **tennis,** try the *Tennisland Racquet Club,* 1330 S. Walnut St., Anaheim, which offers tennis lessons. For water sports, see the Orange County Coast section (Long Beach to San Clemente).

SPECTATOR SPORTS. Featured are the *California Angels* professional baseball team April through September. At times, the *Los Angeles Rams* NFL football team shares Anaheim Stadium with the Angels, since the Rams season runs August through December.

Horse racing is a popular attraction at *Santa Anita Park,* 285 W. Huntington Dr., Arcadia, in the foothills of the San Gabriel Mountains. Internationally rated thoroughbreds are ridden by champion jockeys. Closed May through September. For more information call (818) 574–7223.

HISTORICAL SITES. Visit the *Heritage House Museum* at California State University in Fullerton. Built in 1894, this former residence and office of a once-prominent area physician, Dr. Clark, is restored to its Victorian elegance. Of special interest is the doctor's office and parlor, fully restored, with instruments and furniture actually used for turn-of-the-century medical practice.

Also worth a stop is the *Mother Colony House* (West and Sycamore Sts. in Anaheim). This restored Victorian home once belonged to early German settlers and includes many German artifacts that they brought to this country, plus interesting historical items from Orange County and early Anaheim.

ARCHITECTURE. Take a trip to *Crystal Cathedral,* 12141 Lewis Street, Garden Grove. Philip Johnson, world-famous architect, designed this bold, theatrical auditorium for Robert Schuller's Garden Grove Community Church. The Crystal Cathedral seats 3,000 people in the all-glass, star-shaped structure, which rises 124 feet. Concerts, lectures, and tours are held inside.

LIBRARIES. Open to the public, the California State University Library in Fullerton houses a "Freedom Center," where political pamphlets and dogmatic literature of every sort reside, from interests far left to far right. The library also has an extensive collection of government documents on every subject imaginable.

MUSEUMS. Besides entertainment, the Spanish heritage and early industries of Orange County are remembered in the area's many museums.

The Bowers Museum. 2002 N. Main St., Santa Ana; (714) 558–1133. Built to resemble a Spanish hacienda, this excellent museum features a fine collection of Indian artifacts and early Orange County historical items on permanent display. The museum also owns outstanding works of pre-Columbian art from Mexico and Central America, which are on display periodically. Gift Shop. Admission by donation.

Villa Bianchi Winery Museum. 2045 S. Harbor Blvd., Anaheim 750–4503. A small museum devoted to the early wine industry, with various photos, distilleries, bottles, labels. Free admission.

Movieland Wax Museum. 7711 Beach Blvd, Buena Park; 522–1154. This intriguing collection of stars' likenesses, all created out of wax, features more than 200 such replicas. Original costumes and props are displayed on sets that recreate some famous roles. Both classical and contemporary films are represented here and nearly all are enhanced with special animation, lights, and sound effects.

Another section of the museum, the Palace of Living Arts, displays replicas of famous statues, again in wax, along with 3-D reproductions of well-known paintings. An added treat is to be found at the California Plaza, where visitors walk through the upside-down ship used in the film *The Poseidon Adventure.* $7.50 for adults, $4.50 for children under 11.

Museum of North Orange County. 301 N. Pomona Ave., Fullerton; 738–6545. This museum features a variety of interesting traveling exhibits, covering prehistoric presentations to the space age. Donation.

Museum of World Wars. 8700 Stanton Ave., Buena Park; 952–2323. Houses one of the largest collections of military uniforms and vehicles in the country; featuring WWI and WWII photos and artifacts. Of special interest: Hermann Goering's personal items are on display.

Hobby City Doll Museum. 1238 S. Beach Blvd., Anaheim; 527–2323. Fifty-seven years of collecting dolls from all over the world has resulted in this fascinating doll museum, featuring ancient Egyptian dolls, Indonesian and Chinese miniatures, and space-age Star Trek dolls. Free admission.

MUSIC. *Irvine Meadows Amphitheater* (8800 Irvine Center Dr., Laguna Hills) is an open-air structure offering a variety of musical events from May through October. The amphitheater features special general-admission "meadow seating" and a large, sloping, grass lawn for viewing concerts behind served seating. For information, call (714) 855–8095.

At *Anaheim Stadium,* specialty concerts are performed throughout the year. For information, call (714) 634–2000. The *Pacific Amphitheater* is a recent addition to the music scene in Orange County. On the Orange County Fairgrounds, Costa Mesa, this facility offers musical entertainment as well as stage plays, April through October.

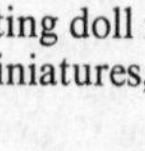

SHOPPING. Orange County offers abundant and distinctive shopping for every taste. There are convenient shopping plazas in every area, not to mention the many small specialty shops and larger department stores.

Anaheim's major enclosed mall, *Anaheim Plaza,* has more than 72 shops, boutiques, restaurants, and services. As a convenience for visitors, the City Shopper bus travels from more than a dozen Anaheim locations to shopping areas. Call (714) 535–2211. Hotels with service are: Sheraton Anaheim Hotel,

Conestoga Motor Inn, Disneyland Hotel, Apollo Motor Inn, Marriott Hotel, Inn At The Park, Quality Inn, Holiday Inn, Hamburger House (at Harbor and Katella), Hyatt Hotel, Grand Hotel, Park Vue Hotel, Tropicana Motor Inn, Anaheim Plaza.

South Coast Plaza Village, Sunflower and Bear Sts., Santa Ana, is an unusual shopping village with unique, quality merchandise. Gifts from most European countries are available, and six international restaurants and sidewalk cafés make shopping easier.

The mammoth *South Coast Plaza Shopping Center,* at 3333 South Bristol Street in Costa Mesa, also has an interesting variety of shops, restaurants, and theaters.

More than 90 stores and services operate at *The City Shopping Center* (2 City Blvd., Orange), where landscaping, fountains, and courtyards add to shopping pleasure. The large *Buena Park Mall* in Buena Park guarantees shopping enjoyment near Knott's Berry Farm.

DINING OUT in Orange County can be a rewarding experience. Restaurants are beginning to follow Los Angeles's lead in offering especially fresh food creatively prepared. There is some ethnic diversity of cuisine and its sophistication of preparation is a growing trend in a growing community. Within a few years, Orange County will undoubtedly become a miniature version of Los Angeles in gastronomy. Dress is usually casual; where it is more formal we'll say so.

Establishments are categorized here according to the price of a dinner from the middle range of their menus. Price categories may be interpreted as follows: *Expensive,* $25 and above; *Moderate,* $10–$25; and *Inexpensive,* below $10. Not included are drinks, tip, and tax. A more complete explanation of price categories can be found in "Facts at Your Fingertips" at the front of this guide.

ANAHEIM

Bessie Wall's. *Moderate.* 1074 N. Tustin Ave.; (714) 630–2812. In 1927, John Wall built a mansion for his bride Bessie. Now it's a lovingly restored restaurant; Bessie's upstairs bedroom has been converted into a cocktail lounge. Authentic photographs of the Wall family and other memorabilia grace the walls. Early California food is featured, including chicken and dumplings, rabbit Madeira, and crab enchiladas topped with sour cream. Casual. All major credit cards.

Mr. Stox. *Moderate.* 1105 E. Katella Ave.; (714) 634–2994. A Continental à la carte menu is kept simple here, with fresh fish, aged beef, and live lobster. There is a cocktail lounge with entertainment, and non-smokers have their own "pure air" section. One of Orange County's best wine lists. Semi-dressy. Valet parking. All major credit cards.

Overland Stage and Territorial Saloon. *Moderate.* 1855 S. Harbor Blvd., in the Hilton at the Park; (714) 750–1811. The theme here is what California was like in the days of the Wild West. Roast buffalo is served nightly; boar, bear, elk, and pheasant are standard specials. The bar is from a Mississippi steamboat, and an actual Overland Stage rests atop the restaurant (this *is* Southern California, after all). Happy hour; Sunday brunch and magic acts during lunch. Casual. All major credit cards.

Acapulco. *Inexpensive.* 1410 S. Harbor Blvd.; (714) 956–7380. One of a chain of Mexican restaurants that excel in quality. Owner Ray Marshall wins a lot of awards for authentic Mexican cuisine, as well as for his creative concoctions. The cold avocado soup is a winner, the crabmeat enchiladas are a renowned specialty. Also in Garden Grove and Santa Ana. Casual. AE, MC, V.

COSTA MESA

Copa de Oro. *Expensive.* 633 Anton Blvd.; (714) 662–2672. Designed like a Mayan temple, this award-winning restaurant offers Mexican Riviera and Continental cuisine. Specialties include Carne Asada and coconut flan. Open daily for lunch and dinner, except Saturday lunch. Sunday brunch. All major credit cards.

Alfredo's. *Moderate.* The South Coast Plaza Hotel, 666 Anton Blvd.; (714) 540–1550. Set in an intimate garden courtyard, Alfredo's offers a wide selection of Italian and Continental cuisine. Veal dishes are the specialty; also featured are beef and pasta dishes. Over 200 varieties of premium California, French, and Italian wines are offered. Live entertainment. Reservations recommended. All major credit cards.

FULLERTON

The Cellar. *Expensive.* 305 N. Harbor Blvd.; (714) 525–5682. This elegant Continental restaurant is impeccably European, both in cuisine and ambiance. Featured entrees are a blend of classical Escoffier and adventurous nouvelle. An outstanding wine list. Dressy. Lunch and dinner daily, no lunch Saturday. All major credit cards.

Mandarin Pavillion. *Inexpensive.* 1050 W. Valencia; (714) 870–7950. A Chinese restaurant explosion has hit Orange County, and this place is at the forefront. Specializes in Shanghai, Peking, Szechuan, and Hunan cuisine. The wine list is good for a Chinese restaurant. There is a sister restaurant, equally good: **Mandarin Gourmet** in Costa Mesa. All major credit cards.

IRVINE

Chanteclair. *Expensive.* 18912 MacArthur Blvd.; (714) 752–8001. They seek to overwhelm. The setting is beautiful, the service is very attentive, and the wine list includes an impressive 100 labels. The cuisine is haute Continental, with an emphasis on French. The menu is à la carte. Dressy; jackets required. Lunch and dinner daily, no lunch Saturday. All major credit cards.

Le Chardonnay. *Expensive.* In the Registry Hotel, 18800 MacArthur Blvd.; (714) 752–8777. A new name and a new restaurant replace the Grand Portage. La Chardonnay, as its name suggests, is a French restaurant. Soft, muted colors and a European atmosphere make this an enjoyable dining experience. Open for lunch, dinner, and Sunday brunch. All major credit cards.

Gulliver's. *Moderate.* 18482 MacArthur Blvd.; (714) 833–8411. Part of a small quality-oriented chain. Picture yourself in jolly old England at the time of Jonathan Swift. Waitresses are "wenches" and busboys are "squires." Walls are adorned with artifacts and old prints. If you can put yourself in this picture, you'll enjoy the food. The single entree is prime rib, and it's roasted tender and juicy; you choose how thick and how well done. The service is youthful and friendly, very California. Casual. Lunch daily, except weekends. Dinner daily. MC, V.

RJ's the Rib Joint. *Moderate.* 4880 Campus Dr.; (714) 752–6023. This popular restaurant, like its Los Angeles counterpart, has ribs, chicken, steak, trout, and one of the largest salad bars around. Specialty salads and sandwiches at lunch. Open for lunch and dinner daily. All major credit cards.

The White House. *Moderate.* 887 South Anaheim Blvd.; (714) 772–1381. In a turn-of-the-century home, recently converted for dining. Features fresh fish, prime ribs, and baby-back pork ribs. Dessert specialties are Amaretto and Grand Marnier mousses. Open for lunch during the week, for dinner daily. Closed Monday. Sunday brunch from 10:00 A.M. AE, MC, V.

ORANGE

Chez Cary. *Expensive.* 571 S. Main St.; (714) 542–3595. The reputation of this Continental restaurant extends far past Orange County. Not only is the food exquisite, but the table settings include the very best china, crystal, and silver. Elegant as well as luxurious, personalized attention is the specialty. If you're a wine enthusiast, you'll love this restaurant—the wine list has 600 labels. Strolling violinist. Dressy. Dinner only. Valet parking. All major credit cards.

The Hobbit. *Expensive.* 2932 E. Chapman Ave.; (714) 997–1972. Dine your way through a charming house. Start in the wine cellar, with Champagne and hors d'oeuvres as you mingle with other guests. Dinner is a Continental multicourse affair, and your table may be in one of many different rooms. There is an intermission, so stroll through the restaurant's own art gallery, and then go on to other courses, such as New York steak with Madeira sauce and a crêpe de maison. Great fun. Dinner only. So popular that reservations must usually be made a month in advance. All major credit cards.

La Brasserie. *Moderate.* 202 S. Main St.; (714) 978–6161. This restaurant is French all the way. A multi-level house with a library-dining room. The accent is on veal and fresh fish. Always fresh vegetables and always homemade soup. A relaxed atmosphere that will not intimidate even those uninitiated in French cuisine. Semi-dressy. No DC or CB.

SANTA ANA

Saddleback Inn. *Inexpensive.* 1660 E. 1st St.; (714) 835–3311. A hacienda-style restaurant, with the decor a blend of Old Spain, Mission California, and modern Orange County. The dining rooms are decorated individually, with a touch of nostalgia. Baby back pork ribs, basted with barbecue sauce, and slow-cooked barbecued beef roast are the house specialties. Filet of sole almandine, barbecued baked chicken, and filet mignon with Bordelaise sauce are other possibilities. A vegetarian plate will be created upon request. Casual. Closed Sunday nights. All major credit cards.

NIGHTLIFE AND ENTERTAINMENT. Concerts, dinner theaters, and a wide variety of musical entertainment are to be found in the Anaheim area, as well as several discos and Country-and-Western bars. Most major hotels have entertainment. For listings in all Orange county cities, check with the Anaheim Area Visitors Bureau, the Sunday *Los Angeles Times*' Calendar section, *Los Angeles Magazine,* and *California Magazine.*

Of particular note in the area is *J.W.'s Cowboy,* a combination disco and country bar complete with large Texas-style room, dance floor, and a game room. At 1721 South Manchester Ave., Anaheim, near Katella; (714) 956–1410.

The best Orange County happy hour (an import from San Diego), weekdays but especially Friday late afternoons, is at *Rusty Pelican* seafood restaurant, 1830 Main St., Irvine; (714) 250–0366. Take the MacArthur exit from #405; the place is right across from John Wayne Orange County Airport, and is an odd building with an Aztec pyramid look. Another good drinking and meeting place is the *Crazy Horse Saloon,* visible from the Newport Freeway (#55) near #405.

Area dinner theatres include: *Curtain Call Dinner Theater,* 690 El Camino Real, in Tustin (714–838–1540); *The Grand Dinner Theater,* Grand Hotel, 7 Freedman Way, Anaheim (714–772–7710); and *Harlequin Dinner Playhouse,* 3503 S. Harbor Blvd., Santa Ana (714–979–5511). Jazz groups and choirs can be heard at The Bridges Auditorium, the Clairmont Colleges, 4th and College Way, Claremont, (714–621–8032).

The *South Coast Repertory Theater,* 655 Town Center Drive, in Costa Mesa (714–957–4033) presents plays in two different theaters—the Main Stage and the Second Stage. The professional theater company offers two seasons of plays each year. The Main Stage seats 507 people and presents 6 plays—general theater fare for the whole family, and a Christmas show each year. The Second Stage is more experimental, offers five shows each year, and seats 161 people. New shows are featured, many by local writers, and this theater has recently begun commissioning new works. The Second Stage has also received a Drama Critics Circle Award for fostering the production of new plays.

LONG BEACH SOUTH TO SAN CLEMENTE

The Coast North of San Diego County

by
MARY JANE HORTON

Mary Jane Horton writes about fitness, fashion, and travel for various national publications; she lives in Santa Monica.

South from Los Angeles, the Pacific coast has often been termed the American Riviera—but it's really something quite different. Coastal communities still almost in their infancy are growing in individuality and prosperity with each passing year. These cities once resembled "Small Town, U.S.A.," with their overabundance of fast-food establishments mixed in with a smattering of stores, one movie theater, a market—and not much more. But with Los Angeles spreading by leaps and bounds, the coastal communities have now taken on some of the richer qualities of urban life.

Beginning with Long Beach, each offers attractions and activities—cultural, historical, and physical—to please all tastes. To contrast with its unique view of technology afforded by offshore oil rigs, Long Beach is a modern, industrial city surrounded by fascinating symbols of the past. Rancho Alamitos, California's oldest standing Spanish ranch, is just a stone's throw from the innovative Long Beach Convention and Entertainment Complex.

Santa Catalina Island, 22 miles off the coast of Long Beach, is an entity unto itself—in many ways, a throwback to simpler days. A short plane ride or a four-hour boat trip takes the traveler to Catalina and a view of the way things must have been in all of southern California before its growth—clean air, green grass, and white picket fences.

Back on the mainland: Coastal Orange County boasts 42 miles of sandy beaches, secluded coves, and sheltered harbors. The "beach boy" atmosphere is prevalent starting in Huntington Beach, where visitors get a feel for this phenomenon whenever the ocean swells: Warm or cold, winter or summer, fair-haired boys and girls of all ages run to the waves with their surf boards ready.

Alongside many of the beaches are new cultural establishments. Some of the coastal cities have their own museums; more and more art

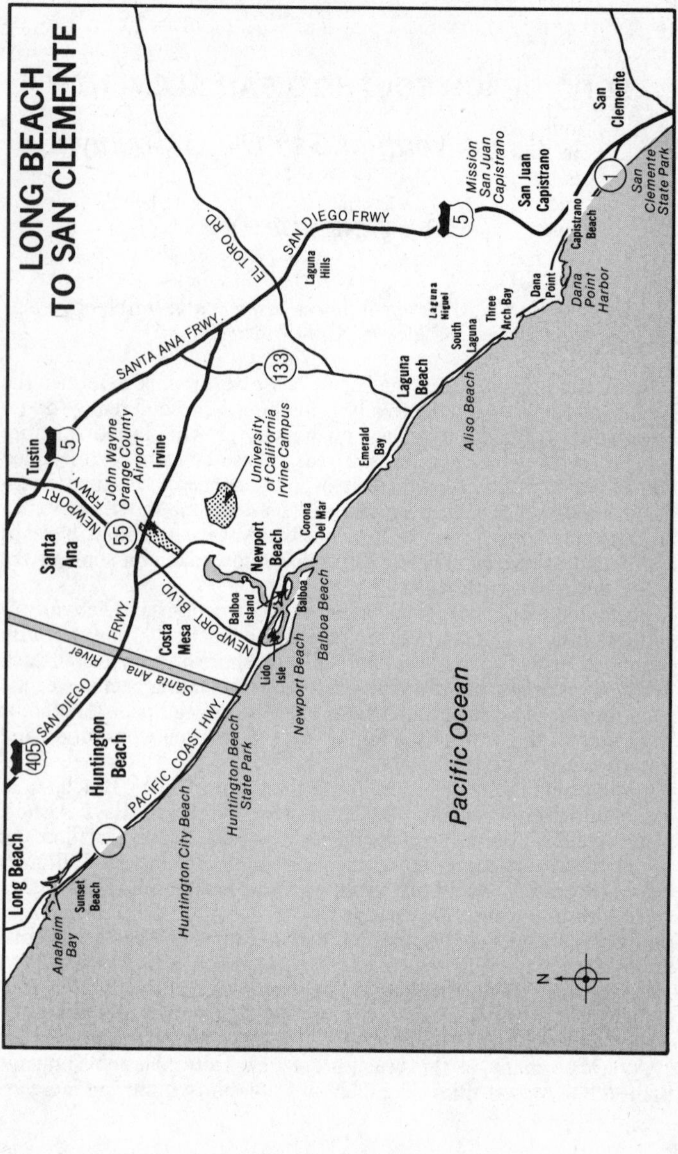
LONG BEACH
TO SAN CLEMENTE
Long Beach
Anaheim Bay
Sunset Beach
Huntington Beach
405
SAN DIEGO
FRWY.
PACIFIC COAST HWY.
1
Huntington City Beach
Huntington Beach State Park
Santa Ana River
Costa Mesa
NEWPORT BLVD.
Santa Ana
55
NEWPORT FRWY.
Tustin
5
John Wayne Orange County Airport
Irvine
SANTA ANA FRWY.
133
University of California Irvine Campus
Balboa Island
Newport Beach
Lido Isle
Balboa
Newport Beach
Balboa Beach
Corona Del Mar
Emerald Bay
Laguna Beach
Aliso Beach
South Laguna
Laguna Niguel
Three Arch Bay
Laguna Hills
EL TORO RD.
SAN DIEGO FRWY
5
Mission San Juan Capistrano
San Juan Capistrano
Dana Point
Dana Point Harbor
Capistrano Beach
1
San Clemente
San Clemente State Park
Pacific Ocean
N

galleries and small theater groups are popping up all the time. Fanciful recreations of fishing villages are also in good supply—take a look at Ports O' Call Village in San Pedro, Fisherman's Village (under construction in Long Beach), and the Dana Point Harbor.

Farther down the coast, the cities of Newport Beach and Laguna Beach, although smaller than Long Beach, have an important role. They are the "big cities" of their area, surrounded by much smaller communities. Newport has an impressive roster of businesses—retail, industrial, and financial—and Laguna Beach has long been known as an artists' colony. Dana Point, just south of Laguna, is an up-and-coming area as it starts to catch some of Laguna's overflow visitors and residents. San Juan Capistrano takes us back in time again, with its inspiring mission. And San Clemente is, of course, well known as the site of Richard Nixon's Western White House, Casa Pacifica.

Long Beach

Long Beach, at present, is undergoing a dramatic facelift. In a surge of redevelopment, six city blocks have been removed to make way for a hundred-million-dollar shopping mall; this is only part of a rejuvenation project totaling more than one billion dollars. The plan will eventually produce one-and-one-half million square feet of office and retail space, hotels, and residential projects.

Part of the redevelopment has resulted in the creation of two new marinas. One contains 1,700 boat slips and the other 131. Both marinas are located adjacent to the Long Beach Convention and Entertainment Center. Shoreline Village, which opened in June, 1983, is a large attraction with restaurants, shops, and a restored carousel dating back to 1906. Slips are available for cruise-up shoppers. A water-ferry shuttle connects the village with area hotels. Shoreline Park completes the picture with fishing, boat rentals, jogging and bicycle paths, and a seaside RV campground.

The Long Beach Convention and Entertainment Center was recently refurbished and now houses one of the major performing arts facilities in Southern California, with its gigantic Terrace Theater, the smaller, elegant Center Theater, and an expansive 90,000-square-foot exhibition hall. In 1984 the center hosted two Olympic events—volleyball and fencing. Howard Hughes's famous huge flying boat, the *Spruce Goose,* is another addition to the city of Long Beach, housed alongside the formidable *Queen Mary* in a 12-story aluminum dome. The seaplane, which was hidden for nearly 40 years, is wood and has a wing span of 319 feet. Multimedia displays surrounding the plane explain its history; Howard Hughes memorabilia are also on view.

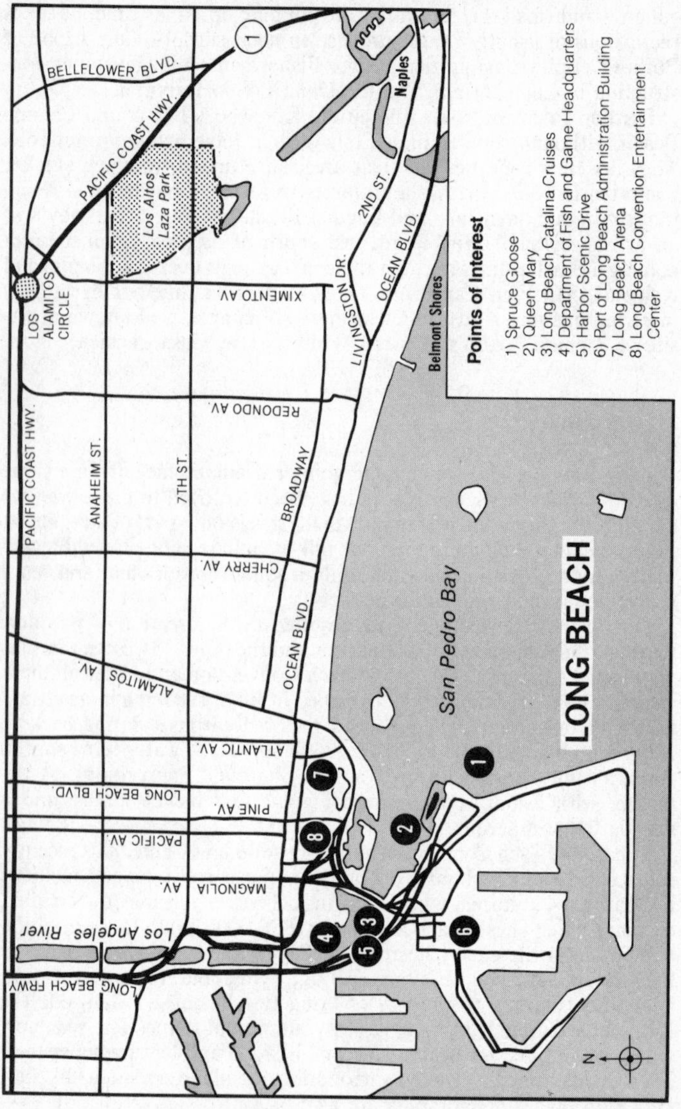
LONG BEACH
Points of Interest
1) Spruce Goose
2) Queen Mary
3) Long Beach Catalina Cruises
4) Department of Fish and Game Headquarters
5) Harbor Scenic Drive
6) Port of Long Beach Administration Building
7) Long Beach Arena
8) Long Beach Convention Entertainment Center
San Pedro Bay
Belmont Shores
Naples
Los Altos Laza Park
LOS ALAMITOS CIRCLE
PACIFIC COAST HWY.
BELLFLOWER BLVD.
ANAHEIM ST.
7TH ST.
BROADWAY
OCEAN BLVD.
LIVINGSTON DR.
2ND ST.
XIMENTO AV.
REDONDO AV.
CHERRY AV.
ALAMITOS AV.
ATLANTIC AV.
LONG BEACH BLVD
PINE AV.
PACIFIC AV.
MAGNOLIA AV.
Los Angeles River
LONG BEACH FRWY
N

So much for the new. Throughout the city, one can look at the architecture and feel the flavor of the Spanish California of yesterday. Fine examples of Spanish residential architecture line Ocean Boulevard —pink and white stucco buildings with immaculately groomed grounds. Two traditional Spanish ranches are open to the public: Rancho Los Alamitos, the oldest standing adobe structure of its type in California, which was built in 1806, and Rancho Los Cerritos, constructed in 1844, which is now a museum/reference library furnished with pieces dating back to the early 1800s.

In nearby San Pedro, visitors get a taste of the world's most famous seaports, such as Singapore and Marseilles, at Ports O'Call Village; the Whale's Wharf is a replica of a New England seaport with quaint cobblestone streets and shops brimming with exotic fare.

Of course, no description of Long Beach is complete without mention of the venerable *Queen Mary.* This most luxurious of luxury liners (built in 1934 at a cost of 48 million dollars) is completely intact, from the extensive wood paneling to the gleaming nickel- and silver-plated handrails and the hand-cut glass. Once the largest, fastest ocean liner on the seas, the *Queen* is now permanently moored at the southern end of the Long Beach Freeway. Tours through the ship are available; guests are invited to browse the 12 decks and witness close-up the bridge, the staterooms, officer's quarters, and engine rooms. Also aboard the *Queen* is The Living Sea, a marine museum created by Jacques Cousteau, where visitors share Cousteau's vision for a futuristic undersea city. Long Beach is also the starting point for a restful and luxurious cruise to Mexico, on the S.S. *Azure Seas,* if one is so inclined.

Palos Verdes Peninsula, a bit north of Long Beach, offers a special treat for the kids: Marineland of the Pacific is a unique park located on a particularly scenic stretch of the coast on Palos Verdes Drive South. In the Family Adventure Swim, the first of its kind in any park, guests paddle among 4,000 fish in a half-million gallon tank. Sea lions romp at Sea Lion Point, and the new Touch Tank allows visitors to feel sea anemones, starfish, sea urchins, and more. Killer whales, dolphins, pilot whales, and sea lions star in regularly scheduled shows.

Santa Catalina Island

On a clear day, if you look out to sea from Long Beach, you'll be able to pinpoint a gleaming spot in the Pacific. This gem is Santa Catalina Island, only 22 miles from Long Beach and, therefore, easily accessible by plane or boat. (See *How to Get There* below.) Originally named San Salvador, this island was discovered and claimed for Spain by Cabrillo in 1542. In 1892, San Salvador was purchased and incorporated into the Santa Catalina Company; present ownership stems from stock purchases made by William Wrigley, Jr., in 1919. The Santa Catalina Island Conservancy, a nonprofit foundation, acquired title to 42,135 acres, or 86 percent of Catalina, in 1974. Through this agreement the island's natural resources are preserved and conserved while public access to recreational opportunities is increased. Hopefully, the agreement will also help to preserve the fresh, old-fashioned country flavor that still pervades the island.

Avalon is the island's only city; Avalon Bay is the site of its most famous attraction—the Casino Building (constructed in 1929 by William Wrigley, Jr.), housing an art gallery, museum, motion picture theater, and ballroom. Guided tours are offered daily.

An array of outdoor activities awaits Catalina visitors. Coastal cruises around the island often pass Seal Rock, where the mammals bark and ham it up for their audience. A glass-bottom boat tour cruises the California State Marine Preserve for a look at the local undersea life, which includes foot-long saltwater goldfish, electric perch, and other unusual species of fish. From May through September, divers take a closer glance at what these waters have to offer.

May through September is also flying-fish season. On another tour, which can be arranged by the local Chamber of Commerce (213–510–1520), a boat equipped with 40-million-candlepower searchlights allows the best view of Catalina's beautiful iridescent flying fish. Soaring out of the water—sometimes as much as 75 yards—these flying fish even land in passing boats from time to time.

Bus tours view other parts of the island, including the 66 square miles of mountainous interior; El Rancho Escondido features performances by pure-bred Arabian horses and wild animals—buffalo, deer, goat, and boar—that wander unhindered in the interior. A tour of the Wrigley Memorial and Botanical Garden is available. Some visitors pursue golf, tennis, fishing, boating, diving, and hiking, while others just take it easy soaking up the sun. Any visit to Catalina is also usually filled with much rambling down the main street sampling the taffy, frozen bananas and other treats.

Huntington Beach

Back on the mainland, and traveling south: The first city you encounter is Huntington Beach. If you come from inland, you'll know you're close when you see the oil derricks. Surfers flock to Huntington Beach; the long pier is a good vantage point from which to watch these dare-devils. This city is also the site of annual surfing competitions in September. Huntington Harbor boasts Orange County's first marina-city: eight separate islands are bordered by concrete bulkheads. The novel waterfronts and water-view homes are a delight to see.

Nearby, Bolsa Chica Ecological Reserve is a must-see for an education on the area's natural environment. Under the management of the California Department of Fish and Game, Bolsa Chica is a protected wetland where visitors witness nature at her best. On Pacific Coast Highway, two miles north of the Golden West exit off the San Diego Freeway (Route 405), the reserve has a mile-long loop trail. The Amigos de Bolsa Chica give tours October through March on the first Saturday of the month.

The coastal wetland, or salt marsh, is home to 100 different animal species. Among various birds are such unlikely sounding creatures as the great blue heron and the common egret. Five endangered species are protected here as well: the light-footed clapper rail, the brown pelican, the peregrine falcon, the California least tern, and the Beldings Spanish sparrow. Some of these birds nest on the two man-made islands. The reserve is still undergoing a restoration, and eventually a total of 150 acres will be turned back to tidelands. At the end of the reserve, you may fish for round stingrays, smooth-hounded shark, topsmelt, and yellow-finned croaker.

Newport Beach

Newport Beach, one of Orange County's oldest communities, is the area's bastion of high society. Numerous yacht and country clubs host a wealth of debutante balls, weddings, and charity functions. Newport began as a small shipping center and vacation spot, but today it is world famous as a recreational community. Newport Harbor is one of the world's busiest small-boat harbors, home to more than 9,000 pleasure crafts.

Many integral parts of Newport's history are still alive today. A 3-car ferry still shuttles cars and passengers between Balboa Island and the peninsula—the Balboa Island Ferry, a bit of history and novelty in Orange County, crosses the main channel from Palm Street to Agate Street and vice versa. Service first began in 1909 due to the necessity of transportation and convenience for the locals. It was then owned and operated by the Wilson Brothers, and was eventually purchased by Joseph Beck, whose family still owns the ferry.

Tourists and locals alike make use of this mode of transportation because it cuts driving distances down 6½ miles and, rather than walking across the Balboa Island Bridge, it gives a scenic main view of the harbor.

Cost is 55 cents for car and driver; 20 cents for each additional adult passenger, and 10 cents for each child. Detailed information on the ferry is available by calling (714) 673–1070.

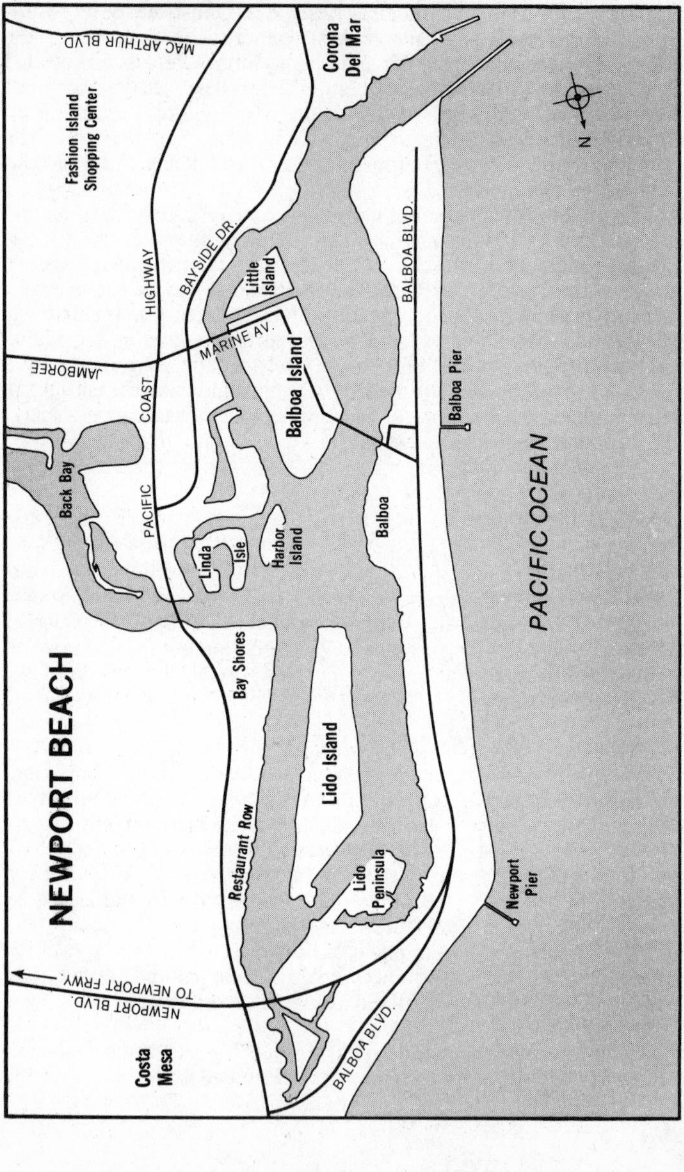
NEWPORT BEACH
Fashion Island Shopping Center
MAC ARTHUR BLVD.
Corona Del Mar
N
PACIFIC COAST HIGHWAY
BAYSIDE DR.
JAMBOREE
MARINE AV.
Little Island
Balboa Island
BALBOA BLVD.
Balboa Pier
Back Bay
Linda Isle
Harbor Island
Balboa
PACIFIC OCEAN
Bay Shores
Lido Island
Restaurant Row
Lido Peninsula
Newport Pier
TO NEWPORT FRWY.
NEWPORT BLVD.
Costa Mesa
BALBOA BLVD.

To get to Balboa Island from Los Angeles, take either the #5 or #405 Freeway south to Newport Beach Freeway #55 west. Then take the Pacific Coast Highway south to Jamboree, and right entering Balboa Island. On Balboa Island frozen banana stands thrive on every corner. (It is said that the frozen banana, dipped in chocolate and rolled in nuts, originated here.)

Another remaining bit of the past is the Dory Fishing Fleet, which still operates at its turn-of-the-century location at Newport Pier. The completely restored Balboa Pavilion serves as a terminal for steamers delivering people to and from Santa Catalina Island. The former South Coast Ship Yard has also been restored as a bayside restaurant; and the Newport Harbor Yacht Club is the oldest sailing club on the harbor.

Before its growth, this area was a cattle ranch above an uncharted estuary, and the Balboa Peninsula was a natural landlocked harbor. It was not until Spanish land grants were sold in the 1860s that this sleepy area began to change. In 1879, Newport received more attention when the sternwheeler, the *Vaquero* from San Diego, started making local stops to take on hide, tallow, livestock, and grain from the Irvine Ranch. Captain S.S. Dunnels is credited with naming the community "New Port."

In 1876, the jetty area was dredged, making it easier for boats to enter the channel, and in 1888, today's Newport Pier was built. In the 19th century, the Santa Ana River was diverted from the lower bay; deep channels and turning basins were dredged, marshlands filled, and the entrance stabilized by two jetties. In 1906, Newport Beach was incorporated as a city.

Today, Newport Beach has more than 60,000 permanent residents, with summer visitors averaging between 20,000 and 100,000 a day. Newport encompasses a total area of 37.5 square miles: 15.5 square miles of land, 1.9 square miles of bay, and 20.1 square miles of ocean.

During the Christmas holidays, a spectacular boat parade finds vessels ablaze with lights and holiday decorations. Balboa Pavilion is the hub of activity. To get there from Los Angeles, take the San Diego Freeway #405 to the Newport Freeway #55 south to the end. This freeway will eventually become Newport Boulevard. Take Newport Boulevard to the end, and bear left onto Balboa Boulevard. Drive two miles to Main Street and turn left. Balboa Pavilion is straight ahead. For information, call (714) 673–5245.

The annual Flight of the Snowbirds in Newport Harbor, the largest small boat race on earth, has been dazzling Pavilion-goers since the first regatta in 1926. Now held in June, this race includes about 150 little Snowbird-class catboats, usually skippered by young people.

The Pavilion was also a hot spot during the days of the big bands—Count Basie, Benny Goodman, and Stan Kenton all played there. An annual dance, the Balboa Hop, commemorates all the "swingers" that once graced the dancing hall.

Sportfishing in modern, comfortable boats is available daily at the Pavilion. And December through February, passengers aboard the whale-watching boats witness the giant gray whale as he passes by on his migratory route. On these trips other marine creatures, such as seagulls, pelicans, pilot whales, and porpoises, can be seen as well. During the summer, the *Pavilion Queen* riverboat leaves each day for a fully narrated cruise of the harbor. Smaller skiffs may be hired for individual rentals throughout the year.

Corona del Mar, just south of Newport Center, is a quaint little town with a lovely state beach. The shopping area, on Coast Highway, has a nautical flavor, and the renovated Eaglet building boasts new, fanciful shops. Sherman Library and Gardens, down the road a bit, is an unusual little stop; this "library cum botanical garden," extremely inviting for browsing, is also the site of many chic social gatherings.

Laguna Beach

Nestled along the shore, among the cliffs, Laguna Beach, with its Saint-Tropez-like flavor, is perhaps the most beautiful of all southern California cities. Bounded by beach for about five miles, the city's 3,328 acres provide a panoramic setting for hillside residents and beauty-seeking travelers.

Entering from the north, you can imbibe one of the most enchanting views of the Pacific; at the same time, stop at the Sunshine Cove roadside stand for a luscious date shake, which may quench your physical thirst with flair. As you travel along Pacific Coast Highway, the ocean glistens on the right. Waves pound against rocks, and the memory of the colorful homes chiseled into the surrounding hills will stay with you forever. On the approach to town lie two of Laguna's most prestigious ocean-side residential areas, Irvine Cove and Emerald Bay.

Farther along, Heisler Park is among the cliffs above the ocean; the Laguna Beach Museum of Art adjacent to the park. Walking south from the park takes you to Main Beach and the center of town. The blue-and-white lifeguard stand and boardwalk are landmarks among the exciting boutiques that fill the streets to the north, east, and south of Laguna's Main Beach.

Laguna's name was applied to this area in the late 1800s by the Indians; *lagonas* means lake, and so the community was named after the town's two freshwater lagoons. Since its incorporation as a city in 1827, Laguna has been widely known as an artists' colony. The Festival of the Arts, an annual event (July and August) that began 40 years ago, insures the city's long-time reputation as a thriving environment for artists and craftspeople.

In the 1960s the city was a haven for hippies; Timothy Leary and other period celebrities hung out at the Taco Bell on Pacific Coast Highway. To this day, a unique mixture of people is drawn to Laguna; the 18,000 permanent residents range in type from rich and famous to countercultural and eccentric.

An enormous likeness of "town greeter" Eiler Larson lends a pleasant historical touch. For years, this friendly man stood on the Coast Highway at the edge of town shouting salutations to everyone who passed by. His "How are you?" and "Leaving so soon?" could be heard eight hours a day as Larson did his job for "the love of Laguna." After his death six years ago, a statue was erected showing his hands eternally outstretched to Laguna visitors. Remarkably enough, a new greeter, looking amazingly like the original, has recently appeared at the entrance to town.

To the outside world, much of Laguna's popularity is linked to the different festivals presented throughout the year. The Festival of the Arts, and the Pageant of the Masters—a human recreation of famous paintings—run concurrently with the Sawdust Festival and Art-a-Fair for six weeks in July and August. All these events combine to present myriad arts and crafts at various prices. February's Winter Festival offers an artist and craftsman fair, a poetry festival, and the Patriot's Day Parade.

Even when no events are scheduled, there's always something to do in Laguna. Quaint boutiques and small malls, packed full with unique stores, prove more than a worthwhile investment of time for those who like to shop. Prices are not always a bargain, but an abundance of items are available that otherwise may be difficult to find. The antique shops, bookstores, craft shops, and art galleries are outstanding, and more goldsmiths and jewelers per square foot fill Laguna than in any other city in the country. As far as restaurants go, there is one for every taste and pocketbook from one end of town to the other.

In the summer, when the crowds gather, a free cable-car-inspired bus runs the length of town. Visitors arrive from all corners of the country, and for this reason it's a good idea to book hotel rooms as far ahead of the busy season as possible.

The Laguna Beach Museum of Art, built in 1972, is a regional institution concerned with community needs. An outgrowth of the Laguna Beach Art Association, founded in 1918, it also tries to carry on that organization's promise: "to advance knowledge of and interest in art, to maintain a permanent art collection, and to create a spirit of cooperation and fellowship between painter and the public"—a truly southern California credo. The art highlights California and the Pacific

Coast from 1900 to the present. Since the museum has quite a large collection, and space is limited, exhibitions are frequently changed.

Visit the shoreline to see what inspired much of this scenic art. Exploring the town's beaches and coves, you will learn the different areas and their different purposes. Main Beach is the center of downtown activity, usually teeming with interesting people from around the world. To get away from the crowds, there is Woods Cove—with rocks to hide behind, to climb on, and to use as a look-out for lurking crabs.

Climbing the steps from Wood's Cove, look up: You'll see a stunning English-style mansion, once the home of film star Bette Davis. When the surf's up, find Salt Creek—that's where the action is. And, for some general relaxation in the sun and sand, you've got quite a choice: A beach or cove awaits you at the end of almost every east-west street in Laguna.

Dana Point

Dana Point is the next stop as you travel south along the coast. A city on the rise, this community is growing in popularity partially because it's so close to Laguna Beach.

Richard Henry Dana, Jr., the city's namesake, tells a bit of history in his book, *Two Years Before the Mast,* as he recalls how cattle hides tossed over surrounding cliffs by Spanish Californian rancheros and Capistrano mission padres were loaded onto trade ships, thus giving the port its start.

Dana also describes the beautiful cove, now the setting of Dana Point Harbor: "There was a grandeur in everything around . . . as refreshing as a great rock in a weary land . . . I experienced a glow of pleasure in finding what of poetry and romance I ever had in me." Dana ended a long ocean voyage at the Point in the 1830s; a bronze statue of the author-seaman sits alongside the harbor today.

When square-rigged sailing ships were in port, Dana Point was the major trading post between Santa Barbara and San Diego. Its new reincarnation has once again taken shape in an enchanting trading port. Mariner's Village sits on the harbor with the backdrop of colorful boats and unique Dana Wharf shops. They share the waterfront with a sportfishing fleet, seagulls, and pelicans. Two marinas are home port to more than 2,500 yachts; for sailors, this is one of southern California's easiest and least crowded marinas to navigate—despite the numerous seals who play on a buoy not far from the harbor.

On the sandy, siltwater swimming beach, kyacks and paddleboats are available for rent. The Orange County Marine Institute conducts tours and offers educational information on tide pools in the area; a replica of Richard Henry Dana's ship, the *Pilgrim,* is on hand to explore. The Dana Point Lighthouse boasts nautical memorabilia. From December through March, whale watching is a popular pastime. Next to the harbor, Doheny State Beach's expansive campgrounds border excellent picnic areas and a picturesque park perfect for long walks or extensive bicycle treks.

San Juan Capistrano

Well known for its historic Mission San Juan Capistrano, this city is also blessed with a breathtaking coastline. The imposing Spanish mission, not far from the coast, is summer home to millions of migrating swallows; these famous birds arrive around St. Joseph's Day, March 19, and go on their way around St. John's Day, October 23. It's a mystery of nature why these swallows unerringly return to Capistrano each year after wintering in Argentina; it has been that way, though, since the mission was built in 1776 by Father Junipero Serra.

Seventh in a chain of California missions established by Franciscan friars, Mission San Juan Capistrano served as the focal point for local Juanero Indians, who were converted to Christianity and taught to raise crops and tend livestock. Because of increasing activity there, by 1797 the mission had outgrown its first chapel and thus the Stone Church was erected. This structure's architecture was awesome: It was said to have had seven domes and a belltower rising from an ornately arched roof. Sadly, the church was destroyed by an earthquake only a few years after its completion. Although Stone Church has never been rebuilt, there is now ongoing construction at the site; completion date for the new church is set for the end of July, 1984.

After Mexico received its independence from Spain in 1821, the mission was confiscated. The ceding of California to the U.S., the gold rush, and California's statehood in 1850 brought about many more changes. The Catholic Church requested the return of Mission San Juan Capistrano and was granted such by Abraham Lincoln in 1865. (The original grant is stored safely in the Mission archives, but a copy is on display in the vestment room.) In 1895, a Los Angeles historical club reroofed the remaining buildings to prevent further decay, but the real restoration came in 1910 with the arrival Father John O' Sullivan. New gardens were planted and foundations and walkways were built. The Serra Chapel was restored in 1924; it now holds a gilded altar from Barcelona.

In November, 1976, in honor of the mission's 200th birthday, and coinciding with the nation's bicentennial, the entire west wing of Mission San Juan Capistrano's quadrangle was rebuilt.

The mission's almost mystical atmosphere must have been the same throughout history. The sheer tranquility and simple character of mission life in old Spanish California comes to life as you walk through the grounds and buildings. Excavation on mission grounds continues to unearth other elements of the past; artifacts, tools, and vestments from these diggings are shown in the vestment room and museum. Self-guided tours by tape-recorder are available, and a visitors bureau with extensive information on the area has recently been established inside the mission.

Swallows arriving from their long journey add even another element of beauty to this enchanted place. The first official mention of the swallows is an entry in the Mission Archives, dated St. Joseph's Day, 1777: "Today, the *pjaritos* returned to the area. The Indians, being joyous over their return, put part of their welcoming ceremony into their evening singing in the neighboring village."

The swallows arrive like clockwork each March; they stay throughout the summer to bear their young and teach them to fly. In October, they're off again to Argentina where it's springtime. One popular legend about the swallows says that these birds come from the Holy Land, carrying in their beaks twigs that are used as a kind of open-air aviary to rest on the ocean, mid-flight. The popular song, *When the Swallows Return to Capistrano,* written by Leon Rene in 1939, etched the mission and its famous swallows into the minds of people throughout the world.

San Juan Capistrano has other historical attractions besides the mission. A restored Santa Fe railroad station, circa 1895, serves as the combination Amtrak terminal and restaurant, the Capistrano Depot. Old adobe buildings, such as the Los Rios Adobe, are also abundant in the area.

San Clemente

As they pass the awesome San Onofre nuclear plant on the coast between San Juan Capistrano's beautiful old mission and San Clemente, travelers may get a strange feeling that the future is, indeed, here. Surfers in the water near the plant confirm that this is, for certain, Southern California.

The San Onofre Nuclear Information Center is a fascinating stop for those interested in learning more about the mechanics of nuclear energy. Displays and self-operated exhibits explain the conversion of an atom into the generation of electricity. Uses of nuclear energy are shown in a film.

San Clemente is probably best remembered as the site of President Nixon's Western White House. This residence, Casa Pacifica, regularly made the news during Nixon's years in office. A Nixon library is slated to be built nearby.

San Clemente also offers more of what makes the beach cities of Southern California proud: lots of sun, fun, and sports activities. Swimming, surfing, sailing, fishing, golfing, and tennis reign among other recreational activities throughout the city. Skeet and trap shooting, lawn bowling, and picnicking are also popular.

The next 20 miles down the coast are lined with the Marine barracks of Camp Pendleton, the country's largest Marine Corps base. Training here involves offshore landing; overland treks are conducted through the camp's three mountain ranges, five lakes, and more than 250 miles of roads. Camp Pendleton was a troop take-off point for the Pacific in World War II, and during the Korean and Vietnam wars.

The next town south is Oceanside, in San Diego County.

PRACTICAL INFORMATION FOR LONG BEACH SOUTH TO SAN CLEMENTE

HOW TO GET THERE. By car. From Los Angeles, the San Diego Freeway (Interstate 405) is the fastest way to get to the coastal cities. There is an exit—or multiple exits—for each city; the way to each city is clearly marked. Long Beach has more than nine exits. Huntington Beach can be reached by going west on Beach Blvd. (Route 39) off Route 405. Newport Beach is accessible from the freeway at the Newport Freeway (Route 55), again west. For Laguna Beach, exit at Laguna Canyon Road (Route 133) and go west. Pacific Coast Highway (Route 1) follows the coast, and is probably the easiest way to get to the cities south of Laguna. (It joins U.S. 5—freeway to San Diego—going south at Capistrano Beach.) From San Diego, get off U.S. 5 onto Rte. 1 at Capistrano Beach. For people who like a leisurely drive along stretches of some of the country's most magnificent scenery, Pacific Coast Highway (Rte. 1) follows the coast through all of these cities.

By train. Downtown Los Angeles' Union Station, at 800 North Alameda, offers train service to both Santa Ana and San Juan Capistrano. The station—an attraction itself with its 52-foot-high ceilings and beautiful carved wood—is one of the last grand railroad stations in this country. For Amtrak scheduling and information in Los Angeles, call (213) 624–0171; in San Diego, call (619) 239–9021 for information on Orange County coastal destinations.

By bus. From Santa Ana, the Orange County Transit Department (OCTD) (714–636–7433) has bus service to Newport Beach. From San Juan Capistrano, there's a southbound bus that stops in San Clemente. Southern California Rapid Transit buses (213–626–4455) leave the downtown Los Angeles terminal (at 6th and Los Angeles Sts.) for various southern destinations. To travel to Long Beach, get the #456 going east on 7th St., or in Beverly Hills, take the #20, which goes west on Wilshire Blvd. To go farther south from the downtown Los Angeles terminal, take bus #800. This leaves approximately 10 and 40 minutes after each hour. The #800 takes you to Knott's Berry Farm, and from there take the #29 bus to Beach Blvd. West. The #29 travels to Huntington Beach. To go south from there, take the #1 bus south. For Long Beach Transit, call (213) 591–2301.

For private bus information, call *Greyhound* at (213) 394–5433 (Los Angeles) or (619) 239–9171 (San Diego) or *Gray Line* at (213) 481–2121 (Los Angeles) or (619) 231–9922 (San Diego).

By boat. Boats to Catalina Island run from San Pedro and Long Beach. Call Catalina Cruises at (213) 775–6111. For the Catalina Express from San Pedro call (213) 519–1212. Service is also available from Newport Beach through Catalina Passenger Service at (714) 673–5245, leaving from Balboa Pavilion.

By air. Catalina is accessible by air on a regularly scheduled basis. Call Helitrans Commuter at (213) 548–1314. Charter services are available at the airport as well.

For more information on general air transportation to the area, see the "How to Get There" section for the City.

TELEPHONES. The area code for the cities south along the coast from Long Beach to San Clemente vary. In Long Beach and Santa Catalina Island, the area code is 213; south from there, in Huntington Beach, Newport Beach, Laguna Beach, Dana Point, San Juan Capistrano and San Clemente, the area code is 714. Parts of the county, however, have been changed to a 619 area code; if in doubt, check with the operator.

You do not need to dial the area code if it is the same as the one from which you are calling. For directory assistance, dial 411. When direct-dialing a long-distance number from any of these cities, you must dial the number "1" (one) *before* you dial the area code and the number itself. An operator will assist you on person-to-person, credit cards, and collect calls if you dial "0" first. Pay telephones now cost 20 cents.

CLIMATE. The coastal area boasts the best of southern California's renowned weather. Devoid of the city smog, this area is also quite a few degrees cooler than inland areas when summer temperatures rise. Also cooler in the winter, the coast can be brisk in the first three months of the year—almost like the New England seaside at times. Temperatures can drop as low as the high 30s and low 40s, especially in the evenings, so be sure to bring a warm sweater or jacket this time of year. However, winter days can also be temperate, climbing up into the 60s. The ususal temperature for other times of year ranges from the mid-60s to mid-70s (with occasional overcast periods during late spring).

The hottest and most uncomfortable weather is definitely a product of a local weather phenomenon called the Santa Ana winds. These dry winds which blow in September and early October create a bothersome dry, hot condition. The line "it never rains in southern California" is not totally true; yet there are some years in which hardly any rain falls. Rainstorms are heaviest in January and February, and sometimes it can storm continuously for a week at a time. June, which some might think to be the beginning of summer, can be disappointing by the coast. Foggy mornings can be deceptive, but often the sun comes burning through around mid-day. The water temperature is cool until July and then stays in the area of the mid-60s until October.

HOTELS AND MOTELS. Since Southern California is the perfect vacation spot, hotels and motels of all description are plentiful. Many are on the ocean, and most operate swimming pools, year-round. Many establishments have seasonal rates, so during winter months you can often find a bargain. Some properties also require a certain length of stay during the busy season—a minimum of three days often must be booked in the summer. To be on the safe side, be sure to call well ahead of your intended visit.

The following is a selection of hotels and motels in the area. Price categories for double occupancy rooms in this region are: *Super Deluxe,* over $70; *Deluxe,* \$50–\$69; *Expensive,* \$40–\$49; *Moderate,* \$30–\$39; and *Inexpensive,* $30 and under. Ranges quoted are for summer season; off-season rates are often considerably lower. For a more complete explanation of categories refer to the "Facts at Your Fingertips" section at the front of this book.

LONG BEACH

The Breakers Hotel. *Super Deluxe.* 210 E. Ocean Blvd.; (800) 221–8941, (213) 432–8781. This completely renovated, 1926 hotel brings Long Beach's elegant past to the present. Ocean views. Two restaurants. Three lounges. Entertainment.

Queen Mary Hotel. *Super Deluxe.* Pier J, at the end of the Long Beach Fwy.; (213) 435–4747 or (800) 421–3732. The *Queen Mary,* one of the most luxurious of luxury liners, has been moored and now serves as a hotel. Staterooms on the ship are guest rooms; guests feel as if they are traveling far and wide though they never leave the pier. The view of the Long Beach skyline is also spectacular. Several restaurants offer gourmet cuisine. Cocktail lounges, entertainment, and shops.

Queensway Bay Hilton. *Super Deluxe.* 700 Queensway Dr.; (213) 435–7676. With its own marina, this hotel has moorings for 100 boats; an additional 100 are planned for the near-future. Many rooms have partial or full marina views. *Adolph's Restaurant* at the hotel is one of the most popular in town. Nightly entertainment. Swimming pool.

Hyatt Regency Long Beach. *Super Deluxe.* 200 S. Pine Ave.; (213) 491–1234; (800) 228–9000. This new resort, across from the downtown marina, has pool, spa, restaurant, and lounge. Business services are also available.

Hyatt Edgewater at Long Beach Marina. *Deluxe.* 6400 E. Pacific Coast Hwy.; (800) 228–9000 or (213) 434–8451. A new section of this hotel offers first-floor rooms with beautiful garden views. The marina-hotel has a coffee shop, restaurant, and lounge.

Golden Sails Inn (Best Western). *Deluxe.* 6285 E. Pacific Coast Hwy.; (800) 528–1234 or (213) 596–1631. Close to the marina, this hotel has a 24-hour restaurant, the *Olive Tree,* and a restaurant-lounge with entertainment. Swimming pool.

Ramada Inn. *Expensive.* 5325 E. Pacific Coast Hwy.; (800) 228–2828 or (213) 597–1341. This member of the familiar chain is close to the ocean. The *Governor's Restaurant* features a piano bar. Swimming pool.

Rochelle's Motel. *Expensive.* 3333 Lakewood Blvd.; (213) 421–8215. Kitchen facilities come with many of the rooms at this motel. Restaurant, entertainment, and swimming pool.

SANTA CATALINA ISLAND

Las Casitas. *Super Deluxe.* P.O. Box 4215, Long Beach 90804; (213) 590–8484. In Avalon, adjacent to the golf course, this hotel is made up of 34 individual studio, one- and two-bedroom cottages or casitas. All units offer full kitchens. Pool, tennis courts, color television.

Hotel Catalina. *Super Deluxe.* 129 Whittley Ave., Avalon; (213) 510–0027. In a residential area, half a block from the beach, the Hotel Catalina offers a choice of rooms and cottages. The charming old-style inn also has a spa, spacious sun patio, free movie theater, and free baggage storage and change lockers.

Villa Portofino. *Super Deluxe.* 111 Crescent; (213) 510–0555. Often called the best-designed hotel in Avalon, this hotel boasts a restaurant, sun deck, and art gallery. It is a popular honeymoon retreat with appropriate accommodations for newly-married couples.

Zane Grey Pueblo Hotel. *Super Deluxe.* P.O. Box 216, Los Angeles 90704; (213) 510–0966. Former home of the famous novelist; the view is fantastic from this hotel. Swimming pool, complimentary toast and coffee, courtesy bus, and television in lobby.

Atwater Hotel. *Expensive.* P.O. Box 4215, Long Beach 90804; (213) 590–8484. Avalon's largest hotel, with 100 rooms. Family oriented; half block from the beach.

HUNTINGTON BEACH

Best Western Huntington Beach Inn. *Deluxe.* 21112 Ocean Ave.; (714) 536–1421. This inn is across the street from the beach, complete with a pool, a restaurant and lounge, and a three-par golf course.

Huntington Shores Motor Hotel. *Deluxe.* 21002 Ocean Ave. (on California Route 1); (714) 536–8861. Pleasant rooms can be found in this motel, which is located across from the beach. Some rooms face the Pacific. Restaurant nearby; heated pool.

NEWPORT BEACH

Hotel Meridien Newport Beach. *Super Deluxe.* 4500 MacArthur Blvd.; (714) 476–2001, (800) 223–9918. Located in the Koll Center, this new, ultramodern hotel is built pyramid style, with a 6-story atrium lobby. Concierge service, gourmet restaurant, cafe, lounge, two snack bars. Health club with Jacuzzi, pool, tennis courts.

Marriott Hotel and Tennis Club. *Super Deluxe.* 900 Newport Center Dr.; (714) 640–4000, (800) 228–9290. A beautiful atrium surrounded by fountains is the trademark of this hotel. A large swimming pool overlooks an adjacent golf course that can be used by guests. Ocean view from the pool as well as from some of the rooms. Fashion Island, a popular shopping area, is across the street. Ten lighted tennis courts, Jacuzzi, two restaurants, a lounge, and entertainment.

The Newporter Resort. *Super Deluxe.* 1107 Jamboree Rd.; (714) 644–1700, (800) 341–1474. Guests have access to the John Wayne Tennis Club on the grounds of the hotel; there are 16 lighted tennis courts in all. Other sports facilities include a three-par, nine-hole golf course, a game field for exercising, jogging paths, shuffleboard, and two large swimming pools. A $12-million renovation has taken place here. Art work by Jim Dine and Kenneth Price in a palm motif is echoed by exotic horticulture spread over 26 acres. Restaurants, lounges, and entertainment.

Sheraton Newport Beach. *Expensive.* 4545 MacArthur Blvd.; (714) 833–0570. One of the newest hotels in this area. Features pool, Jacuzzi, and tennis courts. Also free *Wall Street Journal* and coffee. Restaurant, lounge, and entertainment.

LAGUNA NIGUEL

Ritz Carlton Laguna Niguel. *Super Deluxe.* 33533 Shoreline Dr.; (714) 240–2000, (800) 241–3333. This new resort is on 17½ acres overlooking the ocean. Mediterranean architecture and extensive landscaping gives it a villa-like appearance. Access to beach. Fitness center includes classes, weight equipment, Jacuzzi. Two pools, 2 restaurants, 3 lounges, club with entertainment. Adjacent to an 18-hole golf course.

LAGUNA BEACH

The Carriage House. (Bed-and-Breakfast) *Super Deluxe.* 1322 Catalina St.; (714) 494–8945. A beautiful garden surrounds this charming New Orleans-style house. Stay in the Lilac Suite, the Time Suite, or the Green Palms Suite. Complimentary breakfast, family-style. Welcome gifts of fresh California fruit and wine. No credit cards accepted.

Eiler's Inn. (Bed-and-Breakfast) *Super Deluxe.* 741 S. Coast Hwy.; (714) 494–3004. A beautifully renovated bed-and-breakfast inn featuring a flower-laden atrium and fountain. Continental breakfast is served in this setting; on summer weekends, wine and cheese combines with afternoon entertainment.

With only 13 rooms and a loyal following, it is important to book here well in advance.

Hotel San Maarten. *Super Deluxe.* 696 S. Coast Hwy.; (714) 494–9436, (800) 772–2539. This is one of Laguna's newest hotels, and it is stunning. An atrium and garden decorate the middle of the hotel, with surrounding rooms accented by calicos and antiques. Pool, sauna, restaurant, lounge; Continental breakfast during the week.

Surf and Sand Hotel. *Super Deluxe.* 15555 S. Coast Hwy.; (714) 497-4477. The largest hotel in town, the Surf and Sand is much like a little city. It has a complete shopping area with clothing stores, antiques, shops, and boutiques right on the premises. Private beach, swimming pool, ocean-view lounge, two restaurants, and entertainment.

Hotel Laguna. *Deluxe.* 425 S. Coast Hwy.; (714) 494–1151. The oldest hotel in Laguna is smack in the middle of town, with easy beach access. A patio overlooks a charming garden and the beach for sunbathing. Restaurant, lounge, entertainment. This landmark has just been totally remodelled.

The Inn at Laguna. *Deluxe.* 211 N. Coast Hwy.; (714) 494–7535. This comfortable inn is on the beach, near Main Beach and Heisler Park. Pool, some oceanfront rooms; Continental breakfast.

Seacliff Motel. *Expensive.* 1661 S. Coast Hwy.; (714) 494–9717. Under the same management for 20 years, the Seacliff has many rooms overlooking the Pacific. Private sun decks, heated pool, in-room coffee.

DANA POINT

Marina Inn Best Western. *Expensive.* 34902 Del Obispo St.; (714) 496–1203 (call collect). This lovely marina hotel has a pool and sauna.

SAN JUAN CAPISTRANO

Country Bay Inn. *Super Deluxe.* 34862 Pacific Coast Hwy.; (714) 496–6656. Wood-burning fireplaces grace each room in this inn, located across from a sandy beach. Gracious hospitality is also a plus. The rooms are all differently decorated, some with brass headboards, patios, and balconies. Complimentary Continental breakfast. Jacuzzi.

Capistrano Inn (Best Western). *Deluxe.* 27174 Ortega Hwy; (714) 493–5661. This rambling, comfortable motel is conveniently located. Swimming pool, Jacuzzi; restaurant next door.

Mission Inn Motel. *Expensive.* 26891 Ortega Hwy.; (714) 493–1151. Next door to the mission, this motel stands right in the middle of an orange grove. Restaurant next door.

SAN CLEMENTE

Ramada Inn San Clemente. *Super Deluxe.* 35 Calle de Industrias; (714) 498–8800. A brand-new hotel designed in mission style. Hillside landscape, right off Route 5. Private patios; pool; restaurant; lounge.

HOW TO GET AROUND. Since Southern California coastal cities are so spread out (there are 44 miles between Long Beach and San Clemente), by far the best way to get around is by car. All major car rental firms and a number of local concerns are represented in the Los Angeles/Long Beach and San Diego areas. Check directory assistance or the Yellow Pages for telephone numbers. Public bus service is available, but it is severely limited.

TOURIST INFORMATION. The Chambers of Commerce of the beach cities can be helpful with information on specific questions. In Long Beach, the Convention and Tourism Bureau is at 300 East Ocean Blvd., Long Beach, CA 90802; (213) 436–3645. In Santa Catalina Island, contact the Chamber of Commerce, P.O. Box 217, Avalon, CA 90702; (213) 510–1520.

In Huntington Beach, the chamber is located at 18582 Beach Blvd., Huntington Beach, CA 92648; (714) 536–8888. In Newport Beach, the Convention and Visitors Bureau is at 1470 Jamboree Rd., Newport Beach, CA 92660; (714) 644–8211.

For Laguna Beach information, contact the Laguna Beach Chamber of Commerce and Civic Association, P.O. Box 396, Laguna Beach, CA 92652; (714) 494–1018. For Dana Point, contact the Chamber of Commerce at P.O. Box 12, Dana Point, CA 92629; (714) 496–1555.

San Juan Capistrano has a Visitor's Center inside the mission. For information, contact the Visitor's Center, Mission San Juan Capistrano, Suite 218, San Juan Capistrano, CA 92674; (714) 493–1414. The San Juan Capistrano Chamber of Commerce is located at 31882 Camino Capistrano, San Juan Capistrano, CA 92675; (714) 493–1171. The San Clemente Chamber can be contacted at P.O. Box 338, San Clemente, CA 92672; (714) 492–1131.

SEASONAL EVENTS. Many events in the area are scheduled at the last moment, making it impossible for us to include them. One of the best ways to find out about such happenings is to check the local newspaper in each individual city. The following are established annual events.

January. *Whale watching* begins from the harbors at Dana Point and Newport Beach. Also at Long Beach and San Pedro.

February. The *Laguna Beach Winter Festival,* usually held mid-month, includes a crafts fair and a poetry festival. The *Laguna Beach Patriot's Day Parade.*

March. March 19th is *St. Joseph's Day* when, annually, *the swallows return to Capistrano.* Daylong festivities include Mexican and Indian dances, mariachi music, and other entertainment. In mid-March there is a *Festival of the Swallows,* "Fiesta de la Golindrinas," with a week-long celebration capped off with a parade. *Congressional Cup Sailing Race,* Long Beach.

April. The *Long Beach Grand Prix*—the only formula-one race through the streets of a North American city. Weeklong activities include a chili cook-off, bike race, celebrity race, and a 10,000-meter foot race.

May. Cinco de Mayo, *Mexican Independence Day,* is celebrated with festivals throughout the Southland, on May 5th.

July. Through August, the *Festival of the Arts* is held in Laguna Beach. Included in this popular event is the Sawdust Festival, the Art-a-Fair, and the Pageant of the Masters. On the *Fourth of July,* many coastal cities sponsor fireworks; there is a parade and celebration in Huntington Beach, and fireworks from the *Queen Mary* in Long Beach.

August. *International Sea and Sports Festival,* Long Beach. *Character Boat Parade,* Newport Beach.

September. *Newport Harbor Art Museum Antique Show,* Sept. 19–23. *Huntington Beach Annual Surf Championship. Long Beach Blues Festival.*

October. *Sandcastle Contest,* Corona del Mar, Newport Beach.

December. *Christmas Parade,* San Pedro. *Boat parades* in Newport Beach and Dana Point.

TOURS. In **Long Beach,** tours to the *Queen Mary* (berth J at the southern end of the Long Beach Freeway) include a look at the ship from stem to stern, including bridge, officers' quarters, engine room, as well as all of the public areas. Summer: daily, 9:00 A.M.–9:00 P.M.; winter: Monday through Friday, 10:00 A.M.–6:00 P.M.; box office open until 4 P.M.; (213) 435–3511. The *Spruce Goose* is on view from 10:00 A.M. to 6:00 P.M.; 9 A.M. to 9 P.M. in the summer. Call (213) 435–3511 for further information. *Rancho Los Cerritos* (4600 Virginas Rd., Long Beach), a Spanish house built in 1844, is open to tour daily, Wednesday through Sunday, 1:00–5:00 P.M., (213) 424–9423. *Rancho Los Alamitos* (6400 Bixby Rd., Long Beach), one of the oldest adobe structures in California, also has organized tours. Open daily, Wednesday through Sunday, 1:00–5:00 P.M.; (213) 431–2511. For those who wish to venture out to sea, the S.S. *Azure Seas* might be just the thing. Operated by Western Cuisine Lines, this ship combines an exciting escape, with a large informal party and a chance to see the sights "down Mexico way." For information on the three- and four-night cruises call (800) 421–5866 or (213) 548–8411.

Catalina Island. Various tours are offered around the island. Included are the glass-bottom boat tour, the casino tour, the coastal cruise, skyline cruise, flying-fish boat tour, and the inland motor tour. For information, call (213) 510–2500.

Wrigley Memorial and Botanical Gardens, 1400 Avalon Canyon Road, Avalon, Catalina Island; (213) 510–2288 or (213) 510–1520. This showcase for Catalina Island's native plants comprises more than 37 acres. Grounds are open seven days a week, 8 A.M. to 5 P.M. Admission is 50 cents; children under 12 free. Group tours are available. Tram service is provided between Island Plaza and Wrigley Memorial and Botanical Gardens.

Newport Beach. From the Balboa Pavilion, visitors can take advantage of many tours. Among them: sportfishing (714) 673–1434, and whale-watching and harbor cruises (714) 673–5245.

San Juan Capistrano. Walking tours are conducted each Sunday at 1:00 P.M. to take in the seven remaining adobes built as part of *Mission San Juan Capis-*

trano, the mission itself, and other historical sights in this quaint town. Those wishing to participate should meet at El Peon across from the mission on Ortega Bay. In **San Clemente,** tour the San Onofre Nuclear Energy Information Center; (714) 498–1000.

BEACHES. In addition to city beaches in each community, there are also state- and county-run beaches and recreation areas.

Huntington Beach State Beach is on Pacific Coast Hwy. (near Beach Blvd.). It runs into the city-run beach, and offers miles and miles of coast. Picnic facilities and fire rings for barbecues are available. **Bolsa Chica State Beach** is close to Huntington. This beach also has fire rings for barbecues; it's across the street from the Bolsa Chica Ecological Reserve.

A bit south of Newport Beach, **Corona Del Mar** boasts one of the best walks around, on a rock pier jutting out into the ocean. **Aliso County Park** in south Laguna Beach is a recreation area with a fishing pier. Adjacent to the Dana Point Marina, **Doheny State Park Beach** has a good marine recreation facility for swimming, fishing, and picnicking. Camping is also available here. (For camping information, call 714–496–6171.)

San Clemente State Beach also has camping facilities; for information, call (714) 492–3156. This spot is particularly lovely.

FISHING AND BOAT CHARTERS. Fishing is available in most coastal cities and can run the gambit from a day of leisurely pier fishing to out-and-out deep-sea fishing. No licenses are needed to fish off any public piers in California.

Visit *Belmont Pier,* the place to fish in Long Beach. The pier goes a full half mile into the bay. Half- and full-day deep-sea fishing charters can be arranged at Queen's Wharf Sportfishing (213) 432–8993, or call Belmont Pier Sportsfishing at (213) 434–6781.

Catalina is an excellent fishing spot; rent large or small craft in Avalon at *Avalon Boat Stand Co.;* call (213) 510–1097. *Huntington Pier* in Huntington Beach is frequented by casual and die-hard fishermen alike.

At Newport Beach's *Balboa Pavilion,* more than 40 skiffs and outboard motors are available for full- or half-day fishing. These boats seat four and are equipped with built-in live bait tanks. For information, call (714) 673–5245. Also from Newport, enjoy a day of deep-sea fishing aboard modern boats; rental equipment, license, and anything else you may need is provided at the Pavilion landing; call (714) 673–1434. *Aliso Beach Park* in south Laguna has a fishing pier, as does *Dana Point. Doheny State Beach* boasts surf-fishing.

CAMPING. Newport Dunes Travel Trailer Park. Newport Beach at 1131 Back Bay Dr.; (714) 644–0510. Summer fee is $25 for full hook-up, $14 for tents. 151 campsites, all with electrical, water, and sewage hookup. Sanitary disposal, water, toilets, showers, cooking, tables, swimming, fishing, playground, propane, groceries, laundry.

Doheny State Beach. 2 miles south of San Juan Capistrano; (714) 496–6171. Open all year. Fee $8.00, reservation deposit required; pets allowed for $1.00. 114 tent and recreation vehicle (RV) spaces; 28 days maximum stay for RVs. Sanitary disposal station, water, toilets, showers, cooking facilities, tables, swimming, fishing.

Long Beach Recreational Vehicle Campground, off Shoreline Dr.; (213) 590–6841, 591–6095. 70 spaces for hook-ups and 46 without. Fees are $18 a night with full hook-up and $6 without. Laundry and vending machines.

San Clemente State Beach. 2 miles south of San Clemente off I–5; (714) 492–3156. Year-round, fee $8.00 or $12.00; $1.00 for pets. 56 tent spaces, 100 RV spaces, maximum stay, for RVs June–Sept., 7 days; Oct.–May, 15 days. Sanitary disposal, water, toilets, showers, cooking facilities, tables, and propane; groceries and laundry nearby.

San Onofre State Beach. 3½ miles south of San Clemente, off I–5; (714) 492–4872. Year-round, fee $8.00. Reservation deposit required; fee for pets, $1.00. 157 tent spaces. Sanitary disposal, water, toilet, showers, cooking facilities, tables, swimming, fishing; groceries nearby.

CHILDREN'S ACTIVITIES. Kids will enjoy almost anything grownups enjoy in this area, especially beach activities and biking. Most of the theme parks for which southern California is world famous are located in inland Orange County (see the *Orange County* section above).

Marineland, however, is one exception. The adventure-filled Family Swim is new at Marineland. Here, guests can swim in a half-million-gallon tank with 4,000 fish. At Sea Lion Point, visitors will observe a rare colony of sea lions in their natural environment. Performing whales, dolphins, and sea lions star in regularly scheduled shows. Another attraction at Marineland is the Sky Tower: A glass enclosed bi-level elevator revolves slowly as it takes passengers above Marineland; from the top is a great view of the Palos Verdes Peninsula, and on a clear day, you can see Catalina Island. Marineland is located at Palos Verdes Dr. S., in Palos Verdes Hills; call (213) 377–1571. The park is open daily, 10:00 A.M. to 7:00 P.M. except from mid-April to mid-June, when it is open from 10:00 A.M. to 6:00 P.M., and, until September, from 10:00 A.M. to 7:00 P.M.

While in Laguna Beach, take the children to the *Laguna Moulton Playhouse,* 606 Laguna Canyon Rd.; (714) 494–0743. A special children's theater is sure to entertain the younger members of the family. Open year-round; box office open 1:00–5:00 P.M., Tuesday through Saturday. How to get there: Take San Diego #405 Freeway south or the Santa Ana #5 Freeway south to the Laguna Freeway. The Laguna Freeway ends and becomes Laguna Canyon Road. The playhouse is at the Laguna Festival Grounds, about three miles away. Laguna Moulton Playhouse, 606 Laguna Canyon Rd., closed Sunday and Monday.

PARTICIPANT SPORTS: Southern California is one of the world's most active playgrounds. From walking on the beach and swimming, to wind-surfing and biking, there is a sport for everyone.

Swimming. All beaches mentioned above under *Beaches* are open for swimming; those used to swimming in warm ocean water, however, may think the Pacific a bit brisk in the winter.

Surfing. For those daring enough to try this typically Californian sport, here are some of the popular spots: *Seal Beach,* between the pier and the jetty, is good for morning surfing; *Huntington Beach,* right near the pier, is popular for surfers as well as spectators; in *Newport Beach,* "the Wedge" is known world wide as one of the most treacherous surfing spots—certainly not for beginners, but great for interested spectators; and in *San Clemente,* surfers practice right across from the San Onofre nuclear reactor—an interesting juxtaposition. There is surfing at many more locations; just look for other surfers, gather as much courage as you need, and hit the waves.

Snorkeling. *Corona del Mar,* with its two colorful reefs, is a popular place for snorkeling because it is off limits to boats. In *Laguna Beach,* there is good snorkeling along the whole length of the beach; be sure not to disturb the marine life, though, for it is part of a protected ecological reserve.

Biking. To help bikers throughout California, Caltrans (California Department of Transportation) has a listing of bike paths; call (213) 620–3550. Usually, the bike paths follow the ocean whenever possible, for an indescribably beautiful ride. For weekend and longer trips, call L.A. Wheelman at (213) 533–1707 for planning information.

Golf. Southern California has more than its share of golf courses. There are more through inland Orange County than in the coastal area. Private clubs often honor other memberships. Some of the major courses include:

In Orange County: *Buena Park:* Los Coyotes Country Club (private) (714) 521–6171.

Costa Mesa: Costa Mesa Public Golf & Country Club (714) 540–7500; and Mesa Verde Country Club (private) (714) 549–0377.

Fountain Valley: Mile Square Golf Course (714) 545–3726.

Los Alamitos: Los Alamitos Country Club (semi-private) (714) 828–0402.

Placentia: Alta Vista Country Club (private) (714) 528–1185.

Santa Ana: River View Golf Course (714) 543–1115; Santa Ana Country Club (private) (714) 556–3000; and Willowick Golf Course (par 3) (714) 554–0672.

From Long Beach to San Clemente: *Catalina:* Catalina Island Golf Course (par 3) (213) 510–0530.

Huntington Beach: Huntington Seacliff Country Club (714) 536–7575; and Meadowlark Golf Course (714) 846–1364.

Irvine: Rancho San Joaquin Golf Course (714) 786–5522.

Laguna Hills: Laguna Hills Golf Course (private) (714) 837–7630.

Laguna Niguel: El Niguel Country Club (private) (714) 496–5767.

Mission Viejo: Costa del Sol Golf Course (par 3) (714) 581–9040; and Mission Viejo Country Club (private) (714) 831–1550.

Newport Beach: Big Canyon Country Club (private) (714) 644–5404; Irvine Coast Country Club (private) (714) 644–9550; and Newport Beach Golf Course (par 3) (714) 852–8681.

Long Beach: El Dorado Golf Course (213) 594–0933; Heartwell Golf Park (par 3) (213) 421–8855; Recreational Park Municipal Golf Course (213) 438–4012; Skylinks Golf Course (213) 421–3388; and Virginia Country Club (private) (213) 427–0924.

San Clemente: San Clemente Municipal Golf Course (714) 361–8278.

San Juan Capistrano: San Juan Hills Country Club (714) 837–0361.

Seal Beach: Old Ranch Country Club (private) (213) 596–4425.

South Laguna: Aliso Creek Golf Course (par 3) (714) 499–1919.

Tennis. Southern California also has thousands of tennis courts, many lighted for evening play. These range from the most exclusive private clubs to public tennis courts; check the Yellow Pages in each area for the latter. Some of the major courts include:

Long Beach: The Billie Jean King Tennis Center, 1040 Park Ave., (213) 438–8509, has eight courts which can be reserved; rates are around $1.00 an hour. Six courts, at California State University at Long Beach, 1250 Bellflower Blvd, (213) 498–4111, are open to the public. No reservations here—first come first served.

Catalina: Tennis courts at Las Casitas are open to the public with reservations, for a fee of $6.00 an hour. The hotel has three courts and is located two blocks from the Avalon marina. Call (213) 510–2226 for information and reservations. Catalina Island Tennis Courts has two courts available for $4.00 an hour. The club is located two and a half blocks from Avalon Harbor on Country Club Road; for reservations call (213) 510–0530.

Huntington Beach: Four courts are offered on a first come, first served basis at the Edison Community Center, 21366 Magnolia St. (Magnolia and Hamilton), (714) 960–8870. The fee is $2.00 an hour, and reservations can be made as far as 48 hours in advance. At the Murdy Community Center, 7000 Norma Dr. (off Golden West St., north of Warner), (714) 960–8895, four courts are available for free. No reservations are necessary.

Newport Beach: The Corona del Mar High School, 2101 East Bluff Dr., has eight courts for public use. The Recreation Department uses the courts, so it is best to call and find out when they are free—for the Recreation Department call (714) 644–3151. The same number should be used for information on tennis courts at San Joaquin Road and Crown Drive N. Four courts are available at this location, and can be used for free.

Laguna Beach: In Laguna the tennis courts are located at the Laguna Beach High School on Park Ave. There are eight courts and they are metered. Additional courts are available on Mondays, Wednesdays, and Fridays at the Irvine

Bowl, 650 Laguna Canyon Rd. No reservations and no fees are required for these courts.

San Clemente: Four courts are open to the public at San Luis Rey Park, on Avenue San Luis Rey, off El Camino Real; and another two courts are located at Bonita Canyon Park at the corner of El Camino Real and Calle Valley. All of these courts are available for free on a first come, first served basis. For more information call the Recreation Department at (714) 492–5101.

Water Sports. Sailboat, windsurfing, and other nautical rentals are generally available at or near the piers in each beach city. Some of the major rental groups are:

Long Beach: Leeway Sailing Center, City of Long Beach Recreation Department, conducts sabot sailing instruction (8-foot dingies) and canoeing instruction. Boat rentals are $50 for 20 hours of instruction; sabot lessons are $40 for adults and $30 for youths. From September through June call (213) 435–8447; during the summer call (213) 439–5427. Matlack Windsurfing, 4726 East 2nd St., in Belmont Shores (213) 430–3000, rents windsurfers for $6.00 an hour. They also offer a lesson-and-equipment package for $45.00, as well as individual lessons by the hour.

Newport Beach: Balboa Boat Rentals, Palm and Edgewater, next to the Balboa Ferry, (714) 673–1320, offers 21-foot Victory sailboats for a rental fee of $15.00 an hour. The boats are for use in the bay only.

Dana Point: Sailboat rentals are available from Embarcadero Marina, adjacent to the launching ramp at Dana Point Harbor, (714) 496–6177. Boat sizes range from 14 feet to 23 feet for all-day rentals.

SPECTATOR SPORTS. Because southern California is such an active place, sports activities you might want to take part in outnumber those you just want to watch. However, at the spectator events that take place each year you can be assured that you'll witness some amazing athletics.

Racing. Long Beach is the scene of a grand prix formula-one race in early spring. This race, The *Long Beach Grand Prix,* lures thousands to Long Beach streets for a truly exciting day.

Boating. The *Flight of the Snowbirds Regatta* is held annually at Balboa Pavilion in Newport Beach.

Surfing. In September, an annual *surfing competition* is held in Huntington Beach.

HISTORICAL SITES. With the Spanish influence so prevalent in southern California, historical remnants of the Spanish residents are popular attractions. *Rancho Los Cerritos* is one of these. The adobe house dates back to 1844. It's located at 4600 Virginas Rd., Long Beach and is open Wednesday through Sunday, from 1:00 to 5:00 P.M.; (213) 424–9423.

Rancho Alamitos at 6400 Bixby Rd., Long Beach, (213) 431–2511, is one of the oldest adobe structures. Open Wednesday through Sunday, 1:00 to 5:00 P.M.

MISSIONS. Many areas of California boast old Spanish missions, but probably none are as awesome or well known as *Mission San Juan Capistrano.* This historical fortress, sometimes called The Jewel of the Missions, is known the world over for its swallows, which return faithfully every St. Joseph's Day (March 19). The classic beauty of the mission, its gardens and its flock of white pigeons, attract some 300,000 visitors and photographers each year. Because of this large influx of tourists, the mission has recently opened a Visitor Information Center inside Mission San Juan Capistrano at Suite 218, San Juan Capistrano, CA 92675; (714) 493–1424. The mission itself is located at Camino Capistrano and Ortega Hwy.

MUSEUMS. The cultural focus is growing here by leaps and bounds. In addition to museums, tiny art galleries are plentiful in most of the cities.

Long Beach Museum of Art, 2300 East Ocean Blvd.; (213) 439–2119. Emphasizing art in California, the museum is housed in a beautiful brick-and-lava-stone mansion on a bluff overlooking the ocean in Long Beach. Open Wednesday through Sunday, 12 noon to 5:00 P.M.

In San Pedro, **Cabrillo Marine Museum,** 3720 Stephen White Dr.; (213) 548–7562. Boasts of more than 15,000 foreign and local shells as well as diverse species of fish and other marine life. Open daily 10 A.M. to 5 P.M. Closed Monday.

Newport Harbor Art Museum, at 850 San Clemente Dr.; (714) 759–1122. Newport Beach. Concentrates on "the art of our time," with an emphasis on the last three decades. Open daily from 10 A.M. to 5 P.M.; Closed Mondays.

MUSIC. The *Long Beach Convention and Entertainment Center,* 300 East Ocean Blvd.; (213) 436–3636, offers a selection of different music throughout the year. The Terrace Theater opened in 1978, with a performance by the Long Beach Symphony Orchestra featuring Van Cliburn on piano. Eugene Ormandy, former conductor of the Philadelphia Orchestra, has called the acoustics at the Terrace "absolutely first-class." A 24-hour event line, (213) 432–2233, is available for information on current productions.

The *Golden Bear,* (714) 960–5436, directly across the street from the Huntington Beach Pier, is a popular showcase for bands and musical groups.

STAGE. The *Long Beach Convention and Entertainment Center* has a continuing theater program at the Center Theater. The arena presents extravaganzas such as the Ice Capades. The *Long Beach Community Playhouse* offers outstanding comedy and drama; call (213) 494–1616.

At Laguna Beach, the *Laguna Moulton Playhouse,* (714) 494–0734, offers first-rate plays for children as well as adults. *Sebastian's West Dinner Playhouse* in San Clemente often attracts older, well-known stars such as Kathryn Grayson and Caesar Romero; for information call (714) 492–9950.

SHOPPING. California is the land of the mall; in most areas, all popular department stores, as well as smaller boutiques, are well represented under one roof. Otherwise, look for clusters of stores, usually located in the center of town.

Long Beach. The *Marina Pacifica* shopping center on Pacific Coast Hwy., just north of Second St., is a captivating little shopping area on the water. Redwood buildings and the parklike atmosphere make this an exciting place to shop. *Lakewood Center,* at Lakewood and Del Amo Blvds., is an indoor mall housing more traditional department stores—May Co., Montgomery Ward, J.C. Penny's, Buffums, and Bullocks. *The Market Place,* at the intersection of Pacific Coast Hwy. and Second St., surrounds a lake with theaters, boutiques, and restaurants. *Ports O' Call Village,* in San Pedro, is an "old-fashioned" waterfront complex in one of the world's busiest harbors.

Newport Beach. *Fashion Island* in Newport Center has a multitude of prestigious department stores and boutiques.

Laguna Beach. This small town is unanimously voted the most interesting place to shop in the area, with its tiny malls set off from the street, and more stores than you would ever imagine could fit into such a small town. Laguna offers incredibly diverse items, ranging from silk flowers (at *As Things Are,* in the new Bluebird Canyon Shopping Center) to aloe vera products (at the *Palm Springs Perfume and Cosmetics Company,* in the Lumber Yard Plaza on Forest Ave). Dozens of intriguing art galleries include the renowned *Vorpal Gallery,* 326 Glennyere; the *Watercolor Gallery,* 1416 S. Coast Hwy.; the *Tree of Life Studio Gallery,* 751 Rembrandt; and *Gallery Xyst,* 1412 S. Coast Hwy., just to name a few of the more than 40 galleries. Antiques shops are also abundant in Laguna; there is *Richard Yeakal,* on Coast Hwy., for fine American and European antiques (at very high prices); the *Queen's Head,* at 250 Broadway, with a wide selection for the dollar-wise buyer; *Mage Wind* in the Lumber Yard, which offers antiques as well as contemporary items; and *Off the Wall,* at 950 Glenneyre, with some unusual architectural antiques such as clawfoot bathtubs, brass hardware, mantles, and pedestal sinks. Some of the more out-of-the-ordinary stores include: *Chicken Little Emporium,* Coast Hwy., with whimsical gifts and clothes; *South Seas Rag Co.,* 279 S. Coast Hwy., with some of the barest fashions around; and *Khyber Pass,* at 384 Forest Ave., which features unusual gifts from Afghanistan and the Middle East. *Peppertree Lane* is an adorable shopper's alley at 448 Coast Hwy.; it includes a woman's clothing store, a sweet shop, and an antiques shop, all designed to take you back to simpler, less hectic shopping days, amid trees, white wrought-iron benches, and an array of flowers.

DINING OUT. Restaurants along the Orange County coast are about as varied as the people who live here. This is a high-priced area in general, so the restaurants are fairly expensive. Dining in this area is usually a casual and informal affair; when there *is* a dress code we'll mention it. For those on a budget, there are many coffee shops and cafés. Price ranges are as follows (per person, with no wine or tip included—for more information see "Facts at Your Fingertips"): *Expensive,* $25 and up; *Moderate,* $10–$25; and *Inexpensive,* below $10.

LONG BEACH

La Grotte. *Expensive* 529 East Seaside Way; (213) 437–2119. Located near the Long Beach Convention and Entertainment Center. French and Continental cuisine served in an intimate, European atmosphere. Veal dishes are their specialty, though there is a good selection of seafood. Closed Sunday and holidays. Dinner from 5:30 to 10:00 P.M. weekdays; to 11:00 P.M. weekends. All major credit cards.

Skyroom at the Breakers. *Expensive.* 210 E. Ocean Blvd., (213) 432–8781. Contemporary Art Deco restaurant offers expansive view of the city. French traditional and nouvelle presentations accent fresh products and light sauces. Specialties are stuffed squab, escargot soup, scallops with fresh ginger, and lemon fettucine. Open for cocktails at 4:00 P.M., dinner from 6:00 P.M. to 11:00 P.M., special nightcap menu from 10:30 P.M. to 12:30 A.M. All major credit cards.

Francois Manhattan. *Moderate to Expensive.* 1909 E. 4th St., (213) 436–0620. An institution since 1940, this continental restaurant specializes in flaming duck and rack of lamb. Piano bar. Open for lunch and dinner daily except Monday. All major credit cards.

Adolph's. *Moderate.* 700 Queensway Dr.; (213) 437–5977. In the Queensway Hilton, this restaurant is located in the marina, allowing a beautiful view of the *Queen Mary.* The decor is tropical, with hanging plants and wicker chairs. Seafood is the house specialty. All major credit cards.

Bayshore Fish Market. *Moderate.* 4705 E. 2nd St.; (213) 438–7414. This critically acclaimed restaurant offers Eastern-style seafood such as Maine lobster, calamari, and stuffed shrimp. Daily fish catches. MC, V.

Le Bistro. *Moderate.* 3222 East Broadway; (213) 434–3003. This quiet French bistro has outside dining when weather permits. Specialties are fresh seafood and pepper steak. Open Tuesday through Friday, 11:30 A.M. to 2:00 P.M. for lunch, and Tuesday through Sunday, 6:00 to 10:00 P.M. for dinner. MC, V.

Bobby McGee's Conglomeration. *Moderate.* 6501 East Pacific Coast Hwy.; (213) 594–8627. Looking like an old English farmhouse from the outside, this Elizabethan-style restaurant is filled with antiques and mirrors. The staff is dressed in costumes, each depicting a different storybook character. Choose from a variety of seafood, steak, and prime rib dishes. A discotheque features big band to contemporary music nightly until 2:00 A.M. Restaurant open from 5:00–10:00 P.M. weekdays, until 11:00 P.M. on weekends. All major credit cards.

Domenico's Belmont Shore. *Moderate.* 5339 E. 2nd St.; (213) 439–0261. This restaurant, in the popular Belmont Shores area, has Italian specialties from braciole to fettucine, in a friendly atmosphere. Open for lunch and dinner. All major credit cards.

Hamburger Henry's. *Moderate.* 4700 East 2nd St.; (213) 433–7070. A choice of 38 different hamburgers here; from plain to a polar burger topped with ice cream. Full salad bar; steak, fish, and chicken dishes. A heated patio allows outdoor dining year-round. Open 24 hours, every day. Beer and wine. MC, V.

Houlihan's Old Place. *Moderate.* 6272 A East Pacific Coast Hwy.; (213) 598–9638. Located in the Marina Pacifica Shopping Center, this restaurant offers an interesting setting with a potpourri of old and contemporary posters on the wall. The menu includes burgers and omelettes, as well as duck, shrimp, and fettucine, plus unusual appetizers and desserts. Full bar open until 12:30 A.M. daily, 1:30 A.M. Friday and Saturday. Open weekdays, 11:30 A.M. to 10:30 P.M.; weekends until 11:30 P.M. Sunday brunch from 10:00 A.M. Major credit cards.

SAN PEDRO

Papadakis Tavern. *Moderate.* 301 West 6th St.; (213) 547–5250. The tavern is full of Greek festivity and spirit; decor includes hanging Greek rugs, bronze statues, and marble pillars. Taped music plays continuously as waiters break into Greek dancing throughout the evening. Traditional Greek fare; specialties include lamb wrapped in pastry. Extensive list of Greek and California wines. Open for lunch Tuesday through Friday, 11:30 A.M. to 2:00 P.M. Dinner on Tuesday through Thursday, from 5:00 to 9:00 P.M.; on Friday and Saturday, from 5:00 to 9:45 P.M.; and on Sunday, from 5:00 to 8:45 P.M. Closed Monday. Reservations a must. MC, V.

SANTA CATALINA ISLAND (AVALON)

Flying Yachtsman. *Moderate.* 403 Crescent St.; (213) 510–9177. Situated on the waterfront; a nautical motif prevails here. Variety of seafood, steak, and prime ribs. Open year-round. Lunch, 11:00 A.M. to 2:00 P.M.; dinner, 5:00 to 10:00 P.M. AE, MC, V.

Mr. Gee's Restaurant and Bar. *Moderate.* 888 Los Lomas; (213) 510–1327. Both Continental and Chinese fare. Full bar, entertainment in the summer. Open year-round, 5:00 to 10:00 P.M. for dinner; from 8:30 A.M. to 3:00 P.M. in season. AE, MC, V.

Prego. *Moderate.* 693 Crescent; (213) 510–1218. Primarily Northern Italian cuisine. On the waterfront in an intimate setting. Full bar. Open all year; Fridays through Tuesday in the winter. Open on weekdays from 5:00 to 9:00 P.M.; on weekends until 10 P.M. AE, MC, V.

The Upstairs Place. *Moderate.* 417 Crescent; (213) 510–0333. Located right on the water; arched windows overlook the bay. Fresh seafood dinners. Beer, wine. Open 5:30 to 9:00 P.M. daily during the summer (June to September), weekends only the rest of the year. MC, V.

El Galleon Restaurant. *Inexpensive.* 411 Crescent; (213) 510–1188. A variety of fish, locally caught. The decor is nautical, with portholes and ship rigging. Full bar with nightly entertainment May through October. Dinner, year-round, served from 5:00 P.M. to 9:00 P.M. (11:00 P.M. in season.) Lunch served May through September. All major credit cards.

HUNTINGTON BEACH

Jeremiah's. *Moderate.* 8901 Warner Ave.; (714) 848–2662. Relax in this lush atmosphere, filled with plants, redwood, and leaded glass. Prime rib, fresh seafood, chicken, and steak served in this multi-level restaurant. Guitar music Wednesday through Saturday; disco dancing with live music on weekends. Open 5:00 to 11:00 P.M. on weekends. All major credit cards.

Maxwell's. *Moderate.* 317 Pacific Coast Hwy.; (714) 536–2555. A beautifully decorated restaurant right on the ocean near Huntington Beach pier. Large selection of seafood: local fish and fish from the East coast; live Maine lobster a specialty. Beef and prime rib are also available. One of the largest wine lists around. Breakfast, 8:00–11:30 A.M.; lunch, 11:30 to 4:00 P.M.; dinner Sunday through Thursday, until 10:00 P.M. Sunday buffet brunch from 10:00 A.M. to 3:00 P.M. All major credit cards.

Tibbie's Music Hall. *Moderate.* 16360 Coast Hwy.; (714) 592–4072. A musical revue by the young Americans' Song and Dance Company entertains while you dine on prime rib or chicken. Also a selection of seafood appetizers. Two dinner shows nightly from Tuesday through Saturday at 5:45 and 8:45 P.M.; one seating Sunday at 5:00 P.M. AE, MC, V.

The Golden Bear. *Inexpensive.* 306 Pacific Coast Hwy.; (714) 536–9600; for reservations, call (714) 960–5436. Live entertainment is the primary reason for going to The Golden Bear—food secondary. Sandwiches, salad, chicken, and steak are served during the performances that take place from 8:30 to 10:30 P.M. No credit cards accepted.

NEWPORT BEACH

The Wine Cellar (in The Newporter Resort). *Expensive.* 1107 Jamboree Rd.; (714) 644–1700. Strolling guitarists (why not?) serenade diners in this French restaurant. Seating is from 7:00–8:30 P.M., Tuesday through Saturday. Reservations required, jackets requested. Major credit cards.

Cano's. *Expensive.* 2241 West Coast Hwy.; (714) 631–1381. On Newport Beach's seafood restaurant row south of the junction of the Coast Hwy. with Rte. 55, Cano's is supposed to be a Mexican seafood place, but has more of an eclectic Continental menu. Yachts are moored right outside the windows. The customers are rather dressy; the bar is spacious and slick. Reservations recommended. Valet parking. AE, MC, V.

The Ritz. *Expensive.* 880 Newport Center Dr.; (714) 720–1800. Just as the name suggests, this restaurant is grand. Brass and glass accentuate the richness of the atmosphere, and the food is also first-rate. Specialties include grilled calf's liver and roast duck, and many unusual appetizers are featured, such as steamed mussels and fried oysters. Open for lunch and dinner. All major credit cards.

Amelia's. *Moderate.* 311 Marine Ave., Balboa Island; (714) 673–6580. For 20 years, Amelia and her family have been entertaining visitors (well-known celebrities among them) in the Newport area. This warm and friendly restaurant on the main street of Balboa Island is now a landmark. Fresh fish is a specialty;

Italian cuisine is also served. Reservations a must. Open for dinner only seven days. All major credit cards.

Baxter's Street. *Moderate.* 4647 MacArthur Blvd.; (714) 756–0611. A turn-of-the-century San Francisco street is the setting for this restaurant. Dinner features steak, fresh fish, pasta, and barbecued ribs. Dinner shows nightly by the talented Baxter's Street Singers. Open for lunch, Monday through Friday; dinner nightly except Tuesday. Reservations necessary. All major credit cards.

Capriccio Café (in the Marriott Hotel and Tennis Club). *Moderate.* 900 Newport Center Dr.; (714) 640–4000. An elegant dining room and terrace with a spectacular ocean view. Specialties include crepes, unique sandwiches, and an array of fine desserts. Piano bar. Open daily for breakfast, lunch, and dinner. All major credit cards.

Le Biarritz. *Moderate.* 414 North Old Newport Blvd.; (714) 645–6700. A friendly French restaurant, well known around town for award-winning provincial cuisine. Lunch begins at 11:00 A.M.; treats from 2:00 to 5:00 P.M.; dinner until 11:00 P.M.; Sunday brunch from 10:00 A.M. to 3:00 P.M. All major credit cards.

La Palme. *Moderate.* In the Newporter Resort, 1106 Jamboree Rd.; (714) 640–4182. Seasonal foods are the specialty in this bright, airy restaurant. Diners can overlook a green garden, and fresh flowers add color to the tables. The chef, trained at the famous Bernard's (under the same management), is innovative; some dishes he has offered include oysters with caviar, and grilled prawns with lime and ginger. Open Monday through Friday for lunch and dinner, weekends for dinner only. All major credit cards.

Rusty Pelican. *Moderate.* 2735 West Coast Hwy.; (714) 642–3431. This restaurant, located right at the water's edge, has a fantastic view. The menu offers a wide selection of fresh fish, as well as prime rib. On the second level is a lounge and oyster bar, with entertainment nightly. Open for lunch, dinner, and Sunday brunch. All major credit cards.

The Bistro (in The Newporter Resort). *Moderate.* 1107 Jamboree Rd.; (714) 644–1700. This Parisian café features French onion soup, quiches, and fresh fish. Lovely, casual atmosphere. Open daily for breakfast, lunch, and dinner. All major credit cards.

The Cannery. *Moderate.* 3010 Lafayette Ave.; (714) 675–5777. An authentic cannery overlooking the harbor in old Newport's Cannery Village. This historic landmark restaurant features waterfront views and outdoor dining alongside local fishing boats. The menu features a wide variety of select seafood and steak entrees. Entertainment. Lunch, Monday through Saturday, 11:30 A.M. to 3:00 P.M.; dinner from 5:00 to 10:00 P.M. Sunday brunch from 9:00 A.M. to 2:30 P.M. All major credit cards.

Villa Nova. *Moderate.* 3131 West Coast Hwy.; (714) 642–7880. Since 1933, the Villa Nova on Newport Bay has been serving fine cuisine from central and northern Italy. The versatile menu includes osso buco and mozzarella marinara. Fine wines. Piano bar. Open daily for dinner. Full menu until 1:00 A.M. All major credit cards.

Warehouse. *Moderate.* 3450 Via Osporo; (714) 673–4700. Typical American-style eats with some foreign entries on a gimmicky menu, but here the place is the thing: right at the water. The bar is lively, the waitresses are everyone's idea of young California women. Reserve for large parties only. Major credit cards.

The Crab Cooker. *Inexpensive-Moderate.* 2200 Newport Blvd.; (714) 673–0100. The concept here is to serve very fresh fish, very simply prepared. Your fish is cooked right in front of you over charcoal in this cafeteria-style restaurant. Fresh fish choices include salmon, oysters, sea bass, and crab, and there's shrimp, lobster, and crab claws as well. Entrees come with rice or potato and tomato slices or cole slaw. Comfortable, casual decor with an attention-getting white shark mounted on the ceiling in the center of the room. The shark was caught off the coast of Newport Beach—now that's food for thought! The nautical decor continues with sea-faring pictures, wood carvings and crabs decorating the walls. No reservations. Lunch and dinner, daily. No credit cards.

CORONA DEL MAR

The Five Crowns. *Expensive.* 3801 East Coast Highway; (714) 760–0331. An authentic reproduction of Ye Old Bell, the oldest inn in England, located just outside London. Heavy leaded glass windows, flower boxes, and manicured shrubs adorn the exterior while intimate dining rooms filled with one-of-a-kind antiques and a cozy fireplace complete the interior. Captains, waitresses, and bartenders are garbed in traditional English costumes, including white bonnets for the ladies and knee pants for the gents! Roast prime ribs of beef is the house specialty, carved to your preference. Creamed spinach, a marvelous horseradish sauce, and Yorkshire pudding complete the plate. Other entrees include sauteed prawns with white wine and garlic, Dover sole Varonique and center-cut pork chops finished with brandy, heavy cream, and pink peppercorns. Excellent wine list with over 400 selections. Piano bar most nights, showcase singers on Sunday. All major credit cards.

Hemingway's. *Expensive.* 2441 East Coast Hwy.; (714) 673–0120. This recently refurbished restaurant offers nouvelle cuisine in a warm, intimate atmosphere. Choose fresh seafood, game birds, or veal. Dinner, Tuesday through Sunday, 6:00 to 11:00 P.M.; Sunday brunch on holidays only. Lunch 11:30–2:30, Monday through Friday. All major credit cards.

The Quiet Woman. *Moderate.* 3224 East Coast Hwy.; (714) 640–7440. Famous for its Continental cuisine and friendly atmosphere; a local favorite. Specialties: rack of lamb, veal Oscar, fondue, and charbroiled swordfish. Entertainment. Full bar until 2:00 P.M. Major credit cards.

LAGUNA BEACH

Las Brisas. *Moderate to Expensive.* 361 Cliff Drive, right off the Coast Hwy. north of the junction with Rte. 133; (714) 497–5434. On the cliffs at the north end of the central beach, overlooking the ocean, the beach, and much of the town nestled in the hills, this is a spectacularly sited restaurant, and the Mexican-style seafood in which it specializes is delicious. There is an outside patio that is more or less an adjunct to the bar. All in all a delightful experience, especially at sunset and in the early evening. Both dressy and casual. Brunch on Sunday. Major credit cards.

Ben Brown's. *Moderate.* 31106 Coast Hwy.; (714) 499–2663. Breakfast, lunch, and dinner served in Alisio Canyon, overlooking a 9-hole golf course. Dinner specialties include bouillabaisse, scampi, and veal scallopini. Full bar, cocktail lounge. Open daily. MC, V.

The Beach House. *Moderate.* 619 Sleepy Hollow Lane; (714) 494–9707. With a white-water view of the ocean from every table, this eaterie offers fresh fish, lobster, and steamed clams. Breakfast, 8:00 to 11:30 A.M.; lunch until 2:00 P.M.; and dinner nightly. AE, MC, V.

The Cottage. *Moderate.* 308 North Coast Hwy.; (714) 494–3023. It once was "the thing" to wait on the lovely lawn of this quaint cottage for a table; that was before the establishment started taking reservations. The 70-year-old landmark building, formerly the residence of a pioneer developer, is beautifully landscaped. Daily fresh entree: fish, meat, and vegetarian dishes. Open Monday through Friday, 8:00 A.M. to 3:00 P.M. for breakfast and lunch; 5:00 to 10:00 P.M. for dinner; and until 11:00 P.M. on Friday and Saturdays. Now serving wine and beer. No credit cards.

Diz's As It. *Moderate.* 2794 So. Coast Hwy.; (714) 494–5250. This local institution serves full meals with pate'd'maison soup, salad, and entree. International cuisine. No reservations. Open Tuesday through Sunday from 5:30. Closed Monday.

Partners Bistro. *Moderate.* 448 South Coast Hwy.; (714) 497–4441. An extremely popular local spot. Exquisitely decorated with antiques, beautiful wood, cut glass, and bronze. Favorites include tournedos of beef, veal, and some of the finest fish around. Reservations except Friday and Saturday. Lunch, 11:30 A.M. to 3:00 P.M.; dinner, 5:30 to 10:00; Friday and Saturday until 11. Sunday brunch, 10:00 A.M. to 3:00 P.M.

The Place Across From the Hotel Laguna. *Moderate.* 440 South Coast Hwy.; (714) 497–2625. This restaurant in the middle of town has a woodsy interior. Homemade pastas, vegetarian dishes, omelettes. Open daily, MC, V, DC.

Poor Richard's Kitchen. *Moderate.* 1198 South Coast Hwy.; (714) 497–1667. In the Village Fair mall, this is a comfortable restaurant. Fine soup-and-salad bar. Patio dining with ocean view. Beer and wine. Open daily, 8:00 A.M. to 9:00 P.M. All major credit cards.

The Terrace. *Moderate.* 448 South Coast Hwy.; (714) 497–6769. A new upstairs, outside addition to the popular dining spot, *Partners* (see above). Lattice and greenery are everywhere; pleasant menu as well. Heat lamps take away the outdoors chill. Open daily. All major credit cards.

The Towers (atop the Surf and Sand Hotel). *Expensive.* 15555 South Coast Hwy.; (714) 497–4477. One of the best views of Laguna Beach awaits diners in this sophisticated restaurant. Open for breakfast, lunch, and dinner. All major credit cards.

The White House. *Moderate.* 340 S. Coast Hwy.; (714) 494–8089. A Laguna institution, newly decorated. The menu here is extensive—salads, crepes, pastas, and sandwiches are some of the offerings. Open for breakfast, lunch, and dinner. Entertainment nightly. All major credit cards.

Tortilla Flats. *Inexpensive.* 1740 South Coast Hwy.; (714) 494–6588. Since 1959, Maria Aquilar has prepared the same delicious Sonora-style food at this remodeled Laguna Beach landmark. Tequila flows freely in the upstairs cantina. The architecture reflects the warm welcome of a hacienda—and the view of the Pacific is stunning. Tamales a specialty. Open daily from 11:30 A.M.; Sunday brunch, 11:00 A.M. to 3:00 P.M. AE, MC, V.

DANA POINT

Quiet Cannon. *Moderate.* 34344 Green Lantern; (714) 496–6146. Sitting on a bluff overlooking the marina, the view here is *spectacular.* This woody, split-level restaurant serves prime rib, steak, and seafood. Open seven days. Lunch Monday through Friday from 11:30 A.M. to 3:30 P.M. Dinner Monday through Thursday, 5:00 to 10:00 P.M.; open until 11:00 P.M. Friday and Saturday and on Sunday from 4:30 to 10:00 P.M. Sunday Brunch from 10:00 A.M. to 3:00 P.M. Reservations recommended. AE, MC, V.

Wind and Sea Restaurant. *Moderate.* 25152 Del Prado; (714) 496–6500. Steak and seafood served in a rustic atmosphere with high beamed ceilings, hanging plants, and redwood decor. The house specialty is Alaskan king crab. Full bar with entertainment, Wednesday through Sunday. Open Monday to Friday, 5:30 until 10:00 P.M., and from 4:30 to 11:00 P.M. Saturday and Sunday. AE, MC, V.

SAN JUAN CAPISTRANO

L'Hirondelle French Cuisine. *Moderate.* 31631 Camino Capistrano; (714) 661–0425. This casual French inn has only 12 tables, so a reservation is imperative, especially on weekends. The menu is typically French. Duckling is the specialty, and it is served three ways. Beer and wine. Open from 4:30 to 10:00 P.M. weekends, and until 9:00 P.M. weekdays. Closed Monday and Tuesday. MC, V.

El Adobe. *Inexpensive-Moderate.* 31891 Camino Capistrano; 714–493–1163. The early American setting here highlights a Mexican/American cuisine restaurant packed with Richard M. Nixon memorabilia. Mariachi band entertains on the weekends. Open for lunch and dinner daily, AE, MC, V.

Swallows Inn. *Inexpensive.* 31786 Camino Capistrano; (714) 493–3188. A local hangout, this Mexican eaterie is decorated Western style, complete with sawdust on the floor. Two bars, live entertainment Wednesday through Sunday. Open seven days from 6:00 P.M. to 2:00 A.M. Bar open until 2:00 A.M. No credit cards.

Walnut Grove Restaurant. *Inexpensive.* 26871 Ortega Hwy.; (714) 493–1661. Steak, seafood, and salads in a Spanish-style setting. All baking done on premises. Beer, wine. Open seven days for breakfast, lunch, and dinner. AE, MC, CB, V.

SAN CLEMENTE

Andreino's. *Moderate.* 1925 South El Camino Real; (714) 492–9955. This restaurant is full of antiques, flowers, and lace curtains. Italian cuisine, extensive wine list. Open seven days for dinner only from 5:00 to 10 P.M. Closed Monday during the winter. MC, V.

San Clemente Inn. *Moderate.* 125 Avenida Esplanadian; (714) 492–6103. Seafood, steak, and chicken are served here in a casual setting. Piano bar. The chicken Jerusalem—chicken sauteed in a white wine and cream sauce—is a favorite. Open daily for dinner except Tuesday. All major credit cards.

Swiss Chalet. *Moderate.* 216 North El Camino Real; (714) 492–7931. Swiss-German cuisine served in an authentic atmosphere. Tables surround a fireplace for a cozy setting. Chef's specialty is veal. Open Tuesday through Saturday for lunch from 11:30 A.M. to 2:30 P.M.; dinner from 5:00 to 9:00 P.M. Closed Sunday and Monday. MC, V.

The Fish Tale. *Moderate.* 111 West Palizada; (714) 498–6072. This seafood restaurant features fresh fish carefully prepared. Turn-of-the-century decor. A full bar stocks 50 different imported beers. Open seven days from 11:00 A.M. to 3:00 P.M. for lunch; dinner from 3:00 to 10:00 P.M. Sunday through Thursday, until 11:00 P.M., Friday and Saturday. Reservations recommended. MC, V.

NIGHTLIFE. The largest concentration of nightlife activities is in nearby Los Angeles, but there is also a blend of night-owl activities in all of the coastal cities.

Long Beach. *Bobby McGee's Conglomeration* is one of the best discos around. Located in the Market Place, and popular with a young crowd. DJ's play top 40s for nightly dancing.

In **Huntington Beach,** *Maxwell's* is a disco with an ocean view—right on the pier.

In **Newport Beach** several restaurants accommodate night owls with various types of music. At the *Rusty Pelican,* 2735 W. Coast Hwy., contemporary music is played Sunday through Saturday. The *Cannery Restaurant,* 3010 Lafayette Ave., offers comedy Monday night; soloist Tuesday through Thursday; bands Friday and Saturday; and a jazz quartet for Sunday Brunch. The *Studio Café* at 100 Main St. on the Balboa Peninsula presents jazz nightly. The *Red Onion,* 2406 Newport Blvd., presents a live band that plays top 40s and a little bit of everything else. *Quiet Woman,* 3224 E. Coast Hwy., Corona del Mar, has live mellow music every night except Sunday. And finally: *Bobby McGee's,* 353 E. Coast Hwy., has a disc jockey who plays easy-listening music in the early evening and top 40s for disco dancing later.

In **Laguna Beach,** the *White House,* at 340 S. Coast Hwy., has nightly entertainment featuring rock, jazz, and funk. *The Sandpiper,* 1183 S. Coast

Hwy., offers the music of some of the best local groups around; people flock here from miles away.

In **San Juan Capistrano,** the *Depot,* at 26701 Verdugo Ave., features country, pop, or jazz every night.

INDEX

(The letters H and R indicate hotel and restaurant listing.)